CW00707983

LOGISTICS AND DISTRIBUTION PLANNING

LOGISTICS AND DISTRIBUTION PLANNING

Strategies for Management

Second edition

Edited by James Cooper

First published in 1988
Revised edition 1990
Second edition 1994

Kogan Page Limited
120 Pentonville Road
London N1 9JN

British Library Cataloguing in Publication Data

A CIP record for this book is available from the British Library.

ISBN 0 7494 0948 7

Typeset by DP Photosetting, Aylesbury, Bucks
Printed and bound in Great Britain by
Biddles Ltd, Guildford and King's Lynn

Contents

List of Contributors

Julian Allen is a Research Fellow in the Transport Studies Group at the University of Westminster where his major research interest is the impact of flexible production techniques on logistics and transportation systems. He graduated from the University's Master's programme in Transport Planning and Management in 1992 and was awarded the Freight Transport Association's Centenary Award in 1993 for his dissertation 'Just in time transportation and the environment'.

Michael Browne is the BRS Professor of Transport at the University of Westminster, where he specializes in international logistics. He teaches freight transport and logistics on the University's Master's programme in Transport Planning and Management and is responsible for directing research and consultancy activities in logistics. He is currently involved in major projects on the use of satellite communications, freight transport and the environment and the changing nature of logistics decision-making.

Before joining the University of Westminster he was responsible for international shipping and buying for the Crown Agents and his special areas of interest are often linked to this work. Professor Browne is a member of the International Working Group on Strategic Informatics and has acted as an adviser to the Economic and Social Committee of the European Community. He is a co-author of the book *European Logistics: Markets, Management and Strategy* published in 1991.

Martin Christopher is Professor of Marketing and Logistics at Cranfield School of Management, where he is Head of the Marketing Group and Chairman of the Cranfield Centre for Logistics and Transportation. In addition he is Deputy Director of the School of Management responsible for Continuing Executive Education. Professor Christopher has worked for major international companies in North America, Europe, the Far East and Australasia. In addition he is a non-executive Director of a number of companies. He has written numerous books and articles and is on the editorial advisory board of a number of professional journals in the marketing and logistics area. He is co-Editor of *The International Journal of Logistics Management* and his recent books have focused upon relationship marketing, customer service and logistics strategy. Professor Christopher is a Fellow of the Chartered Institute of Marketing and of the Institute of Logistics, on whose Council he sits. In 1987 he was awarded the Sir Robert Lawrence medal of the Institute of Logistics and Distribution Management for his contribution to the development of logistics education in Great Britain.

Jacques Colin is Professor of Management Science at the University of Aix-Marseille II. He is Director of the CRET (Research Centre for the Study of Transport Economics) in the Faculty of Economic Sciences, at the University of Aix-Marseille II. He is a specialist in logistics and more specifically his interests lie in the study of strategies developed by big companies (in industry, distribution and transport) and in the effects of the development of logistics on planning and on the environment. He has carried out many research projects for government bodies. He is also a consultant for important companies, such as IBM, SNCF, OTIS, SAGA, ELF. He has published widely, for example two important works: *Logistics Within the Firm*, published by Dunod (written in collaboration with D Tixier and H Mathe) and *Logistics in Distribution* published by Chotard and co-authored with G Paché.

Professor James Cooper is Director of Cranfield Centre for Logistics and Transportation at Cranfield School of Management, where he is also Exel Logistics Fellow. After graduating in Economics at Nottingham University, he worked in the distribution division of Kodak, later returning to academic life at the Transport Studies Group, Polytechnic of Central London (now the University of Westminster).

Professor Cooper has extensive research, consultancy and teaching experience in both freight transport and logistics. He has led a number of major studies on these topics for both the UK government and many companies and he participates in the DRIVE 2 programme of the European Commission as a partner in the COMBICOM consortium. He led the Cranfield team on a joint study with Andersen Consulting for the Council of Logistics Management. The results of the study were published in a report *Reconfiguring European Logistics Systems* in February 1993.

Professor Cooper teaches regularly at the University of Linköping in Sweden and the Catholic University of Brabant in the Netherlands. As UK representative on the OECD expert group on advanced logistics and communications, he has contributed to establishing a wider appreciation of the importance of logistics. Together with colleagues, Professor Cooper has written another best-selling book *European Logistics: Markets, Management and Strategy*, which was published by Blackwell Publishers in November 1991.

Nathalie Fabbe-Costes is Assistant Professor in Management Science and Director of Research at the CRET (Research Centre for the study of Transport Economics) in the Faculty of Economic Sciences at the University of Aix-Marseille II. Her principal area of research is logistics. More specifically, her interest lies in the strategic application of logistics, and in the design of associated information and communication systems; she has produced various publications in this area, including contribution to the work of the logistics specialists' group in the OECD, Paris, 1992.

Dr John Fernie is a senior lecturer in marketing at Dundee Business School, Dundee Institute of Technology. His main research interests are in the field of retail distribution management, especially in the areas of manufacturer–retailer relationships and contract distribution. He edited *Retail Distribution Management*, published by Kogan Page in 1990. Dr Fernie is editor of the *International Journal of Retail and Distribution Management* and is a member of the Chartered Institute of Marketing and the Institute of Logistics and Distribution Management.

Gordon Hill is Vice President and Director of A T Kearney, the international management consultants, with a specialist interest in logistics and materials management. He has been responsible for the development of A T Kearney's logistics practice which now covers all aspects of supply chain management from sourcing, manufacturing and distribution through to the end customer. He was formerly a research scientist with the National Coal Board and Experimental Engineering Manager with Johnson Wax International. He is a member of Council of the Institute of Logistics and is the author of a number of publications on management subjects.

Bernard J La Londe holds a BA in Economics from the University of Notre Dame, an MBA from the University of Detroit, and a PhD in Business Administration. In addition to this academic background, he spent several years with the Ford Motor Company on the staff of the Vice President of Sales and Advertising and in field sales operations. He is author or co-author of a number of books and monographs and is a frequent contributor of articles to professional journals and the trade press. His most recent books include *Customer Service: A Management Perspective* (with Martha C. Cooper and Thomas G. Noordewier), 1988; *Partnerships in Providing Customer Service: A Third-Party Perspective* (with Martha C. Cooper), 1989 and *Evolution, Status, and Future of the Corporate Transportation Function* (with James M Masters), 1991.

Professor La Londe has been active as a consultant on logistics issues and as a lecturer in executive development programs for a wide range of companies. He serves on the Editorial Review Board of *The International Journal of Logistics Management* and served as Founding Editor of the *Journal of Business Logistics* from 1978 to 1989.

Marvin L Manheim was appointed to the William A Patterson Distinguished Chair in Transportation at Northwestern University's Transportation Centre in 1983. The Patterson Chair is the intellectual focal point of the Transportation Centre's extensive research and education activities in transportation. He has written two books and published extensively in the areas of globalization, information technology and competitive strategy, management decision-making, decision support systems, transportation management, transportation systems analysis and application of microcomputers. Professor Manheim is Chairman of the Board of Cambridge Systematics, Inc; and a director of The Harper Group, a publicly-traded international freight forwarder with 300 offices in 46 countries.

James M Masters is an Assistant Professor of Logistics Management in the Department of Marketing in the Max M Fisher College of Business at The Ohio State University. He teaches undergraduate and graduate courses in the quantitative aspects of logistics management. His work has been published in the *Journal of Business Logistics*, the *International Journal of Logistics Management*, the *International Journal of Systems Science*, the *Transportation Journal* and *Decision Sciences*. Professor Masters is a member of the Decision Sciences Institute, The Institute for Management Science, the Production and Operations Management Society, the Society of Logistics Engineers and the Warehousing Education and Research Council.

Alan C McKinnon is a senior lecturer in the Heriot-Watt University Business School, Edinburgh. He obtained a masters degree in transport from the University of British Columbia and PhD from University College London for research on physical distribution in the food industry. He has undertaken research and consultancy work in a wide range of logistics-related topics including the distribution strategies of retailers, warehousing development, inventory management, customer–supplier relationships and freight transport policy. Since 1990, he has been European editor of the *International Journal of Physical Distribution and Logistics Management*.

Ken Ogden is Professorial Fellow and Head of the Monash Transport Group in the Department of Civil Engineering at Monash University in Melbourne, Australia. His research interests cover a range of topics in transport planning and traffic engineering, and he is the author of over 100 technical papers. He currently holds the Chair of the Advisory Committee of the Australian Road Research Board, is a member of the Urban Goods Movement Committee of the US Transportation Research Board, and is former Chair of the National Committee on Transport of the Institution of Engineers Australia. His book *Urban Goods Movement: A Guide to Policy and Planning* has recently been published by Ashgate.

John Oxley read Mechanical Sciences at Cambridge and then worked in industry, initially on chemical plant design and then in plant management. Subsequently he was involved in investigations into plant profitability and operating efficiencies, and in management training. He joined Cranfield Institute of Technology in 1978, consulting and lecturing in logistics, but concentrating primarily on materials handling and warehouse system design and management. He has written tutorial material, and also examines for professional bodies in logistics and distribution. He is co-author of a standard text on Logistics and Distribution Management.

Ivy Penman is Head of International Planning with Exel Logistics, the contract distribution division of NFC plc. Responsible for strategic development, Ivy has been involved for several years in planning and implementing strong expansion into mainland Europe and North America. She is also a regular speaker at conferences and has written numerous articles. For three years Ivy has also worked on an environmental initiative for Exel Logistics. This was launched as a comprehensive policy in June 1991 and has won numerous awards in the UK. A former management consultant with A T Kearney, Ivy was educated at St Andrews University (MA in Philosophy/Psychology) and has an MBA from Cranfield. She spent her formative years in industry with the BOC Group.

Cees Ruijgrok is Professor in Transport and Logistics Management at the Tilburg Institute of Advanced Studies (TIAS) of the Tilburg University, where he holds the position of Director of Studies on the Postgraduate Course in Transport and Logistic Services. He is also head of the Department of Logistics at INRO TNO in Delft. He has studied econometrics at the Erasmus University in Rotterdam and has been involved in research on transport and logistics related subjects since 1972. Previously he has been fellow of the Netherlands Institute of Transport (now NFA) at Rijswijk and has been part-time professor in transport economics at the Free University in Amsterdam.

Alan Rushton is the Director of Graduate Programmes for the Centre for Logistics and Transportation, Cranfield School of Management. He has worked for many years in the field of logistics and distribution. Prior to his academic appointment at Cranfield, he spent some time in industry and as a consultant. He was involved in the initial development of the MSc programme in Distribution and Logistics at Cranfield and now runs the full and part-time programmes. He has particular interest in the development and modelling of distribution and logistics strategy, freight transport and third party distribution. He is co-author of the Handbook of Logistics and Distribution Management. He continues to undertake consulting and to lecture in the UK and internationally.

Minoru Saito is a senior analyst in Nittsu Research Centre Inc, which is a subsidiary company of Nippon Express Co. and the only private research institute specializing in logistics in Japan. After obtaining a Masters degree in Economics from Hosei University, he became an analyst in Nittsu Research Centre Inc. In recent years, he has undertaken research on the location and function of the logistics centre. He has published *Door to Door Delivery Service – Innovator in Transportation*, Seizando, Toyokeizai (Japanese). His second book, *Logistics Strategy*, Toyokeizai (Japanese), was published in Autumn 1993.

Philip B Schary is Professor of Marketing and Business Logistics at Oregon State University in the US. He holds a Bachelor's Degree in Aeronautics from St. Louis University, an MBA from the University of California at Berkeley and a Ph.D from UCLA. He has worked in the airline, aerospace and oil industries before entering academic life. He has also held academic appointments in England, Australia and Denmark. His publications have appeared in a variety of academic and professional journals. From 1973 to 1982, he served as North American editor for the *International Journal of Physical Distribution and Materials Management*. His current interests are issues in international logistics and managing the global supply chain.

Geoff Tweddle, currently working at the Institute for Transport Studies, the University of Leeds, has been engaged in research in the field of transport and distribution for a number of years. He has written numerous articles, mainly concerned with competition between modes and on road goods transport. Prior to 1982 he gained considerable experience in industry, particularly the distribution of bulk materials by road, rail and sea, while employed by a large mining company. He is a member of the Institute of Logistics.

Jos Vermunt is currently Manager of Strategic Innovation of the Royal PTT Netherlands in The Hague. Before that he fulfilled a wide variety of positions in different companies (Bruynzeel, Ahold, Coopers and Lybrand), all dealing with logistics management issues. He has been director of PTT Post Logistics, a subsidiary of the Royal PTT Netherlands which specializes in logistic services for the distribution of small consignment sizes business to business. He has recently finished his PhD at Tilburg University on the subject of professional logistic services. His chapter in this book is a summary of this dissertation.

Matthew Walker graduated from the University of the West of England where he specialized in transport and strategic issues. He then spent several years in retailing before returning to the academic world as a researcher and lecturer in logistics at the Universities of Westminster and Huddersfield. He has published widely on logistics costs, the impact of information technology and customer service. Matthew is now a logistics consultant working on European projects for P-E International. He holds an MSc from the University of Westminster and is a member of both the Chartered Institute of Transport and Institute of Logistics.

Donald Waters graduated in Physics and then developed his interests in Management Science at the University of London. He worked in industry and local government before lecturing at the Strathclyde Business School. Since 1987 he has been a Professor of Operations Management at the University of Calgary. During this time he has acted as a consultant to government and business organizations in Europe, the Middle East, Australia and North America. He has published widely, primarily on topics related to logistics, and has just finished the fourth of a series of text books on Operations Management.

Dr Carl Watson-Gandy has been studying and working in the area of distribution and logistics modelling since 1965. He has written many papers, a book and commercial software. Originally with a mining engineering background, he is a founder and Fellow of the Institute of Logistics, and was instrumental in generating and promulgating many of the original logistics concepts. He has held posts at Imperial College and The Royal Military College of Science and has been a visiting Professor at the University of Copenhagen. He is currently a freelance academic and a consultant with Burman Associates.

Introduction

This second edition of *Logistics and Distribution Planning: Strategies for Management* has been completed to follow on from the success of the original book, which first appeared in 1988. Importantly, it reflects the many changes that have occurred in the field of logistics management since then. In particular, the wider integration of logistics has advanced with great speed, helped by developments such as the Single European Market and the North American Free-Trade Agreement. The successful management of logistics across borders represents one of the major challenges faced by many companies today.

In a similar vein, logistics professionals working in industry, consultancy or the universities, are looking beyond their own borders for sources of ideas and inspiration. They no longer feel tied to a home-grown framework – witness the growing international scope of conferences and journals on logistics, as well as research and consultancy projects.

While the first edition of *Logistics and Distribution Planning: Strategies for Management* enjoyed a substantial international audience, both as a text book for courses and as a guide for managers, its UK origins were strongly reflected in both topics and writers. This has now changed. Some of the original chapters have been retained and updated where they are relevant both to an international readership and to contemporary issues in logistics management. But most are new and written by internationally-renowned authors drawn from around the world, representing eight countries and four continents.

Most of the authors have a professional link with Cranfield in one way or another. Some have contributed to our teaching programmes in logistics, which include our executive development courses as well as our long established Masters course in logistics and transportation. Others have worked with Cranfield in research programmes of various kinds, ranging from 'Reconfiguring European Logistic Systems' for the US-based Council of Logistics Management, to studies of advanced logistics and communications for the inter-governmental Organisation for Economic Cooperation and Development, based in Paris. Networking of this kind plays a vital part in developing our knowledge and understanding in a rapidly changing business environment. It is especially important in the context of logistics where the crossing of organisational and disciplinary boundaries is essential to the achievement of success.

Yet, not so very long ago, logistics did not feature so much in the thinking of even some major companies. This has now changed dramatically, partly as a result of an expansion of scope to include the entire supply chain which offers significant potential for realising benefits through the integration of previously separated activities.

Definitions of logistics vary, both over time and according to the authors. The following description, which is a synthesis of several definitions, aims to encapsulate the widened scope and purpose of logistics management in the 1990s.

> Logistics is the strategic management of movement, storage and information relating to materials, parts and finished goods in supply chains, through the stages of procurement, work-in-progress and final distribution. Its overall goal is to contribute to maximum current and future profitability through the cost effective fulfilment of customer orders.

The intention of this book is not so much to be an encyclopaedia on logistics, to cover everything implicit in the above definition, but rather a forum in which a selected number of key issues are addressed. As in the previous edition, the aim has again been to cover a wide span of logistics interests, ranging from the formulation of strategies, to the effective management of operations. Contributions from a variety of world-wide experts means that it has been possible to count on an authoritative view for each of the topic areas covered in the book.

In my role as editor, I have already had the opportunity to read the thoughts and ideas expressed in each of the chapters. Indeed, one of the greatest pleasures of being editor was to be the *first* to enjoy the riches of the chapters as they converged into this book. I now leave it to new readers to explore the chapters that follow, in the anticipation that they too will benefit, both professionally and personally, from the wealth of knowledge and expertise that they contain.

James Cooper
Cranfield
January 1994

Chapter 1

New Directions in Logistics

Martin Christopher
Cranfield School of Management

In recent years there has been a growing recognition that the *processes* whereby we satisfy customer demands are of critical importance to any organization. These processes are the means whereby products are developed, manufactured and delivered to customers and through which the continuing service needs of those customers are met. The logistics concept is the thread that connects these crucial processes and provides the basis for the design of systems that will cost-effectively service customers.

Accompanying this recognition of the importance of process has been a fundamental shift in the focus of the business towards the market-place and away from the more inwardly oriented production and sales mentality that previously dominated most industries. This change in orientation has necessitated a review of the means whereby customer demand is satisfied – hence the dramatic upsurge of interest in logistics as a core business activity.

The 1990s: The Value Decade

Recession in many markets, combined with new sources of competition, has raised the consciousness of customers towards value. 'Value' in today's context does not just mean value for money – although that is certainly a critical determinant of purchase for many buyers – it also means perceived benefits. Customers increasingly are demanding products with added value, but at lower cost; hence the new competitive imperative is to seek out ways to achieve precisely that.

Michael Porter[1,2] was one of the first commentators to highlight the need for organizations to understand that competitive success could only come through cost-leadership or through offering clearly differentiated products or services. The basic model is illustrated in Figure 1.1. Porter's argument was that a company with higher costs and no differential advantage in the eyes of the customer was in effect a commodity supplier, with little hope of long-term success unless they could find a way out of the box. His prescription was that the organization should seek to become either a *low-cost producer* or a *differentiated* supplier.

However, in reality it is not sufficient to compete only on the basis of being the lowest-cost supplier. The implication of this is that a competitor in the bottom right-hand corner has to compete on price – if a

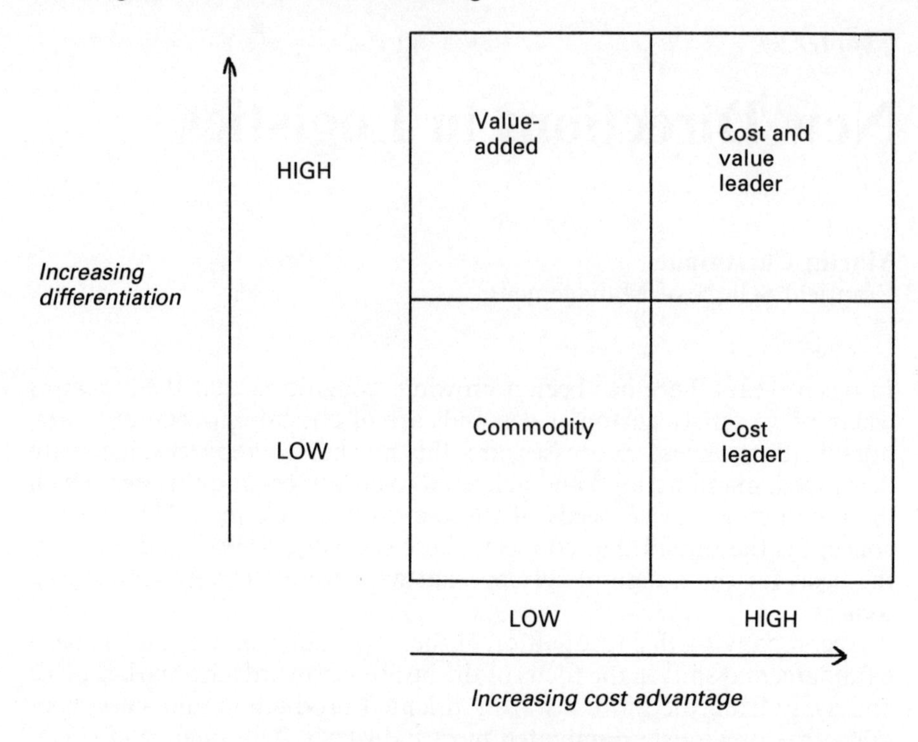

Figure 1.1 *The Competitive Options*

company is only a cost leader, how else can it compete? Competing solely in terms of price will merely reinforce the customer's view that the product is a commodity – the very thing the company wishes to avoid. On the other hand, a strategy based upon differentiation will make it possible to compete on grounds other than price. Whilst value for money will always be an issue, the aim is to increase the customer's perception of the values they are receiving and hence their willingness to pay a higher price.

Because effective logistics management is capable of both reducing costs and enhancing differentiation through superior customer service, it has a unique capability to assist the organization in its journey to the top right-hand corner of the matrix.

An argument that is being heard more frequently is that logistics is a *core capability* which enables the firm to gain and maintain competitive advantage. More and more the view is expressed[3] that it is through capabilities that organizations compete. These capabilities include such processes as new product development, order fulfilment, marketing planning and information systems. There can be little doubt that companies which in the past were able to rely upon product superiority to attain market leadership can no longer do so, as competitive pressure brings increasing technological convergence. Instead these companies must seek to develop systems that enable them to respond more rapidly to customer requirements at ever lower costs. Hence, as well as being the decade of value, the 1990s is the decade when logistics management becomes a central business concern.

Logistics and Supply Chain Management

Logistics management is essentially an integrative process that seeks to optimize the flows of materials and supplies through the organization and its operations to the customer. It is essentially a planning process and an information-based activity. Requirements from the market-place are translated into production requirements and then into materials requirements through this planning process.

It is now being recognized that for the real benefits of the logistics concept to be realized, there is a need to extend the logic of logistics upstream to suppliers, and downstream to final customers. This is the concept of *supply chain management*.

Supply chain management is a fundamentally different philosophy of business organization and is based upon the idea of partnership in the marketing channel and a high degree of linkage between entities in that channel. Traditional models of business organization were based upon the notion that the interests of individual firms are best served by maximizing their revenues and minimizing their costs. If these goals were achieved by disadvantaging another entity in the channel, then that was the way it was. Under the supply chain management model the goal is to maximize profit through enhanced competitiveness in the final market – a competitiveness which is achieved by a lower cost to serve, achieved in the shortest time-frame possible. Such goals are only attainable if the supply chain as a whole is closely co-ordinated in order that total channel inventory is minimized, bottlenecks are eliminated, time-frames compressed and quality problems eliminated.

This new model of competition suggests that individual companies compete not as company against company, but rather as supply chain against supply chain. Thus the successful companies will be those whose supply chains are more cost-effective than those of their competitors.

What are the basic requirements for successful supply chain management? Figure 1.2 outlines the critical linkages that connect the market-place to the supply chain.

The key linkages are between procurement and manufacturing, and between manufacturing and distribution. Each of these three activities, while part of a continuous process, has a number of critical elements.

Procurement

Typically in the past, supply management has been paid scant attention in many companies. Even though the costs of purchases for most businesses are the largest single cost, procurement has not been seen as a strategic task. That view is now changing, as the realization grows that not only are costs dramatically impacted by procurement decisions and

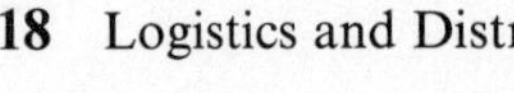

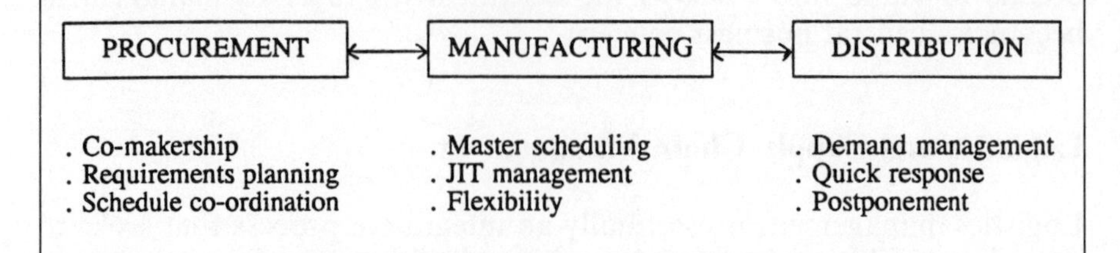

Figure 1.2 *Critical linkages in the supply chain*

procedures, but also that innovation and response-to-market capability are profoundly affected by supplier relationships.

The philosophy of *co-makership* is based upon the idea of a mutually beneficial relationship between supplier and buyer, instead of the more traditional adversarial stance that is so often encountered. With this partnership approach, companies will identify opportunities for taking costs out of the supply chain instead of simply pushing them upstream or downstream. Paperwork can be eliminated, problems jointly solved, quality improved and information shared. By its very nature, co-makership will normally involve longer-term relationships, based upon single-sourcing rather than multiple supply points. Rank Xerox in Europe has adopted the co-makership philosophy which has resulted in their supplier base falling from 5,000 to 300.

A fundamental feature of this integrated approach to supply chain management is the adoption of some form of *materials requirements planning* linked to *schedule co-ordination.*

Basically, materials requirements planning (MRP) is a time-phased approach to managing the inbound flow of materials, which potentially has the capability to link the factory to its suppliers. By itself, however, it lacks the connections to the customer in that it is a 'push' system rather than a 'pull' system. More recently there have been a number of developments to the concept which have enabled a more flexible demand-based approach to be adopted.[4]

Beyond the idea of requirements planning is something much more fundamental, which requires the linking of suppliers' production schedules with those of their customers. The aim should be to view your suppliers' operations as merely an extension of your own. Companies like Nissan, in their UK manufacturing facility, have developed closely linked systems with all of their suppliers so that those suppliers have full visibility not only of the production schedule at Nissan's Washington plant, but also the real-time sequence in which cars are moving down the assembly line. By the use of electronic data interchange (EDI) and open communications, Nissan has been able to reduce lead-times, eliminate inventories and take costs out of the supply chain. Other companies may have introduced similar JIT systems but often, in so doing, have added to their suppliers' costs, not reduced them.

Manufacturing

The key word in manufacturing in today's environment is *flexibility* – flexibility in terms of the ability to produce any variant in any quantity, without significant cost penalty, has to be the goal of all manufacturing strategies. In the past, and even still today, much of the thinking in manufacturing was dominated by the search for economies of scale. This type of thinking led to large mega-plants, capable of producing vast quantities of a standardized product at incredibly low unit costs of production. It also has led many companies to go for so-called 'focused factories' which produce a limited range of products for global consumption.

The downside of this is in effect the possibility of hitting the 'diseconomies' of scale. In other words, the build-up of large inventories of finished product ahead of demand, the inability to respond rapidly to changed customer requirements and the limited variety that can be offered to the customer. Instead of economies of scale, the search is now on for strategies that will reduce total supply chain costs, not just manufacturing costs, and that will offer maximum flexibility against customer requirements. The goal must be 'the economic batch quantity of one', meaning that in the ideal world we would make things one at a time against known customer demands.

One of the lessons that the Japanese have taught us is that the route to flexibility in manufacturing does not necessarily lie through new technology, e.g. robotics, although that can help. A lot can be achieved instead through focusing upon the time it takes to plan, to schedule, to set up, to change over and to document. These are the classic barriers to flexibility and if they can be removed then manufacturing can respond far more rapidly to customer requirements. In a factory with zero lead-times, total flexibility is achieved with no forecasts and no inventory! Whilst zero lead-times are clearly an impossibility, the Japanese have shown that impressive reductions in such lead-times can be achieved by questioning everything we do and the way in which we do it.

Distribution

The role of distribution in the supply chain management model has extended considerably from the conventional view of the activity as being concerned solely with transport and warehousing. The critical task that underlies successful distribution today is *demand management*.

Demand management is the process of anticipating and fulfilling orders against defined customer service goals. Information is the key to demand management: information from the market-place in the form of medium-term forecasts; information from customers, preferably based upon actual usage and consumption; information on production schedules and inventory status and information on marketing activities such as promotions that may cause demand to fluctuate away from the norm.

Clearly, while forecasting accuracy has always to be sought, it must be recognized that it will only rarely be achieved. Instead the aim should be to reduce our dependence upon the forecast by improved information on demand and by creating systems capable of more rapid response to that demand. This is the principle that underlies the idea of *quick response* logistics.

Quick response logistics has become the aim for many organizations, enabling them to achieve the twin strategic goals of cost reduction and service enhancement. In essence, the idea of quick response is based upon a replenishment-driven model of demand management. In other words, as items are consumed or purchased, this information is transmitted to the supplier and this immediately triggers a response. Often high speed, smaller consignment quantity deliveries will be made; the trade-off being that any high transport costs will be more than covered by reduced inventory in the pipeline and at either end of it, yet with improved service in terms of responsiveness. Clearly information technology has been a major enabling factor in quick response logistics, linking the point of sale or consumption with the point of supply.

A further trend that is visible in distribution is the search for *postponement* opportunities. The principle of postponement is that the final configuration or form of the product should be delayed until the last possible moment. In this way maximum flexibility is maintained, but inventory minimized. The distribution function takes on a wider role as the provider of the final added value. For example, at Rank Xerox the aim is not to hold any inventory as finished product but only as semi-finished, modular work-in-progress, awaiting final configuration once orders are received. Similarly, one of the USA's largest video rental chains, Blockbuster Video, is developing a system where only blank tapes are held in individual stores but when a customer requests a video, this is rapidly copied through an electronic link to a central point. When the video is returned it can be taped over for the next customer, and so on.

What is apparent is that distribution in the integrated supply chain has now become an information-based, value-added activity, providing a critical link between the market-place and the factory.

The New Competitive Framework: The Three Rs

We began this chapter with a brief review of how today's customer is increasingly seeking added value and how logistics management can provide that value. In the past, the primary means of achieving competitive advantage were often summarized as the 'four Ps' – product, price, promotion and place. These should now be augmented with the 'three Rs' – reliability, responsiveness and relationships – and logistics strategies need to be formulated with these as the objectives. Let us briefly examine each in turn.

Reliability

In most markets and commercial environments today, customers are seeking to reduce their inventory holdings. Just-in-time practices can be found in industries as diverse as car assembly and retailing. In such situations it is essential that suppliers can guarantee complete order-fill delivered at agreed times. Hence a prime objective of any logistics strategy must be reliability.

Responsiveness

Very closely linked to the customers' demands for reliability is the need for responsiveness. Essentially this means the ability to respond in ever-shorter lead-times with the greatest possible flexibility. Quick response, as we have seen, is a concept and a technology that is spreading rapidly across industries. For the foreseeable future, speed will be a prime competitive variable in most markets. The emphasis in logistics strategy will be upon developing the means to ship smaller quantities, more rapidly, direct to the point of use/consumption.

Relationships

The trend towards customers seeking to reduce their supplier base has already been commented upon. The concept of 'single sourcing' has now received widespread support. The benefits of such an approach include improved quality, innovation sharing, reduced costs and integrated scheduling of production and deliveries. Underlying all of this is the idea that buyer/supplier relationships should be based upon partnership. More and more companies are discovering the advantages that can be gained by seeking out mutually beneficial, long-term relationships with suppliers. From the suppliers' point of view, such partnerships can prove formidable barriers to entry to competitors. Once again, companies are finding that logistics provides a powerful route to the creation of partnerships in the marketing channel. Logistics management should be viewed as the thread that connects the inbound and outbound flows of channel partners.

The challenge to marketing and strategic planning in any business is to construct a corporate strategy that specifically builds upon logistics as a means to achieving competitive advantage, through a much stronger focus on the three Rs. It is still the case that many organizations have not fully understood the strategic importance of logistics and hence have not explicitly tailored logistics into their corporate strategies and their marketing plans.

The Organizational Challenge

One of the most significant changes in recent years has been the way in which we think of organization structures. Conventionally, organizations have been 'vertical' in their design. In other words, businesses have organized around functions such as production, marketing, sales and distribution. Each function has had clearly identified tasks and within

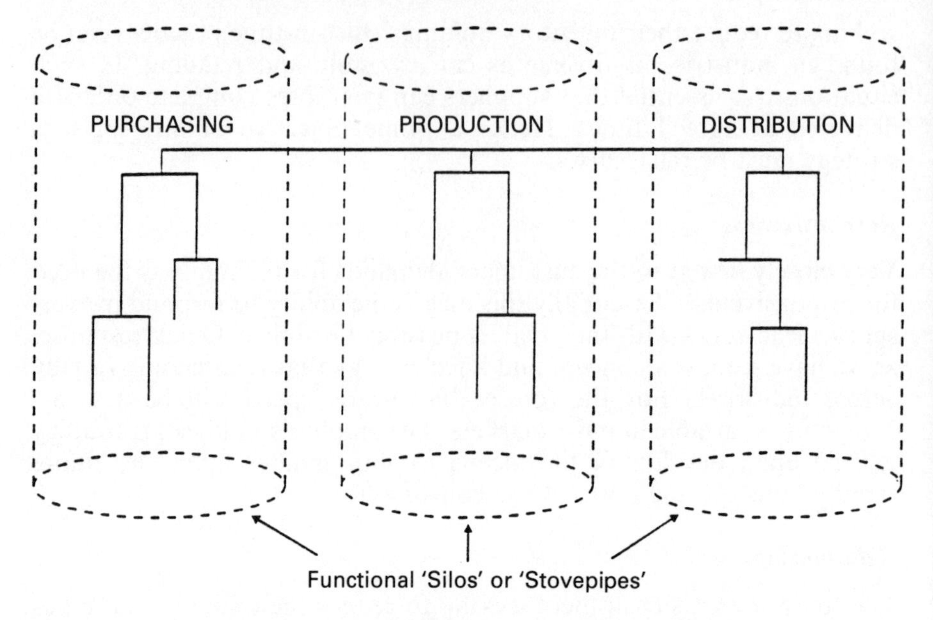

Figure 1.3 *The vertical/functional organization*

these functional 'silos' or 'stovepipes' (as they have been called) there is a recognized hierarchy up which employees might hope to progress. Figure 1.3 illustrates this functionally oriented business.

The problem with this approach is that it is inwardly focused and concentrates primarily on the use of resources rather than upon the creation of outputs. The outputs of any business can only be measured in terms of customer satisfaction achieved at a profit. Paradoxically, the achievement of these outputs can only be achieved by co-ordination and co-operation *horizontally* across the organization.

These horizontal linkages mirror the materials and information flows that link the customer with the business and its suppliers. They are in fact the *core processes* of the business. Figure 1.4 highlights the fundamental difference of the horizontal organization.

In the horizontal organization, the emphasis is upon the management of processes. These processes, by definition, are cross-functional and include new product development, order fulfilment, information management, profitability analysis and marketing planning.

The justification for this radically different view of the business is that these processes are in effect 'capabilities' and, as we have observed, it is through capabilities that the organization competes. In other words, the effectiveness of the new product development process, the order fulfilment process and so on determines the extent to which the business will succeed in the market-place.

How does a conventionally organized business transform itself into a market-facing, process-oriented organization?

One of the major driving forces for change is the revolution that has taken place in information technology and systems enabling the supply

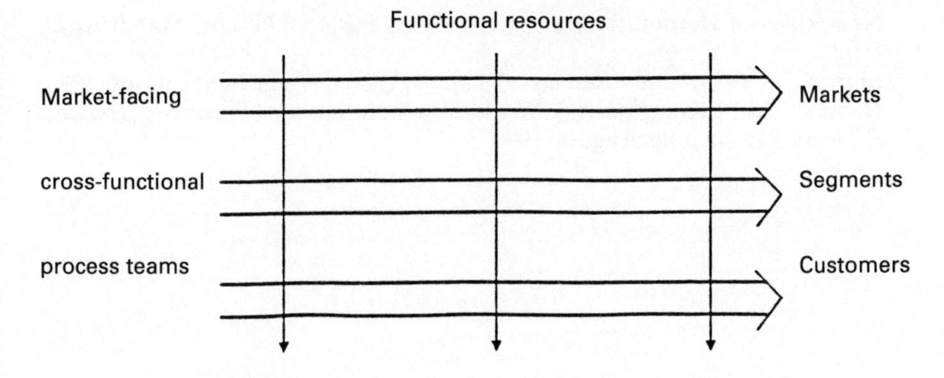

Figure 1.4 *The horizontal/process organization*

chain linkage to become a reality. More and more, the business will find itself organizing around the information system, in other words the processes for capturing information from the market-place (forecasts, anticipated requirements, customer schedules and orders) will be linked to the processes for meeting that demand.

It is not coincidental that one of the biggest priorities for management today is *business process redesign*, a philosophy and a set of tools for fundamentally reviewing the systems and procedures in use within the organization.[5] Emerging from such reviews is the inevitable conclusion that logistics processes are central to the efficient and effective working of the business.

Summary

- Businesses in all types of industries are placing far greater emphasis on the design and management of logistics processes and the integration of those processes upstream and downstream with those of suppliers and customers.
- The business of the future will undoubtedly be market-driven, with logistics processes providing a critical means for achieving corporate goals.
- It will be a highly co-ordinated network of out-sourced flows of materials and supplies, integrated through an information system that reaches from the ultimate consumer to the far end of the supply chain.
- The era of logistics and supply chain management, which many have predicted for some time, seems finally to have arrived.

References

1 Porter, M., *Competitive Strategy*, Free Press, 1980.
2 Porter, M., *Competitive Advantage*, Free Press, 1985.
3 Stalk, G., Evans, P. and Shulman, L.E., 'Competing on Capabilities: The

New Rules of Corporate Strategy', *Harvard Business Review*, March/April, 1992.

[4] Martin, A., *Distribution Resource Planning*, Oliver Wight Publications, 1983.

[5] Hammer, M., 'Re-engineering Work: Don't Automate, Obliterate', *Harvard Business Review*, July/August, 1990.

Chapter 2

Assessing the Cost of Customer Service

Gordon V Hill
Vice President
A T Kearney Limited, Management Consultants

Introduction

The distribution market has undergone a fundamental change within the last 20 years. No longer are distribution services driven by the producers of consumer goods. Now the large retailers are in the driving seat and this has brought considerable change to the market-place.

Retailers have placed much greater emphasis on the customer service elements of distribution. The providers of distribution services have therefore had to ensure that they can respond to the requirements of their major customers. If a retailer demands a delivery to be made at 10.00 on Wednesday morning, say, then the distributor has to be able to guarantee that the load will be there at that time.

For the retailer, an emphasis on customer service in distribution can help to add value to products. Take, for example, the delivery of a product with a limited shelf-life to a retail store. Perishable products of this kind (eg cream, yoghurt, fish, bread) cannot be slow-moving within the distribution system. In economic terms, the extra revenue resulting from fast delivery, with the attendant quality and freshness, outweighs any extra cost incurred, and adds value to the product.

High levels of customer service appeal to retailers because value can be added to products. But the distributors must always be asking themselves the key question, 'Are my customers paying me what it costs to provide increasingly exacting distribution services to them?' Distributors cannot afford to allow retailing customers to add value to products at their expense. When the costs of delivering to a particular customer have been identified, and that customer is found to be paying too little for the service, a further question has to be addressed: 'What steps should I be taking to ensure my customer pays equitably for the services I provide?'

Both the above questions underpin the formulation of a customer service strategy by distributors; yet neither question is easy to answer. One reason is that some producers quote a price for their products that includes the cost of delivery to the customer. A distributor working on behalf of such producers may find it difficult to initiate a dialogue on distribution costs because these are often not quantified or well understood. The producer may be unable to evaluate the differing costs to deliver, say, to different parts of the country.

Within this environment, the distributor has the unenviable task of formulating a successful customer service strategy. This chapter begins by examining two sets of attributes that influence a customer service strategy. The first comprises what may be termed 'physical distribution service attributes' and the second 'trading service attributes'. Examples are used whenever possible to demonstrate how these attributes affect the cost structure of distribution activity.

There follows a further section which demonstrates the need to measure, monitor, control and cost the operation of a customer service strategy.

Physical Distribution Service Attributes of Customer Service

The components of a physical distribution service may be expressed in the following terms:

- Availability of stock – that is the availability of product for on-schedule delivery
- Order cycle time
- Frequency of delivery
- On-schedule delivery
- Reliability of delivery.

Together, the components are responsible for giving distribution a particular customer service profile. It helps, however, to consider each component in turn, to establish its contribution to the profile.

Availability of Stock

The most frequently used measure of customer service in physical distribution management is that of stock availability. Distributors often sell their services on the basis of a customer service promise that includes, say, '95 per cent of all orders will be delivered from stock'. Also, contracts are often negotiated on the basis of stock availability measures, with a given percentage of orders or items to be met from stock. Penalty clauses may be introduced whereby a failure to reach or maintain a given level of service will result in the distributor being effectively fined for poor performance.

It is important, therefore, to define precisely the basis of measurement. Consider the simple example of a wholesaler receiving an order calling for ten units of each of ten different types of battery – a total requirement for one hundred batteries. However, only five of one type of battery were available and these were supplied to the customer. The customer service performance would be said to be:

- Batteries supplied: 95 per cent

- Battery types (line items) fully satisfied: 90 per cent
- Orders fully satisfied: 0 per cent.

It follows that a distributor must pay a great deal of attention to the costs of stock availability. Research has demonstrated the curvilinear character of the cost of investment in stock. Figure 2.1 shows a typical relationship between cost and levels of stock availability. It demonstrates that, with rising levels of stock availability, costs at first rise in an almost linear relationship. However, when stock availability levels exceed 90 per cent, there is exponential growth in stock investment.

Clearly, it is essential for companies to understand the relationship between stock availability and cost. This is especially true for companies with many stock lines, where dramatic increases in safety stock requirements, and hence in cost, become apparent as the stock availability is increased beyond the 90 per cent service level.

Most companies are acutely aware of the costs of holding stock. This awareness was most recently demonstrated during the early 1990s, when companies sought to reduce their stock levels as the recession and high interest rates increased the cost of holding stock. One solution adopted to reduce stock costs was the centralization of inventory holdings from several depots into one main location.

There are potential savings to be achieved in manpower, buildings, handling equipment, administration and inventory financing costs through centralization. However, some of these savings may have to be traded-off against increases in transport costs. As Figure 2.2 shows, fewer depots can bring increases in transport cost.

Yet, overall, centralization will often mean that companies can maintain, or even increase, stock availability while total distribution costs are reduced. This is a major factor influencing the trend towards centralization within the UK retail sector. Most of the major multiples in grocery retailing now operate centralized distribution systems.

Order Cycle Time

Order cycle time is the elapsed time between a customer intimating a need and that need being satisfied. It is wrong to regard order cycle time simply in terms of the time interval over which the supplying company chooses to exercise direct control. A mail-order warehouse, for example, may claim to be offering a 24-hour service if it despatches goods the day after receiving the order for those goods. However, the customer would almost certainly see the order cycle time as being longer than 24 hours.

It follows that order cycle time should be defined as the sum of three time intervals, which are:

- The inbound order communication
- The order processing as well as the preparation and despatch of goods
- The outbound transportation of the goods.

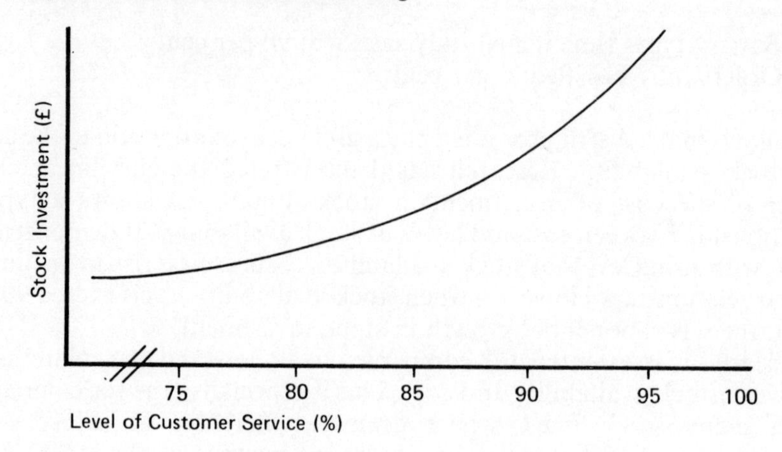

Figure 2.1 *Stock investment*

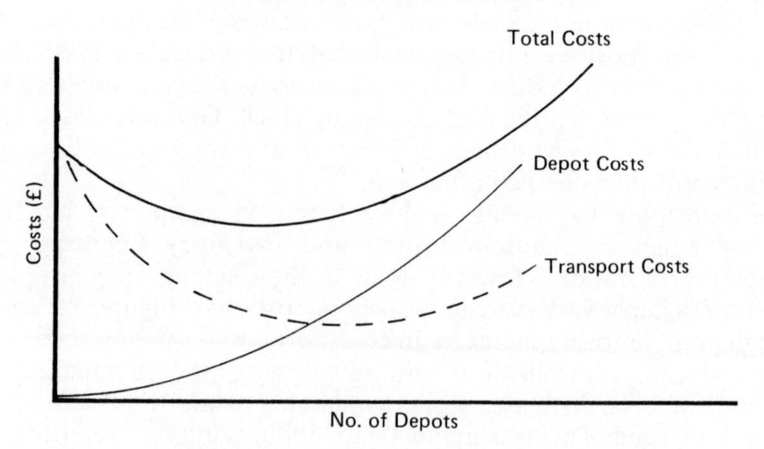

Figure 2.2 *The depot cost-transport trade-off*

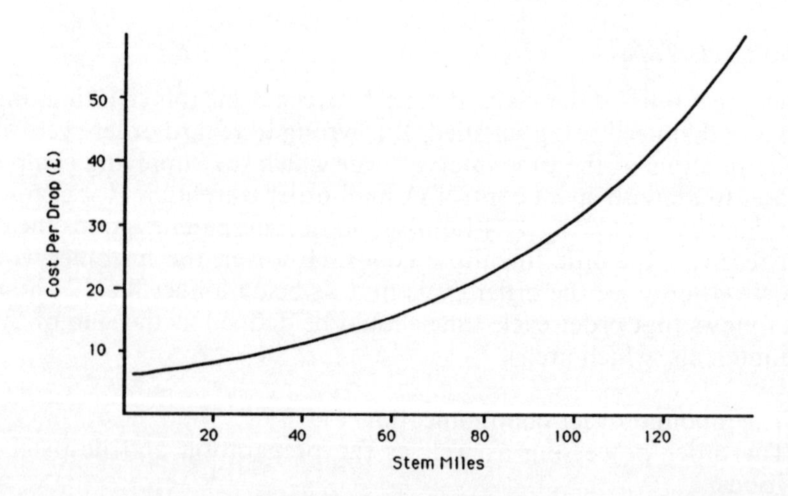

Figure 2.3 *Cost per drop*

If the order cycle time is to be shortened, then one or more of the above time intervals must be reduced correspondingly. This almost always leads to increased costs, resulting from wages paid for working unsocial hours, inefficient resource utilization and the need to use stockholding depots. There is an important trade-off between the extent to which such costs can be tolerated and the commercial benefits that a shorter order cycle time may bring.

Frequency of Delivery

While the *timing* of deliveries is important to many retail customers, the *frequency* of delivery can also be a key consideration in customer service. Many retail outlets now have little or no stockroom capacity and large consignments cannot, therefore, be readily accommodated. Smaller, more frequent, consignments are more usual.

This pattern of deliveries implies multi-drop journeys by distributors when delivering to many of their customers. Multi-drop journeys are intrinsically expensive, especially at a time when depot networks are being thinned in an attempt to reduce the total level of stockholding. The more distant the delivery area, the more time the vehicle and driver spend in reaching that delivery area, and hence the amount of productive time spent in multi-drop work is correspondingly reduced. Figure 2.3 shows an example of how much more expensive multi-drop operations become as deliveries are made at greater distances from the depot.

A further aspect of delivery frequency is the cost of fulfilling incomplete orders. When a company does not have the stock to deliver all the goods requested, it has three choices. Firstly, it may delay sending the whole consignment until new stock of the missing goods arrives. This is not, however, a popular option. Secondly, it may despatch the available goods upon receipt of order and make a further delivery immediately after the missing stock finally becomes available. Thirdly, it may send the top-up consignment to the customer along with his next, regular, consignment.

Order top-up is an issue in delivery frequency, because the costs associated with the three options will not be the same. In most cases, the second option will be appreciably more expensive than the others because a special delivery arrangement is made. Yet the second option may be the one sought by customers insisting on high levels of service. If this is the case, then the distributor must be prepared to take action in two respects: he must first ensure that stock availability is set at an appropriate level and kept there; then he must endeavour to recover the costs of providing these special deliveries.

On-Schedule Delivery

As distribution has become increasingly retailer-driven, meeting the delivery requirements of retailers has become of paramount importance. In particular, on-schedule delivery is now an integral part of many distribution operations serving the retail sector.

In the grocery sector, many multiples have diversified their product lines, placing an increasing emphasis on short shelf-life products, such as dairy produce, fish and meat. This development has meant an increase in the frequency of deliveries.

In order to avoid queues and in an effort to smooth their workload, many grocery retailers have instituted delivery control systems. These require that deliveries are made at specific times determined by the retailers. All deliveries must be booked in. Any vehicle that arrives without a predetermined delivery time, or any vehicle that is late, may well be refused access to the unloading bay. Meeting the exact delivery requirements of a customer is therefore an important facet of customer service.

On-schedule deliveries, however, do impose costs on the distributor, especially when a delivery service is offered to more than one customer. The distributor will be attempting to meet a number of booked deliveries, all set independently of one another. As a result, delivery schedules will become complex and vehicles under-utilized. It is reasonable to expect the distributor to try to recover the cost of meeting on-schedule deliveries from those customers requiring them.

Reliability of Delivery

Regular delivery not only satisfies customer service requirements, but can benefit the distributor, since distribution planning becomes relatively simple. In particular, there is scope for grouping calls on a geographical basis with all deliveries to, say, the Wokingham area being made on a Tuesday. The simplicity of the arrangement has a certain appeal for the distributor and will help to reduce some costs. Vehicle routeing and scheduling, for example, will be less complex and therefore less costly.

However, there is also the risk of inefficiency in some areas of the distribution operations. Consider a consistently maintained order cycle with all deliveries being made within 48 hours of receipt of order. As the distributor has no control of the size of the order, considerable fluctuations in demand may occur within a defined geographical area designated for a delivery service on a particular weekday. During one week there may be high demand, requiring the use of additional vehicles. In the following week, vehicles may be under-utilized. There will be no possibility of evening out fluctuations in demand across the whole distribution system if delivery area boundaries are fixed. These considerations must be fully evaluated when a company is costing out its distribution service for customers.

The above examination of distribution service attributes shows their contribution to customer service and their impact on the structure of distribution costs. However, it is important to emphasize that attributes will vary in importance from customer to customer, according to the characteristics of the distribution markets served. For example, one multiple retail chain may wish to compete in terms of the freshness of its products. It will therefore require regular daily deliveries. Another may compete on the cheapness of its goods. In this case, a weekly delivery may be sufficient.

Distributors should be prepared to assess which service package to offer potential customers, by making a close assessment of likely needs. Relevant factors will include market sector, turnover, location of outlets and the distribution strategies of competitors.

It invariably pays for a distributor to assess the likely needs of customers and to prepare a number of distribution options for the customer to consider. The choice by the customer can then form the basis for the service provided. This approach will avoid the unhappy situation where a customer requests an inappropriate distribution service, the distributor provides it, the customer then finds it unsuitable and blames the distributor for its failings.

The Trading Aspects of Customer Service

It is vital to recognize that physical distribution service attributes of customer service are complemented by a series of trading service attributes. These apply to the wider trading environment of companies, rather than just to distribution. The most important trading service attributes are:

- Debt financing
- Stock financing
- Materials-handling techniques
- Technical support facilities.

Debt Financing

Many companies, whether providing goods or services, allow customers to delay payment for some time after invoices are received. Very often there is an accepted period of time that suppliers will allow their customers. This may be 30, 60, or even 90 days.

Delayed payment amounts to suppliers giving interest free loans to their customers and it is often justified because increased turnover may be promoted by the practice. The disadvantage, however, is that strains on cash flow can result.

A further refinement of extended credit is 'credit stretching'. This occurs when the customer places an order at the end of an accounting period, in the knowledge that administration procedures within the supplying company will delay the raising of the invoice until the following accounting period. As a result, the customer could enjoy protracted credit at the expense of the supplier.

Distributors can be affected just as much by the above practices as the producers of goods. They may find they are paying interest on loans to bridge the time interval between the provision of distribution service and the receipt of payment for that service. Clearly any interest paid is a cost of serving the customer concerned. Furthermore, there are opportunity costs resulting from delayed payment which should also be taken into account. They too represent debt financing by the company. Distributors should consider the scope for recovering the cost of debt financing from their customers by reflecting it in the rates charged.

Stock Financing

In many cases, stock is held in anticipation of the orders from a variety of customers and it is difficult to attribute the costs of holding the stock to any one customer in particular. However, on occasions, some customers require special product lines to be held exclusively for them. In these circumstances, it is appropriate to recognize the cost of financing stock held on behalf of such customers and, if appropriate, to charge for the service.

The need to make a charge is, indeed, justified if a customer asks the supplier to hold extra stock in anticipation of increased demand. In effect, the supplier is making it unnecessary for the customer to hold stocks. Yet the supplier will be bearing the expense of holding the extra stock within his own distribution operation.

Materials-Handling Techniques

No longer is the choice of equipment for materials handling purely a distribution decision. Many high street retailers, for example, have developed specialized equipment for use both in the store and in the vehicle. Much of the equipment is designed to improve the smoothness of both vehicle unloading and shelf-filling.

When the distributor provides materials-handling equipment, he should take account of the benefits to the customer which arise subsequent to the distribution operations. Yet roll cages, pallets, boxes, barrels and storage cartons may all require substantial investment. It is right that all the service benefits enjoyed by the customer are evaluated as a basis for justifying the investment, but that the cost of the investment is recognized as a cost of serving the customer.

Furthermore, it is often the case that goods have to be transferred from one type of equipment to another to suit the demands of particular customers. For example, goods to most large distribution centres are delivered on wooden pallets. Yet many retail outlets require their goods to be supplied in roll cages. It is the responsibility of the distributors to make this transfer from one type of equipment to another. The additional time and expense involved should be appropriately reflected in the charges to the individual customer.

Similarly, all forms of technical support, from vehicles to computers, are put at the disposal of customers by suppliers as part of the distribution service. Yet individual customers invariably have different requirements for technical support, making the overall task complex and expensive. The costs incurred are often not met by the recipients of technical support, because this is seen as an aid to selling and not a customer service. Distributors would be wise to review this practice, with the aim of reflecting in the rates charged the full costs of technical support attributable to individual customers.

Planning a Customer Service Strategy

The previous sections have outlined the multi-faceted nature of customer service. Creating an awareness of the many components of customer service is the first step in designing a distribution service. A subsequent step should be to quantify the impact and cost of customer service attributes in distribution service.

In some cases, a potential customer will already have devised a set of distribution performance criteria against which the supplier of the service will be monitored. Rarely will these criteria satisfy the needs of both the user and the provider of the distribution service. The distributor is likely to wish to monitor additional criteria. For the user, operational standards in distribution (eg service reliability) may be the main consideration. The distributor, however, will need additional data as a basis for costing and pricing the distribution service provided.

A number of criteria, however, will be of common interest, and can form the basis for establishing a sound cooperative relationship. In broad terms, the criteria can be either positive or negative in character. An example of a positive measure is the percentage of all goods despatched within 48 hours of receipt of order. Negative measures include the number of user complaints about the distribution service and the number of invoice queries.

Once a measure has been established, distribution performance can be monitored, and this forms the basis of deciding how much it will cost to correct any aspect of the service provided. In this way, the costing and controlling of customer service is given a firm footing.

However, there is usually a need for distributors to develop a second stage of service analysis in an attempt to allocate joint service costs between individual customers. As discussed in the previous sections, there are a number of service attributes where costs are not covered by direct charges to customers. This second stage requires a form of distribution audit in which the key service characteristics are identified and assessed according to their capacity for cost generation. The distributor must then try to ensure that any costs generated by providing a service for a particular customer should be recovered from that customer.

Additionally, there are important marketing reasons for proceeding to the second stage of customer service measurement. In particular, it will help to identify the contribution made to profits by the separate market segments, retail chains or product groups. This gives a foundation for successful business development by identifying the most profitable trading areas for the distributor. It is vital to recognize that distributors, no less than producers, will benefit if they identify their most profitable markets and plan accordingly.

The Implications of a Customer Service Analysis

The process of analysing the costs of customer service should ideally include the following components:

- Price discounts on the products sold
- Gross margins achieved by individual products
- Customer service levels
- The cost of distribution
- Order soliciting costs
- Merchandising costs
- Point of sale support costs.

It may then emerge that some customers, or indeed, whole market segments, do not contribute to the corporate profits. Appropriate action can be taken with respect to any of the above components to improve that contribution. In particular, customer service levels may need to be modified.

An example will help to illustrate the application of this approach to customer profitability assessment. Using CASCADE, the computer model developed by A.T. Kearney for customer profitability evaluation in distribution, the customers of a manufacturing company were ranked according to their contribution to fixed overheads and profits. From the analysis, three broad groups of customer accounts emerged. There were those accounts which contributed greatly to the company's profits because the distribution costs were relatively modest. Then there was a broad base of customers whose contribution to profit was small but positive. Finally, there was a group of accounts that attracted so much cost that their contribution was negative and they had an adverse effect of overall profits.

Different consequences result from identifying the costs of customer service by means of a customer service audit. Sometimes there is an element of cross-subsidy between customers or outlets. This is most probably the result of two factors within distribution. The first is a failure by many distributors to undertake a detailed customer service analysis and to attribute costs appropriately. The second factor is the use of an equalized delivery pricing policy to customer outlets. This allows for the same charge to be made for each delivery, irrespective of location within the country or service provided. Its merit may be simplicity, but it serves to conceal the true costs of distribution.

The Implications of a Contribution Analysis for Customer Service

The implications of identifying the full costs of customer service are potentially far-reaching, for both the providers and users of distribution. Consider, for example, a retail user with a dedicated delivery operation. This operation may be provided on the basis of equalized delivery pricing, with each retail outlet receiving goods at a given price per case. Cross-subsidization in the delivery service means that the true costs of servicing the customer outlets is hidden. For remote locations, the true delivery cost could be very high, reducing the commercial viability of the outlet.

Transparency in distribution costing therefore gives the retailer a proper basis for an evaluation of his own trading environment. There is the possibility that some outlets might be closed. Alternatively, the retailer may simply regard the additional costs as a justifiable price for continued presence in a particular market. Whatever the outcome, the commercial judgement has a firmer foundation than before.

Distributors, too, need to be aware of the potential dangers of cross-subsidization. Take, for example, a large producer which sells to two high street chains. The first asks the distributor to take receipt of the goods and to deliver them weekly in bulk to their regional distribution centres. The second asks for daily delivery to all their outlets. Clearly the cost profiles of the two delivery operations will be markedly different.

Any tendency for the distributor to blur the differences in cost profile through cross-subsidization, either deliberate or inadvertent, can be potentially disastrous. This is because one customer may be paying more than he should for his distribution service. If he discovers this and takes his business elsewhere, the distributor may find it difficult to find replacement business on the same terms. The prospects will be even worse if there is a contract which does not allow the distributor to charge a realistic price to the remaining client, once undercharging is discovered.

The proper costing of the customer service elements is, therefore, the key to developing a rational relationship between the users and providers of distribution services. Only when all the cost elements of a service are identified and appropriate rates charged to customers will distribution develop as a business. The strategy is clear. It now requires the industry to apply it.

Summary

- The increasing domination of retailers in the distribution market place, at the expense of producers, has led to an increasing emphasis on customer service
- Customer service has two sets of attributes; those relating to the distribution service, itself, and those relating to the wider trading environment
- Many distributors are unaware of the costs of the distribution services they provide. It is therefore essential for performance criteria to be devised against which the costs of distribution can be assessed
- Performance measures for customer service are also important for distributors because they can help identify their most profitable customers. This helps provide a firm foundation for planning business strategies which are aimed at profitable sectors of the distribution market.

Chapter 3

Formulating Logistics Strategy

Nathalie Fabbe-Costes and Jacques Colin
CRET
University of Aix-Marseille II

Why Formulate Logistics Strategies?

Commercial and industrial organizations can be thought of as systems which are composed of operational processes structured and regulated by a set of functions that can become strategic; they are currently the object of intense environmental pressures. Never have these forces been so diverse: they are disrupting previous equilibriums and call for rapid and coherent responses, as shown in Figure 3.1.

The multiplicity of corporate responses implies coordination and integration in an approach with a clearly defined strategic character. Indeed, only through the use of strategy, this 'art of using information

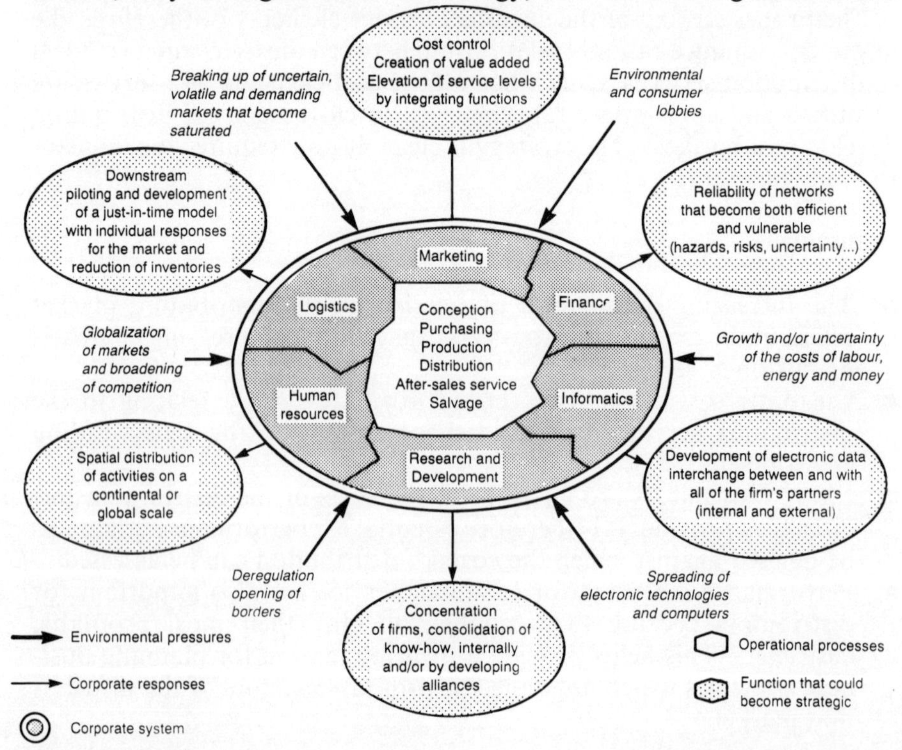

Figure 3.1 *Corporate responses to environmental pressures*

obtained in operating, integrating it, quickly formulating plans of action and having the ability to gather a maximum of certainties in order to confront the uncertain'[1] will companies be able to overcome the extreme environmental instability that appears to be characterizing the end of the millennium. Strategy will enable companies to formulate and achieve their objectives, allowing them to seize and take advantage of opportunities as they arise, while, at the same time, remaining in tune with their environment.

It appears that one of the priorities that is considered essential today by numerous firms is an understanding of logistics. Logistics, defined as the technology of control of the physical flow of materials and goods and related information that a firm sends, transfers and receives, appears as an organizational approach that can conserve and improve the flexibility and reactivity of the firm *vis-à-vis* its environment.

In order to satisfy its ideal objectives of continuity (preventing stock-out) and fluidity (limiting overcapacity), logistics has progressively left behind its original operational role, which was a combination of transport, handling and warehousing operations. The concept of a logistics chain enabled firms to control flow from downstream to upstream and to optimize, in terms of cost and level of service, the whole physical movement pulled by demand. The field of logistics has therefore been considerably broadening, as illustrated in Figure 3.2.

Logistics has now become a very far-reaching 'total' approach, which is both transversal and very ambitious. Its main role is to synchronize overall physical flow, and it is indeed in permanent interaction with all of the classic functions of a firm, constituting an active interface between the firm and its environment.

It is paradoxical to note that while the environmental pressures that appear in Figure 3.1 are not specific to logistics, the same cannot be said of the responses that firms in most sectors must now make. Their for-

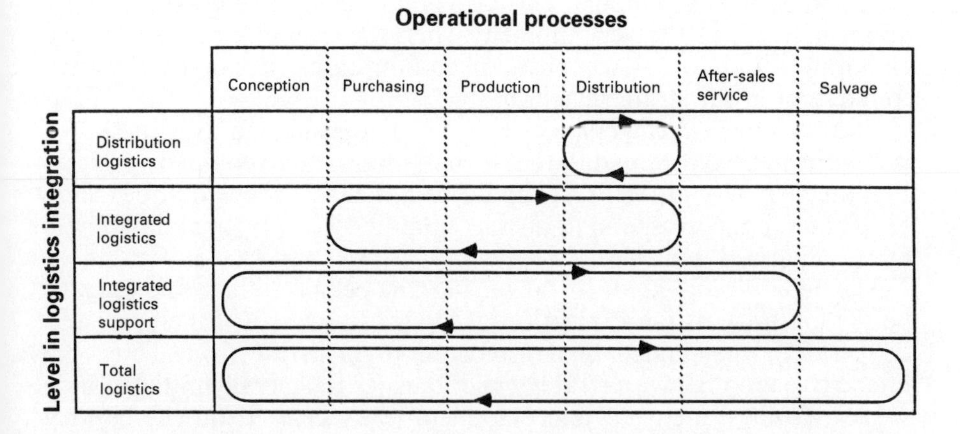

Source: Adapted from Mathe, H., Colin, J., Tixier, D., *La logistique*, Dunod, Paris, 1983.

Figure 3.2 *Evolution of the field of action of logistics*

mulation conceals options that imply a logistics approach, especially when responses are combined. For challenges that are not specifically logistic, the firm conceives solutions and strategies that are, or that become logistic.

The profound transformations that have taken place in the structure of firms, as well as the extension of their activities, have confirmed the need for a strategic approach to logistics. Its aim is to control the areas where the firm operates, the timing of these operations and finally, the inherent risks involved in the firm's choices.

How can one identify the strategic projects in which logistics could play a key role? To answer this question in a 'creative' manner, we thought it indispensable to propose an innovative approach to strategy formulation.

A Conceptual Approach to Formulating Logistics Strategy

The classic approach to formulating a logistics strategy consists in beginning with the firm's overall strategy and then defining the logistics strategy that will enable the firm to reach its objectives. Logistics is thus conceived as a functional support system and a tool for global strategy; logistics strategy should appear as a subset of the overall strategy. The control of the flow of materials and goods today constitutes a key factor for success in numerous domains which justifies this downward approach.

Logistics, like other functions such as marketing and informatics, also opens new strategic lines of action. In order to formulate these new lines, it is imperative to reverse the classic approach, to think strategic logistics rather than logistics strategy.

Strategic logistics consists in imagining and developing strategic actions that would be impossible without strong logistics competences. From being seen first as a key factor for success, logistics is becoming a fully competitive advantage. This viewpoint makes it necessary to think about logistics at the very moment when the overall strategy is being elaborated and to foresee how, in certain cases, it can be the very foundation of the strategic action.

The two interrelated perspectives between logistics and strategy shown in Figure 3.3 lead to very different formulations and to company projects that are also very different. It should be noted that they do not exclude each other, but correspond to distinct finalities. The principal differences are summarized in Table 3.1.

The determining factor for 'reversing' the perspectives would seem to be the maturity of the perception of logistics as a cross-functional and deliberately open-ended management domain in the firm. Thus, the interactive loop between strategy and logistics is generally initiated by a request from strategy to logistics, historically centred on the control (reduction) of logistics costs.

The experience, know-how and systems developed in logistics action then retroact on the strategy, becoming the vector of its (re)formulation,

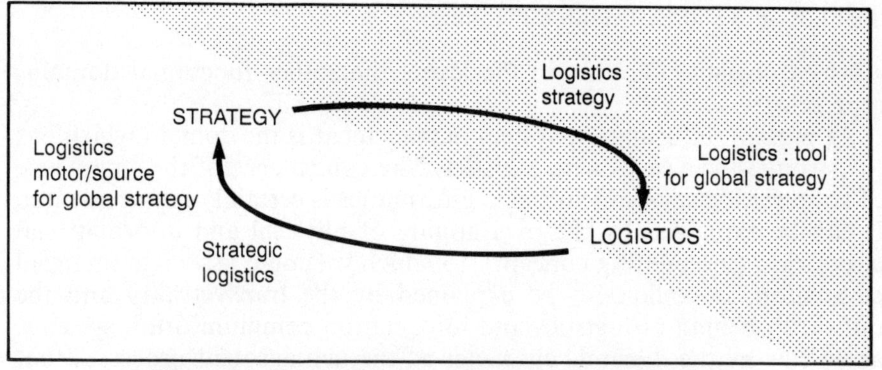

Figure 3.3 *From logistics strategy to strategic logistics*

enabling the firm to differentiate itself by the logistics services it provides, increasing its range of combined products and services, or even diversifying into logistics activities.

Finally, strategic logistics formulations emerge from this repeated transversing of the interactive strategy/logistics loop, which becomes a 'progress spiral'[2] for the firm. The purpose of running through this loop is to have a logistics organization that is adapted to the firm's objectives, and to be able to identify, exploit, or even better, create opportunities for the firm.

The strategic formulation of logistics can be expressed by two 'classic' concepts of strategy: the profession and the mission. In concrete terms, to formulate a logistics strategy, one defines the ranges of movement that it 'produces', how it produces them (technologies, know-how, organization), to whom they are directed (internal or external clients) and the needs that they satisfy. Consequently, this formulation can identify several 'sectors of activity' that are more or less synergistic. Among them, some can be considered supports for the firm's overall strategy (logistics strategy perspective), while other sectors can be vectors of its strategy (strategic logistics perspective).

Formulation is then oriented to the choice of organizational solutions to adopt in order to achieve defined objectives. It should be noted that as a transversal function of coordination for all stages of movement and for management for both internal and external interfaces, logistics can only be efficient if it is linked with the other functions, rather than replacing them. Options that are chosen in the domain of logistics must in particular be congruent with those in the domains of marketing, finance, information systems, manufacturing and human resources. Ideally, logistics strategy should be combined with the other strategies, and

Table 3.1 *Main differences between logistics strategy and strategic logistics*

	Logistics strategy	*Strategic logistics*
Perception of logistics stakes	strategy support	strategy foundation
Effects on organization	improvement, evolution	change, transmutation

strategic logistics should use the levers that other functional domains represent.

At present, information-system management is the domain which has the strongest synergies with logistics. The coincidence of the emergence of strategic logistics and strategic informatics is certainly not accidental. It can be explained by the overlapping of physical and informational circulation (the piloting concept), to which we could associate financial circulation. It could also be explained by the transversality and the outward opening of logistics and information communication systems, as well as by the dynamic character of the management processes that they support. In addition, the control of physical and informational flow develops and is the support for a flexibility and adaptability of the firm that is now indispensable for durability and growth.

The formulation of logistics strategy also deals with the 'make or buy' decision. The strategic or non-strategic character of a logistics organization provides information on the originality and confidentiality required for the necessary know-how, the expected reliability of the processes and the significance of the planned organization. In the cases of delegated operations or organizations, it brings about the definition of the means required to ensure control. It therefore creates networks of complementary skills and ensures their consistency.

It is not our intention, at this point, to go into existing organizations in detail. However, we do wish to illustrate through actual examples of logistics projects how firms have taken into account the strategic dimension of logistics.

Illustrated Typology of Possible Logistics Strategies

In order to specify and illustrate the conceptual approach to the strategic formulation of logistics, we have selected several case studies of distributors, manufacturers and genuine 'logistics firms' that have now become transporters and logistics suppliers. They represent a variety of strategies and are dealt with by category. Our typology, presented in Table 3.2, contains six 'classic' generic strategic axes and considers strategic formulations by adopting both perspectives described in Figure 3.3.

Certain axes correspond to actions conceived (at least initially) without changing the domain of activity (cost domination, differentiation and innovation), or imagined in order to move to new domains of activity (expansion and diversification), with alliance, *a priori*, allowing for both.

Cost Domination

Logistics Strategy: Reduce Costs That Are Specific To Logistics

- **Becton-Dickinson**, a multinational firm in the medical sector, has centralized its stock in a single European site in order to reduce its

Table 3.2 *Typology of logistic strategies and strategic logistics*

<table>
<tr><th colspan="2">Approach</th><th>Logistics Strategy</th><th>Strategic Logistics</th></tr>
<tr><td colspan="2">Cost domination</td><td>Reduce logistics costs</td><td>Reduce overall costs with logistics</td></tr>
<tr><td colspan="2">Differentiation</td><td>Quality of logistics service</td><td>Logistics factor of differentiation</td></tr>
<tr><td colspan="2">Innovation</td><td>Logistics support for innovation</td><td>Logistics as a source/ motor for innovation</td></tr>
<tr><td colspan="2">Alliance</td><td>Logistics as a means of alliance</td><td>Logistics as a source/ motor for alliance</td></tr>
<tr><td rowspan="2">Expansion</td><td>Profession</td><td>Logistics as a support for integration</td><td>Logistics as a new product</td></tr>
<tr><td>Mission</td><td>Logistics as a support for extension</td><td>Logistics in order to win new clients</td></tr>
<tr><td colspan="2">Diversification</td><td>Use of logistics synergies</td><td>Diversify through or in logistics</td></tr>
</table>

inventory level and at the same time the financial costs of immobilized capital.

- After reducing the number of their factories and specializing the remaining ones at a European level (economies of scale on production costs), **SKF** and **Roussel-UCLAF** had to construct a distribution logistics scheme in order to control costs that threatened to soar.
- In order to limit the costs of stock possession, **Bull** distributed its stock of spare parts in a hierarchic network with local, national and European warehouses.
- **Carrefour**, a French hypermarket chain, gave up systematically supplying its stores directly from manufacturers; it now has products delivered to warehouses maintained by logistics suppliers in order to reduce the cost of supplying.

Strategic Logistics: Through Logistics, Reduce Overall Costs

- **Auchan**, a French hypermarket chain, has a network of warehouses, permitting it to considerably reduce purchasing costs through the ability to stock massive quantities that it imports or buys on promotion from its suppliers.
- **Intermarche**, a French supermarket chain, works in the same manner: two-thirds of its inventory corresponds to a speculative stock of promotional products and products bought at a high discount for quantity.
- In the automobile industry, logistics approaches to external flow

control by reducing the number of suppliers have succeeded in diminishing supply costs. **Renault** and **PSA (Peugeot)** now have only 950 primary suppliers who were all due to be registered (with stricter certification than ISO norms) in 1993 to deliver just-in-time. Qualitative and quantitative controls on delivery were to be totally eliminated.

Differentiation

Logistics Strategy: Improve the Quality of the Logistics Service

- By rationalizing their logistics, **Becton-Dickinson** and **Bull** were able to improve their performances in terms of quality of service, availability of references, complete deliveries, guaranteed delivery times.
- **Mory-Protect**, a French logistics supplier in the Novalliance group, has specialized in the logistics of dangerous products (chemical) and has become a recognized specialist.
- **Philips-Eclairage** has a highly automated central warehouse in the Paris area that is controlled by computerized logistics, making it possible to deliver to its clients every day. Thus wholesalers no longer need to hold more stock than is needed in between deliveries: they choose to be preferentially supplied by Philips.
- **Nozal**, a merchant in metallurgy and a subsidiary of Usinor-Sacilor Stell, is developing regional warehouses equipped with cutting machines and which are able to make daily deliveries of custom-cut steel to clients. The client orders on the eve of delivery: there is no need to maintain stocks, or to rely on merchants who deliver weekly.

Strategic Logistics: Permit An Increased Differentiation

- **PSA** and **Renault**, like many car-makers, have developed a just-in-time logistics that permits them to feed very flexible production lines that are capable of assembling vehicles that conform exactly to client specifications, with synchronized and single deliveries. The Renault Clio, for instance, can be delivered with the following options: air-conditioning, power-steering, 80 different engine types, 20 different gearboxes, and 5 different bodies: a total of 32,000 theoretical combinations, without taking into account the range of paintwork and upholstery options. The Peugeot 205 is available in 28,000 combinations. Over its entire automobile range, PSA can offer 500,000 combinations to its customers. The customer can even change his mind up to ten days before the delivery date, thanks to a logistics information and products system that controls its manufacturing system.
- In order to increase its range of aircraft, **Airbus-Industrie** elaborated a logistics system capable of supplying work stations one by one, depending on the type of aircraft being assembled.

Innovation

Logistics Strategy: Logistics As a Support for Innovation, Logistics Innovation

- **La Redoute**, a French mail-order firm, promises its customers a two-day delivery service which has enlarged its market. This commercial innovation depends on a very strong integration of physical and information flows and on the automation of the sorting centre created for it by the French postal service.
- In order to exchange logistics information with its suppliers (information concerning its suppliers' shipment notification, etc), the French automobile sector has set up an EDI (Galia/Odette) network, which is a genuine support for the just-in-time model of production planning.
- In order to recapture a share of the refrigerated goods market, the **SNCF** (French National Railways) operates an overnight service between the south of France and Paris with refrigerated wagons. These trains are very fast (160 kph). They are loaded in the early evening and arrive at the Rungis wholesale market outside Paris at dawn.

Strategic Logistics: Logistics As a Source or Motor for Innovation

- The **IBM** factory in Montpelier, which manufactures the large ES/9000 systems, has linked some of its suppliers to an EDI network. A work station can therefore make a direct request to a supplier, who then has 48 hours to deliver (15 per cent of factory orders are sent by this system). IBM has thus been able to reduce the duration of production cycles by 70 per cent (better reactivity), reduce costs and take full advantage of the technological innovations proposed by its suppliers, without being penalized by the obligation to use parts that are still in stock but are already obsolete. By the same token, IBM can produce tailor-made products for its customers.
- By adopting a very strong reliability–maintainability–availability approach, that depends in large part on a very efficient spare parts logistics, **Bull** has been able to guarantee a rate of breakdown downtime with its large systems equal to at most 2.5 hours per year.

Alliance

Logistics Strategy: Logistics as a Means of Alliance

- In negotiating a 'logistics charter' with its supplier, the **PSA** automobile group seeks to stabilize and perpetuate its client–supplier relations. This logistics charter identifies the rights and duties of suppliers in terms of delivery requirements transmitted by PSA factories. Members of this 'network' are interdependent to the point that in certain cases the car-maker transfers its skills to the supplier (design of new parts, quality control at the source). Some suppliers are no longer 'parts suppliers' but have become 'function suppliers' (for example, tightness supply as opposed to rubber joint supplier).

- **IBM** has become an affiliate with the French transport company **Calberson** (IBM holds 49 per cent of the capital). This new firm, **Logic-Line**, has taken over the physical distribution of IBM microcomputers and has become a specialist in just-in-time delivery from completely automated warehouses.

Strategic Logistics: Logistics as a Source/Motor for Alliance

- By developing its own powerful centralized logistics system, that is dedicated to the stores operated by 'independent' members, the French distribution group **Intermarche** has placed them in a position of total dependence *vis-à-vis* the group.
- In order to set up in France, **UPS** (United Parcel Service) chose to buy **Prost**, a French parcel service that has developed very innovative technical solutions for both transport and parcel tracking.
- **Tailleur Industrie**, a designer and operator of advanced warehouses specialized in the synchronized delivery of parts to factories organized on a just-in-time basis, is now associated with **CAT**, a transport subsidiary of Renault, in order to respond to all invitations to tender made by automobile and aeronautical manufacturers.

Expansion by Profession

Logistics Strategy: Logistics as a Support for Integration

- Integrators, former messenger services (urgent letters), have become express delivery services by integrating various activities: air transport, sorting, pre- and post-routing, all of which is coordinated and followed up by a very powerful communication and information system.
- **Andre**, a French shoe distributor (a chain of both urban shops and specialized supermarkets), strengthened by its logistics organization, has taken over some ready-to-wear clothing chains (Kookai, Caroll, Creeks).

Strategic Logistics: Logistics as a New Product

- The **Bull** group, by innovating in a very efficient after-sales logistics, no longer sells machines but a complex, powerful and very reliable computation package (hardware, software, and a 24-hour technical support).
- For **Otis**, **DEC**, **Dassault, Eurocopter** and others, after-sales logistics has now become a product which is a source of revenue and sometimes of profits which are superior to those made when the products were originally sold.

Expansion by Mission

Logistics Strategy: Logistics as a Support for extension

- **SKF**, **Roussel-UCLAF**, **IBM** etc, can only ensure their internationalization by entrusting European subsidiaries with specialized factories and by including them in a complex logistics network composed of central and national warehouses that are in constant contact.

- In the same manner, it has taken a powerful logistics system to enable **Renault** to coordinate its two complementary factories in Douai (France) and Valladolid (Spain).

Strategic Logistics: Logistics in Order to Win New Clients/Customers

- **Continent**, a French hypermarket chain, supplies its new Greek stores in Salonika and Athens with the same logistics tool it uses for its stores in the South of France.
- **Marks and Spencer** supplies its stores in France from a logistics site in Kent.
- The organization of the **Philips-Eclairage** central warehouse in France could enable it to serve certain European neighbours.

Diversification

Logistics Strategy: The Use of Logistics Synergies

- Numerous road haulage firms, in all of the European countries, have become specialized logistics suppliers for special traffic or goods that present homogeneous logistics characteristics: **TFE** (Transport Frigorifiques Européens) for fresh products; **Salvesen** for frozen products; **Ducros** (France) and **UPS** (Germany) for deliveries in dense urban zones; **FDS** (France Distribution System), **NFC** and **Exel** Logistics (United Kingdom) for supplying large distribution chains.
- Automobile makers, with their great capacity (commercial and logistic) to mobilize the resources (industrial and technological) of their suppliers, are becoming vehicle designers (imagining more attractive combinations of components for the client) and assemblers (by just-in-time converging of everything necessary to assemble the vehicle ordered by each customer).

Strategic Logistics: Diversifying Through or in Logistics

- Through exploitation of its automated warehouse, **Philips-Eclairage** diversified into the creation of a parcel service that allowed it to deliver to all of its clients, large and small, everywhere in France and every day, to the point where it now sells more logistics services than electric equipment. The company has started to deliver articles made by other manufacturers, provided that they are not in direct competition with its own products.
- **Telemarket**, a subsidiary of the Monoprix-Galeries Lafayette distribution group, offers its customers who order by phone or Minitel (the French videotex system) home delivery by appointment. These customers are obviously different from those who shop in the Monoprix stores in city centres.
- **Logic-Line**, which specializes in just-in-time deliveries from highly

automated warehouses, has diversified its services; **Logic-Line** Consultant develops skills in diagnostics and logistics advice, as in systems engineering and automated warehousing.

Strategic Action Itineraries in Logistics?

The above examples provide evidence that on one hand firms do not centre their strategy on logistics alone (informatics and marketing, in particular, are always implicitly if not explicitly associated) while on the other hand they do not strictly aim for a single result only (differentiation, for example). The generic strategies mentioned and separately illustrated (for convenience) in the previous section are not only dependent but are also more generally combined. Three strategic action 'itineraries' can be detected:

- The firm is aiming at a privileged axis and obtains other advantages from 'spin-offs'
- The firm deliberately aims at several axes that may be spread out in time but are conceived as being interdependent
- Once the firm has aimed at one or several strategic axes and has built a new logistics system, it discovers that it can 'rebound' and, from that point on, aim at new axes.

For each of these itineraries, which can, of course, be used linked together by firms, we present a figure setting out the various options, followed by several examples. In order to simplify the presentation, we have used the abbreviations lS (logistics strategy) and sL (strategic logistics) to identify the perspective adopted by the firm.

The Possible Spin-offs From a Strategic Move

- Andre, by expanding through professions (lS) that were in large part founded on logistics and commercial abilities, will probably endeavour to find logistics synergies in its distribution network in order to reinforce its cost domination (lS).
- Nozal first sought a differentiation (lS) in terms of its clients but then discovered that the principal advantage of its service was in reducing the costs of its clients (sL) who could then limit their inventory level and order only when necessary, without risk of stock-out.
- The technologies for tracking parcels, logistics innovation (lS) developed by a growing number of express delivery services constituted at first a differentiation approach (sL) *vis-à-vis* competitors (attempting to obtain a modern image, without great value in terms of exploitation). By making transfers more reliable (increased control of risks), such technologies make it possible to reduce the level of the consignee's inventory and therefore it costs (sL), while at the same time reducing production cycles (as in the case of IBM). The most dynamic express delivery services now integrate such technologies

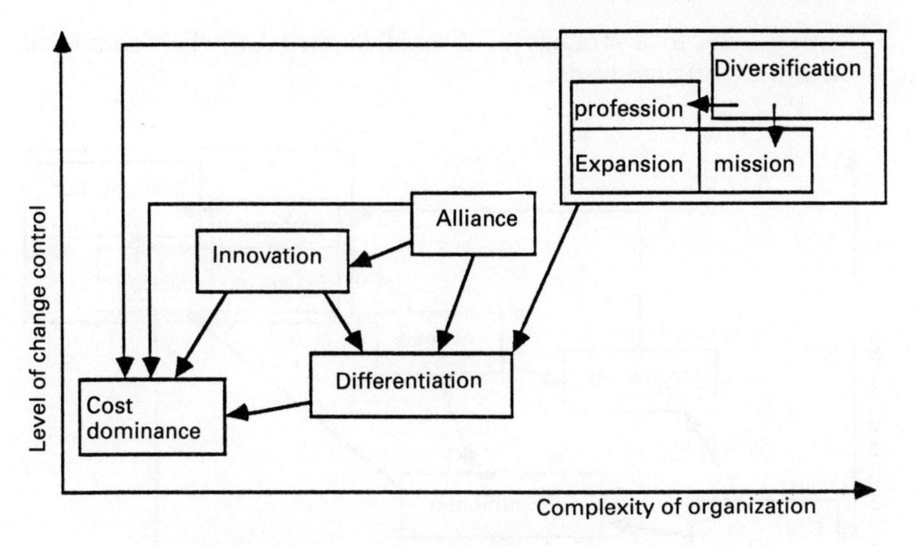

Figure 3.4 *Possible spin-offs from a strategic move*

into their commercial approach and thus move again by expanding their mission (sL).

It should be noted that spin-offs are always in the direction of decreasing organizational complexity and towards a lower level of change. Because spin-offs are not *a priori* foreseen, they are not automatic and, in any case, are of less intensity than when strategic moves are deliberately played in a combined manner.

Combination of Articulated Strategic Moves

- In distribution, the intention of a firm to equip itself with its own and/or subcontracted logistics means corresponds to a combination of deliberate logistics moves: reduction of direct logistics costs (lS) (Carrefour) and overall supply costs (sL) (Auchan and Intermarche); the will to differentiate (Auchan, with its broad range of food products, approximately three times that of Carrefour); the desire to make alliances (sL) (Intermarche) or to permit geographic expansion (sL) (Continent), or even, in certain circumstances, to open to diversification (sL) (Telemarket). Monoprix-Telemarket is an example of a firm which has more or less implemented all of these strategic dimensions, others will follow the same path.
- The IBM–Calberson joint venture, conceived on the basis of an alliance (lS), has rapidly led to a diversification approach (sL) (Logic-Line).
- Integrators, with their knowledge of complementarities and alliances (sL) (UPS), have sought to integrate mobilized means (lS). Certain firms, such as DHL and TNT, offer their networks to dispatch parts between industrial sites working with the just-in-time system. This

corresponds to a strategy of diversification (sL), when compared with their original trade.

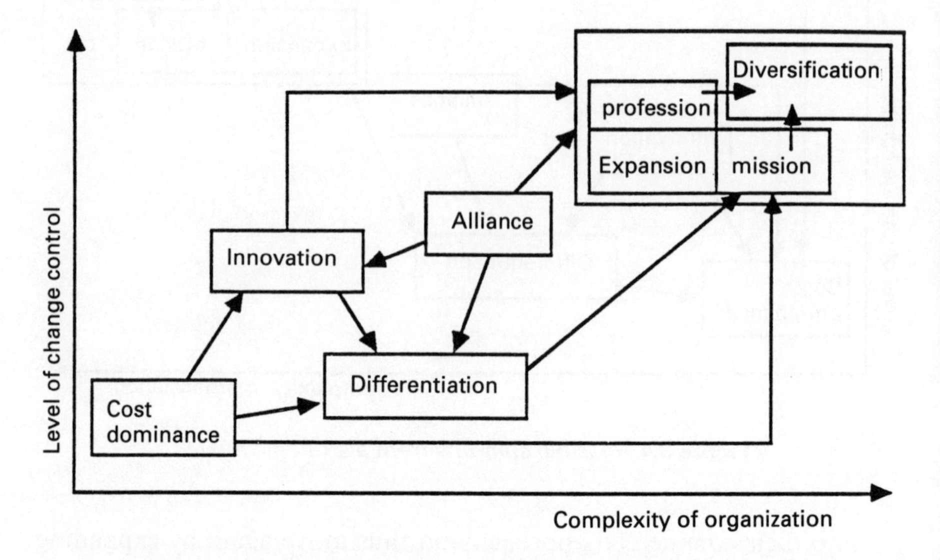

Figure 3.5 *Possible combination of articulated strategic moves*

This level of strategic maturity is not yet very widespread, which explains the most frequent situation where the firm rebounds by making *a posteriori* discoveries of new means of action.

Rebounding With New Strategic Moves

It should be noted that the possibilities illustrated in Figure 3.6 are not as numerous as those in Figure 3.5 as the moves are not intended to be linked together.

- Medis is a purchasing centre equipped with extensive logistics means (with some automated warehouses) developed jointly with several chains of food retailers (minimarkets and hypermarkets in the South of France). MEDIS is the result of an alliance founded on logistics (lS) and is now in the process of diversification (sL) by supplying a chain of 'hard discount' stores, Les Mutants, who offer some 600 products with a single 'first price reference' for each item.
- With a major investment of several hundred million francs (lS) in an automated distribution warehouse, Philips- Eclairage initially sought to differentiate itself from its competitors (lS). With its acquired experience, it then took over the distribution of materials complementary to or different from its range and made by other manufacturers. Can it be said that this diversification (sL) has transformed Philips-Eclairage into a logistics distribution firm? Where are the margins: through the sale of products or the sale of logistics services?

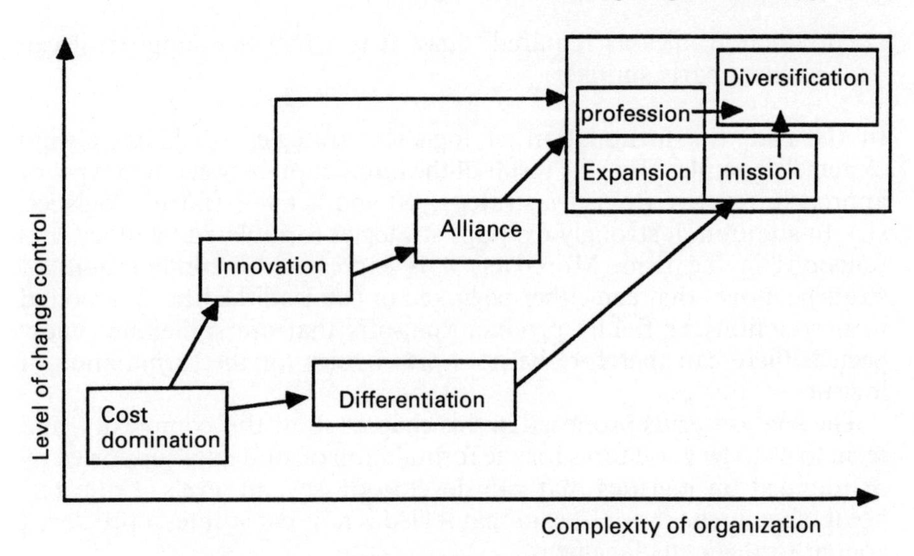

Figure 3.6 *Rebounding with new strategic moves*

Note that a second rebound has led the firm to geographic expansion (sL) by delivering to customers in regions beyond France.

- The automobile industry (PSA, Renault, etc) has operated a very complex combination of logistics approaches of overall cost reduction through logistics (sL), differentiation (sL), innovation in logistics EDI (1S), that go through alliances with logistics suppliers and parts suppliers (sL) and expansion by internationalization (lS). On the strategic level, starting with logistics synergies (lS), a diversification phase can lead the firm to make a radical change in paradigm. With their strong logistics skills, the car-makers are becoming conceivers and assemblers, able to offer either very differentiated ranges of cars (Clio and 205 examples), or, on the contrary, very standardized vehicles. Thus the time from conception to industrialization of the Twingo, the latest Renault model, was only 33 months, for an investment of only 3.7 billion francs. This very original car is only available in 32 combinations (options: air-conditioning, sunroof, eight body/seat colours). It is built on the same production lines as the Clio, which is available in tens of thousands of different versions. In our opinion, this constitutes a strategic logistics (sL) diversification that essentially depends on both the perfect control of logistics processes and communication and information systems.
- The logistics suppliers Tailleur-Industrie developed know-how for advanced warehouses and just-in-time synchronized industrial deliveries by first following an innovation approach (lS) and then by alliances founded on logistics (sL). It is now rebounding on diversification (sL) by proposing to its customers (car-makers) that it should perform assembly phases in its advanced warehouses for parts that it already manages. It can therefore assemble certain parts (eg bumper, lights and electrical system) and deliver them directly to the

production lines as required. Since it is a logistics supplier, it can become a parts supplier.

In the end, the formulation of logistics strategies is almost always extremely complex. It is the result of the interaction between two types of approach: reactive (logistics strategy, lS) and active (strategic logistics, sL). In addition, it strongly overlaps strategies formulated by other vital functions in the firm. Moreover, it is expressed by combinations of strategic moves that can either be linked or can lead the firm to rebound to new actions or finally produce spin-offs that are sometimes unexpected: there can therefore be no *a priori* rules for the formulation of logistics strategies.

The analysis grids proposed in this chapter show this complexity, and seem to us to be good tools for the formulation of strategies supported by or founded on logistics that can develop on several levels. From this point of view, can it not be said that logistics now constitutes a privileged area in strategic management?

Summary

- Firms formulate their strategies in response to intense environmental pressures
- Logistics is an essential element of that strategy
- The field of logistics has become progressively broader and is now very far-reaching
- A trend from the perspective of logistics strategy to that of strategic logistics is apparent, representing a source of competitive advantage
- A variety of 'classic' generic strategic axes and formulations can be identified.

References

[1] Morin, E., *Science avec Conscience*, new edition, Le Seuil-Points, Paris, 1990.
[2] Martinet, A.C., *Stratégie*, Vuibert, Paris, 1983.

Further Reading

Ansoff, I (1979) *Strategic Management*, Macmillan, London.
Chandler, A D (1962) *Strategy and Structure*, MIT Press, Cambridge, Mass.
Mathe, H, Collin, J, Tixier, D (1983) *La logistique*, Dunod, Paris.
Wiseman, C (1985) *Strategy and Computers*, Dow Jones-Irwin Inc, USA.

Chapter 4

Organizing for Logistics

Philip Schary
Oregon State University

Logistics has been described as 'the corporate traffic cop,'[1] directing the flow of material and finished products from source through production and distribution to the final customer. The scope of its potential responsibility is staggering, but the ability of logistics management to take direct action is limited. This presents the fundamental problem: how to build and guide an integrated management system which spans the entire organization through the actions of other managers.

The ultimate objective of the logistics manager is to support corporate goals by delivering products to the final customer, at a time and place of their choosing. This normally means not only managing individual shipments, but a continuing series of transactions which provide genuine service to customers. Logistics service involves the taking on of tasks that the customer would otherwise perform, and creating interdependence between customer and supplier. These objectives must be balanced against the costs of providing service. The task of the logistics manager is then to direct a system involving multiple functions, organizational units and external organizations to achieve an optimal balance of service and cost.

The perspective on logistics has been shaped in recent years by three forces: the concept of the supply chain, the movement towards globalization, and the process of deintegration of industry – the 'hollowing out' of the industrial corporation. The first of these forces focuses logistics on integrating the entire set of activities in procurement, production and distribution into a single decision system. The second emphasizes that logistics has developed in a world of international markets and supply links, organized through corporations with global perspectives. The environment of logistics must take into account differing operating parameters and environmental conditions. The third is a fundamental change in the organization of industrial production. Corporations focus on their core activities, contracting for the rest from other suppliers and service organizations. This last presents both challenge and opportunity for logistics management. The challenge comes from the necessity to coordinate across organizational boundaries. The opportunity is that this is a natural extension of the traditional role of logistics management.

This chapter addresses three areas: the logistics task, organizational issues and the relationship between management and the information system. They are closely related. They are also characteristic of modern organizations in general, that actions take place as a lateral process across organizations, rather than as a vertical process completely contained within the organization.

The Logistics Task

The central characteristic of logistics management is coordination across functional areas. Studies over the years describe an evolutionary process toward expanding responsibility under the umbrella of logistics management.[2]

The core of logistics management begins with direct control over these areas:

- Outbound transportation
- Logistics administration
- Intra-company transportation
- Distribution centre management
- Logistics system planning.

In addition, other companies also include some or all of the following functions within the scope of logistics:

- Order processing
- Customer service
- Factory warehousing
- Inbound transportation
- Production planning
- Production materials and work-in-process inventory
- Sales forecasting.

Adding to this list, there are other areas which are also necessary for global supply management:

- Customs relations and trade documentation
- Global production allocation (for multiple plant operation)
- Currency exchange management.

All of these functions are important to the material and product flow process. However, setting them apart in a separate department is not the only solution to this coordination problem. The task is to bring them together in a cohesive system. Moreover, there is always a limit to the functional span of a separate logistics organization. Once the boundary is determined, there are always activities excluded which are also part of the logistics process. This is what one writer has described as the 'functionalism–coordination dilemma'.[3]

There is also the inter-organizational coordination task. This concerns more than the problem of delivering finished products to customers, or bringing material from a supplier to production. Whether organizations are directly under the corporate umbrella, or participate as outside contractors, is becoming less important than how they perform their functional assignments. The logistics task is both to arrange transportation and communication, and coordinate operations, inventory management and possibly production schedules for these outside organizations. This coordination may involve multiple stages of distribution or production, each of which must be linked together to meet the objectives of the supply chain. It may require passing customer orders through the system to take actions. At mangement level, it may require balancing the activities and capacities of several organizations simultaneously to enable product flow to take place. This coordination role is becoming the most important aspect of logistics management.

Organizational Solutions

The purpose of any organization is to process and communicate information. The traditional approach to organizations has been to establish separate functional departments, with control emanating from the top toward the bottom. This hierarchical or vertical orientation has never fitted well with the logistics orientation toward horizontal flow across functional areas. For one thing, it separates departments and leaves them to pursue individual goals, ie to suboptimize. Communication between departments becomes difficult, as functions are performed in isolation. It also leads to costly efforts to insulate departments from each other. Further, it defeats the purpose of logistics, which is to integrate the entire supply chain as a single unit.

Many logistics management units today operate with a combination of departments and coördination. Usually, there is one set of activities controlled directly by logistics management – the minimal core which we described above. Everything else involves coordination. Alternatives involving larger departments or greater coordination present difficulties.

There is another problem: the position of logistics within the corporation. Where should logistics management be located, and who should have ultimate responsibility for its activities? One argument says that logistics should be clearly identifiable as a separate area. This approach may satisfy the need for management control, but it may limit political support within the organization because it threatens to absorb functions which may also fit logically in other departments.

A second argument would place logistics under manufacturing, close to the core supply problems, following a materials management approach.[4] Much of the current discussion of manufacturing strategy has common ground with logistics over coordination, supplier relations and just-in-time delivery. Product variety going to distinctly different markets argues for placement under marketing. This argument is further reinforced by the need for customer service.

There is, however, an overarching link between production and distribution which becomes almost totally ignored. Make-to-order products are directly delivered to customers. Make-to-inventory products usually go through intermediate distribution facilities as field stocks. The balance between these activities is changing. The advent of flexible manufacturing is changing it from make-to-inventory to manufacturing-to-order, which means that more products are delivered directly to customers. The strategic concerns of supply chain management now deal with total throughput time from material source to final product delivery to a customer, having enough capacity to supply product variety and having the flexibility to respond to changes in demand volume. As the chain responds to customer demands, it must also contend with intermediate customers such as retailers and distributors who influence it through their order practices and inventory management. This suggests a third alternative, that of making logistics into an adjunct of marketing.

The lack of resolution to this problem points to a different kind of solution – horizontal management across functional boundaries, oriented to process rather than function. Boundaries become less important than the object, product movement. This is also an increasing pattern of other organizational areas, to stress coordination over authority.

Jay Galbraith has provided us with a useful framework with which to examine the problem of the lateral organization.[5] He divides potential solutions into two camps: those that limit information flow and those that increase the capacity to handle information. Reducing information flow is an argument for departments. Departments and other organizational units can be buffered from each other by using slack resources. Holding stocks of inventory is a typical and particularly relevant example of this – having lots of finished product inventory allows production to go on its own way, while inventory insulates it from the market. Control systems allow departments to operate independently of each other. Similarly, it can also insulate production from suppliers. One of the major thrusts of logistics, production operations and supply chain management, however, is to reduce inventory. Another related solution is for management to create self-contained tasks, isolating them from the environment through management actions. Again, this opposes the primary logistics objective of coordination and creates suboptimization.

The alternative of increasing information capacity may take one of several forms, emphasizing lateral coordination: using the manager as an integrator, managing by committee (or in its most permanent form, through a matrix organization), or reliance on information systems. Integrators operate through personal persuasion. They are leaders who get their primary satisfaction from the success of their groups, rather than their own individual accomplishments or power positions.[6] They manage conflict, work out compromises and by their own efforts arrive at solutions. They manage, rather than make decisions.

Matrix organizations are *de facto* standing committees. In a typical logistics context, a matrix organization would include members from each major department. The manager is in effect a permanent chairman, constantly pushing a logistics agenda on to the committee. The advantages are that it can include key functional areas without change in the departmental organization, it can be flexible in membership to meet the needs of specific problem situations, and it can be a highly effective means of communication. It is probably not as effective in making fast decisions, and it also generates internal conflict between the matrix manager and functional area managers, sometimes expressed within the matrix committee. Logistics management by matrix makes logistics into a centre of responsibility without direct authority. It is used because the breadth of the problems exceeds the authority, and the extent of the knowledge required exceeds the limits of any single individual.[7]

A third solution is to rely on information systems. Frederick Beier once conceived of logistics management as controlling the information system and setting the decision rules, but then letting individual functional managers provide information to the system.[8] This was a partially prophetic view of the future. With cooperation across the corporate organization, the logistics information system can often perform this coordination role more easily than formal organizational assignments. A logistics information system centralizes data for planning and control, while it decentralizes operating decisions. Centralization extends the reach of the logistics manager for both system planning and control. Decentralization allows local managers to gain access to important information for their own decision-making purposes. The information system therefore changes the emphasis of logistics management from the decisions themselves to the management of information for decisions.

The Role of Information

The conceptual model of the information system is a pyramid of data and applications, based on a flow of transactions. Transactions are messages between organizational units requesting some kind of action, such as delivery of products from a preceding stage of processing. Each transaction leaves a data trail which can be captured for use in operating status reporting, scheduling and related applications. It can be stored in a common data base accessible to all organizational units, providing information to everyone connected to the system. These data can be manipulated, interpreted and used for operational scheduling, planning and long-range strategic planning, depending on the level of management.

The organizational effect is to unite all functional units through common information flow, giving them the power of immediate access to information that was formerly only available to managers at higher levels in the organization. This development supports the concept of a lateral organization, with organizational units such as procurement, processing, production and distribution connected to each other and exchanging operating data for product flow. No longer do functions and operations have to be merged into a common department to achieve coordination.

A further development is electronic data interchange (EDI), standardized data communication between separate organizations, such as suppliers and customers. This allows the same types of data which are passed within the organization to be connected to outside parties also involved in the production process. The common denominators are prior agreements to participate in the logistics flow process and to share relevant information using a uniform message standard. Suppliers can now be coordinated through common production schedules with manufacturing. Customer forecast and sales demand data can be transmitted to distribution.

The Transaction Cost Model

Organizational boundaries are defined in current economic theory by the cost of transactions. Transactions can be either internal to the firm or external between firms. They have a cost which must be taken into account along with production. Transactions include the costs of negotiation, planning, adapting, execution and monitoring. Actions by the firm to minimize these costs define its boundaries. The firm will incorporate functions within its boundaries when the cost of securing the performance of these functions, including both production and transaction costs, is less than that of securing these costs in the market from outside suppliers.

Transactions are internal, within the organization, when they are less costly than taking them outside to the market. Otherwise, a firm would secure its services in the open market. The firm's boundaries are determined by the balance of these transaction costs but are modified by two other factors: bounded rationality and opportunism. Bounded rationality refers to the limits of the ability of managers to solve complex problems, such as directing complex logistics networks. It favours the use of the market to limit the scope of decisions. However, there is an opposing force, opportunism, which emphasizes the self-interests of each party. It involves the notion of conflicting objectives and potential conflict, leading to internalizing operations.

Market-based transactions are favoured over internal transactions where there are fixed investments, or specialized knowledge and skill. Demands can be aggregated for economies of scale and scope. These transactions, however, become more costly as they become more specific to a single purpose, such as specialized investments. When they result in a bilateral exchange between a single buyer and a single seller, they lose the advantages of their market orientation and are then internalized within the organization.

Transactions and the Logistics Concept

The transaction cost approach is useful to logistics through its emphasis on the role and cost of coordination. The decision whether to perform logistics functions internally depends on the combination of negotiation, management (including coordination) and operation. The decision whether to use internal functions or outside organizations to perform part of the functions of the supply chain is determined by the combination of costs and the limits of management skill and specific knowledge. Using outside contractors in transport and warehousing provide examples of these decisions. Transport operations involve operating costs which are often lower for external suppliers. Similarly, warehousing is a specialized function which requires unique skills. It also involves levels of investment that a firm may not wish to make. Only if the warehouse requires intense coordination, or there is a sufficient volume of throughput, would it be operated within the firm. If the costs of coordination and operation for outside agencies are low, there is a tendency to contract for them outside, because this conserves assets and provides flexibility.

Coordination with external partners is made possible through two types of communication, One is the informal network of personal contacts which always exists between organizations in a business relationship. It is necessary but not sufficient for effective integration. The second is perhaps more important: electronic data interchange (EDI). EDI enables the transfer of data files between computer systems, connecting operations directly through standardized communication. All kinds of transactions can take place through EDI: purchase orders, funds transfer, production scheduling, shipment instructions and forecast data, to name only a few. EDI has many advantages over other means of doing business: more accuracy, because data are entered only once, and instantaneous transfer of data ready for action. However, it also requires previous agreement on communication and message standards, and compatibility of internal computer and record-keeping systems among the parties involved. It promotes frequent transmission of coordinating communications in standard formats, placing partners who may previously have been at arm's length into closer operating relationships to each other.

The Electronic Organization

The impact of information systems and EDI on logistics organization is twofold. First, the direct costs of transactions are decreasing because of the declining costs of data transmission and management. Second, the capacity to transmit data is expanding, making it possible to increase the content of messages, and easier to deal with complex coordination problems. EDI supports a conclusion that logistics organizations do not have to be internalized but can be managed through outside departments and organizations.

These units become part of a larger network of communication and interaction, noted in management information systems literature under the terms 'virtual organizations'[9], 'electronic hierarchies'[10] and 'quasi-integration'. Where they formerly dealt with each other at arm's length, they now coordinate operations through electronic connections on a long-term basis.

How then should we define the limits to logistics organization? With EDI, the span of the information system potentially becomes as broad as the reach from customer to supplier. As customer orders enter the system, they generate data which become the basis for functional commands: order fulfilment, production scheduling, delivery instructions, purchasing orders and other related documents. Each of these also leaves a data trail to be stored in a data base, accessible to any party which needs the data.

The organizational effects of EDI are neutral. Unless the message standards are proprietary, they facilitate 'electronic markets' as easily as they do more permanent forms of organization. Message standards promote system compatibility and the ability to connect with multiple buyers or sellers. Proprietary standards have power to limit contact with outside parties, but these appear to be losing out in favour of common and more flexible standards.

To encourage the development of extended organizations, there must also be other forms of commitment and communication. Contracts bind network-based organizations for specific periods of time. The organizational connections can be reinforced through informal supplementary e-mail connections, establishing a sense of participation. Sproull and Keisler, however, found that decision processes were as much as four times as long, compared with face-to-face situations.[11]

Information system-based organizations become defined by their communication networks. One dimension is physical access, whether this is direct or through another party. A second lies in the currency of the data. Some units must operate in real-time, such as delivery transactions between supplier and production. Others can operate with lagged and summary data.

In effect, several organizational networks operate within the same information system. These networks may cut across organizational boundaries to embrace vertical relationships between supplier and market, bringing parts of several organizations into close contact, without involving other parts of their parent establishments. These functional networks are subsets of the logistics information system but reach beyond it for accomplishing specific tasks.

One example is the Quick Response systems which are becoming widely adopted in the American garment and retail industry sectors.[12] The industry has reached agreement on bar-coding, message standards and, equally important, on processes for transmitting demand information through the entire supply chain. The objective is to coordinate the order process through successive stages of production and distribution, to reduce total order cycle time. This in effect becomes a functional network that becomes a part of several organizational information systems.

The impact of this information system on management is only beginning. We have seen severe reductions in management ranks as a result of the communication capacity and decision power incorporated within the management information system. The ability to transmit large quantities of information makes possible a degree of coordination which changes the perception of what is an organization. Questions remain, however. Who will plan and direct this new organizational form – the customer or the supplier? Or does the scope of decisions become so great that it is too broad to be managed by any single party?

The impact of the logistics information system (LIS) parallels the general development of management information systems. It allows management to gain access to operations data of other units, limited only by willingness to cooperate. The effect makes transactions activities of every unit visible to management. At the same time, it allows each unit to 'see ahead', to observe the entire process in operation. The logistics manager is no longer the only place where operating information is available. Information is now shared among all participants in the product flow process.

The logistics information system operates at two levels: internal operations, and as an extension to a larger network of suppliers and service providers. Sharing data becomes a dominant criterion in establishing relationships with outside parties. The result is the creation of a larger *de facto* organization, all members of which are then visible to other members and to a centralized logistics management.

The logistics organization takes on a new appearance – a chain of separate operating units coordinated through an information system. This larger organization is defined by connectivity – the general access to the system, the currency of data, the need to coordinate, and whether this data must be interpreted prior to use. There may be several information networks within a logistics system, distinguished by their data connections. The supply chain requires that suppliers should be able to see through the manufacturing and intermediate stages to see final demand. Distribution should be able to track progress of individual shipments to market.

The role of logistics managers as leaders of this new organization is still being defined. The lateral nature of the organization maintains a role for integrators and matrix organizations. The manager assumes more the role of leader, facilitating operations rather than direct involvement in routine decisions, negotiating rather than asserting direct supervision, securing resources and asserting decision rules, rather than dealing with operations directly. The primacy of information suggests that the future role of logistics management will be to design the information flows and the data requirements, as much as managing the physical flow directly.

Conclusion

This discussion began with the requirements for logistics management. The demands for widening the scope to encompass the entire supply chain are now becoming apparent. Traditional forms of organization are inadequate to the task and the result has been a search for new forms of management to match the nature of the product and material flow process, the lateral organization.

The future of logistics management appears to be evolving toward a combination of integration through personal action and information systems. The new technology of EDI extends functional boundaries beyond the traditional limits of organizations. The organizational task is to extend common objectives and relationships to this larger arena. Coordinating the logistics process requires a new type of training for the rapidly evolving field information systems. Directing information flows to manage product and material flow is a logical role for logistics managers. If the profession doesn't accept it, there must be someone else in the organization who will.

Summary

- Logistics service involves the creation of interdependence between customer and supplier
- A changing global industrial structure is leading logistics towards a role of integrating the entire set of procurement, production and distribution activities, expanding the scope of traditional logistics responsibilities
- Traditional forms of organization are inadequate to the evolving role of logistics
- Inter-organizational coordination is becoming an increasingly important task
- The advent of flexible manufacturing is leading to new strategic concerns
- The flow of information between organizations is being revolutionized by electronic data interchange, which is itself leading to the development of extended organizations.

References

[1] Muller, E.J., 'Linking Logistics to Corporate Goals', *Traffic Management*, September, 1989, pp. 28–34.

[2] See Jack W. Farrell, 'Distribution Departments Gain Ground', *Traffic Management*, September, 1981, pp. 44–50; Kearney Management Consultants, 'Organizing Physical Distribution to Achieve Bottom Line Results', *Proceedings of the National Council of Physical Distribution Management*, NCPDM, Chicago, 1981, pp. 1–14; also see Donald J Bowersox, Cornelia L. Dröge, Dale S. Rogers and Daniel L. Wardlow, *Leading Edge Logistics: Competitive Positioning for the '90s*, Council of Logistics Management, Oak Brook, Il, 1989.

[3] Frederick J. Beier, 'Information Systems and the Life Cycle of Logistics Departments', *International Journal of Physical Distribution*, 3 (3), 1973, pp. 312–21 at p. 314.

[4] See John F. Gustafson and Robert G. Hagemann, 'Logistics: Growing Intellectual Entourage', *Production and Inventory Management*, 17 (3), 1976, pp. 1–21; Jeffrey Miller and Peter Gilmour, 'Materials Managers: Who Needs Them?', *Harvard Business Review*, 56, January–February, 1978, pp. 145–53.

[5] Jay Galbraith, *Organizational Design*, Addison-Wesley Publishing Company, Reading, Mass., 1977.

[6] Paul R. Lawrence and Jay W. Lorsch, *Organization and Environment*, Richard D. Irwin, Inc, Homewood, Il, 1967, p. 244.
[7] Cf. Christopher A. Bartlett and Sumantra Ghoshal, 'Matrix Management: Not a Structure, a Frame of Mind', *Harvard Business Review*, 68, July–August, 1990, pp. 138–45.
[8] Beier, op. cit., p. 321.
[9] Stuart E. Madnicjk, 'The Technology Platform' in Michael S. Scott Morton (ed) *The Corporation of the 1990s*, Oxford University Press, New York, 1991, p. 32.
[10] Thomas W. Malone, Joanne Yates and Robert I. Benjamin, 'Electronic Markets and Electronic Hierarchies', *Communications of the ACM*, 30, 1987, pp. 484–96.
[11] Lee Sprouill and Lee Keisler, 'Computers, Networks and Work', *Scientific American*, September, 1991, pp. 116–23.
[12] Cf. Bernie Krill, 'Quick Response: Now for the Hard Part', *Material Handling Engineering*, March, 1990, pp. 67-8; Bernie Krill, 'Quick Response 90: Manufacturing Gets More Respect', *Material Handling Engineering*, June, 1990, pp. 48–57.

Chapter 5

Beyond the Logistics Pipeline: Opportunities for Competitive Advantage*

This chapter is dedicated to the memory of Gary Biddle

Marvin L Manheim
J.L. Kellogg Graduate School of Management

Objectives and Approach

Firms today face increasingly severe competitive pressures. In response, the logistics function has become increasingly visible and central to firms' competitive strategies. Much has been written about the integration of the logistics pipeline, and especially 'supply chain integration'. While this is an important focus for management attention today, it is essential to put it in perspective.

In this chapter, our objective is to analyse the role of logistics in globally competing firms. The central question which we address is: 'What does it take to gain competitive advantage through the logistics function today?' Put another way, 'Will supply chain integration provide a competitive advantage?' If not, 'What other strategies should a firm pursue?'

To answer these questions, we need to look beyond the logistics function, to two related issues: the changing structures of globally competing organizations, and the critical role that information technology plays in today's competitive environment. These then provide a basis for addressing the central question.

Organization Change – The Drivers

Our starting point is the evolution of organization structure in globally competing organizations (GCOs). We first summarize the major business drivers affecting GCOs, looking at several competing thrusts: business process integration, global regionalization, and the emergence of business teams.

* The hypotheses presented here are based on about 90 interviews with more than 30 companies and organizations in the US, Europe, and Japan.[1] Interviews were conducted with general and functional managers at a variety of levels, and with managers in the IST function. Some of these interviews were done as university research, while others were done for strategy studies for particular organizations. Early versions of these results were reprinted in Manheim (1990, 1991, 1992).

Business Drivers

To compete successfully in this dynamically changing environment, firms need to be able to address effectively several key strategic issues.[2]

Cost-quality improvement through coordinated manufacturing
Competitive pressures push strongly to reducing product delivered cost and at the same time to improve the quality of the product and all aspects of customer service. One key element of many firms' strategies is to tighten all aspects of the manufacturing process. This includes such coordination strategies as 'just-in-time' and overall quality improvement programme.[3]

Cost-quality improvement through simultaneous engineering
Another key element is better design of the product for manufacturability. Integrated design teams are formed, pulling together product design, engineering and manufacturing. In some cases, packaging and distribution, and marketing and R&D functions are also brought into the simultaneous engineering process.

The order cycle
In many industry sectors, such as motor vehicles and appliances, the product is built to customer order and customer specifications. The order cycle begins when the customer places an order, and ends with the delivery of the completed product to the customer. In these sectors, a key competitive issue is to be able to deliver the product to the customer as soon after order placement as possible.[4]

After-sale customer support
In many cases, customer support after the sale is a critical issue. Customers are demanding a high level of service for maintenance, including spare parts availability and technical skills in service staff. Add-on products and services, such as training, documentation, and product upgrades, are also required. A high level of customer support capability is required, but it can also be profitable. In some product sectors, 10–20 per cent or more of total product-line net profit comes from after-sales support.

The design cycle
In many sectors, intense competition is resulting in ever-shorter product lives. The time it takes to conceive a new product, design it, and put it into manufacturing, and deliver it to the market with a fully support network in place – the design cycle – is becoming shorter and shorter. This means that newer technology can be put on the market; the company that takes six years to design a new car model today is putting on the 1993 market a vehicle with 1987 technology, while the company with a three-year design cycle is competing with 1990 technology.[5]

Globally coordinated flexible manufacturing
Global sourcing of components and sub-assemblies, global distribution into multiple markets, and efficient use of a network of global manu-

facturing and assembly plants, is leading to globally coordinated manufacturing. In this new style of 'flexible manufacturing' – FMS II, for flexible manufacturing systems of the second type – the objective is to coordinate production planning and scheduling among multiple plants in many countries, and across product lines, to respond to changing market and production conditions.

Globally coordinated R&D

Global coordination of research and development is driven by the need for product development for global markets,[6] and by the recognition that unique research competencies exist in many different countries and cultures. At the same time that a company strives to tap these competencies, it also usually wants to minimize undesired duplication and overlap. Managing R&D in a global situation is especially critical. For example, in the pharmaceutical industry, clinical trials and regulatory approval applications must be undertaken in many countries relatively simultaneously.

Integration of the Core Business Processes

As companies change to respond to these new forces, what will they focus on? The first focal process is, of course, the fundamental one: what business should we be in, and what strategy should we follow in this business? Beyond this, are there other key business processes? Based on the issues identified above, we have hypothesized[7] that businesses will increasingly focus on three major, critical business processes.* These processes integrate a number of functions and cut across departmental and other organizational boundaries. These integrating processes are: the order cycle, the product development cycle, and the customer relationship management cycle:

- The order cycle begins when the customer places the order, and ends with delivery of the final product to the customer. It includes production planning and scheduling, logistics for inbound and finished products, production coordination between schedulers and suppliers, and other types of integration and coordination.
- The product development cycle involves all aspects of designing a new product and getting it to market. It includes R&D, product planning and design and the related market research and design for manufacturing.
- The customer relationship management cycle involves all interactions with prospective customers prior to a sale, the sales process itself, and serving the customer after the sale, with maintenance, upgrades, training and other services.

* This line of argument was developed in collaboration with Jacques Roure, SEMA Group; and the late Gary Biddle, formerly of American Standard, Corp., to whom this chapter is dedicated. (Biddle, 1990; Roure, 1990; Manheim, 1991).

Several key functions support these three integration foci:

- The 'people management' process – human resources management, in its broadest definition
- Information systems and telecommunications
- Technology and finance
- Finance
- Logistics and transportation.

Impact of the Single European Market

The emergence of the Single Market in Europe is proving a major force in this evolution of organizations. While certain elements of the original concept have not yet been (and perhaps may never be) implemented, such as a single financial institution and universal currency, the dominant goals of the Single Market are already on the way to implementation.

In 1987, a group of experts made these predictions:[8]

> Europe 1992 will bring about significant changes in globally competing organizations, especially in manufacturing, merchandising, logistics and transportation services, and information systems and telecommunications products and services. Three major forces will cause these changes: the opportunities to restructure production and distribution to exploit opportunities for product harmonization and production and distribution efficiencies; the opportunity to exploit new thinking about inter-organizational coordination through information technology and especially EDI; and the newly open market for provision of IST services and products.

These processes are already well under way.[9] The creation of an integrated market in the European Community is having a significant effect, not only because of the special legal and administrative actions which have been or are being taken, but also because of the shift in the psychology and perspectives of managers and government officials. European and non-European companies are investing in significant restructuring of their production and distribution systems in Europe.

This is being driven largely by the fact that, under the implementing regulations for the Single Market, many rules and regulations that impact on product design have been or are being changed. For example, a company no longer has to produce in twelve countries to meet local market pressures, or produce twelve different country-specific versions of the same product. In addition, as a practical matter, the distribution area extends beyond the twelve to the other countries of Western Europe, not already part of the EC.

This is causing accelerated introduction of new manufacturing, merchandising and distribution approaches. For example, the Japanese motor manufacturer, Nissan, has consolidated all of its automotive parts distribution activities in Europe into a single distribution centre located in Amsterdam. To exploit these opportunities, companies are investing significant resources in developing restructured production, distribution, logistics, marketing and management systems. Naturally, these often reflect the latest thinking in manufacturing technology and logistics, incorporating just-in-time and other new approaches.

Extensive use of information systems and telecommunications (IST) is a part of these innovations, being used to coordinate and in some cases to integrate many important functions, both within the firm (organizational information systems), and between firms (inter-organizational information systems). Significant progress is being made in the development of data transmission standards for electronic data interchange, especially among manufacturers and their suppliers, distributors and customers (the EDIFACT standards are particularly important). The new production systems will use IST based on these standards.

In parallel, the deregulation of telecommunications in Europe, and related deregulation and privatization activities elsewhere, are creating the potential for major changes in all aspects of the offering of telecommunications and related information systems services, such as value-added networks.

The Single Market is thus serving as a testing ground for new approaches, organizations, systems, and processes. Organizations which innovate in Europe will gain competitive advantage in implementing similar elements in other regions and in their global organization. Firms which fail to exploit the European opportunity will likely suffer fundamental global disadvantage.

However, while change eventually will be quite significant, in general it is not moving as fast as some experts had anticipated. Global economic conditions are one factor, and management failures to understand the opportunities and take significant actions are another.[10] Obviously, 1992 has been more a symbol than a point of instantaneous, rapid, and major change, but nevertheless, globally competing organizations are already facing the need for change in Europe. This, together with the opening of Eastern Europe to economic and social change is driving rethinking about how to organize not only for the Single Market, but also for global competition. By restructuring to deal with Europe, globally competing organizations are learning lessons that will be carried over to the restructuring of their global organizations. Any firm that wishes to be a successful global competitor in the latter half of the 1990s and beyond, must be active in Europe to learn from Europe.

Interestingly, from the point of view of transportation and logistics service providers, the major forces of change are already well under way; these are the shifts in the structure of production and distribution described previously and the related shifts in the demands for transportation and logistics services.

The Challenge: Evolving Organization Processes

So far, we have seen that there are important forces driving organization change: the business processes described first, the need to create coordinated and integrated business processes, and the changing structure of the European market. All of these forces together are calling forth major changes in the ways in which organizations organize for global competition.

Critical to this process will be the role of information technology. We now turn to examine the information technology dimensions of coordination by focusing on the order cycle, one critical business process.

Strategic Opportunities Through Information Technology: Order Cycle Integration

Many companies are attempting coordination of their order cycle, in various ways.[11] Sometimes called 'supply chain management', this integration process involves moves to tighten the linkages among production and logistics functions, and including purchasing, finance, and other elements.

Pipeline Management Systems (PLMS)

To accomplish integration in the order cycle, tightly- linked 'pipelines' of information flows are being developed, paralleling the pipelines of goods flows. Thus, the pipeline for managing the materials flows is supported by an information systems 'pipeline', or pipeline management system (PLMS). The PLMS utilizes electronic data interchange (EDI) and other forms of computer-to-computer interconnections, and consists of transaction processing (TP), management information systems (MS), executive information systems (EIS), and decision support systems (DSS) components.

Many firms in manufacturing, merchandising, logistics and transportation are already well-embarked on this strategy. For example, in order to implement order cycle integration through 'supply chain management', EDI is beginning to be widely accepted as the primary form of information technology linkage among various partners in the production and distribution of goods (in addition to the presently-used fax, voicc, tclcx, and mail). EDI is being used to connect the transaction processing (TP) systems of various trading partners. Management information systems (MIS) (and executive information systems – EIS) sit on top of these systems to provide management reporting and analysis of the materials flows through the supply chain. These are supported increasingly by decision support systems (DSS) for operational and managerial control of these processes. For example, a DSS might be used to support decision-making for evaluation of alternative routings of a shipment when expedited transportation is needed.

Some of the major functions performed by components of the PLMS include:

- **Shipment status tracking** location of a shipment at each major transition point as it moves through the transportation segments of the supply chain

- **Inventory status tracking** current inventories by item (usually, SKU, stock-keeping unit) while in production and warehousing processes, or in movement through transportation carriers
- **Movements of ancillary information in document or electronic form** waybills, manifests, etc.; and associated documentation for customs, insurance, financial and other processes associated with the movements of materials through the order cycle.

Are Pipeline Management Systems a Source of Competitive Advantage?

Is this a direction through which a firm can obtain a competitive advantage? The concept of integrating the order cycle is now well-known. While there are certainly many difficulties in implementing this concept successfully, it *is* a well-known and widely recognized management task.

Assessing Strategic Opportunities: Concepts

In order to examine PLMS, we will draw on concepts from the study of information systems as a competitive weapon.

The possible uses of information technology as a competitive weapon are well-known, and continually debated.[12] It is useful to assume that, under some circumstances, IST *can* help a firm achieve a competitive advantage; and to apply a simple framework to stimulate development of candidate strategies and to assess strategy proposals.

Competitive Advantage vs. Competitive Necessity

A *sustainable competitive advantage* means that an organization or a region is more effective than any competitor for a substantial period of time, say five to ten years. In the case of a business entity a sustainable competitive advantage can be defined as producing profits which are significantly above the average for firms in the same industry.

A *competitive necessity* is some feature of an organization's strategy which must be adopted if an organization is to remain at least equally competitive with other leading organizations of the same type.[13]

Components of a Multi-thrust Strategy

Based on these distinctions of competitive advantage and competitive necessity, we have hypothesized a 'multi-thrust strategy', requiring four basic elements:[14]

Base
Actions intended to build a sound foundation – the technology, organization and human resource base necessary for survival as a viable organization and for laying a foundation for seeking competitive advantage.

Parity
Actions intended to seek 'parity', ie, to maintain competitive equality, based on an analysis of actions taking place in the industry and emerging competitive forces. Often, a 'benchmarking' analysis of competitors and of other industry sectors is useful in identifying potential parity actions.

Incremental initiatives
Focused actions which, by targeting specific segments of the organization's markets, seek to achieve an incremental lead over competitors. Competitors are likely to respond and match these actions. Therefore, it is necessary to have a continual process of moving forward with next-step actions to keep ahead of competitors in focused areas.

Breakthrough
Actions which seek to achieve a 'breakthrough' and thereby a restructuring of the market and the firm's role in it, such that a sustainable advantage is achieved.

The multi-thrust strategy model is useful both for generation of strategy alternatives, and for evaluation of a programme of strategic actions. To generate strategy alternatives, this model suggests the elements of a programme of strategic actions. From a normative perspective, we hypothesize that an organization's basic strategy should be developed by taking those actions necessary to be sure that a sound base exists and will be retained, by taking those additional actions that are necessary in order to maintain parity with leading competitors, and in addition taking actions which collectively form an effective programme of rolling, incremental, focused initiatives. In addition, it is often, but not always, desirable to include 'breakthrough' actions, which may have potential for achieving a sustainable competitive advantage.

From the perspective of evaluation of strategy proposals, the model can be used as a framework to classify candidate strategy elements in terms of their likely significance. For example, of the actions proposed, which will achieve a breakthrough? Which will gain only an incremental advantage? Which will, at best, enable the organization to keep up with its competitors? Of course, these questions involve substantial and substantive judgements, based wherever possible on analysis (eg competitive intelligence, benchmarking, etc), but also inevitably based on assumptions as well.

We now apply these concepts to assess strategic opportunities in the order cycle.

Assessing Pipeline Management Systems: Competitive Advantage or Competitive Necessity?

To summarize our earlier discussions: in a manufacturing or merchandising firm, one key task is managing the order cycle–supply chain integration. Many companies are moving to do this. Is implementation of PLMS a source of competitive advantage?

Pipeline Management Systems

The critical tasks in implementing PLMS include, among others:

- Integration of transaction processing capabilities between firms (suppliers, customers)
- This integration is achieved in part through utilizing widely-accepted EDI standards for message formats. While implementing EDI has many practical difficulties, knowledge of how to implement EDI is widespread and readily available
- MIS and EIS for executive monitoring and reporting of the pipeline processes are essential elements. Shipment status and tracking systems on a carrier-specific and multi-carrier or forwarder basis are one key element of the MIS
- DSS for operational purposes (eg planning and scheduling, dispatching) are also important.

In addition to these technical steps, organizational changes will also often be required, to exploit the information available and to be able to respond to the new customer needs. Effective order cycle integration requires major organizational changes as well as significant changes in information systems. Some companies will do this, and do this well, and thus will be leaders in their sectors, and will thereby gain some significant advantage over competitors. This advantage will show up in reduced costs, through reduction of inventory and logistics facilities and services, and improved customer services.[15]

It is a competitive necessity to have a world-class capability to manage the order cycle.[16] A company which fails to do this is likely to have higher inventory costs than its competitors, higher order processing and related costs, and to provide a lower level of service to its customers.

Pipeline management systems implementation is particularly important for firms already competing in Europe. If our hypotheses are correct, the European market will transform rapidly over the next few years as leading firms move rapidly to invest in new production and distribution capabilities, and in the process of making these strategic investments, develop pipeline management systems. No company can expect to ignore this and survive through the 1990s.

Does a company which leads its competitors in integrating the order cycle gain a significant competitive advantage?

Many firms have been engaged in these processes for several years. There are many individuals and firms with expertise in the necessary skills, so any company can catch up, if it wishes, by using internal expertise or hiring external consultants and using products which are widely available in the market-place (eg EDI software and commercial value-added networks for data communications with partners).

Therefore, the know-how is not unique, and the technology is widely available. If there is a key differentiating variable, it is the management capacity to lead and implement effectively. While effective implementation of PLMS is indeed a difficult management and technical task, the knowledge about what to do and how to do it is widespread. Therefore, we conclude that effective implementation of PLMS is a competitive necessity and is not likely to be a source of a sustainable competitive advantage.

Assessing Other Information Systems Options

In the same way, we can analyse a broad range of IST options. We apply the conceptual framework of the multi-thrust strategy introduced previously. Table 5.1 gives a summary of the two basic strategy thrusts, 'Base' and 'Parity', and the corresponding technologies.[17]

Seeking Opportunities for Competitive Advantage: Concepts

Where are there opportunities for a competitive advantage, if PLMS are only a competitive necessity? We now introduce some additional concepts which will help us think about this question.

The Life Cycle of a Strategy

Competition is a highly dynamic process. Every strategic move has a finite life. We can define the 'life' of a strategy as the period during which a company will retain a competitive advantage. For example, if company A takes an action, it will be countered by an action by B. If A's move is successful and if it takes a long time for B to counter A's move, then A may achieve a sustainable competitive advantage through achieving a significant market share and profitability; thus A's action will have been a 'breakthrough' action. The 'life' of A's strategy will be relatively long. If, on the other hand, B counters quickly, and A's advantage is relatively short-lived, then A will have achieved only a short-term, incremental advantage. The life of A's strategy will be short.

If a strategy has a short life, then a company must be prepared to follow launching that strategy with the launch of a next-phase, or second, strategy. Thus, the need for a series of staged, incremental actions is rooted in the short life cycle of a strategy.

The Life Cycle of IST-based Strategies

The life of a strategy is a particularly critical issue when strategies are based on the use of IST. In general, it is quite difficult, in today's world, to find an information technology-based strategy which cannot be copied by competitors. Each new piece of technology, whether hardware, software, computers, communications, or whatever, evolves rapidly, and typically evolves in many places roughly simultaneously. In some cases, a piece of IST innovation can be protected by patent or copyright; in that case, a strategy based on that protected innovation may have a significant life. However, the rate of innovation is so rapid, and the streams of research so diverse, that even if one particular approach is protected,

Table 5.1 *Basic strategies*

Strategy thrust	*Technology*	*Examples*
To build the base	Transaction processing systems	Order entry, accounts payable
	Management information systems	Monthly financial reporting system; weekly sales reporting system
To achieve parity	Decision support systems – management, operations	Marketing management, production scheduling, financial planning and budgeting
	Electronic mail	Unstructured messages (memos, notes, reports)
	Telecommunications infrastructure	Voice, data
	Executive information systems	On-line reports, on-line queries
	Electronic data interchange (EDI) – basic	Purchase orders, invoices, payment orders
	Value-added networks (VANs)	Store-and-forward messaging
	Application development process	CASE tools
	End-user controlled application development process	Fourth-generation languages; IS department support of user-generated applications
	Shipment status systems	Carrier or forwarder-based shipment tracking systems (container, pallet, item levels), with associated documentation of shipments (insurance, customs, others)
	Pipeline management systems (PLMS)	Integration of EDI and non-EDI communications among trading partners, together with transaction processing, management information system, and decision support systems for each trading partner, and including shipment status systems (see text)

competitors are likely (but not certain) to find an alternative path to achieving the same objective.

Thus, there is a premium on speed in developing and implementing an IST-based strategy, and on being prepared to follow it up with another in order to protect the advantage created.

We define the 'market life cycle' of a strategy as the period during which a company has implemented a strategy and has achieved a competitive advantage which can be discerned in measurable and meaningful differences in market share and/or profits. The total life cycle of a strategy includes the time from the conception of an idea, through decision to implement, development, testing, refinement, and implementation, and retirement, and includes the market life cycle.

Strategic Capacity

How effective can a company be at mounting not just one, but a sequence of successful strategic moves?

For a company to be successful, it must mount a series of strategic initiatives over time. Because each initiative consumes resources, a company can mount only a certain number of initiatives at any time. We define the number of strategic initiatives which a company can mount over a specified period of time as the 'strategic capacity' of the organization.

This leads to the notion that a company can also consider strategic actions which are intended to increase its strategic capacity. Clearly, investing in R&D is one such strategic action; investing in the development of people skills is another.

The HRIS Hypothesis

Information technology by itself is rarely a source of sustainable competitive advantage,[18] for the reasons discussed above: most often, the knowledge of how to do something with information systems spreads rapidly, and other firms can quickly counter a firm's move. The market life cycle of a purely technology-based strategy is often only one or two years, or even less. There are two major exceptions, however: where there is a unique aspect to the technology which can be protected through patents or other legal devices; or where the investment in the technology is so great that competitors are turned away by the risks involved.

The ability to duplicate the human resource asset of a company is much more limited. It takes years and special efforts to develop a unique culture, people trained in the necessary skills, and effective and efficient business processes which exploit that culture and those skills. Clearly, investing in people, processes, and culture is a potential source of sustainable advantage.

Therefore, one way to think about the uses of information technology to gain competitive advantage, is to consider ways in which the technology components can be used to lever the people skills in the organization. We call this the 'HRIS hypothesis' (for human resources integrated with information systems and telecommunications):

- **The HRIS hypothesis** A potential source of competitive advantage through IST is to use IST to lever unique people skills and organization strengths.

Influence of HR on the Life Cycle of IST Strategies

Operationally, the HRIS hypothesis has three major implications.

Effect on IST adoption and implementation
First, as we invent and/or assess potential IST options and corresponding strategies, we need to consider the human dimensions of the organization, insofar as these factors affect its ability to take a decision on a strategy and to implement that strategy effectively.

Taking a decision involves all aspects of readiness and willingness to understand possible strategies, to face up to the need to take decisions, to take decisions in an effective manner, etc. For example, Bollo *et al.*[10] have observed that senior managers of small and medium-sized transport companies have great difficulty in seeing the need to take such major steps as implementing EDI and other elements of PLMS.

With respect to implementation of a strategy, there are a wide range of ways in which individuals and groups can support or resist the effective implementation of a strategy; often, carefully-managed organization change strategies are needed for successful implementation. Thus, the total life cycle of an IST-based strategy can be affected by the human resource dimensions of an organization, including the HR elements of its overall business strategy.

Effect on IST effectiveness
Secondly, as we invent and/or assess potential strategies, we should address explicitly the interrelationship of the IST and HR components of the strategies. Is the IST strategy essentially independent of the people elements?

For example, introduction of a simple EDI link may not involve any difference in the ways in which people work, as when an existing manual function is replaced by a computerized version. Or, the differences which do result do not enhance people's skills, responsibilities, empowerment, or satisfaction with work. In either case, people presently performing the tasks may be unenthusiastic about the change, or may even resist it.

On the other hand, it may be that the IST strategy is carefully coordinated with a series of steps to increase people's skills and control over their own work tasks. For example, introduction of EDI may be coordinated with a change in a credit authorization process and related software. The resulting changes relieve the employees in the credit check function of the routine drudgery of the job, and allow them to concentrate on the small number of credit approval cases which require judgement and perhaps consultation with sales and management personnel in other departments. Thus, their work becomes more involving, less routine, more challenging, and more satisfying.

Effect on strategic capacity
Third, strategies may be specifically intended to increase the capacity of the organization to develop, manage, and implement strategies, through enhancing the basic capabilities of the organization. For example, a strategy may be designed to increase significantly the level of education and training of people throughout a global organization; and at the same time, to encourage innovation and employee-initiated improvements.

Organization Change and Information Technology: Opportunities for Competitive Advantage

We now turn to look at opportunities for a competitive advantage based on the concepts introduced in preceding sections. In order to explore these implications, in this section we examine the organizational change dimensions related to the Single European Market, global competition in general, and the three integrating foci identified earlier.

Organization Structure and Coordination

As a consequence of the changes in manufacturing, merchandising, and distribution described in earlier sections, globally competing organizations (GCOs) in these sectors will be restructuring their formal organizations within the European region and on a world-wide basis. A number of formal organizational approaches are being taken or will be taken in the future. Regardless of the formal organization structure, however, the use of teams, both informal and formal will be increasing substantially.

Alternative organizational structures have been emerging.[19] In the search for new coordination mechanisms which integrate the organization, the tensions of the previously cited critical integration foci are causing two different forms to be considered.

One form is the evolution to global product groups. This is typified by Philips, Siemens, and others, which have been evolving away from multinational organizations to product groups on a world-wide basis.

The second form is the evolution to a geographic, regional structure. The emergence of the Single European Market is a major factor in managerial thinking. Clearly, to many managers, a unified market requires a single organization to manage production, distribution and marketing for the EC as a whole. Many Japanese companies – and some American and European companies as well – are putting into place a global structure with, typically, a four-region organization: Europe, North America, Japan, and the rest of the world. Each of these regions has significant authority and responsibility to act independently, to respond to its particular market and production conditions.

There is a tension between these two forms. In the product group organization, there is still a need for some regional structures; after all, logistics issues within Europe do not require day-to-day management attention of the logistics managers in Asia. In the regional structures, there is still a need for some product breakdown, and the regions must coordinate globally: development of new products, coordinated roll-out and marketing strategies, coordination of R&D are all major coordination issues in these new structures. So at the same time as authority is being restructured and decentralized to the regional level, new coordination mechanisms must be established between regions.

In many companies, these two forces are not completely articulated. Our interviews with Japanese companies have indicated movement toward regional structures. However, in few cases has significant responsibility for the integration functions been moved out of Japan; of course, Honda is one major exception. Honda North America has independent design and manufacturing responsibility, as well as sales. In the case of Philips, it appears that in most product groups, the power has been taken away from the national (country) organizations and placed in the global product groups, but the need for regional structures has not yet been resolved. In the case of Procter and Gamble, a matrix structure has been put in place, with strong power in the product groups but also almost equally strong power in geographic regions.

Organization Structure – Multiple Power Centres

Given this tension between alternative organization structures, which will be dominant? Several researchers have observed that the organization structure which is emerging in some leading companies is different from either of these traditional organization forms.

Bartlett and Ghoshal[19] identify three major forces shaping GCOs: the need for efficiency drives a firm for global integration, while the need for responsiveness to markets drives the firm to local differentiation and the need to have continual and rapid learning throughout the organization drives an organization to seek innovation on a world-wide basis. This results in their identification of several different types of company organizations:

- **Multinational** A multinational manages a portfolio of portfolio national entities. Its key strategic capability is building a strong local presence through sensitivity and responsiveness to national differences
- **Global** A global company treats the world market as an integrated whole, and products and strategies are developed to exploit an integrated unitary market. The key strategic capability is the ability to build cost advantages through centralized global-scale operations
- **International** In the international company, 'the parent retains considerable influence and control, but less than in a classic global company; national units can adapt products and ideas coming from the centre, but have less independence and autonomy than multinational subsidiaries'.

Bartlett and Ghoshal argue that a new form of organization is emerging, which they call a 'transnational', and which others have called a 'hetarchical' organization:[19]

> One of the critical assets of a well-functioning MNC is its cadre of internationally experienced personnel, well versed also in the intricacies of intra-firm communication. This together with the hardware and software of information management, constitutes the nervous system of the firm – its perceptive apparatus, information processing systems, and activators for response to opportunities and problems...
>
> It is obvious from the above that the most important part of structure is, not the formal organization, but the less easily describable management systems, communication processes, and the corporate culture.

Drawing on the observations of both sets of researchers, and our own interviews and observations, we can extend and modify the arguments of these researchers to characterize the hetarchical organization as follows:

- There are many centres, of different kinds, in different countries
- Different centres have different roles, many of which are specialized; both domestic and foreign subsidiaries may have particular strategic roles
- The assets of the organization are dispersed, with different centres managing various assets
- Each centre has significant independent decision-making responsibility, whether or not it is a profit centre
- Formal accountability, responsibility and authority is hierarchical, especially for budgeting and finance, and for management of managers
- There are multivalent power relationships: the formal hierarchical structure is balanced by a strong matrix thrust, sometimes a matrix with more than two dimensions, so that the mechanisms of coordination and integration are primarily by persuasion and negotiation, rather than by dictate, and the primary decision-making processes of each independent centre involve lateral relationships with other centres, as much as, or more than, hierarchical relationships
- These multilateral relationships create an integrated network forming the basic structural framework of the organization
- In this environment, firm culture is very important in establishing reference frames for negotiating agreements
- Important power centres are located outside the firm boundaries, in strategic partners of various types (customers, suppliers, distributors, etc)

In this type of organization, the critical assets are:

- the personal networks of relationships
- human resource management processes and systems

- information channels of all types
- information technology systems
- processes of change management which can be effective in this multivalent decentralized environment.

Hetarchical Organizations and the Single Market

In the processes of putting in place new organizational structures to deal with the Single Market, many GCOs will go through two phases. At first, some GCOs will organize hierarchically by regions, while others will organize by product groups globally. Then, GCOs will discover that extensive informal lateral linkages are important to retain flexibility and responsiveness in global competition, and so will transition, in a second stage, to explicit hetarchical organizations.

This hypothesis is at least partially verified by one example, that of IBM in Europe:[20]

> The company's European operations are being reshaped into a novel structure that could become a model for how a multinational corporation should organize itself to do business in post-1992 Europe. The European plan will also guide financial performance in a region that last year supplied nearly half of the company's $6.02 billion net income and 37.5% of its $69.02 billion revenue....
>
> The planning and implementation of the IBM Europe reorganization began more than a year ago. The blueprint was developed in a series of Paris management meetings and calls for IBM's European operations to become over the next five years or so *more centralized in some respects and increasingly decentralized in others. [Emphasis added.]*

A key element of this plan is improvement of the 'pipeline management systems' and other internal systems. However, the approach being taken is not a uniform centralization strategy, but rather a decentralization strategy for some functions, resulting in a strategy that looks somewhat hetarchical:[21]

> The result, if the program is successful, will produce a structure that simultaneously takes advantage of possible savings from a unified European Community market and also avoids alienating local customers, who will still have parochial tastes. That is the hope, at least, and the plan is getting some flattering reviews even from a few IBM competitors.

Clearly, the processes of organization change necessary to deal with the Single Market and globalization have only begun.

Hetarchies and Teams

One way of interpreting the preceding discussion is to conclude that no formal organization structure can ever be 'right'. Rather, the hetarchical structure is the only one that can work in this dynamic environment of global competition. The formal structure is not stable; it is the process of using teams to cut across the structure which is indeed the stable feature of these organizations.

Increasingly, organizations are using informal or semi-formal teams, which cut across the formal functional lines of the organization. For example, in a globally-competing manufacturing organization, a design team may be constituted of 10–300 people, from functions ranging through engineering, manufacturing, packaging, distribution, marketing, R&D, finance, and others; from 5–30 different locations, on 2–5 continents and in 2–20 countries.

Teams may be short-lived or may last for years, may be formally organized, semi-formal, informal, or even loose networks. Teams are fluid; many teams come and go as issues arise and are resolved, or opportunities are perceived and seized.

The working arrangements for teams and their members raise complex issues. Regardless, teams are being used very frequently, and are major elements of an organization's strategy to deal with the critical strategic issues identified previously. Teams provide the capability to cut across formal barriers for communication and coordination. Teams can provide an effective mechanism for rapid response. Teams also serve, often, to give individuals greater freedom and opportunity to be innovative and effective in dealing with the issue at hand.

Increasingly, teams are cutting across the boundaries of the firm.[22] Often, teams will involve members from other companies which are strategic partners: partners in a joint venture, in an R&D activity, or suppliers of critical components or important distribution partners.

The use of teams is found in all types of organizations, and especially in the hetarchical organization.

Example: Emergence of Logistics Coordination Teams

Teams are emerging in critical roles in logistics management and in related areas such as production management. In several leading companies, the logistics function is emerging as a leading element of the movement toward a hetarchical structure. In these companies, a corporate logistics function has been created to coordinate logistics globally. Examples include Hewlett-Packard (announced in 1990), Apple Computer, Xerox, Philips (accomplished several years ago) and Siemens.[23]

These coordination capabilities may prove to be leading-edge innovators in global coordination, since the logistic function is usually leading in establishing an integrated supply-chain management function. These logistics teams are examples of the hetarchical organization: these corporate logistics functions rarely operate with line authority over global logistics. Rather, they serve as coordinators, working through committees, task forces, or other types of team mechanisms to bring about coordination on selected issues. Generally, the line management of the logistics function on a day-to-day basis is in the product groups, the geographic regions, or at even lower levels, such as a country or a plant.

There seems to be significant variability in how these functions are organized, and in their power and likely impact. It seems clear, however, that these corporate logistics groups will tend to centralize procurement of carrier and logistics services or at least the policies, criteria, and coordination mechanisms through which these services are procured. The role of the central team is often:

- Establishing overall policy
- Leading the process of coordinated procurement of services, or ensuring that some other entity designated to lead a particular procurement acts effectively
- Standardizing where appropriate, such as coordinating the implementation of EDI.

Coordination teams are emerging in other functional areas as well.

Strategic Opportunities in the Order Cycle: Teamwork Support Systems

What can we learn from this discussion of organization structure, hetarchical organizations, and teams? If pipeline management systems are no longer sources of sustainable competitive advantage, what possibilities are there in, or related to, the order cycle?

Managing the Order Cycle: The Need for Teams and Team Support Systems to Complement Pipeline Management Systems

Managing the pipeline of materials flows illustrates the need for, and potential of, information systems which support teams.

Consider a product group in which components and subassemblies are sourced in five to ten countries on three continents, production takes place in a three to six factories on two or three continents, and distribution of finished product is global. Further, assume that in this product group there is some significant interchange of material across continents. A production line for widgets goes down in California, which usually supplies widgets primarily to Ohio. This information is reported, on an 'exception' basis, to a logistics team which is working closely with a production management team to coordinate the management of the pipeline supporting this particular product group. This team immediately goes into action: where are there widgets in transport anywhere in the world? What using plants are they being shipped to? What are the relative priorities of these shipments for different using plants? Are there inventories anywhere which could be diverted to meet the need? What are the opportunities for diversion of shipments in transit, and the consequences of those diversions? Can other steps be taken to minimize the consequences of a proposed diversion?

This is a complex task: how can a production problem be overcome by a combination of production and/or logistics actions, possibly on a global basis? This is also a *team* problem: who needs to be involved in finding out critical information? In developing possible courses of action? In assessing their consequences? In making a decision? Where the decision will probably require a negotiated agreement among a number of individuals in several different countries and several different roles?

At present, this task is resolved using telephone, telex, fax, and possibly e-mail. How could information technology support more rapid and effective accomplishment of this task in the future? What is needed is a system which supports the team working on a particular task.

Task/Team Support Systems

We use the term 'task/team support system' (TTSS) to designate a system designed to support the team working on a specific task such as that described in the preceding section. A TTSS in a globally competing organization is designed explicitly to support work by team members who are scattered geographically across different time zones and, often, across different languages and cultures.

As illustrated by the hypothetical example, TTSSs are an important complement to pipeline systems. Pipeline management systems have as their very objective the goal of routinizing the operations of the order cycle. By themselves they are not well-suited to handle group problem-solving issues although they can be designed to support the handling of the non-routine. They can be separate systems, or closely integrated with pipeline systems; but their functionality is very different.

There are many applications for TTSS in supporting order cycle integration:

- Supporting the team responsible for resolving a production or distribution problem in managing the global pipeline
- Supporting teams responsible for operations, such as coordinating production schedules, coordinating logistics or transportation procurements, coordinating purchasing of materials and components, etc
- Supporting the global logistics team described earlier, in our discussion of the hetarchical organization
- Supporting the process of 'team selling', in a logistics or transportation organization, or in any other geographically-distributed organization.

Example: A Task/Team Support System For Global Sales

Task/team support systems are particularly promising for team support to tasks such as team selling: managing a coordinated sales process in which a number of geographically scattered individuals participate.

The Rose Company (a fictitious name; the example is real) is a multinational logistics service provider, with several hundred offices in more than 25 countries. Rose uses a mainframe computer and several regional minicomputers, integrated in a network, as the backbone of its pipeline management information system. A mixture of leased and public lines are used for telecommunication of data. Most offices are either on-line with the network or have dial-up access over public-access networks. In addition to MIS capabilities, an e-mail system is used widely throughout the company.

About 12 months ago, Rose senior management decided to have a more focused and more globally coordinated sales effort. The strategy which was implemented had these elements:

- Identification of a certain number (*N*, say) of target customers (actual or future)
- For each customer, designation of a senior Rose manager as the sales coordinator
- Establishment in the e-mail system of a 'bulletin board' where company staff could post messages for each separate target customer
- Operating process for team coordination:
  - Rose employees who visit a target account are requested to post an e-mail message summarizing any information acquired
  - at least once a month, the sales coordinator for that account reviews the messages, prepares a summary, and sends out additional messages with comments, suggestions, queries, etc. to all of the Rose employees, world-wide, concerned with marketing to that account
  - a global sales coordinator overviews the process, assists in preparing account summaries, and manages the various 'conversations' from the perspective of a 'facilitator'.

This TTSS is credited with providing important assistance in Rose's gaining at least one major global account soon after its introduction.

This use of an electronic bulletin board and messaging system is a simple example of a TTSS. It shows what can be done with a mixture of available technology and appropriate management strategy. What could be done with current technologies, integrated into TTSS, to gain competitive advantage, and lever the human resources of the organization?

Task/Team Systems: An Opportunity for Competitive Advantage in Hetarchical Organizations

As organizations become more hetarchical, a greater and greater premium will be placed in the ability to coordinate laterally among individuals in multiple organizational units. This capability will be especially important in organizations with units scattered geographically across different time zones.

Task/team support systems will have the potential of creating major opportunities for competitive advantage for globally-competing organizations. Because this technology is new and emerging, few organizations have expertise in it. Further, reflecting the HRIS hypothesis, because the technology of TTSS leverages people skills, it is possible that an organization may be able to combine the technology with human resource development and management strategies that create together a unique and sustainable competitive advantage. For example, implementing a TTSS for global pipeline management may allow development of a globally coordinated order cycle integration capability that is a source of significant competitive advantage.

Towards a Comprehensive Strategy: Creating the Knowledge-Based Organization

The application of task/team support systems to order cycle integration is a particularly promising strategy (or class of strategies) and reflects the concepts of the HRIS hypothesis, and the recognition of the limited market life cycles of strategies based purely on technology. Can this same perspective lead to identification of other, promising strategic opportunities as well? Particularly importantly, can we identify some directions which will increase the strategic capacity of the organization?

Table 5.2 summarizes a number of promising directions.[10] Based on the conceptual framework of the multi-thrust strategy, we identify a number of opportunities for competitive advantage. At this stage of development, these are concepts, or pointers to possible strategies. These elements need to be translated into a fully fledged strategy in a particular firm before such an assessment can be made. As such, it is difficult to gauge in the abstract whether such strategies can be 'breakthrough' or are only sources of possible incremental advantage. Therefore, we discuss incremental and breakthrough elements together.

In the rest of this section, we discuss some of the ideas presented in Table 5.2.

Principles Underlying a Broader Strategy

The need for a broader strategy is established by the line of argument laid out in preceding sections:

- To compete effectively in the rapidly-changing world exemplified by the Single Market, organizations will have to evolve to hetarchical structures
- In this organizational environment, lateral relationships, and especially the ability to work in teams across internal and external boundaries, will be especially important
- Information technology to support teams – task/team support systems – will be one source of competitive advantage
- In general, technology by itself will be imitated and so the major basis of a sustainable advantage must be in development of unique skills in the organization. These may involve developing the capability for rapid innovation and rapid implementation, as well as other cap-

Table 5.2 *Potential strategies for competitive advantage*

Advantage through	*Technology*	*Examples*
'Beyond EDI'	Advanced EDI – beyond the basics	Integrated application systems exploiting EDI: accounts receivable, purchase orders and order entry systems, production scheduling, others; value-added services for customers: shipment tracking, order-status tracking
	Effective implementation	Management of organization change process to exploit EDI integrated with application systems
Customer-focused logistics	Performance measuring and management	Performance measurement and monitoring systems
	Customer-service focused organization	Customer service measurement, monitoring and evaluation systems; DSS for operations and for management focused on customer service measures
	Customer relationship management	Customer-focused data bases and reports; customer relationship management teams and support tools
	Customer-tailored services	Customer-focused customizing capabilities, including, queries, reports, tracking capabilities, DSS for customer use, team support for customer service coordination
Individual work support	Personal information management support	Lotus Agenda and other personal information management tools
	Location-independent computing	Notebook computers; palmtop computers (Poquet, Sharp Wizard, Kyocera Refalo, Apple Newton); handwriting tablets (NCR, GridPad); with appropriate application software
Intelligent work support	Intelligent agents	Processing of messages using 'intelligent' agents; scanning of data

Table 5.2 *Continued*

Advantage through	*Technology*	*Examples*
	Messaging focal point	Multiple-message dialogues covering multi-step transactions, with multiple media, intelligent agents; universal messaging focal point
	Symbiotic DSS	Intelligent agents in DSS
Teamwork support	Same location – same time	Group DSS
	Same location – different time	Electronic bulletin boards
	Different locations – same time	Teleconferencing, video, conferencing, computer conferencing; screen-sharing software
	Different locations – different times	Lotus Notes
	Task/team support systems (TTSS)	Applications of teamwork support software to specific team tasks: pipeline management coordination and contingency management; logistics teams; production planning contingency management; team selling, national and global account management, customer relationship management; product design; environmental scanning
	Workflow management	TTSS with agents flowing work among individuals
Intelligent team-based decision support	Task/team support systems with intelligent agents	Intelligent agents in team-based DSS
	Integrated task/team support systems	TTSS with intelligent agents, an SDSS architecture, organizational learning elements, integration of multiple tools

Table 5.2 *Continued*

Advantage through	*Technology*	*Examples*
Business process redesign	Business process redesign approach and techniques	Process change methods and techniques; use of TTSS for support of business process redesign team, for client management of process
Organizational learning	Enhance people's skills, capability for growth	Immediate help, context-sensitive help, in-depth help; study help, including electronic bulletin boards
	Collaborative learning	Using experts, peers; using TTSS
	Intelligent aids to learning	Learning-on-demand; organizational learning
Information systems management capacity	IST management capability	Capability to manage information technology globally in an appropriate mix of centralized/ decentralized management

abilities based on expanding the strategic capacity of the firm, as suggested by the HRIS hypothesis and other elements discussed previously

- Strategies which enhance the people skills of the organization will be especially important.

The 'Tight–Loose' Dilemma of Logistics Organizations and Opportunities for Competitive Advantage

Many organizations today face a significant challenge. They must be 'tight' at the same time that they are 'loose'. They must have a lean, disciplined operation, in which there is a strong and ceaseless attention to keeping costs down and providing quality service at the same time, while also being innovative, responsive to customers' needs, flexible and adaptive to changing conditions and changing customer needs. This requires, for example, the ability to be able to customize capabilities so as to provide customer-specific tailored services, together with customized information systems support.

The need to be simultaneously tight and loose, in these terms, is especially critical in logistics organizations. In today's environment, where cost, quality, and service are all critical, all three goals must be met simultaneously.

Developing and maintaining this style can be assisted by a number of information systems elements:

- Performance measuring and monitoring systems
- Customer service measurement, monitoring and evaluation systems
- Customer-focused data bases and other customer relationship management capabilities
- Support to customer-focused team-based customer relationship management, such as 'team selling', to support multi-phase, large-account, multi-function and multi-geography sales efforts (eg extensions of the Rose example described earlier)
- Customer-focused customization capabilities, eg by using a client-server architecture, with customer-focused tools, to develop and modify applications for specific customers. Example: develop specific EDI interfaces to enable the customer to exploit value-added services provided by a transportation carrier or forwarder; develop a sophisticated inventory management and outgoing shipment consolidation system for a customer in a particular sector.

In addition, the human resource dimension is critical; we address this separately in the following sections.

Organizational Learning

There is an acute need for continued learning in GCOs. As new teams are formed, individuals must be able to learn rapidly what is needed to deal with a new set of issues. As new knowledge is developed, it must be made available to other members of the team and to individuals in other parts of the larger organization. While responsibilities for maintaining formal assemblies of knowledge (eg libraries, data bases) may lie in specific formal organization units, making that knowledge available on an as-needed basis throughout the larger organization is an important element of competitive advantage.

There are a number of modes of learning which can be supported.

Immediate help
When there is a problem, or a piece of information is needed quickly, a person wants to be able to get immediate help. This may come from:

- A data base, available from the workstation in text, hypertext, hypermedia, or other forms
- An expert, available asynchronously, ie with time delay until a response is received, by the posting of a question or discussion on a discussion bulletin board (either a stand-alone bulletin board or a module in a team support environment)
- An expert, available synchronously, that is, on demand and at the time of the need, to respond immediately to a query.

In-depth help
Often, an issue cannot be resolved quickly. Then, the user engages in a

dialogue with one or more resource persons, with multiple interactions over time. The resource persons may be peers, experts, or both.

Study help
When a user wants to go deeper into an issue, he/she can access a module of instructional material to pursue at leisure. The module may include self-test examinations or other evaluation material, so that the individual may also be certified upon completion of self-study. The module may be complemented with in-depth help from peers or experts.

Collaborative learning
Team support can be utilized to enhance the collaborative nature of learning. An instructional environment might utilize a mixture of all of the above elements: previously prepared tutorial material, peer-to-peer conversations, peer-to-expert conversations, peer-prepared material, conversations with external experts, intelligent agents for certain kinds of evaluation and advice, and other components.

Intelligent Agents to Support Scanning of Data

In today's computer-based world, there is an increasing problem of too much data and not enough information. The user is overwhelmed with potentially useful data. There is a major need to provide tools which will act, with little or no guidance from a user, to scan large volumes of data and identify that information which is most likely to be useful to the user. A variety of approaches and applications are emerging, and can be applied to order cycle integration.

Early work by Malone dealt with scanning of e-mail messages.[24] In this approach, a user defines a variety of rules for processing messages, depending on key words in the FROM, TO, SUBJECT, DATE or other structured fields, or on key words found in the body of the message. This approach is directly applicable to the processing of messages in PLMS.

Stiles[25] has pointed out that the interpretation of a message depends on its context. For example, a shipper may receive a large number of shipment status messages from carriers and forwarders, reporting the processing of a shipment as it moves from origin to destination. Of these messages, almost all contain, in essence, only the information that everything is going according to plan (the committed schedule for the movement). Only a small fraction contains 'real information' which must be inferred by examining other data. This requires inferring from information in one or more data bases, in addition to the information in the message itself. To do this requires use of an 'intelligent agent' which can apply sophisticated sets of rules to data in several data bases.

Thus, in order cycle integration, there is a need, and an opportunity, for development of intelligent agents which will provide true information. This is a major opportunity.

Universal Messaging Focal Point

Stiles and colleagues[25] have proposed the need for a multiple-media message-processing facility in implementing order cycle integration. The observation on which this proposal is based is that, for the foreseeable future, many companies and many units of companies will continue to use a variety of media for communication, including fax, voice, telex, as well as mail and non-standard computer messages. Thus, while EDI is emerging in standard forms, there will still be many companies, and many message types, which will not be part of the EDI world.

Stiles proposed the concept of a multiple-medium messaging focal point, which could translate messages among various media. Two additional features are also important in the concept: the ability to interface with existing mainframe and other 'legacy' systems, without requiring reprogramming of those systems; and sophisticated intelligent agent capabilities especially designed for the complexities of managing information in the order cycle, as discussed above.

This universal messaging focal point capability is packaged as an application-development tool-kit, allowing developing of specific applications for particular unique business situations. Because of this, an organization possessing such a tool-kit can also develop unique skills in business process redesign to implement processes which exploit the tool-kit in powerful ways.

Symbiotic Decision Support

Symbiotic DSS (SDSS) is a major extension of the concept of intelligent support to human problem-solving. A prototype SDSS for assisting individual schedulers in production planning in an integrated steel mill has been developed and tested.

The approach taken in this design is general. In an SDSS, the user works on a problem. The 'intelligent assistant' component of the system observes what the user does and, occasionally, sends constructive advice or criticism to the user. In addition to observing the user work, the assistant learns about the problem the user is working on by also working on the problem, using the same tools as the user, but without explicit direction from the user. Thus, the assistant may sometimes look at aspects of the problem closely related to what the user has been looking at; at other times, the assistant may go off and do things very differently.

While at present this approach is being applied to provide intelligent assistance to a single individual, the overall architecture can be extended to providing intelligent support to a team or to a formal organizational unit, eg for contingency management in PLMS, for production planning or for product design.

Team-based decision support

SDSS could be especially powerful when extended to the teamwork environment. For example, while many DSS are available today for carrier scheduling of equipment and drivers, they all assume a single individual is the decision-maker supported by the DSS. In many situations, the actual decision processes involve multiple interactions among individuals, with different roles and responsibilities, in a team-based approach.

Integrating TTSS with intelligent agents in an SDSS architecture could be especially promising for many tasks in the order cycle, in particular in team situations where individuals from two or more organizations would participate. For example, an emerging trend in order cycle integration is for 'cross-partner transparency'. In one example, a retailer captures sales data in real time through point-of-sale (POS) terminals at the check-out counters. This retailer requires each major vendor to access this POS data and to provide replenishment stock as needed to maintain store inventories at pre-agreed levels. A third partner in this process is the transportation carrier, who is responsible for picking up the vendor's products from one or more plants or distribution centres, consolidating or breaking down shipments as necessary, and delivering to the retailer's stores in a timely fashion to meet the retailer's requirements.

In this context, a TTSS would involve the retailer (store managers, department buyers, others), the vendor (production planning, outbound logistics managers, account representative in the sales department, etc), and the carrier (account representative, operations manager, dispatchers, etc). Because much of the time the system would operate relatively smoothly, intelligent agents would play an important role in scanning data, identifying problems, and developing advice messages to various parties on possible actions to resolve problems, actual or anticipated.

Workflow Management

One particular form of task/team support systems involves applications in 'workflow management'. In these applications, the objective is to replace the flow of paper documents in an organization through electronic documents. Workflow management systems are particularly effective in supporting processes where there is a substantial amount of structure. One example would be a typical travel expense reimbursement process.

This type of structured process is very common in the order cycle. For this reason, workflow management is a form of TTSS that should be particularly effective in logistics applications. As these systems are just beginning to be marketed, few firms have any experience in these applications, and early movers should be able to capture significant incremental advantage.

Process Redesign

In our previous discussion of EDI and PLMS, we discussed the need to redesign application systems such as accounts receivable and order entry, and to redesign the work processes around these systems to take advantage of these capabilities. In a more general sense, business process redesign is in itself a major strategic initiative.

Various forms are currently fashionable under different terms, such as 'business process re-engineering', 'business process transformation', and others. In some cases, the terms and their advocates represent a deep, thoughtful process; in others, the terms reflect only rhetoric. In general, though, the fundamental concept is sound: business process redesign can be an effective strategy, when conducted as an integrated process to redesign the nature of the work, the information systems support to that work, and the organization (both formal and informal) around that work.

Today, process redesign is being undertaken in many companies, so that by itself is not a source of advantage. However, effective redesign requires several key elements:

- Understanding of the substantive issues in the business and the business processes
- Understanding of the best practices and state of the art in similar processes in other businesses and other business sectors
- Ability to diagnose and understand the existing organizational environment
- Ability to develop and implement effectively a change management strategy
- Ability to utilize information technology in a deep and thoughtful way in the redesigned processes
- Ability to develop a strategy for process change implementation which will be both innovative and far-reaching in its impacts, and conservative and relatively minimal in risk in its implementation
- Ability to get management and staff buy-in on the need for change in processes and the plan for implementing those changes.

In order cycle integration, the opportunities for process redesign are significant. In many cases, the existing processes have never actually been 'designed'; they have simply evolved over time as a series of *ad hoc* procedures to get a job done. Often, different people in the same organization are following different processes, and even the same individual may vary the process for no obvious reason.

Developing the capability to do process redesign can be, potentially, a source of competitive advantage for logistics firms. First, process redesign is essential for effective implementation of EDI and PLMS. Second, it can be a valuable support to the internal process of developing specialized capabilities for particular customers. Third, it can be an effective tool for use in helping customers to adapt rapidly to unique capabilities provided by logistics functions or logistics service providers.

There are several ways in which a business process redesign capability can be developed. Today, there are many consultants offering process redesign services. A firm can utilize such consultants, or it can develop its own internal capabilities, or it can do both. The consultant can be used as a one-time activity, or as a strategic partnership.

Task-Team Support Systems: an Integrating Focus

Many elements of the technologies described previously can be integrated into a unified architecture for providing support to individuals and teams for critical strategic tasks.

For example, to support a globally dispersed production planning team, a TTSS would provide individual (private) and team support, with intelligent agents, an SDSS architecture, and organizational learning elements. The TTSS would sit on top of a telecommunications infrastructure with MIS and EIS tools. The basic data structure would be a marriage of PIMs, hypertext, and other techniques. Various DSS components would be available, including CAD, spreadsheets, analytical, engineering, financial and data base tools.

A TTSS for production planning would have similar features, but would be closely tied to EDI, VANs, and transaction-processing capabilities.

Information Systems Management Capacity

The above discussion suggests that, perhaps, there is no single technology, and no single system, which *by itself* can be a source of competitive advantage today. Rather, IST must be managed as a combination of systems and technologies, which are incrementally evolved, in the context of dynamically changing technology, competition, markets, and organizational and individual capacities. Most importantly, IST must be managed as an essential part of business strategy. Perhaps the GCO with the greatest competitive advantage will be the one that builds a strong strategic management capability around the IST functional area.

For the logistics function, this poses a challenge: logistics must catalyse the kind of dynamic IST management capabilities which are required, to enable the logistics function to achieve its objectives. In some cases, this may require the logistics function to establish its own departmental resources to meet this need.

Strategic Opportunities: Summary

The Basic Strategy

- It is a competitive necessity for a firm which wishes to compete globally to be active in Europe in some way. Being active in Europe in the time of transition to the Single Market is an important opportunity to learn about changes which will affect competition globally.
- It is a competitive necessity to be using information technology together with other elements of management to integrate the order

cycle, integrate the product cycle, and integrate customer relationship management
- To integrate the order in a manufacturing or merchandising company, it is a competitive necessity to have a pipeline management information system (PLMS), transaction processing, MIS/EIS, shipment location and tracking, and appropriate operational and management DSS
- The critical competitive necessities for logistics services providers or transportation carriers today are already well understood, and follow from the preceding:
  - Effective use of information technology
  - A totally-integrated PLMS, supporting the customer's pipeline system
  - Effective logistics service delivery, including high-quality service, and offering multiple services including not only transportation but also various value-added services
  - Capability to perform as an integrated logistics service provider taking responsibility for outsourced logistics services for major shippers
- Simply integrating the order cycle is, today, a competitive necessity, rather than a source of sustainable competitive advantage.

Seeking Significant Competitive Advantage

- The directions of potential competitive advantage for transportation carriers and other logistics service providers, and for information systems services and products vendors, appear to lie in targeting these evolutionary forces and especially the need to build the people as well as the technology dimensions of a strategy. The specific directions to be considered carefully include:
  - Learning from manufacturing and merchandising organizations where global coordination is emerging as a key issue, and where logistics or transportation can be leading-edge innovators in this role. Concentrate especially on the three critical integration foci: integration of the order cycle, the product cycle, and customer relationship management. Look for leading-edge customers with whom to work to develop new kinds of systems and services
  - Learning how to combine human resource and information technology strategies to provide coordinated support to task-specific teams, such as logistics or production coordination teams. In general, the direction for seeking competitive advantage will require exploiting information technology and human resources, including organization design, in new ways
  - Developing expertise in task/team support systems. Such TTSS can be very valuable in internal operations. The best way to learn about TTSS in order to develop services and marketing strategies is to use them
  - Pursuing the options identified in Table 5.2.

A Comprehensive Strategy for Long-term Sustainable Advantage

- For those firms who really want to achieve a sustainable advantage, we believe there is an option: to move ahead with the full range of options listed in Table 5.2. The key to this is a logical progression:
  - Use EDI and PLMS implementation to develop basic skills in information systems and in business process redesign
  - Move rapidly beyond basic EDI to advanced EDI, using this as a testing ground to develop and refine advanced skills; include basic business process redesign activities, basic intelligent messaging, and universal messaging focal point-like capabilities to exploit and consolidate PLMS achievements
  - Place priority on customizing customer service capabilities, on team support, and on organizational learning initially; reflecting the HRIS hypothesis, investing in these capabilities will expand the strategic capacity of the organization
  - As these objectives are achieved, move into advanced areas, including advanced intelligent agents (with learning), symbiotic DSS, and integrated multifunctional team support; and providing business process redesign for customers and strategic partners.
- Senior management rarely understands the potential of this range of options; even when it does understand, it rarely has the management breadth and depth to implement such a comprehensive strategy effectively while also keeping the core business profitable and growing. Because the capability to implement such a comprehensive, multifaceted strategy is rare, the firm that does this, and does this well, is likely to gain a substantial, sustainable competitive advantage.

The Opportunity for Logistics

- The changes in the ways businesses are competing and are organizing for global competition are profound. For example, the role of teams in the context of the emergence of hetarchical organizations is very important. This creates a tremendous challenge, and opportunity, for the logistics function in shipper organizations and for logistics providers. At the same time, the role of information technology in business in general, and in logistics in particular, is becoming critical.
- In many companies, logistics is leading or is among the leading functions. This is occurring because the global coordination of production and distribution is emerging as a major issue and opportunity. Logistics can be a leading innovator in developing and exploiting strategic options such as those described here.
- Those logistics professionals who understand these issues and opportunities have two significant opportunities: the opportunity to help their organization gain a significant competitive advantage; and the opportunity to become leaders in their organizations. To do this, logistics must understand the full range of information systems opportunities, as well as the broad range of issues in globalization;

they must also have the capability to lead in innovating in their organizations.

Acknowledgements

Research support from the following is gratefully acknowledged: the Strategic Informatics Research Program and the companies supporting it – British Airways, Consolidated Freightways, Consolidated Railroad Corporation, Harper Group, IBM, System One, and Yellow Freight Co; and the William A. Patterson chair at the Transportation Center, Northwestern University. Portions of the fieldwork underlying this research were supported by the Japan Foreign Trade Council, Tokyo; by the Center for US–Japan Relations, Northwestern University; by the International Center for Information Technologies, Washington DC, the City of Amsterdam, the Netherlands National Physical Planning Agency, the Province of North Holland, the Amsterdam Chamber of Commerce, Mitsubishi Research Institute, Fujitsu Research Institute, and Cambridge Systematics, Inc.

This chapter benefited from numerous conversations and joint activities with Peter Keen, ICIT; Eric Clemons, Wharton School; Benjamin Mittman, Northwestern University; Joyce Elam, University of Texas; Shinroku Tsuji, Kobe City University of Commerce; Moriaki Tsuchiya, Tokyo University; John Robinson, Harper Group; Frank Le Clerq, Amsterdam City Planning Department and TNO; Gary Biddle, American Standard Corporation; Jacques Roure, Sandoz Corporation and the Sema Group; Kyoji Kunitomo and Yasumasa Shinohara, Ricoh Company Ltd, and Tatsuro Ichihara, Fumio Tateishi, and Nobuo Tateishi, Omron Corporation.

I gratefully acknowledge the benefits of the research support of the sponsors and the collaborations of colleagues, but I alone am responsible for any errors or biases presented here.

References

[1] Biddle, G.J., presentation on 'Global Information Technology', at DSS-90, Boston, Mass., May 1990.

Ives, B., and Jarvenpaa, S., 'Global Information Technology: Some Conjectures for Future Research', in Sprague, R.H., Jr., (ed.) *Proc. 23rd Annual Hawaii International Conference on System Silences*, IEEE Computer Society Press, Los Alamitos, Cal., 1990

Manheim, M.L., 'Global Information Technology: Issues and Strategic Opportunities', *International Information Systems* **1** No 1, 38–67 (January), 1992

Manheim, M.L., 'Global Information Technology: Issues and Opportunities', in Sprague, R. (ed.) *Proceedings of the 24th Hawaii International Conference on System Sciences*, IEEE Press, Los Alamitos, California, 1991.

Manheim, M.L., 'Global Information Technology: Globalization and Opportunities for Competitive Advantage through Information Technology', *Tijdschrift voor Vervoerswetenschap* (Journal for Transport Science), **2**, 138–59, 1990.

Manheim, M.L., Keen, P.S. and Elam, J. *Strategic Assessment: the Use of Telecommunications as an Element of Competitive Strategy by the City of Amsterdam*, Cambridge Systematics, Inc, Cambridge, Massachusetts, 1989.

Roure, J., 'Integrated logistics management system', presentation to International Working Group on Strategic Informatics, Paris, March 1990.

[2] Ives, B., and Jarvenpaa, S. 'Global Information Technology: Some Conjectures for Future Research' in Sprague, R.H., Jr. (ed.) *Proc. 23rd Annual Hawaii International Conference on System Sciences*, IEEE Computer Society Press, Los Alamitos, Cal., 1990.

Levitt, T., 'The globalization of markets', in Vernon-Wortzel, H. (ed.) *Global Strategic Management: the Essentials*, Wiley, New York, 1990.

Manheim, M.L., Keen, P.S. and Elam, J. *Strategic Assessment: The Use of Telecommunications as An Element of Competitive Strategy by the City of Amsterdam*, Cambridge Systematics, Inc., Cambridge, Massachusetts, 1989.

[3] Flaherty, M.T. 'Coordinating International Manufacturing and Technology', in Porter, M. (ed.) *Competition in Global Industries*, Harvard Business School Press, Boston, Mass., 1986.

Roure, J., 'Integrated logistics management system', presentation to International Working Group on Strategic Informatics, Paris, March 1990.

[4] Roure, J., 'Integrated logistics management system', presentation to International Working Group on Strategic Informatics, Paris, March 1990.

Stalk, G.A., Jr., and Hout, T.M., *Competing Against Time*, Free Press, New York, 1990.

[5] Stalk, G.A., Jr., and Hout, T.M., *Competing Against Time*, Free Press, New York, 1990.

[6] Levitt, T., 'The globalization of markets', in Vernon-Wortzel, H. (ed.), *Global Strategic Management: the Essentials*, Wiley, New York, 1990.

[7] Manheim, M.L., 'Global Information Technology: Issues and Opportunities', in Sprague, R. (Ed.), *Proceedings of the 24th Hawaii International Conference on System Sciences*, IEEE Press, Los Alamitos, California, 1991.

[8] Strategic Informatics, 'Emerging Issues in Strategic Informatics', Working Paper, International Working Group on Strategic Informatics, Transportation Center, Northwestern University, Evanston, Illinois, 1987.

[9] OECD, *Advanced Logistics and Road Freight Transport*, OECD, Paris, 1992.

[10] Bollo, D., Hanappe, P., and Stumm, M., 'New Means of Communication to Serve Commercial Carriers: An Experiment on a European Basis', in Sprague, R.H., Jr. *et al.* (eds), *Proc. 24th Annual Hawaii International Conference on Systems Sciences*, IEEE Computer Society Press, Los Alamitos, Cal., 1991.

[11] Council of Logistics Management, *Proceedings*, Oakbrook Council of Logistics Management, Oakbrook, Il, 1992, 1991, 1990, 1989.

Flaherty, M.T., 'Coordinating International Manufacturing and Technology', in Porter, M. (ed.), *Competition in Global Industries*, Harvard Business School Press, Boston, Mass., 1986.

OECD, *Advanced Logistics and Road Freight Transport*, OECD, Paris, 1992.

Roure, J., 'Integrated logistics management system', presentation to International Working Group on Strategic Informatics, Paris, March, 1990.

[12] Manheim, M.L., Keen, P.S., and Elam, J., *Strategic Assessment: The Use of Telecommunications as An Element of Competitive Strategy by the City of Amsterdam*, Cambridge Systematics, Inc., Cambridge, Massachusetts, 1989.

[13] Clemons, E.K., and Row, M., 'A Strategic Information System: McKesson Drug Company's Economost', *Planning Review* **16** No. 5, Sept./Oct., 14–19, 1988.

Clemons, E.K., and Row, M., 'Structural Differences Among Firms: A Potential Source of Competitive Advantage in the Application of Information Technology', *Proc. 8th Intl. Conf. on Information Systems*, Dec., 1–9, 1987.

Manheim, M.L., and Mittman, B., 'Opportunities to Use Information Systems as a Strategic Tool to Achieve Competitive Advantage in the Steel Industry', Research Report, Northwestern University: University Steel Resource Center, 1988.

[14] Manheim, M.L., Keen, P.S., and Elam, J., *Strategic Assessment: The use of Telecommunications as An Element of Competitive Strategy by the City of Amsterdam*, Cambridge Systematics, Inc., Cambridge, Massachusetts, 1989.

[15] Clemons, E.K., and Row, M., 'A Strategic Information System: McKesson Drug Company's Economost', *Planning Review* **16** No. 5, Sept./Oct., 14–19, 1988.

Roure, J., 'Integrated logistics management system', presentation to International Working Group on Strategic Informatics, Paris, March, 1990.

[16] Manheim, M.L., and Mittman, B., 'Opportunities to Use Information Systems as a Strategic Tool to Achieve Competitive Advantage in the Steel Industry', Research Report, Northwestern University, University Steel Resource Center, 1988.

[17] Manheim, M.L., 'Global Information Technology: Issues and Strategic Opportunities', *International Information Systems* **1** No. 1, 38–67 (January), 1992. Adapted with substantial modifications.

[18] Manheim, M.L. (1985) 'Information technology and organization change: Strategies for managers', fourth annual William A. Patterson lecture, Northwestern University, unpublished working paper.

[19] Bartlett, C.A., and Ghoshal, S., *Managing across Borders: the Transnational Solution*, Harvard Business School Press, Boston, 1989.

[20] Hedlund, G., and Rolander, D., 'Action in Hetarchies – New Approaches to Managing the MNC', in Bartlett, C.A., Doz, Y., and Hedlund, G. (eds.), *Managing the Global Firm*, Routledge, London, 1990.

[21] Hudson, R.L., 'IBM Again Revamps European Sector: It Seeks to Find Proper Mix as Market Grows Tougher', *Wall Street Journal*, 4/22/91.

[22] Johnson, R., and Lawrence, P.R., 'Beyond Vertical Integration: the Rise of the Value-adding Partnership', *Harvard Business Review*, 1988.

[23] Council of Logistics Management, *Proceedings*, Council of Logistics Management, Oakbrook, Il, 1992, 1991, 1990, 1989.

[24] Malone, T.W., Grant, K.R., Lai, K-Y., Rao, R., and Rosenblitt, D.A., 'The Information Lens: An Intelligent System for Information Sharing and Coordination', in Olson, M.H. (ed.), *Technological Support for Work Group Collaboration*, Erlbaum, Hillsdale, NJ, 1989.

[25] Stiles, P., paper on Universal Messaging Focal Point presented at the Sixth World Conference on Transport Research, Lyons, France, July, 1992.

Chapter 6

The Global Logistics Challenge*

James Cooper
Exel Logistics Fellow and Director of Cranfield Centre for Logistics and Transportation, Cranfield School of Management

Introduction

As business continues to globalize, attention has increasingly turned to logistics. Several key factors influence the choice of global logistics options for business.

A basic consideration must be the characteristics of the product itself. A primary product characteristic, such as value density, is an important determinant of its 'logistics reach', and hence the structure of logistics operations on a global scale. Similarly, secondary characteristics of the product, such as its branding, formulation and peripherals (which include packaging), are vital considerations in deciding global logistics strategies based on postponement principles. It is also possible, on the basis of secondary product characteristics, to define four major options for postponement which apply at different points in the supply chain, from the production point, through to theatre warehouses.

In addition, sourcing and production requirements make it possible to develop a taxonomy of businesses according to their logistics needs on a global scale. Importantly, the accelerating dynamics of global businesses may demand a variety of approaches over a period of time in order to secure success. The critical success factors for management at one point in time will change as the company and its global logistics requirements are repositioned in response to competitive pressures. It is vital that managers anticipate these requirements as a key part of the global management process which increasingly necessitates both a change in management roles and major changes in organizational structure.

Background

Over the past few years there has been a sustained trend towards the globalization of businesses. The driving forces behind this trend are several. Ohmae,[1] for example, points to the spread of similar life-style preferences among the young around the world, which creates ever-wider markets for products such as trainers and personal stereos. He calls this the 'Californianization' of the young. Upstream of the market, in

* This chapter is based on a paper first published by the author in the *International Journal of Physical Distribution and Logistics Management*, Vol 24, No 4, 1993, entitled 'Logistics strategies for global businesses.'

manufacturing, there are also important factors which drive the process of globalization. Increasingly, it is too expensive to duplicate best manufacturing practice in each of an organization's major markets.[2] Manufacturing facilities have therefore become more focused, both by product specialization and geographical location.

Inevitably, as the process of globalization continues, the character of companies must change. The following quotation by Levitt captures this point:

> The multinational and the global corporation are not the same thing. The multinational corporation operates in a number of countries and adjusts its products and prices in each – at high relative costs. The global corporation operates with resolute certainty – at low relative costs – as if the entire world (or major regions of it) were a single entity; it sells the same things in the same way everywhere.[3]

Inevitably, considerable discussion has arisen on how far global standardization can go. Whereas Levitt refers to products being sold in the same way everywhere, others such as Kotler,[4] Douglas and Wind[5] and Jain,[6] have identified significant barriers to the standardization of marketing in many industries. Similarly Piore[7] and Bartlett and Ghoshal[8] point to the rejection of standardization in many products by a large and growing group of consumers.

Just as standardization can be related to both the processes and content of marketing,[9] so it is a similar story for logistics. Theatre operations in logistics, for example, are highly variable throughout the world and the priorities for management in Europe, for instance, will differ significantly from those elsewhere.[10]

As a consequence, managing logistics at a global level represents a challenge of considerable complexity, and it seems fair to say that many companies have yet to get to grips with the challenge of managing global pipelines.[11] Indeed, among some US managers there seems to be a dichotomy in their thinking about global logistics. According to one survey,[12] US managers did not expect much globalization of logistics channels, yet simultaneously held the view that manufacturing facilities would become more centralized.

It therefore seems timely to review the process of business globalization and to consider the implications for logistics, with the aim of bringing more clarity to our understanding of both the strategic and the management issues. In particular, we need to embrace the point that global logistics management implies the making of choices between options, with respect to both content and process. There is no single standardized model for all companies to follow: each company must cater for the particular business environment in which it operates.

This examination of global logistics begins with a brief overview of the globalization of company operations, to provide a working context. The discussion then moves on to assess the development of global logistics strategy, taking a bottom-up approach. To begin with, the impact of product-market characteristics on strategy formulation is assessed, followed by an evaluation of logistics strategy at the level of the business unit or company. Finally this chapter considers the implications of global logistics strategies for management, notably the critical success factors that apply and the need for organizational change.

The Globalization of Company Operations

It has been estimated[13] that trade between subsidiaries of the same company accounts for more than half of all trade between OECD countries. One third of all US exports is to the overseas subsidiaries of US firms. Another third of US exports is accounted for by foreign manufacturers sending goods back to their home countries. Not all of this trade represents the activities of fully global businesses; many firms will be more restricted in scope. Nonetheless, the figures do illustrate the importance in world trade of companies which are already global or have gone some way towards achieving global status.

A further important point is that these trade flows are not only larger than in the past (as a result of global economic growth) but they are also qualitatively different than before. Trade used to be based on relatively fixed locations with raw materials sourced from where they were found or grown, and production taking place in the industrialized centres of Europe and North America. Now the process is much more footloose than it once was. Industrial components can be sourced from a variety of alternative locations and the assembly even of advanced products is less tied to established centres; for example, the Shanghai Aviation Industrial Corporation (SAIC) assembles civilian aircraft in China on behalf of McDonnell Douglas.[14]

A number of key, but interdependent, factors have been responsible for reshaping the activities of major companies, including:

- The globalization of markets
- Cheaper communications
- Removal of barriers to trade and foreign investment
- Achieving economies of scale in business
- Innovation in logistics.

Each of these factors is very briefly reviewed in turn below, both to expand on the trends outlined above in the Background section and to provide examples from companies which are either partly or fully globalized.

The Globalization of Markets

This represents a phenomenon which is different from the simple growth in world trade. Rather it means that the same products (or variants tailored to local tastes) are sold in more countries than before.

Probably the archetypal global product is Coca-Cola, which is sold in just about every country. Hamburgers from McDonald's are not far behind, but the list is not exclusively American. Other products with a strong global reach include Benetton clothing (Italy), Sony consumer electronics (Japan), Rolls-Royce aero-engines (UK) and Mercedes-Benz cars (Germany).

Some of these products represent useful illustrations of the limits to standardization in global marketing. Mercedes-Benz cars, for example, are not sold with left-hand drive in all export markets; several, such as Japan, Australia and the UK, require the steering wheel to be on the right of the car. Benetton, in its clothes range, balances standardization with some local adaptation. Others follow the path chosen by Pizza Hut, which:

> protects the core elements of its brand by copyrighting its individual product brand names eg Perfect Pizza. It also ensures standardisation across markets by operating a strict specification of product ingredients. However the concept is adapted to suit local needs. For example some elements of the menu (such as desserts) will vary, as will store design and even the way products are served to the customer.[15]

These examples seem to point to a clear enough message on the issue of standardization in global marketing; namely, that marketing is consumer-oriented and if consumers prefer a non-standard product, then companies must oblige to achieve or maintain success.

Cheaper Communications

The process of market globalization is inextricably linked with cheaper communications of various kinds. For example, the spread of television allows advertisements for goods to be directed at previously untapped markets. In this way, people can be persuaded that they have unrealized wants or needs that can only be satisfied by the purchase of a particular product. The spread of satellite television, which spans national boundaries, must have contributed to the development of global markets, particularly in consumer products.

Furthermore, communications in the transport field are crucial to this process of globalization. Cheaper transport, through technical developments such as containerization, now makes it economic to serve new markets or source from new locations. Also, communications, in the form of information systems designed to control the flow of goods, are now becoming a vitally important consideration. Developments such as electronic data interchange (EDI) are fast reducing transaction costs and are making global trading more attractive to an increasing number of companies.

Removal of Barriers to Trade and Foreign Investment

The General Agreement on Tariffs and Trade (GATT) has had an important influence on world trade, which has been stimulated by the application of the most favoured nation (MFN) rule 'under which a government has to extend trade benefits granted to one country to all other GATT members and GATT's simple concept that protection against imports should be achieved by means of non-discriminating tariffs.'[16]

In the area of foreign investment there have also been major changes. Take, for example, the case of Ford in Spain. In the early 1970s the Spanish car market was heavily protected. Tariffs on imports were very high, at 81 per cent on cars and 30 per cent on components. Moreover there was a requirement that cars built in Spain had to have 95 per cent local content. Finally, no foreign company was allowed more than 50 per cent ownership of a company operating in Spain, which conflicted with Ford's policy of 100 per cent ownership of foreign subsidiaries.[17] Because the Spanish government was keen to establish a strong local motor industry and increase car exports, these conditions were relaxed. The pay-off for Spain was 19,000 new jobs and opportunities for export. With the further establishment of plants by General Motors and SEAT (now owned by Volkswagen), Spain is now a major European producer of cars.

Economies of Scale

Achieving economies of scale in business has been an important parallel development in line with the above changes, not least in manufacturing. If economies of scale exist that extend beyond the size of national markets, then there is a potential cost advantage to companies through centralized production.[18] In other words, it will be worthwhile making in one location, to serve a number of national markets, rather than to have national manufacturing units.

This has been the strategy of companies such as Procter and Gamble (P & G) in Europe. Toothpaste, for example, is made in Germany for sale throughout Europe. Furthermore, such focused production appears to be on the increase. Unilever, a major competitor of P & G, has recently changed its strategy from making most of the product range at plants in its main country markets to a series of specialized factories located at strategic centres in Europe.[19]

A vital point about single sourcing of production is that it distances many final customers from production, as shown in Figure 6.1. For the multinational company (MNC), operating a host-market production strategy, customers and production are in close proximity. As Figure 6.1 shows, this is less true for the global or transnational company (TNC) practising single-source production; it follows that there are major implications for logistics management in this transition from multinational to global operations.

Innovation in Logistics

This has played a key role in making sure that global companies can still react effectively to local market demands, even when their production

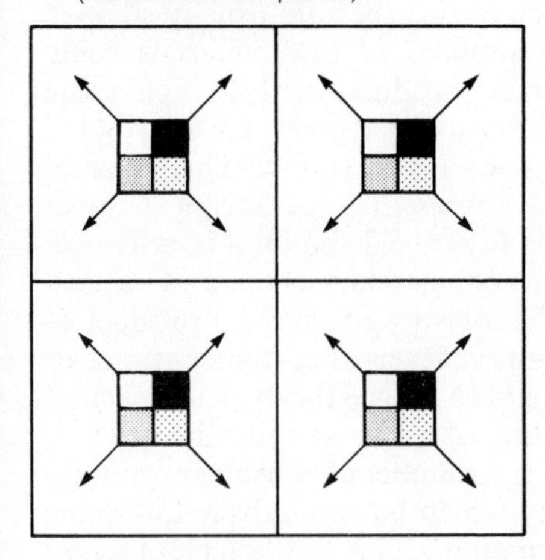

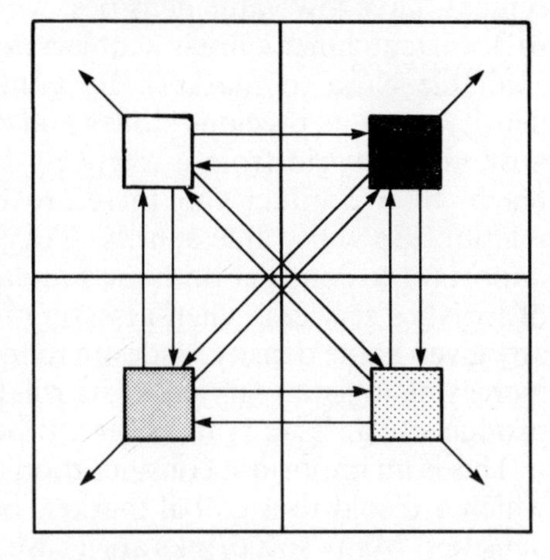

Distribution paths

Source: Adapted from Dicken, P., *Global Shift: Industrial Change in a Turbulent World*, Harper and Row, London, 1986

facilities are distant. The application of the principle of 'postponement' is an important case in point.[20] This allows for some activities normally associated with production to be performed downstream in the supply chain, delaying the point in time when goods become dedicated to particular markets or customers. Take, for example, the case of Caterpillar in its production of lift-trucks. In order to save on production costs the company moved manufacturing away from the United States. Lift-trucks come with a variety of options, and it would have been excessively costly to stockpile lift-trucks fitted with a host of option permutations at an American warehouse, so that any one customer order could be rapidly fulfilled from stock. Much better to ship across part-finished lift-trucks and to finish assembly, using the required options, at the warehouse. The important point here is that the warehouse has become an extension of the assembly line, allowing Caterpillar to maintain (or even improve) levels of service, at an acceptable cost.

Logistics strategy is therefore a consideration of growing importance for Caterpillar and companies like it. Yet the precise formulation of a logistics strategy for any one company depends crucially upon a number of key product variables. In the following section we examine these variables and consider how global companies can thereby reconfigure their logistics operations in order to gain or sustain competitive advantage.

Product Variables and Global Logistics Strategy

One of the key product variables in determining global logistics strategy is value density; namely the value of a product in relation to its weight and volume. The general rule is that the lower the value density, the more localized the logistics system. Many commodity products, such as cement, have low value densities, which means they are usually shipped to local catchment areas (subject to supplies of raw materials being available close to market). By contrast, products with a high value density, such as precious stones and expensive perfumes, are distributed around the world from a relatively few points of supply. The 'logistics reach' of a product can therefore be represented as having a direct relationship with value density. Yet, as Figure 6.2 shows, it is extremely important to consider both the standard of customer service and the cost of logistics services, when assessing the logistics reach for a product of any given value density. A desire to improve levels of customer service or increasing logistics services costs will tend to reduce the logistics reach of products (e.g. from r_2 to r_1 for a product of constant value density v_1).

This is an important consideration for a number of consumer products which are sold to a global market, but which have relatively low value densities. Many soft drinks are a case in point. Each bottling plant serves a well-defined area around it and the radius of operation is largely determined by both customer service and the cost of logistics services for delivery to customers. (The radius of operation varies according to local conditions, but in Europe it is about 150 miles.)

The configuration of the bottling plant network is therefore highly dependent upon logistics reach. It follows that a change in logistics reach

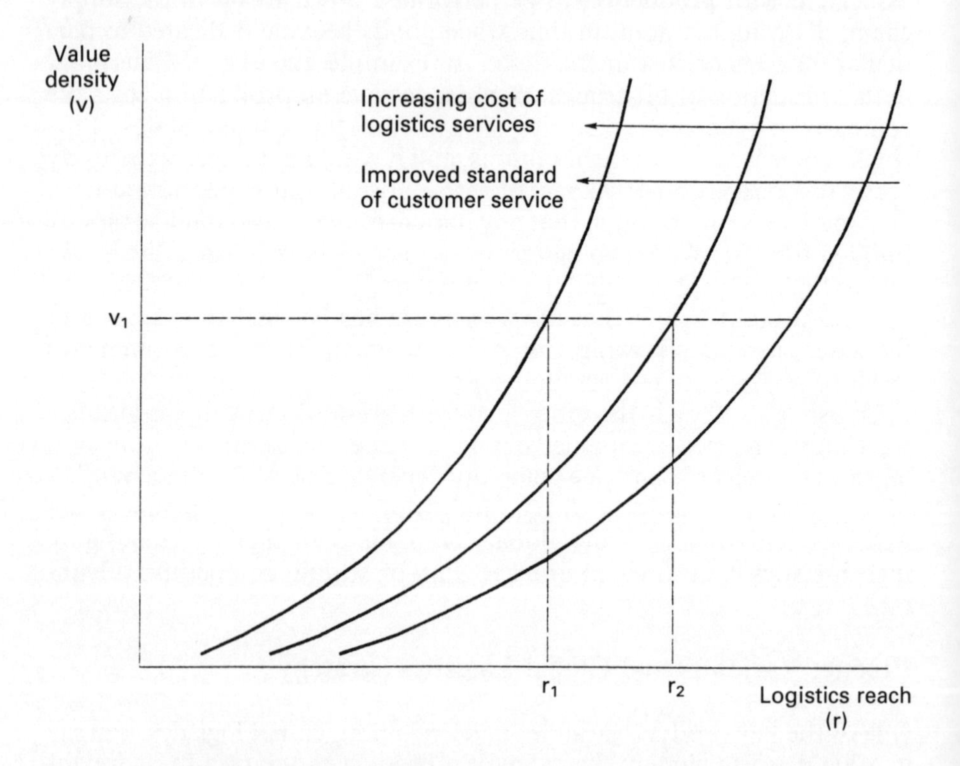

Figure 6.2 *Product value density and logistics reach*

as a result of, say, changes in transport costs, will impact upon the bottling plant network. There must be continuous monitoring of the costs of production, as measured against the costs of distribution, to ensure that no imbalance develops in the network. Over the long term it must be a key logistics objective to maintain a production network that is neither too dense, nor too sparse, when judged against the twin criteria of customer service and supply chain economics.

However, it would be wrong to construct a logistics network for a global product entirely on the basis of a primary product characteristic such as value density. In many product markets (not least soft drinks), brand or technical superiority (or both) are also vital considerations, especially when they are key factors in secured market share. Taking the healthcare sector, for example, two of Johnson and Johnson's healthcare products have high value densities, yet the logistics strategy for Vistakon contact lenses is entirely different from the strategy appropriate to Ethicon sutures. This is because Vistakon operates in a highly competitive market place where product price is an extremely important driver. By contrast, Ethicon sutures hold 80 per cent of the market, so price is relatively unimportant next to high levels of customer service which deter the entry of rivals with competing products. Accordingly, the logistics strategy for Vistakon is focused upon the centralization of production and inventory in the USA, with world-wide distribution taking place from this single location. For a non-standard, high value product such as Vistakon, this strategy makes a great deal of sense, since economies of scale in production can be enjoyed, together with savings in inventory from centralization. World-wide airfreight charges for a product with such a high value density can readily be accommodated within this strategy.

The logistics strategy for Ethicon sutures is entirely different, given its dominant position within the market-place. Customer service, rather than cost, becomes the driver, so the logistics strategy is geared to high quality delivery in each theatre of operations; neither production nor inventory is centralized, given the need to provide unfailing supply to demanding customers.

The different priorities in formulating logistics strategies for products in the healthcare market are summarized in Figure 6.3. It emphasizes the importance of secondary product characteristics (price as a driver in the market-place) as well as primary product characteristics (product value density) when framing logistics strategy. Clearly, it is important for management to appreciate that the position of a product in the Figure 6.3 matrix is not always static. Priorities in logistics strategy must therefore change as market conditions change. For example, products at an early stage of their life-cycle will often enjoy high profits, encouraging rival companies to offer competing products. So while product price may not initially be a driver in the market, it will often become one eventually. As a result, the logistics strategy in the beginning (when competing products are not a threat) might emphasize very short lead times, with cost being a lesser consideration. Later, the strategy may well focus on

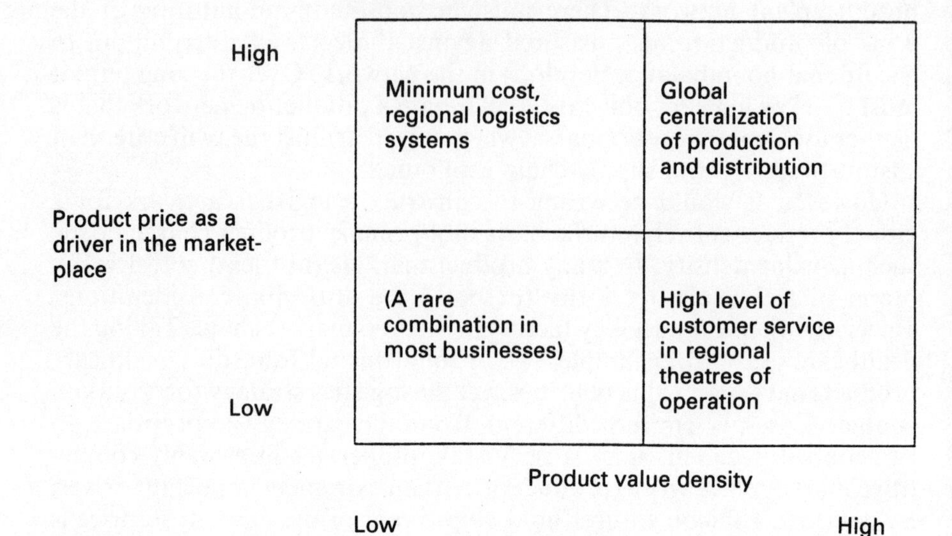

Figure 6.3 *Product-market factors and priorities in logistics strategy formulation*

Source: Adapted from *Reconfiguring European Logistics Systems*, a report for the Council of Logistics Management, jointly prepared by Cranfield School of Management and Andersen Consulting, 1993

cost-efficiency through centralized inventory and consolidation in transport movements.

Postponement

There are, however, a number of other secondary product characteristics which can play an important role in configuring logistics systems to best advantage. In a number of cases these can be related to the principle of postponement, the application of which can lead to superior systems in logistics, not least because inventory levels can be cut and problems associated with uncertainty of demand in particular markets can be considerably reduced. Postponement in a global context can be very readily related to 'yes' or 'no' answers to three questions that relate to secondary product characteristics. These questions are:

- Brand: Is it global?
- Formulation: Is it common to all markets or different between countries/customers?
- Peripherals: Are labels, packaging and instruction manuals common to all markets?

Starting from the perspective of global brands only, there can be only four different combinations of answers to these questions, as indicated in

Table 6.1, using illustrations from consumer markets. These combinations underpin four strategy options in logistics which are based upon different kinds of postponement in the supply chain.

The postponement option which applies furthest upstream in the supply chain is *bundled manufacturing* (see Figure 6.4). This is where the product formulation differs by market, either because of customer preference or varying technical standards. In the case of bundled manufacturing, the postponement aim is to retain product commonality for as long as possible in the production process. Only at the last possible opportunity should the product be configured to meet the needs of a particular market. This approach is exactly that taken by Sony in its Welsh factory, which makes television sets for Europe. The company began production by making different product ranges for countries, according to the broadcasting and technical standards used locally. Each product range had a very different manufacturing specification. Sony then succeeded in simplifying production through the introduction of a 'Eurochassis', which was a base design for all European television sets. Only at a late stage in the production process was the Eurochassis tailored specifically for, say, the French or German markets.[21] Key benefits, alongside not having to commit production to specific countries until a late stage, were the rationalization of the range of components required for television manufacture, the simplification of inbound logistics planning, and improved product quality.

The *unicentric* postponement option takes effect downstream from the manufacturing plant. Under this option global branding, together with common labels and peripherals, mean that the decision to allocate products to particular customers in world markets can be postponed until the product reaches a central warehouse; there is no need to earmark particular batches in production for given customers on account of their unique branding, formulation or packaging requirements.

Further downstream in the supply chain come the *deferred assembly* and *deferred packaging* options, both of which take place at theatre warehouses serving regions of the world or specific countries. Deferred assembly means that it is the final configuration of the product itself which happens at theatre warehouses, rather than at production plants.

The Caterpillar example, discussed earlier, shows the application of deferred assembly in an industrial market. A common application in consumer/business markets is for computers, as identified in Table 6.1, where different combinations of monitor, base unit and keyboard can be brought together at a late stage in the supply chain.

Lastly, deferred packaging can be a useful strategy when the brand and product formulation are common to all markets, but where packaging/labelling are country or customer-specific. Again, this is an operation that can take place at a theatre warehouse, close to several customers with different packaging/labelling requirements, so that production need only be committed to particular customers at an advanced stage in the supply chain.

It is important, however, to point out that the logistics strategies

Table 6.1 *Logistics strategies for global products in consumer markets*

1. Global logistics strategy	**Unicentric** Fully centralized production and distribution	**Bundled manufacturing** Design product so that customization can take place at latest possible stage of production process	**Deferred assembly** Final configuration of product at theatre warehouse	**Deferred packing** Labelling and packing at theatre warehouse
2. Product variables				
Brand – is it global?	Yes	Yes	Yes	Yes
Formulation – is it common to all markets?	Yes	No	No	Yes
Peripherals (labels etc) – are they common to all markets?	Yes	Yes	No	No
3. Potential strategy benefits	Economies of scale in production and distribution	Rationalization of components range simplifies inbound logistics and contributes to improved quality	Economies of scale in production and distribution, savings in inventory with high levels of customer service.	Economies of scale in production, savings in inventory with high levels of customer service.
4. Examples	Marlboro duty free cigarettes	Sony television (countries have different colour systems, electrical standards)	Compaq computers (countries have different keyboard requirements, especially for language symbols such as the umlaut and cedilla. Instruction manuals must also be in appropriate language).	Wash & Go shampoo*

* Economies of scale in the bottling process limit the extent to which deferred packaging can be applied for products of this kind.

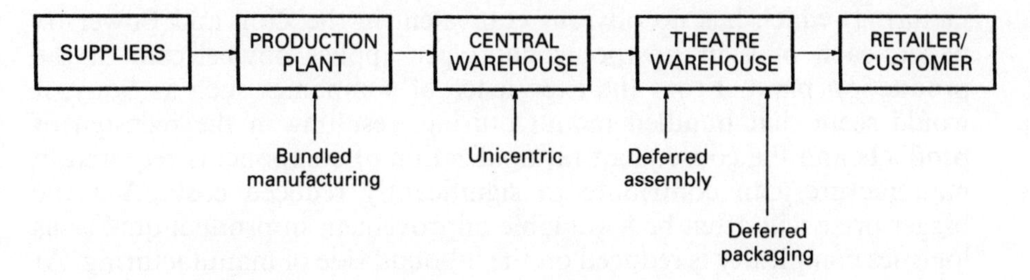

Figure 6.4 *Postponement points in the supply chain*

identified in Table 6.1 represent an upper bound to producers of global products. This is because not all products readily lend themselves to global logistics strategies, and many activities will need to remain more localized. The following factors will favour some degree of localization in logistics:

- Products with a relatively low value
- Limited economies of scale in production
- Need to produce in local markets as a result of political considerations
- Uneven development of global markets, with some regions taking much more product than others.

Nonetheless the four strategy options (bundled manufacturing, unicentric, deferred assembly and deferred packaging) do represent distinct and realistic opportunities for companies, as the examples cited in Table 6.1 testify.

Moreover, this approach of defining strategic logistics options based on combinations of secondary product characteristics gives an opportunity to compare and contrast the results with those of Zinn and Bowersox.[22] In their key work in the area of postponement, they identify five different postponement types (labelling, packaging, assembly, manufacturing and time) rather than the four which arise from making all possible combinations of secondary product characteristics (see Table 6.1).

In broad terms, assembly and manufacturing postponement differ mainly in the degree of warehouse assembly which occurs; they therefore relate closely to the deferred assembly option as defined above. Similarly the labelling and packaging postponement types are strongly linked and correspond to deferred packaging.

The fifth of Zinn and Bowersox's postponement types (time postponement) mean that 'products are shipped to customers only following order receipt, resulting in centralized inventories'. This compares with distribution in anticipation of orders, where products are shipped to warehouses on the basis of forecasts. Clearly, this postponement and the unicentric option are strongly related.

This leaves one option in postponement strategy (bundled manufacturing) which has no obvious equivalent in the Zinn and Bowersox paper; each of their postponement types applies downstream of the production plant. From the experience of companies such as Sony, it would seem that bundled manufacturing, resulting in the redesign of products and the consequent rationalization of components required in manufacture, can contribute to significantly reduced costs. Yet the bigger prize will often be a valuable improvement in product quality as logistics complexity is reduced on the inbound side of manufacturing. At a time when total quality management is paramount in the thinking of management at all levels, superior logistics performance through bundled manufacturing must be an attractive postponement option for those companies which sell complex, but non-standardized, products to different markets.

Company Strategy in Global Logistics

The discussion so far has focused on the characteristics of finished products and their market-place. Clearly, several key characteristics (value density, product price as a driver in the market-place, and the commonality of branding, formulation and peripherals) are closely linked to the formulation of logistics strategy for finished products, from the point of manufacture to the point of final consumption.

However, it is important also to consider logistics upstream of production, to gain a complete picture of the logistics options for companies operating at a global level. For example, the sourcing of raw materials or components represents a major consideration when decisions are made on developing new markets or relocating production. The formulation of global logistics strategy must therefore take full account of production processes as well as product-market characteristics.

At this point, it is important to recognize that some companies will have not just one logistics strategy, but several. This is most often the case where business units of the same company manage product groups with varying logistics needs. Yet there are some companies which are less differentiated than others with respect to logistics strategy. As a result, it is possible to give them some overall classification according to their global logistics strategy.

Analysis of the strategic development of a variety of global companies suggests that there are five distinct clusters, one of which can be unsustainable beyond the short term. These are summarized in Figure 6.5, which also indicates the global logistics requirements of companies.

Invaders

The unsustainable logistics cluster is evident for companies which can be called invaders. Classic examples of invaders in the recent past are Japanese companies such as Sony and Nissan. They established plants to serve local markets in the 1970s (Sony) and 1980s (Nissan) mainly on an assembly basis, using components sourced from Japan. However, with

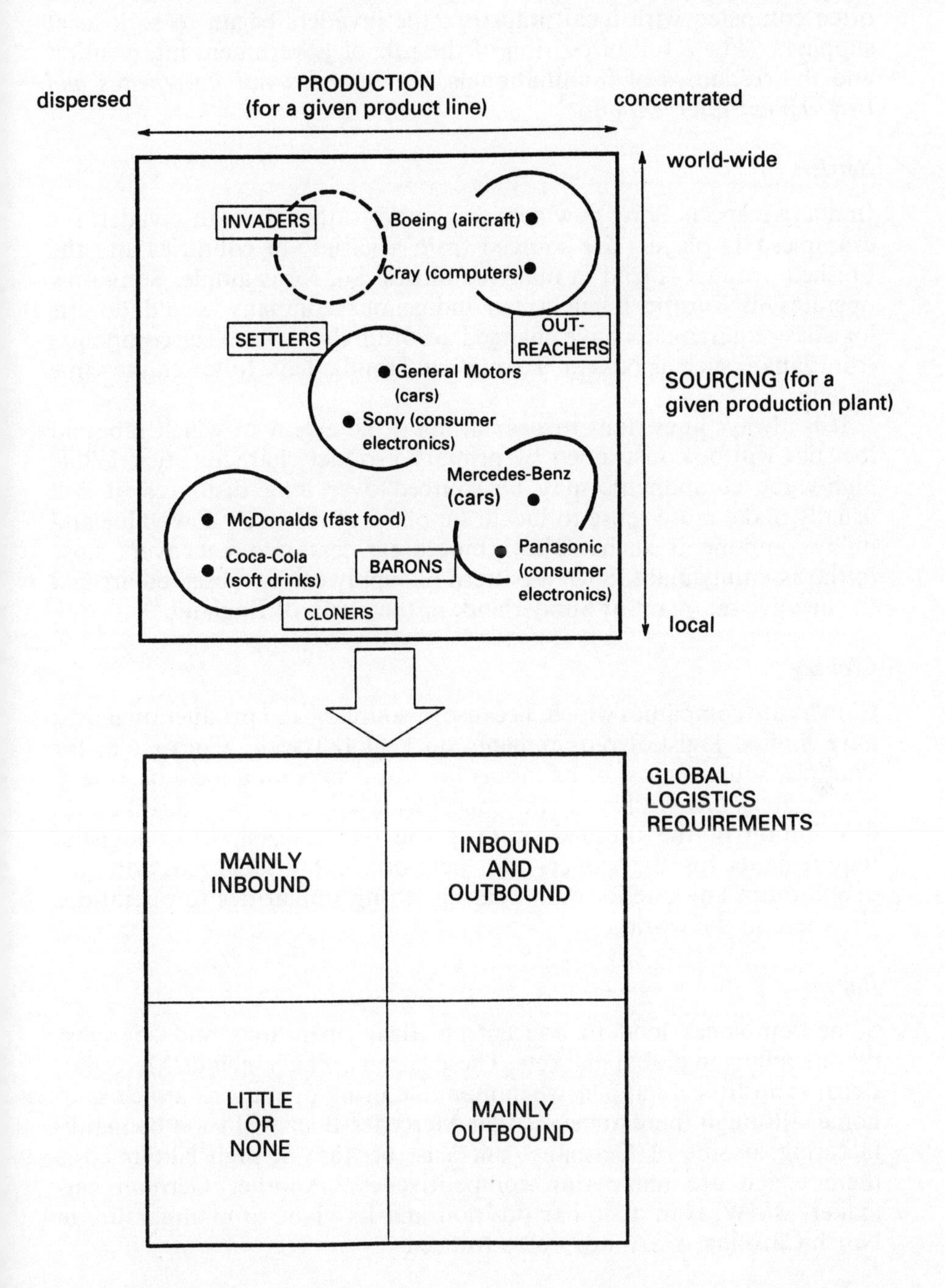

Figure 6.5 *Production process and global logistics requirements*

the diminishing political acceptability of 'screwdriver' operations (which often competed with local industry), the invaders began to seek local suppliers. (For a full discussion of the role of government intervention and the responses of multinationals, see *International Enterprises and Government Intervention*.)[23]

Settlers

In many respects Sony now acts as a settler rather than an invader; for example, CD players are sourced from a variety of countries and the finished product is sold in many countries. So, for example, Sony now operates in Europe much as an indigenous company would do. Its logistics requirements have changed accordingly. Several car companies from Japan, such as Nissan, Toyota and Honda, have followed the same pattern.

It is always important to bear in mind the extent to which inbound logistics will be constrained by primary product characteristics. While high-value components may be sourced over long distances, it will usually make more sense to locate suppliers of relatively low-value and bulky components, such as plastic mouldings, seats and seat covers, close to the assembly plant. Such a pattern of supply can be observed around the new Nissan plant at Sunderland, in the north of England.[24]

Cloners

Cloners are companies which, because of sourcing and production needs, have limited logistics requirements on a global scale. Coca-Cola, for example, sources most of its inputs for soft drinks on a local basis (e.g. cans, water). Generally only the concentrate will be imported. Likewise, distribution of the finished product will be localized. Most logistics requirements for the cloners are therefore highly localized, with the operation in any one location bearing strong similarities to operations elsewhere in the world.

Barons

Some companies tend to concentrate their operations and sourcing, despite selling in global markets. These barons, which include Mercedes-Benz, seem to feel happier when manufacturing operations are close to home, although there are signs that Mercedes-Benz will soon be manufacturing outside of Germany, not least because of high labour costs there which are hampering competitiveness. Another German carmaker, BMW, is in a similar position and its plans to manufacture in North Carolina, USA, are well advanced.

Outreachers

Lastly, there are the outreachers: global companies which manufacture in perhaps just one location (e.g. Cray computers in Minneapolis, USA), but which source from around the world. Companies of this kind, which sell in global markets, have extensive inbound and outbound logistics requirements.

It follows from the above discussion that global companies often need to pursue very different logistics strategies from one another, depending upon a variety of factors relating both to procurement and production processes. In turn, this has a major impact upon how they should approach the management of their logistics systems. The following section considers the key issues that arise.

Managing Global Logistics Systems

There is no doubt that the successful management of all kinds of global logistics systems depends, in turn, on the successful management of information. Crucially, in the context of global logistics, the 'expansion of the information network makes possible a degree of control which could not be envisioned only a short time ago.'[25] Networking, together with electronic data interchange (EDI), frequently represents the foundations upon which global operations are built.[26]

Just as global companies vary in their logistics requirements, information needs are also different, not just between companies but very frequently within them as well. Reck identifies many companies having to operate in 'mixed mode' when managing information systems.[27] Financial systems may require an 'imperialistic' approach, in which a system is effectively imposed on all business units, whereas sales and marketing may be better advised to adopt a 'multidomestic' approach to reflect the national focus of operations. Yet, as Cooper and Browne[28] point out, global companies often need to integrate their own information systems with those of global customers, a point emphasized by Morris[29] when outlining the global strategy of Univar, the chemicals company.

Clearly information systems management represents a critical success factor for all kinds of global company, and one which is increasing in importance. There are, however, three other critical success factors which are strongly linked to the cluster classification of global logistics strategies, summarized in Figure 6.5. These are:

- Diffusion of best practice, which principally applies to cloners
- Partnershipping, particularly with logistics service providers, which is critical to the success of many outreachers
- Flexibility in switching between different global logistics systems especially those of invaders, settlers and barons (see Figure 6.6).

Diffusion of best practice is a critical success factor for cloners because logistics operations, although localized, are extensively replicated around the world. It is therefore important for any logistics breakthrough in one location to be recognized and then adopted by all the operational centres.

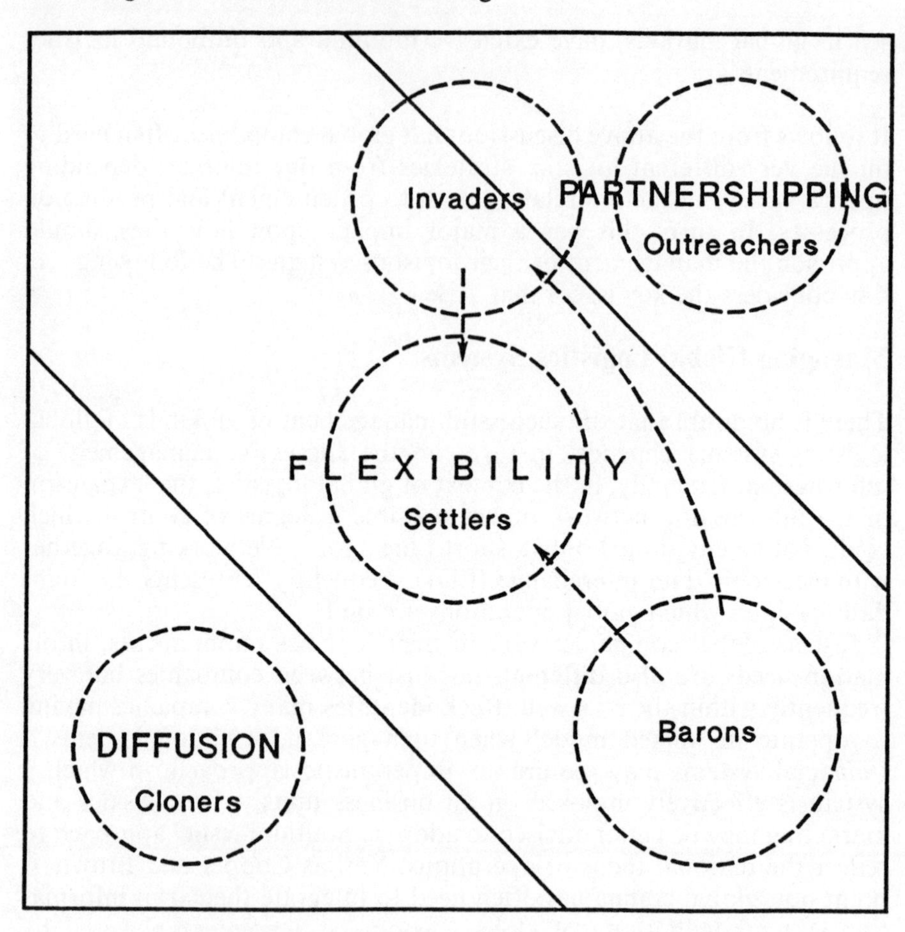

Figure 6.6 *Critical success factors in global logistics*

Generally, it will be insufficient to expect best practice in one location to be leveraged effectively and rapidly by management in other locations without some intervention by head office. In effect, there has to be a 'change management' team to act as a catalyst for spreading best practice through the organization. This process is not without its dangers, one of the greatest of which is to think in terms of 'transferring' rather than 'translating' best practice between operational centres. Transferring has connotations of taking a logistical innovation and implementing it without modification somewhere else. Costly failure can be the result, since theatres of operation may only be slightly different, but these differences may be crucial to local success. It follows that translation of ideas between different theatres should be the preferred approach, since this implies taking account of local conditions when bringing in best practice.

Outreachers, by their very nature, have a heavy reliance on both inbound and outbound logistics. Moreover, because production often relies on a highly skilled and specialized workforce, the scope for relocating manufacturing facilities may be limited. A production site will therefore be considered as having a fixed location for at least the medium term.

These factors point to relatively stable networks for inbound and outbound logistics, focused on the production centre. Yet, because of the extensive reach of the networks, it is most unlikely that outreachers will want to undertake many of the operations themselves. Invariably they find it preferable to outsource their global logistics services.

Service quality will be a crucial consideration. For example, on-time deliveries for inbound logistics will be one of the highest operational priorities, because production delays will be extremely expensive in the making of the high value products which are typical of outreachers. Every step must therefore be taken to ensure a first-class logistics service. A key consideration will often be the development of a partnership in logistics which is based upon a relationship rather than a series of single transactions between the outreacher and the provider of global logistics services.[30] A consequence of this must be for outreachers to form relationships on a more restricted basis than before. In effect, outreachers must work with fewer carriers (say) and in a more involved way.[31] Managers of outreach companies need new skills in forging such essential relationships; amongst other things they must be skilled in the art of negotiating and be capable of recognizing and developing win-win opportunities. In addition, as noted by Rinehart,[32] a high degree of commitment to the formation of relationships is a vital factor in the successful negotiation of partnerships in logistics.

Fortunately for outreachers seeking partnerships, recent years have seen the genesis of a freight mega-carriers on a global scale,[33,34] whose growth will depend both upon information systems and scale of operation acting as a barrier to entry. At the same time, it would be wrong to suggest that the future prospects for forging effective relationships between outreachers and these larger carriers is straightforward. For example, many companies (including outreachers) would like to see their logistics partners almost as extensions to their businesses. This may seem an attainable goal when few significant relationships have been developed. But as Bowersox acutely observes: 'cultural absorption admittedly gets tricky when a service provider is simultaneously engaged in multiple alliances'.[35]

Flexibility in switching between global logistics systems is arguably the most interesting of the critical success factors in global logistics. This factor applies principally to companies which fall into the classification of invaders, settlers or barons (see Figures 6.5 and 6.6). A key point about these global companies is their propensity to switch between classifications, notably from invader to settler, or baron to settler. This is an entirely different set of circumstances from either the cloners or the outreachers and demands a special critical success factor, namely the ability to switch smoothly from one global logistics classification to another – in other words, flexibility.

So far, the ultimate requirement has been for companies to join the settler classification, for reasons ranging from political pressures to high operating costs (see above). Yet the settler classification may soon require a great deal of flexibility by companies operating *within* it. Up until now, the emphasis in many manufacturing operations has been the achievement of economies of scale which has tended to emphasize the management of ever-lengthening supply lines.[36] Yet the increasing need to revamp international distribution channels may in future be driven by flexible manufacturing, rather than economies of scale.[37] To date, the quest for economies of scale has introduced an element of inflexibility into global logistics systems,[38] but the literature increasingly speaks of new technologies which can overturn these prevailing economies of production.[39,40,41] Developments such as numerically controlled (NC) manufacturing, computer-integrated manufacturing (CIM), flexible manufacturing systems (FMS) and cellular manufacturing systems promise much, once their current costs can be reduced, as seems likely. Already Nissan has been able to develop a car model which is profitable on a production run of only 20,000 units;[42] Japanese companies are well to the fore in achieving economic flexibility in manufacturing.[43] Furthermore, *The Economist* foresees the disbursement of production toward smaller manufacturing units and the diminished importance of labour costs – an important consideration when global companies want to retreat from low-wage countries.[44]

Flexible manufacturing as a reality, rather than as a prospect, will inevitably transform the logistics requirements of global companies, not least for the settlers. In particular, future settlement would mean manufacturing taking place in more, rather than fewer, locations. (An early example of this trend is in newspapers, where new technology has promoted the decentralization of printing facilities.)

The wider-development of flexible manufacturing certainly has its attractions. Shorter supply lines to market raise the possibility for more companies of making to order, rather than making to stock. Also, in many cases there would be a reduced dependence upon transport, resulting in a number of environmental and pollution benefits.

New ways of manufacturing, rather than new technologies in transport or the penetration of new markets for products, may therefore be the next big challenge in global logistics. Unquestionably, the companies that succeed best in facing this challenge will be those that have flexibility built into both their logistics systems and their management.

The Challenge of Organizational Change

The globalization of markets, together with intensifying competition, new methods of manufacturing and changing relationships with both suppliers and customers, represent a considerable challenge to logistics managers with global responsibilities. As this chapter has attempted to illustrate, global logistics management is a complex, fast-changing environment in which to work, and demands ever more sophisticated strategies. But as Bartlett and Ghoshal have accurately observed,[45] many companies are organizationally incapable of carrying out these strategies. The issue of how to reconfigure organizations to secure effective logistics management is now a growing preoccupation in many boardrooms.

At the heart of the issue is a change in what the new organizational configurations should be expected to deliver. Bartlett and Ghoshal summarize it as follows:

> The critical strategic requirement is not to devise the most ingenious and well coordinated plan but to build the most viable strategic process; the key organisational task is not to design the most elegant structure but to capture individual capabilities and motivate the entire organisation to respond cooperatively to a complicated and dynamic environment.[46]

For logistics managers, *process* is a vitally important word in the reconfiguration of organizations. All too frequently, within traditional, functionally-based organizations, responsibilities for logistics have remained fragmented. Reporting structures which are focused on major functional areas such as production and marketing create divides between each area and limit the effectiveness of overall supply chain management.

Increasingly, however, companies such as Hewlett-Packard have moved towards a process-oriented approach which helps to bridge these divides.[47] This approach puts the emphasis on processes such as financial and information control, new product development and order fulfilment (the latter essentially being a synonym for logistics, but which has the virtue of suggesting a strong customer orientation in the logistics process). Crucially, important linkages *between* processes can foster changes in organization to the benefit of logistics management. Schary and Coakley, for example, point to ways in which the development of information technology is reshaping logistics organization.[48] In a similar vein, Rockart and Short agree that information technology provides a new approach to the long-standing management problem of effectively managing interdependence – by which they mean linkages between areas of functional, product and geographical responsibility.[49]

In a growing number of companies, the need to manage interdependence is expressed in the development of networking. Central to the idea of networks is the encouragement they give managers to evaluate problems from the perspective of what is right both for the customer and the company, rather than from the often conflicting viewpoints of business functions or departments.[50] The importance of networking to logistics, where effective management greatly depends on the breakdown of sectional interests within the organization, and where customer service is paramount, is clear here.

Yet it is essential to realize that many senior managers, long used to working within highly formalized organizational structures, are likely to find themselves culturally challenged by networking and will need help, understanding and time to adapt. Also there must be a recognition that new career paths will be needed for those just entering management.

In this respect, Unilever has successfully adopted a programme of short- and long-term assignments overseas for managers, along with careful and systematic proselytization of Unilever's strategic vision and organizational values to contribute to effective networking on a global scale.[51]

Increasingly, however, the cultural challenge has become wider in scope as management paradigms which are not rooted in Western culture are seen to bring successful results. In particular, it is important to consider the extent to which the adoption of Japanese management styles (albeit in some modified form) can make a significant contribution to competitive advantage in Western-based companies. For example, Berkowitz and Mohan, in their study of the steel industry, noted the US steel companies were more highly integrated than their Japanese rivals.[52] But they also found that 'the unique nature of Japan's procurement and logistical system created significant economies of scale by virtue of industry-wide cooperation and learning, and through buyer–supplier arrangements that offered all the benefits of vertical integration without its disadvantages'.

The need for organizational change is, of course, based upon much wider considerations than logistics alone. Much of the general management literature of the late 1980s focuses on organizational change as one of the major issues facing businesses of all kinds, [53,54,55,56] and many questions still have to be resolved.

New organizational forms are by no means easy to introduce, especially when they represent a radical departure from long-established paradigms. Yet, for global businesses in particular, the need for change can no longer be denied. As companies reinvent their own forms of organization, many of them – perhaps for the first time – have the important opportunity to redefine logistics management roles. For global companies, where logistics is highly complex and where management flexibility is often a key requirement, this opportunity is not one to be missed.

Summary

- The trend towards the globalization of business increasingly necessitates both a change in management roles and in organizational structure
- Globalization has important manufacturing and marketing implications. Industries are now much more footloose
- Globalization of markets, cheaper communications and the removal of barriers to trade and foreign investment are reshaping the activities of many companies
- Managing logistics at a global level represents a challenge of considerable complexity
- There are certain key product variables which are important in determining global logistics strategy
- Certain distinct 'clusters' of logistic strategy can be identified.

References

[1] Ohmae, K., *Triad Power – the coming shape of global competition*, The Free Press, New York, 1985.
[2] Porter, M., *Competition in Global Industries*, Harvard Business School Press, Cambridge, Mass., 1986.
[3] Levitt, T., 'The Globalization of Markets', *Harvard Business Review*, May–June, 1983.
[4] Kotler, P., 'Global Standardization – Courting Danger', Panel Discussion, 23rd American Marketing Association Conference, Washington DC, 1985.
[5] Douglas, S., and Wind, Y., 'The Myth of Globalization', *Columbia Journal of World Business*, XXXI, (4), 1987.
[6] Jain, S., 'Standardisation of International Marketing Strategies: some research hypotheses', *Journal of Marketing*, 53, January, 1989.
[7] Piore, M., 'Corporate reform in American manufacturing and the challenge to economic theory', working paper, Sloan School of Management, MIT, Cambridge, Mass., 1987.
[8] Bartlett, C.A. and Ghoshal, S.J., *Managing Across Borders*, Century Business Press, London, 1989.
[9] Raffée, H. and Kreutzer, R.T., 'Organisational Dimensions of Global Marketing', *European Journal of Marketing*, 23, (5), 1989.
[10] Cooper, J., Browne, M. and Peters, M., *European Logistics: Markets Management and Strategy*, Blackwell Publishers, Oxford, 1991.
[11] Braithwaite, A. and Christopher, M., 'Managing the Global Pipeline', *International Journal of Logistics Management*, (2), 1991.
[12] Zinn, W., and Grosse, R.E., 'Barriers to Globalisation: Is Global Distribution Possible?', *International Journal of Logistics Management*, (1), 1990.
[13] Julius, D.-A., *Global Companies and Public Policy*, Royal Institute of International Affairs, London, 1990.
[14] Rosenthal, T.M., 'McDonnell Douglas in China', *Global Trade*, February, 1989.
[15] Segal-Horn, S. and Davidson, H., 'Global Markets: the Global Consumer and International Retailing', *Journal of Global Marketing*, 5 (3), 1992.
[16] Dullforce, W., 'The Final Showdown', *Financial Times*, 1 November, 1991.
[17] Dicken, P., *Global Shift: Industrial Change in a Turbulent World*, Harper and Row, London, 1986.
[18] Lee, W.J., 'Global Economies of Scale: the case for a world manufacturing strategy', *Industrial Management*, 10 (9), 1986.
[19] Cooper, Browne and Peters, op. cit.
[20] Zinn, W. and Bowersox, D.J., 'Planning Physical Distribution with the Principle of Postponement', *Journal of Business Logistics*, 9 (2), 1988.
[21] Ferguson, A., 'Britain's Best Factories', *Management Today*, November, 1989.
[22] Zinn and Bowersox, op. cit.
[23] Poynter, T.A., *International Enterprises and Government Intervention*, Croom Helm, London, 1985.
[24] Hudson, R. and Sadler, D., 'Just-in-Time Production and the European Automotive Components Industry', *International Journal of Physical Distribution and Logistics Management*, 22(2), 1992. Hudson and Sadler also point to a significant difference in logistics system development, with respect to the USA and Western Europe, in the case of component supplies to the Japanese automotive industry. A key factor was the extent of outsourcing,

which was generally greater in Western Europe (typically around 50–60 per cent) compared with Chrysler, Ford and General Motors operations in North America (averaging around 35–40 per cent). Thus, 'whereas the Japanese vehicle assemblers openly encouraged parts suppliers to follow them into production in the USA, there was from the outset greater potential opportunity and incentive for Japanese vehicle builders ... to work with the existing West European automotive components base'.

[25] Schary, P.B. and Coakley, J., 'Logistics Organization and the Information System', *International Journal of Logistics Management*, 2 (2), 1991.

[26] Runyan, L., 'Global IS Strategies', *Datamation*, December 1, 1989.

[27] Reck, R.H., 'The Shock of Going Global', *Datamation*, August 1, 1989.

[28] Cooper, J. and Browne, M., *Logistics Strategies for Global Industries: The Consequences for Transport and Information Technology*, Paper to the 6th World Conference on Transport Research, Lyon, June/July, 1992.

[29] Morris, G.D.L., 'Univar: Poised for Global Reach', *Chemical Week*, April 3, 1991.

[30] Bowersox, D., 'The Strategic Benefits of Logistics Alliances', *Harvard Business Review*, July/August, 1990.

[31] Copacino, W.C. and Britt, F.F., 'Perspectives on Global Logistics', *International Journal of Logistics Management*, 2 (1), 1991.

[32] Rinehart, L.M., 'Global Logistics Partnership Negotiation', *International Journal of Physical Distribution and Logistics Management*, 22 (1), 1992.

[33] Sparks, D. and Mathe, H., 'Survival of the Quickest: the challenge of the international express market in Europe', in *Managing Services Across Borders* (ed Hervé Mathe), Volume 8 in series 'Research in Operations and Service Management', Eurolog Press, 1991.

[34] Browne, M., 'Freight Mega-Carriers in the 1990s: the strategic importance of information technology in the race for global scale', *International Information Systems*, April, 1992.

[35] Bowersox, op. cit.

[36] Fawcett, S.E. and Birou, L.M., 'Explaining the Interface Between Global and JIT Sourcing', *International Journal of Physical Distribution and Materials Management*, 22 (1), 1992.

[37] Anderson, D.L., 'International Logistics Strategies for the 1980s' in 'Strategies for International Logistics', (ed. M. Christopher), a monograph edition of the *International Journal of Physical Distribution and Materials Management*, 15 (4), 1985.

[38] Braithwaite and Christopher, op. cit.

[39] *The Economist*, 'Beyond Robots', July 5, 1986.

[40] Fife, W.J., 'Why Flexible Manufacturing Systems are Here to Stay', *AACE Transactions*, 1991.

[41] Goldhar, J.D. and Lei, D., 'The Shape of Twenty-First Century Global Manufacturing', *The Journal of Business Strategy*, March/April, 1991.

[42] Hamel, G. and Prahalad, C.K., 'Corporate Imagination and Expeditionary Marketing', *Harvard Business Review*, July–August, 1991.

[43] De Meyer, A., Nakane, J., Miller, J.G. and Ferdows, K., 'Flexibility: The Next Competitive Battle – The Manufacturing Futures Survey', *Strategic Management Journal*, 10, 1989.

[44] *The Economist*, op. cit.

[45] Bartlett, C.A. and Ghoshal, S., 'Matrix Management: Not a structure, a frame of mind!', *Harvard Business Review*, July–August, 1990.

[46] Bartlett and Ghoshal (1990), op. cit.

[47] Marr, C.J., 'How to Achieve Global Logistics Coordination', *Competitive Global Logistics Symposium*, Cambridge, 7–10 April, 1991.
[48] Schary and Coakley, op. cit.
[49] Rockart, J.F. and Short, J.E., 'IT in the 1990s: Managing Organizational Interdependence', *Sloan Management Review*, Winter, 1989.
[50] Charan, R., 'How Organizations Reshape Organizations – for results', *Harvard Business Review*, September–October, 1991.
[51] Bartlett and Ghoshal (1989), op. cit.
[52] Berkowitz, M. and Mohan, K., 'The Role of Global Procurement in the Value Chain of Japanese Steel', *Columbia Journal of World Business*, Vol XXXI, (4), Winter, 1987.
[53] Bower, J., *When Markets Quake: The Management Challenge of Restructuring Industry*, HBS Press, Boston, 1986.
[54] Miles, R.E. and Snow, C.C., 'Organisations: A New Concept for New Forms', *Californian Management Review*, 28 (3), 1986.
[55] Drucker, P.F., 'The Coming of the New Organization', *Harvard Business Review*, 66 (1), 1988.
[56] Kanter, R.M., *When Giants Learn to Dance*, Simon and Schuster, New York, 1989.

Chapter 7

Logistics Strategies for Europe

Michael Browne
BRS Professor of Transport, University of Westminster
and Julian Allen
Research Fellow, Transport Studies Group, University of Westminster

Introduction

Two logistics strategies form the focus for the chapter that follows. The first is the trend to concentrate production and storage in fewer but larger manufacturing and stockholding sites. The second concerns logistics innovation, and specifically the increasing interest in flexible production techniques. One of the most influential and well-known techniques used in a flexible manufacturing strategy has been just-in-time (JIT) production. Concentration and JIT production are closely linked to changes in transport, since they often involve a trade-off between savings in inventory and storage costs and higher spending on transport. It is therefore essential to consider how transport and logistics services companies can respond to manufacturers' changing strategies. The chapter concludes by considering the key issues for the future.

The key role of logistics is to integrate the functions of buying, production and distribution within a company. The scope and need to develop new logistics strategies has been stimulated by the steps taken to create a Single European Market (SEM) from 1 January 1993.* The steady implementation of measures to create the SEM has encouraged many manufacturing companies to reconsider the way they produce and market their products within Europe. In addition, the development of market economies among the countries of Central and Eastern Europe has encouraged some companies to plan for an even larger European economic area. Through the latter half of the 1980s and the early 1990s there has been, for larger companies, a discernible shift away from a

* The primary objective of the Single European Act has been the attainment of a Single European Market, which came into being on 1 January 1993; this is intended to facilitate the freedom of movement for persons, goods, services and capital. The realization of this economic unit has required the removal of numerous barriers; in order to achieve this, the Commission of the European Communities has defined 282 measures, not all of which have yet been implemented. The most important of these measures involve the elimination of physical frontiers (through the proposed removal of checks on persons and goods), technical frontiers (through the creation of uniform European standards and harmonization of certain national laws) and fiscal frontiers (by means of the gradual harmonization of VAT rates and excise duties).

mainly national or multidomestic approach to a more unified, pan-European strategy.

Concentrated Production and Storage

SEM Factors Encouraging Concentration

Central to the logic of forming the SEM has been the desire to encourage the development of European companies able to compete on level terms with companies from Japan and the USA. It is often claimed that fragmented national economies within Europe have resulted in too many small companies in certain key industrial sectors.[1] This in turn, it is argued, means that European companies do not have the critical mass needed to compete in the global market-place. Dismantling barriers to trade and opening up public procurement within the EC will result in new opportunities for companies to grow and become more competitive. Inevitably this is also likely to result in the relocation of certain economic activities as some companies become larger and others fail.

To create the SEM, certain specific barriers to trade have had to be removed:

- Physical barriers (such as border crossing controls)
- Technical barriers (such as different product standards in different member states)
- Fiscal barriers (such as different taxation regimes).

Despite working to a common deadline set out in the Single European Act of 1986, progress on dismantling the barriers and implementing the necessary national legislation has not been uniform across the EC and some countries are ahead of others. However, in broad terms the removal of the barriers will:

- Increase intra-EC trade flows (ie trade flows between member states of the EC)
- Reduce the need for product differentiation
- Expand the opportunities for European branding and marketing
- Reduce research and development costs
- Reduce unit costs of production
- Increase the scope for economies of scale.

Companies will increasingly regard the whole of the Community as their home market, rather than having their trading horizons restricted to a single country. This in turn has important implications for logistics services. For example, increased trade between member states will create new demands for logistics services such as transport and warehousing.

European Scale Production from Single Sites

Increasing market integration enables companies to pursue a number of strategies designed to take advantage of their size. The scope to concentrate production at a small number of carefully selected locations is one that has a special importance within Europe. Until recently, the strategy followed by many companies has been based on production for separate national markets. The requirement to produce product variants for different markets, the complexity of border-crossing formalities and the added costs of international trade transactions has led, typically, to a rather fragmented approach to production. Although for many companies the changes in strategy have been part of a broader response to growing global opportunities and increased international competition, the creation of the SEM has undoubtedly encouraged plant and warehouse rationalization.[2]

Two factors which strongly influence the concentration of production and storage are the value per tonne of a product and the frequency of delivery (Figure 7.1). The closer a product is to the top left-hand corner, the greater will be the propensity for concentration. Economies of scale in production will, however, tend to favour concentration, even where the product value density is rather low.

The manufacturing approach of Colgate-Palmolive provides a good example of the move to fewer production sites. In 1990 Colgate-Pal-

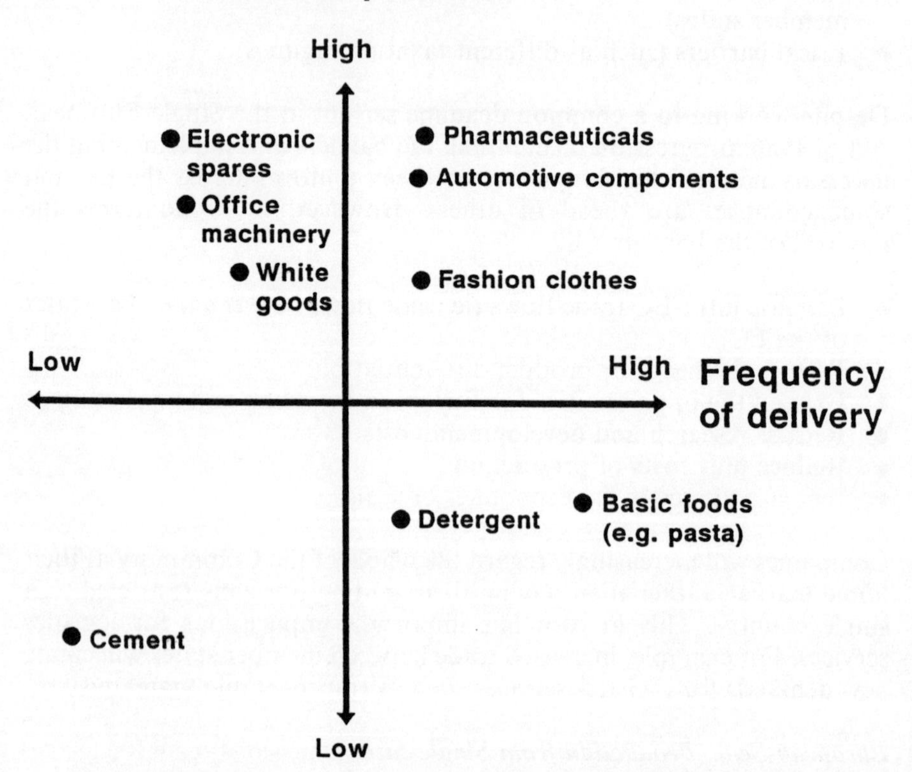

Figure 7.1 *Factors encouraging centralization*

molive operated 15 manufacturing plants across Europe and each plant had local national warehouses which fed products into the national distribution system.[3] Cross-border shipments were limited. By 1992, only ten plants were being used and the mix of products sourced from each plant had been reduced. Technologies had become focused and 'Europlants' established (eg in the 1980s eight plants had produced soap, whereas by 1992 only two were being used). This change in production strategy was accompanied by a change in marketing, with the development, where possible, of 'Europroducts', which in turn had an impact on logistics arrangements. One result has been that although total European demand for a product may have remained the same, there has been much more trade between markets. Now approximately one-third of Colgate-Palmolive's products are made in one European country and sold in another.

Concentrating production at fewer sites will, generally, increase transport costs because products need to be carried further to markets. But it will be worthwhile financially if there are sufficient economies of scale in production, as well as in related areas such as R&D. Many areas of manufacturing exhibit economies of scale. In the food sector, for example, it has been estimated that a modern plant producing chocolate bars needs a minimum capacity of 200 tonnes a day to reach optimal scale[4].

However, not all products readily lend themselves to these pan-European logistics strategies, and many activities will need to remain more localized. The following factors will favour some degree of localization in logistics:

- Products with relatively low value densities
- Limited economies of scale in production
- Need to produce in local markets as a result of political considerations
- Uneven development of markets, with some regions taking much more of a product than others.

Pan-European Inventory Holding

One of the classic relationships in logistics is the trade-off between warehousing and transport: as the number of warehouses is reduced, the total cost of operating them decreases but transport costs rise, for a constant throughput of goods through the system.[5] This choice is usually presented in the form of a diagram to illustrate the implications for combined warehouse and transport operating costs and the choice of the optimum number of warehouses in a distribution system (see Figure 7.2). Concentrating inventory holding into a smaller number of warehouses may enable a firm to reduce the amount of inventory that is actually held, since separate safety stocks are no longer required.*

* There is a large literature on the benefits that can be derived from the concentration of stockholding.[6,7,8,9]

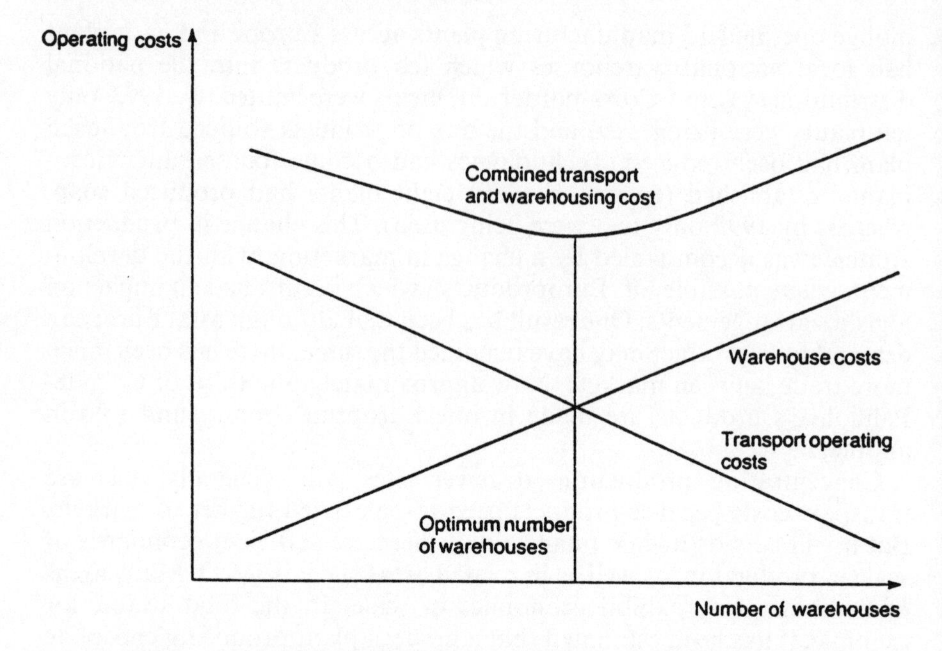

Figure 7.2 *Trade-off in transport and warehouse operating costs*

Source: Ballou, R.H., *Basic Business Logistics*, Prentice-Hall, Englewood Cliffs, NJ, 1987

At present many manufacturing companies find themselves holding too much stock in too many warehouses. The reasons for this are a complicated mix of factors, including historical ownership patterns, the importance of nationalistic public procurement policies, and over-complex transport and product regulations. This pattern has been changing and some national distribution centres have been replaced by international ones serving a much wider market. The SEM means that firms can increasingly hold stock irrespective of national borders, as simplified customs procedures should make it possible to guarantee delivery times which previously could be achieved only by maintaining national warehouses.

The extent to which a company will find it desirable to move towards a centralized warehousing system is very much influenced by the products concerned and the rate of product flow through the supply chain. A single warehouse serving a large part of Europe may be appropriate for spare parts (especially slow-moving items); Rank Xerox has already focused its spares storage for Europe in a single central warehouse at Venray in the Netherlands. However, the same will not be true for certain consumer goods and many food products, which move in large volumes. Here the speed of stock-turn, combined with the high volumes, mean the best European solution will certainly involve a number of warehouses in an appropriate hierarchy. For example, some warehouses may serve international needs, while others will be dedicated to national or regional requirements.

Although it is true that many stockholding points also act as break-bulk points, there may well be an argument for supplementing centralized stockholding warehouses with local break-bulk facilities. Companies have attempted to limit total transport costs by maximizing the trunk-haul component (where the goods are usually moved in bulk loads) and minimizing the local delivery distance where the goods are usually moved in smaller consignments (leading to a higher cost per tonne-kilometre). Minimizing total freight transport costs:

> is achieved by breaking bulk as close as possible to the customer and hence maximising the number of break-bulk points. The minimisation of stockholding costs requires the concentration of stock into as few locations as possible. The locational pressures of the two main depot functions of stockholding and the breaking of bulk are, therefore, in conflict.[10]

In order, at least in part, to overcome this conflict, the functions of stockholding and breaking bulk can be spatially separated. Stock may be held in a small number of warehouses from which goods are despatched in appropriate unit loads to a much larger number of stockless transit points, where the break-bulk operation takes place.

Flexible Production

In recent years the concept of 'flexible production' (also referred to as 'lean production and post-Fordism') has received considerable attention. Gertler has argued that firms have increasingly adopted practices which are founded on the concept of flexibility.[11] He suggests that such practices include:

- A more flexible use of workers and machines
- More flexible inter-firm relations (vertical disintegration, subcontracting, alliances etc)
- More flexible relations with the market – driven by competition and a consequent shortening of product life cycles (resulting in greater product diversity and reduced lead times for new products)
- A reduction in unrealized capital tied up in inventory
- Changes to social institutions to foster more flexible employment relations
- The breaking down of barriers to the mobility of capital between sectors and between places through the deregulation and restructuring of many product, service and capital markets.

The best known and most widely documented flexible production method is that of just-in-time (JIT) production. JIT eliminates processes which do not add value and will involve reducing machine set-up times, improving the flow of materials, reducing lead times, and improving customer service and product quality. JIT involves a trade-off between inventory and transport costs; as inventory levels are reduced, the supply chain is likely to become increasingly transport intensive.

Implicit in much of the literature on JIT and flexible production is the assumption that flexibility and mass production are alternatives. However, as Hirst and Zeitlin have recognized, 'flexible specialization as a general theoretical approach is compatible with a broad spectrum of possible forms of productive organization – including the predominance of mass production.'[12] There is no reason why large firms operating from sites producing for a pan-European market cannot take advantage of flexible production methods. A strategy of concentrated production can also incorporate flexible production methods. Such an approach enables the firm to enjoy the benefits of each strategy in unison.

European references to JIT tend to emphasize rapid transport and control of suppliers. While the latter is also true of Japanese JIT, the transport requirements are usually simplified in Japan by the proximity of supplier and producer. In a European context, JIT has the following implications:

- A closer relationship between supplier and manufacturer
- A closer relationship between manufacturer and transport company (reduced or zero inventory means there is no margin for late or erratic delivery of raw materials or components)
- More frequent delivery, but of smaller amounts
- Intensive flows of information between supplier, manufacturer and transport operator.

Organization structure may have to be changed in order for companies to accommodate the new relationships listed above. For instance, to achieve a closer relationship between manufacturer and transport operator it may be necessary to reduce the number of contractors used and to coordinate transport purchasing in a more systematic way.

The implications of JIT delivery for transport are indeed dramatic. Instead of a large vehicle delivering, say, weekly, the requirement may be for much smaller vehicles to deliver daily or, in some cases, several times a day. For many large Japanese manufacturers, this has not caused a problem, since component suppliers are often located near the factory gate. However, in Europe, planning controls and the complexity of the existing pattern of industrial linkages mean that when JIT production techniques are implemented they can lead to a more extensive use of the public road network.

Implementing JIT practices is not evenly spread across industry sectors and countries. Even within a single industry there appear to be considerable national variation, according to a survey by PRS Consulting International Limited. Their survey of the EC auto-component industry found that in France, over 60 per cent of the companies polled claimed to be supplying on a JIT basis, while in the UK the figure was just over 50 per cent and in Italy 25 per cent.[13]

The logistics innovations and strategies described above tend to involve an increase in the consumption of transport services within the supply chain. This can occur as a result of either increasing trip length (as is the case with the concentration of production and storage locations) or greater frequency of deliveries (as occurs in a JIT system). It would appear that transport is regarded by companies as a relatively cheap input, in comparison with other logistics costs. Therefore companies are willing to spend more on transport in the knowledge that this additional expenditure will be easily recouped in savings in other areas such as inventory costs. It is also evident that the logistics services demanded by manufacturers have been changing – both concentration of stock and JIT production put more emphasis on reliability in the supply chain. In view of these developments, it is essential to consider the way in which logistics service providers should respond to these new challenges.

Implications for the Suppliers of Logistics Services

European deregulation, the abolition of internal frontiers and harmonization of fiscal and technical standards will all help to boost trade among the member states of the EC, and make it simpler for all carriers to participate in that trade. We can expect to see not only increased cross-border traffic but also the growing internationalization of carriers' activities, with companies providing full national distribution services in more than one country. Companies with a customer base that includes multinationals manufacturing in several European countries need to decide their best strategy.

In deciding how to take advantage of the new European opportunities, logistics service providers need to be clear about which of the following strategies they wish to adopt. Do they want to be:

- **Pan-Europeans** providing a Europe-wide service offering distribution both within and between a number of European countries
- **Multidomestics** providing national services which are in several European countries
- **Eurolinkers** providing a network of mainly international services between major European markets?

The network implications of each strategy are illustrated in Figure 7.3.

Clearly the most ambitious strategy is the first – to provide a truly pan-European service. A few integrated express companies have achieved this level of service provision (eg TNT and UPS), but if we consider a wider portfolio of logistics services it is apparent that even the prospective mega-carriers such as Nedlloyd and Danzas cannot be said to provide a wide range of both national and international services on a European basis.

The multidomestic approach would seem to have been the one adopted by NFC, Britain's largest logistics and transport company. About one-third of their operating profits now come from outside the

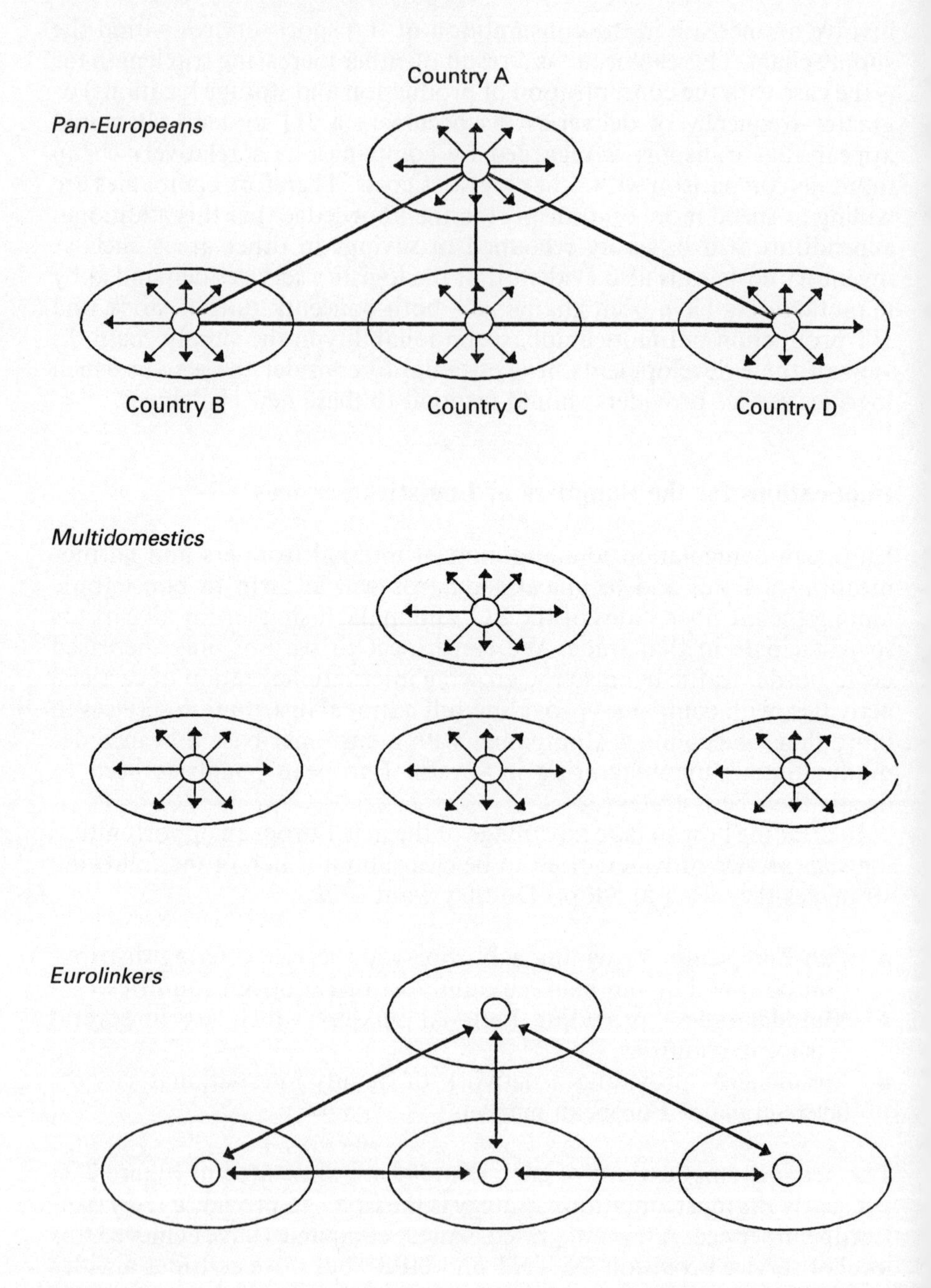

Figure 7.3 *Strategy options for providers of logistics services*

UK, and as their 1992 Annual Review makes clear, the NFC strategy has been to 'make the company a fully international organisation by using its skills and expertise to extend into new geographical areas'. The Annual Review goes on to state: 'Increasingly, our major clients are companies which operate on an international scale and use NFC services in several markets.'[14]

The foundations for the strategy appear to lie in the successful duplication of domestic services in other countries. The original services are, of course, adapted as required.

Among the companies which appear to be following the Eurolinking strategy are P&O and Ducros. The strategy pursued by the latter is especially interesting. Ducros (France), Tuffnells (UK), Transerra (Spain) and Mazzoni (Italy) have formed a European Economic Interest Group called 'Eurotraf', to transform these mainly national companies into a more truly European network.[15]

The choice of strategy for any one company providing logistics services will be influenced by:

- Company culture and background (for example, the size of the company and their ability to absorb the financial and management consequences of rapid change)
- customer profile (such as industry, speed of reaction to European opportunities)
- customer culture (are the logistics services customers European in their business-to-business purchasing, or largely national?).

There are parallels between the options for logistics service providers and those available to manufacturing companies responding to their own customers' changing requirements. In an integrated European market, there was an expectation that industrial buyers who previously had dealt at a national level would change their tactics and centralize their purchasing. In anticipation of this, some multinationals created a European HQ specifically to deal with their pan-European customers. However, it has been suggested that this 'supermarket' theory of business-to-business purchasing has been largely discredited and that most companies still buy products at a national level, even if they are operating in several European countries. If this is true then there are important implications for logistics service providers market strategies.[16]

It is essential that a logistics service provider matches the needs of the customer – it is little use providing an excellent service that no one wants or knows how to use. One problem for companies that aimed at mega-carrier status in the late 1980s appears to have been that they were ahead of their time.[17]

Whichever strategy, or strategic variation, is chosen by major suppliers of logistics services they, and their customers, need to bear in mind external developments such as government policy towards transport, and growing concern about the environment.

Issues for the Future

Forecasts suggest that demand for transport will continue to outstrip the ability of governments to supply sufficient infrastructure capacity.[18] The effects of this mismatch between demand and supply could influence the logistics strategies outlined in this chapter. If congestion increases, then road freight transport will become less reliable, less productive and more expensive. There is increasing pressure on road transport users to cover the external costs they generate, and the imposition of a carbon tax is one option being considered by policy makers. Road haulage prices would rise if fuel taxes were sharply increased, since fuel, typically, accounts for between 20 and 30 per cent of total lorry operating costs. In turn, this would alter the ratio between stock and warehouse costs on the one hand, and transport costs on the other. It might also encourage the use of combined transport for some longer distance transport movements. But would increased transport costs and growing congestion fundamentally alter the rationale for the logistics developments discussed in this chapter? There appear to be several conflicting possibilities.

Increased congestion may mean that companies supplying over a long-distance network will be unable to achieve the necessary reliability with low stock levels. This delivery disruption could force managers to review their logistics systems; it may mean switching to a more localized system of stockholding and a changing emphasis on transport. For example, key component suppliers may decide to relocate in order to be nearer their customers. Certain firms are already beginning to reconsider their centralization policies and are opting instead for a more local approach; for example, Honeywell have abandoned the idea of a single European site.[19]

Increasing the cost of transport in a more systematic way (eg by increasing fuel tax) could also have an impact on logistics strategy. Weigel has suggested that when modelling a given distribution system, which served a large part of the EC, a logistics cost minimum was reached with only three warehouses.[20] When the model was developed to include a specific allowance for external costs (ie the model incorporated higher transport costs), the trend to centralization became economically less favourable and the cost minimum was reached with five warehouses. It would appear then that in certain circumstances, logistics strategies could be fairly sensitive to changes in transport costs.

In view of the evident uncertainty that exists about forthcoming changes in transport costs, manufacturing companies need to avoid planning and implementing an inflexible logistics system that is dependent upon relatively high levels of transport consumption. For example, the best strategy at present may be to postpone investment in a centralized warehouse with high levels of automation, correspondingly high capital costs and a lengthy pay-back period, when it may become necessary to reconfigure the system in the near future. There may be opportunities to use information technology in order to gain the benefits of centralized control of inventory, even though the physical stock-holding is dispersed.

Summary

- Moves to concentrate production and stock-holding have been encouraged by the creation of the SEM
- There has been a trend to reduce stock levels by more careful management of production and implementation of JIT techniques
- Increasingly, suppliers of logistics services must develop pan-European strategies
- Hitherto, producers have treated transport as a relatively cheap resource. Liberalizing freight transport within the EC may strengthen this tendency, increasing the consumption of transport as a means to achieve savings in inventory and production
- In the longer term, it is possible that transport costs may rise in real terms and companies will then have to develop different logistics strategies.
- Companies planning their logistics strategies for the late 1990s and beyond need to be wary of adopting inflexible methods, rooted in past relationships, between the cost of transport and economies of scale in production and storage.

References

[1] Cecchini, P., *The European Challenge: 1992*, Wildwood House, Aldershot, 1988.

[2] Braithwaite, A., 'Managing European Logistics Assets (Part I and Part II)', *Logistics Today*, 9 (4), 1990, pp. 17–19; 9 (5), pp. 22–3.

[3] Machell, P., 'Supply chain strategy in a multi-national environment'. Institute of Grocery Distribution Conference on *Improving Supply Chain Effectiveness in the Grocery Trade*, 1993.

[4] Watts, H.D., 'Manufacturing trends, corporate restructuring and spatial change' in Pinder, D. (ed)., *Western Europe – Challenge and Change*, Belhaven, London, 1990.

[5] Ballou, R.H., *Basic Business Logistics*, Prentice-Hall, Englewood Cliffs, NJ, 1987.

[6] Star, M.K. and Miller, D.W., *Inventory Control: Theory and Practice*, Prentice-Hall, Englewood Cliffs, NJ, 1962.

[7] Williams, J., *Food distribution costs: Results of an inter-firm study of wholesale, transportation and warehousing costs*, National Materials Handling Centre, Cranfield, 1975.

[8] Das, C., 'A Re-appraisal of the Square Root Law', *International Journal of Physical Distribution*, 8 (6), 1978, pp. 331–6.

[9] Sussams, J.E., 'Buffer stocks and the square root law', *Focus on Physical Distribution and Logistics Management*, 5 (5), 1986, pp. 8– 10.

[10] McKinnon, A., *Physical Distribution Systems*, Routledge, London, 1989, p. 108.

[11] Gertler, M., 'The limits to flexibility: comments on the post-Fordist vision of

production and its geography', *Transactions of the Institute of British Geographers*, 13 (4), 1992, pp. 419– 32.

[12] Hirst, P. and Zeitlin, J., 'Flexible specialisation versus post-Fordism: theory, evidence and policy implications', *Economy and Society*, 20 (1), 1991, pp. 1– 56.

[13] Hambros Bank Ltd, *Transport in Europe in the 1990s*, 1991.
NFC Annual Review and Summary Financial Statement, 1992, p. 9

[14] NFC, op. cit., p. 11

[15] *Transport Magazine*, 'Ducros renforce son réseau européen' July/August, 1992, p. 17.

[16] Lorenz, C., 'Second thoughts about moving in', *Financial Times*, Monday, February 1, 1993.

[17] Cooper, J., Browne, M. and Peters, M., *European Logistics: Markets, Management and Strategy*, Blackwell, Oxford, 1991.

[18] Group Transport 2000 Plus, *Transport in a fast changing Europe*, 1990.

[19] Colin, J., 'Strategies de réstructuration des firmes et polarisation de leurs éspaces logistiques, un défi pour les réseaux Européens de transport?', Paper presented at the *Sixth World Conference on Transport Research*, Lyon, France, June 1992.

[20] Weigel, B., 'Integrating ecological aspects into the simulation and planning of warehouse locations', Paper presented at the Sixth World Conference on Transport Research, Lyon, France, June, 1992.

Chapter 8

Logistics Strategies for the USA

Bernard J La Londe and James M Masters
The Max M Fisher College of Business
The Ohio State University

> 'All men can see these tactics whereby I conquer, but what none can see is the strategy out of which victory is evolved.'
> Sun Tzu, The Art of War, 500 B.C.

Identifying Key Logistics Strategies

The Nature of a Corporate Logistics Strategy

Our purpose in this chapter is to identify and describe what we believe to be the two most important business logistics strategies which have emerged in the American marketplace over the last decade and which will remain the two dominant logistics strategies well into the twenty-first century. Our analysis will argue that these two strategic concepts, namely, 'supply chain management' and 'cycle time compression', represent distinctly different yet complementary approaches to corporate logistics that form the frameworks around which hundreds of American firms are building successful logistics systems.

'Strategy' is a term which is often used very broadly in the business setting. For example, we might speak of a strategy for coping with an impatient customer or a strategy for unloading a truck. Our use of the term strategy here will be more formal and traditional. By the term strategy we refer to a general concept of operations which guides all of our activities towards an ultimate goal. Many writers have defined the term in many different ways, but some general characteristics of a strategy are widely accepted. A strategy is global in scope rather than local. A strategy is long-term in perspective rather than short-term. A logistics strategy, for example, might take several years to fully implement and might guide the operation of the entire firm for a decade or more. A strategy is general rather than specific, and a successful logistics strategy will provide a general unifying coherence to what might otherwise have become a set of conflicting activities, functions, and goals within the firm.

A business strategy exists for a purpose, and that purpose is quite simple. The strategy is the tool chosen to accomplish the fundamental objectives of the firm. In this sense, the firm's strategy is secondary and is very much a means to an end. Just as the firm chooses an appropriate strategy to accomplish its objectives, the choice of a strategy leads to decisions of a more tactical or operational nature which will guide the activity of the firm on a month to month and day to day basis.

The choice of an appropriate and effective logistics strategy must be guided by the objectives of the firm as well as by its capabilities and resources. In addition, the development of a successful logistics strategy must recognize and deal with important factors and conditions in the firm's external business environment. For that reason a brief overview of what are perhaps the most significant of these factors in the American business environment is appropriate.

The US Business Environment

A number of general forces have affected most firms in the American marketplace, and these forces will continue to drive logistics decision making in the years to come.

- **Increasing globalization** American firms are becoming increasingly involved in global enterprise for a number of reasons. Rising standards of living in the developing economies and the elimination of barriers to commerce related to the dissolution of the command economies of the Eastern Bloc have worked to increase world trade. For American firms, this has meant opportunities for new markets overseas, new sources of raw materials and components, as well as new manufacturing sites. In most cases these options have led to more complicated logistics systems. While increased globalization of business has led to new opportunities, it has also resulted in new levels of competition for many firms which have often added to the pressure on the logistics system of the firm.
- **Mergers and acquisitions** Throughout the 1980s many American firms went through a series of buy-outs and mergers. In some cases individual firms went through as many as five reorganizations in ten years. In many cases these reorganizations created powerful new firms, but these mergers were often disruptive to logistics operations and frequently created excess and redundant logistics capacity in the newly formed enterprise. The wave of mergers has now ended, but not all of the new combinations have proven to be successful, and many firms are continuing to struggle with the rationalization of the logistics structures of the combined firms.
- **Downsizing** Throughout the last ten years scores of major American firms have announced and executed plans to 'downsize' their operations. In some cases this involves reducing the number of plants and facilities and eliminating excess production capacity, but in many other instances the basic idea is to simply reduce the cost of a given level of operation by eliminating personnel. These firms are looking for ways to permanently reduce the number of employees, both workers and managers, by eliminating unnecessary functions

and increasing the productivity of the remaining workforce. Some companies have been forced into these actions by the urgent need to survive, while other firms have taken a more deliberate, long-range view and have made their downsizing decisions as part of long-term plans to improve their competitive position. In any case, and regardless of the motivation, logistics functions have frequently been involved in downsizing plans, since logistics is a traditionally labour-intensive function, and since the costs and benefits of a specific logistics function are often difficult to quantify. Pressures to down-size the logistics workforce have often affected the selection of an appropriate logistics strategy.

- **Increased competition, complexity and uncertainty.** In addition to the forces of globalization, merger/acquisition, and downsizing which have affected the American firm, many other factors in the business environment have generally acted to increase both the level of competition and the level of uncertainty facing the firm, and hence the complexity of business decisions. The economic deregulation of the domestic transportation industry has resulted in new opportunities for creative shipper/carrier relationships and has produced lower freight bills. Deregulation has also resulted in a shrinking of the carrier base and a great deal of turbulence in the industry. Environmental awareness, recycling and energy conservation have created challenges for logistics operations in many industries. Hazardous material regulation, product recall requirements and product liability issues have increased the cost and complexity of logistics operations throughout the economy. All of these issues, among others, affect the choice of the appropriate logistics strategy.
- **New Information Technology** While many factors have increased the burden on the logistics system over the last decade, we can also identify the environmental factor which has had the greatest positive influence on the operation of the logistics system, and that factor is surely the development and implementation of powerful and inexpensive information technology to operate and control the logistics system. Dramatic progress has been made in increasing the power and reducing the cost of computer hardware, particularly in the area of desktop or personal computers. These machines have become the platforms on which powerful new software packages can reside. In addition to the ubiquitous spreadsheet and database software packages, which have proved to be extremely useful to logistic operations and management, a new generation of special purpose, user-friendly software applications has emerged to handle MRP, DRP, demand forecasting, facility location, vehicle routing, shipment rating, and many other problems and tasks. Finally, effective telecommunications linkages have been developed to enter large amounts of data into these computers and to move data between them. Optical bar code scanners and other automatic identification technologies are widely available to eliminate the need to enter data manually. Electronic Data Interchange allows the direct, machine to

machine transfer of data in standardized format so that firms can automatically process transactions. These capabilities give the firm the ability to design truly automated logistics information and control systems to deal with the increasing complexity of the business world, and these capabilities help to determine the choice of an appropriate logistics strategy.

Contemporary Logistics Strategies

Many American firms began to employ the logistics concept during the 1970s; that is, at that time many firms began to integrate the traditional business functions of traffic management, warehousing, inventory control, and in some cases purchasing, into a single organizational entity in order to make appropriate trade-offs between the costs and benefits associated with the flow of material throughout the firm. The decision to embrace the logistics concept was often considered to be a strategic decision in itself because the integrated logistics approach was new and unusual and was seen as a way to differentiate the firm from its competition by providing equal or better customer service at a lower total logistics cost.

As the logistics concept became more commonly adopted during the late 1970s and early 1980s, the prevailing view of logistics strategy began to resemble a traditional market segmentation approach. The management of a firm would recognize that logistics system performance, measured along such dimensions as product availability, speed of delivery, consistency of delivery times, loss and damage rates, flexibility to special requirements etc, was an essential element of the marketing mix or product offering. The logistics system could always develop a higher level of customer service performance at some increment of total logistics costs. The strategic decision consisted of determining where the firm should be operating on this cost/service trade-off curve. One firm might decide to be the high service/high cost provider in the marketplace, while another firm, with an otherwise directly comparable product, might choose to be the low service/low cost provider who would target a different segment of the market with a package of tailored logistics services. In this traditional framework, choosing a logistics strategy was a matter of discovering what specific levels of logistics performance the firm's customers wanted and were willing to pay for, and then developing a logistics system which could deliver that package of services at a competitive cost. To a very large extent, this rather basic view of logistics strategy remains relevant today. However, many American firms have moved beyond these basic concepts to an expanded view of logistics strategy.

Some American firms may seem to be applying what might be called an 'Inventory Reduction Strategy' to their logistics operations. Many firms have reported on their use of MRP and DRP, as well as other similar techniques such as Just-In-Time, Quick Response, Efficient Consumer Response, Continuous Replenishment, and a host of other approaches, to manage their material flow and reduce their aggregate inventory levels. Many firms have used these approaches and have improved their operations as a result, but in our view it would be a mistake to view these initiatives as inventory reduction strategies. Inventory is a powerful logistics tool, but it is not without cost. As new management techniques become available, it becomes possible to alter the mix of inventory, transportation, information, and other logistics assets employed in the logistics system so as to improve the total system performance. In this sense, inventory reduction is not the major focus of a successful logistics strategy. If it were possible to improve total logistics performance by increasing some inventory levels, as is frequently the case, then such an increase would undoubtedly be appropriate. It is certainly true that over the last ten years many American firms have reduced their inventory levels and improved their total performance. What this demonstrates is that many firms had unnecessarily high levels of inventory, and that new inventory control procedures were able to extract higher levels of service out of smaller amounts of inventory. In this respect, then, inventory management is an important issue, but it is primarily tactical in nature.

However, our analysis of contemporary logistics practice does indicate that two fundamental logistics strategies are emerging. American firms are using these strategies to deal with the challenges in the logistics environment and achieve their long-term objectives of market share and profitability. The first such strategy is Supply Chain Management. This strategy involves expanding the integrated logistics concept beyond the corporate borders of the firm to include the logistics operations of vendors and customers. The second strategy is Cycle Time Compression. This strategy involves managing the flow of material so as to minimize the time needed to respond to customer demands. These two basic strategies are being successfully applied in many American firms in a number of different ways, and they are changing the nature of competition in the American marketplace. The remainder of this chapter will offer definitions of these two strategies and examples of how they are being employed in American firms, and the chapter will close with a discussion of implementation issues.

Supply Chain Management

The Supply Chain Concept

Throughout the 1970s and early 1980s, many American firms were working very diligently to implement integrated logistics management. The idea here was that the movement of material throughout the firm could be managed in an organic and systemic way, and that by doing so, both the effectiveness and the efficiency of the operation could be dramatically improved. Implementing this concept has proved to be a difficult and time consuming task for many firms, and in fact, many American firms are still working towards this goal. But major progress has been made, and most firms have benefited from the effort. Taking the system-wide perspective allows the firm to make appropriate trade-offs between purchasing costs, transportation costs, and inventory and warehousing costs. Close coordination between these operations can produce high levels of service and performance while reducing the total costs incurred.

While integration of the logistics process within the firm has produced dramatic improvements, most consumer and industrial products are not totally created by a single firm. Normally, several independent firms are involved in manufacturing a product and placing it in the hands of the end user. One firm might produce a raw material and sell it to a second firm which uses the material to produce a component. A third firm buys the component and assembles it into a product which is sold to a fourth firm such as a wholesale distributor. The wholesaler in turn sells the product to a fifth firm, such as a retail merchant, and the fifth firm sells the product to a consumer. The set of firms which pass these materials forward can be referred to as a supply chain. The example described here is a fairly simple supply chain; in actual practice, supply chains for technologically complex products may involve scores or hundreds of firms. Even if each individual firm in such a chain is performing integrated logistics management of its own internal operations, there still exists a great potential to increase the overall efficiency and effectiveness of the supply chain as a whole by practising integrated logistics management on the total flow of material throughout the entire supply chain. We will refer to the strategy of applying integrated logistics management to all the elements of a supply chain as 'supply chain management'.

The strategic concept of supply chain management has been employed in many different variations and under several different names in American firms over the last ten years. Some firms refer to the practice as developing 'strategic alliances'; other firms describe the activity as 'partnering'; while some firms feel that they are establishing special logistics relationships with 'key vendors' or 'key customers'. Whatever the process is called, the strategy generally involves the following elements:

- Two or more firms in a supply chain enter into a long-term understanding – although typically not a legally binding contract – to do business with one another on mutually favourable terms with closely integrated and synchronized logistics processes. The firms can include buyers and sellers, as well as carriers, warehousers and other third parties.
- The firms work hard to develop high levels of trust and commitment to the relationship. The goal is to change the buying–selling relationship from an adversarial, winner–loser, bargaining–haggling, arms-length exchange into a cooperative, team-oriented enterprise where each party is looking out for the interests of the other party as well as their own concerns.
- The logistics integration activity typically involves the sharing of very

timely and very sensitive demand and sales data, inventory data, and shipment status data. Data sharing often involves a firm giving direct access to its computerized databases to its supply chain partners.

- The visibility and flexibility provided by the supply chain approach will often lead to changes in the locus of control of the traditional logistics processes. For example, a retailer might allow a manufacturer to 'read' its demand and inventory data and launch replenishment orders automatically, merely notifying the retailer's purchasing function after the fact. With mutually satisfactory quality assurance procedures established in a vendor's manufacturing facility, a buying firm may dispense with the inspection of goods received from the vendor.
- Application of the supply chain approach leads to service improvements and cost reductions to member firms at all levels in the chain, with members in the chain negotiating how the benefits will be shared. The chain as a whole becomes more competitive compared to other firms in the industry which are not members of such a chain.

In developing a supply chain strategy, most firms attempt to reduce the number of vendors and carriers, and in some cases the number of customers, with which they do business. Many firms have established deliberate plans, for example to reduce their vendor base by up to 90 per cent over a period of a few years. This represents a fundamental shift from the traditional purchasing philosophy which held that buying from many sources created competition and insured low prices and high service. Under the supply chain approach, the firm very carefully reviews a set of potential sources according to a set of strict criteria including, for example, quality assurance programs, financial stability, environmental standards, and so forth. The firm then selects one or a small number of vendors and works to build a long-term relationship with each, based on the promise of close working relationships and nearly guaranteed order streams. As a result, the buying firm becomes a larger and more important and profitable customer to the vendor, and the vendor becomes a larger and more important source for the buyer. These changes tend to reinforce the relationship and provide incentives to strength the supply chain further.

In the earliest versions of the supply chain concept, firms sought to achieve vertical integration. That is, a firm would establish control over the chain and obtain the desired efficiency and responsiveness by owning each element of the chain. The supply chain management strategy represents the recognition that most of the benefits of vertical integration can be obtained simply by coordinating the logistics operations of independent firms in the chain. This intense level of cooperation and coordination has been described by Janice Hammond of Harvard as the 'virtual' integration of the channel.

While a successful supply chain management strategy involves the cooperation of several firms, generally one firm takes the lead in establishing and directing the supply chain activity. In many cases the retailing firm is the chain leader, for example in the case of Walmart. In other situations, the supply chain approach is initiated further back in the supply chain. In any case, there is often an issue of channel power involved in the supply chain approach, since the stronger members of the chain have the ability to dictate terms and conditions to the less powerful chain members. In the most successful applications of the concept, the emphasis has been on developing a chain strategy which is seen as mutually beneficial to all of the participants, rather than on using coercive power to extract concessions from weaker chain members.

An Implementation Tactic: Quick Response

Many American firms have developed and implemented what they describe as 'quick response' systems to handle the physical distribution of finished goods. These systems are often thought of as inventory control procedures and are often compared to the Just-In-Time procedures widely used in material management systems for production facilities. In most cases, however, these systems can be readily seen as examples of the supply chain strategy. In a typical quick response implementation, a retailer and a manufacturer agree to closely coordinate the deployment and control of retail inventories. Key components of such systems usually include:

- The retailer captures accurate and timely sales data, typically via POS scanning of bar-coded merchandise.
- SKU level sales and inventory data are shared with the manufacturer on a weekly or daily basis via EDI transmission.
- The manufacturer is authorized to initiate automatic or nearly automatic stock replenishment action against pre-established target inventory levels.

The term 'quick response' originated in the textile industry, and Milliken Industries, a major manufacturer of fabrics as well as finished textile goods, played a key role in promoting and developing the concept, as well as in developing the data processing and telecommunications standards which are necessary to use the concept on an industry-wide basis. The technique has now spread beyond the clothing and apparel industry and is being applied in many consumer goods settings. The Automatic Identification Manufacturers (AIM), a trade organization of manufacturers of bar-coding equipment and software and other forms of automatic identification technology, sponsors an annual meeting of executives who are working on the quick response approach in their firms. At Quick Response 93, held in Atlanta in June 1993, over 2,000 executives gathered to describe their programmes and to discuss the problems and potential of quick response in many different product settings.

Target Stores has enthusiastically implemented quick response in a general retail environment. Target operates over 500 large stores in the

USA and is growing at a rate of approximately 15 per cent per year. Target stores carry clothing, household goods and appliances, health and beauty aids, and a wide variety of general consumer goods. Target is a discounter, and generally competes with stores such as KMart, Walmart and Sears.

Target bar codes all items, and point of sale data on all transactions are captured. Daily data are relayed to corporate headquarters each evening via satellite transmission. Daily sales and inventory data on specific items are shared with key vendors who participate in the quick response programme. Target does not permit truly automatic replenishment, but they do guarantee to the vendor that a weekly order will be placed. Since the vendor has access to the inventory objectives, on-hand inventory and actual sales data for the entire firm, the vendor can readily anticipate the size of the order and can use this information in its production and distribution planning.

Once a week, the actual order is made and the vendor ships it to each of Target's six distribution centres, with the product arriving within a week. Once the product arrives at the distribution centres, Target management has an additional week's worth of sales data to consider and then sends replenishment shipments to each store. Thus the store will receive a replenishment shipment for each item every week based on a two week cycle to the vendor.

Target's primary objective in this system is not to reduce the total inventory in the stores. Target's marketing philosophy, rather, is that the consumer likes and expects the store to be 'full', that is, that each item carried should be available, and available in depth, and that the shopper should be able to see that depth. Thus all inventory at the store should be on display, with none out of sight in a storeroom. Shelf facings are designed to be wide and shallow rather than narrow and deep, so that the shopper can readily see the abundance of stock on offer. Standards in stock availability are set quite high; Target expects a 95 per cent in-stock rate, where 'in stock' is defined to mean 'at least 40 per cent of the maximum designed inventory is on the shelf'. Using this standard, the traditional out of stock percentage in the stores is virtually zero. To support this standard, Target relies on the quick response approach to increase the 'fit' of the replenishment shipment. The goal of the replenishment system is to bring each item as close as possible to 100 per cent of designed shelf capacity without creating an over-stock, which would result in diverting part of the shipment to backroom storage. Diversion of partial shipments to backroom storage is undesirable because backroom stock is not on display and hence is not productive, because backroom stock has a greater tendency to become lost, damaged or stolen, and because of the expensive triple handling required to move the property in and out of the storeroom.

Target has found that its quick response system has been a great success and has been an important element of the firm's success. Key vendors involved in the programme have benefited from the assured stream of orders and the increased predictability of those orders which comes from the sharing of sales and inventory data. Target benefits from higher item availability at the vendor, at its distribution centres and at the stores. Cycle inventories at the centres are lower due to frequent replenishment, and safety stocks are lower due to the shorter forecasting horizons involved. While the system involves higher transportation costs and incremental data systems costs, these costs are offset by savings in inventory costs at the distribution centres as well as by substantial savings in handling costs at the stores due to the increased 'fit' of the replenishment orders provided by the system. In addition, the sales data needed to drive the system have proven to be extremely useful in fine tuning the merchandising operation, and the closer vendor relations which have developed have led to price reductions and other purchase savings. Overall, Target is extremely enthusiastic about its quick response system and is aggressively expanding its programme to include more key vendors, with a goal of becoming 100 per cent quick response on all high volume items.

Cycle Time Compression

The Importance of Cycle Time

Logistics managers have long recognized the importance of order cycle time, and this concept has entered into the planning and operation of inventory control and distribution systems for decades. More recently, American logistics executives have come to recognize the strategic significance of planning, and indeed reducing, the cycle times in their systems. Throughout many different industries, and taught by the example of successful Japanese competitors, American firms are working to reduce the total time required to bring products to the marketplace. As George Stalk and Thomas Hout explain in their best-selling book *Competing Against Time*,

> Today, time is on the cutting edge of competitive advantage. The ways leading companies manage time – in production, in sales and distribution, in new product development and introduction – are the most powerful new sources of competitive advantage (p 39)

A cycle time compression logistics strategy can be applied to distribution and production, and American firms have also shown how the strategy can be employed in product development and roll out.

In one frame of reference, cycle time can be thought of as the time which elapses between the point at which a customer places an order and the point at which the product is received. Traditionally, logistics managers have attempted to control or reduce this order cycle time by increasing in-stock availability rates, pre-positioning field inventories close to customers or using premium freight services to speed delivery. While effective, these tactics are not without cost.

From another point of view, customer order cycle times are

obviously important, but they do not measure the true response time of the firm since the finished goods inventory performs the function of uncoupling the demand process from the production process. In this respect, the cycle time is the length of time material remains in the firm as it flows from raw material, to production, to finished goods and on to delivery to the customer. Attacking this cycle time has several benefits. First, it makes the firm more responsive; that is, the firm may be able to produce and distribute a product to a given customer faster. Second, cycle time reduction will reduce the time that material is held as inventory, and hence will increase inventory turnover and return on assets.

This form of cycle time compression can be observed in the use of MRP and DRP in the production/distribution system. In a traditional material control system, for example, raw materials are stockpiled in inventory to support the manufacture of a wide range of end items which are periodically produced according to some schedule. Stockpiles are maintained according to long run, aggregate demand for the raw materials and without regard to the current production schedule. Items are simply drawn from stock when needed for production and replenished when the stockpile is low. As a result, many items are stockpiled for long periods of time since most items are actually in production for only a small fraction of the year. In an MRP environment, material control is envisioned as a scheduling process rather than as a stockpiling process. The MRP approach is to examine the master production schedule, calculate the raw materials requirement implied by the schedule and order the required materials to arrive as they are required. In such a system, the 'dead time' that property spends as inventory waiting to be used can be dramatically reduced. A DRP system applies the same tactic to finished goods in the distribution system, scheduling the production and distribution of product to coincide with the sales and marketing plan for the product. Thus the use of MRP and DRP systems can be seen as a tactic to achieve cycle time compression of the second type – reducing the total time that materials are held by the firm. Note, also, that this goal is typically achieved without resorting to premium, high speed freight. The cycle time reduction is gained through postponement, no property moves until it needs to. The logical extension of this 'scheduling' approach can be seen to be operating in most JIT systems, which can be thought of as MRP systems with very small 'time buckets'; that is, the production period over which requirements are defined in a JIT system is considered to be as little as one hour, rather than the day or week normally employed in an MRP system.

The third form of cycle time is the time it takes the firm to bring a new product to market. For some products, the design and development cycle time is not closely related to logistics processes. However, where individual product life cycle times are short, as in the case of style or fashion goods, logistics processes can make critical contributions to a successful cycle time compression strategy.

American firms have employed many different tactics to achieve cycle time compression in their logistics processes, but most successful applications share these common characteristics:

- The responsiveness of the total system is increased. The firm can respond more quickly to changing customer requirements because the logistics system has become more flexible and adaptive, and more easily able to react to changes in plans.
- Inventory levels are reduced at all points in the system as on hand stocks come to reflect true customer requirements more closely.
- Risk and the associated costs of risk are reduced. As the cycle time falls, the demand forecasting horizon can be reduced, which reduces the risks of stockouts, lost sales, obsolescence, redistribution, and all the other problems associated with forecast error.
- The information content of the system increases. The system comes to rely on fast and accurate transmission of information as a substitute for the inventory previously used to operate the system.

An Implementation Tactic: Crossdocking

In an attempt to reduce the time that material is held as inventory in the logistics system, many American firms are employing a tactic which is often referred to as crossdocking. In a crossdocking operation, shipments (normally of finished goods) move through a warehouse or distribution centre without being held in storage. In a traditional retail distribution system, for example, the distribution system might receive a single shipment of several truckloads of a given item. The shipment would be received, inspected, and moved to storage. The inventory control system would then recognize the availability of the property and release many small orders for the item to satisfy requirements at the retail outlets. The orders would be picked from stock, assembled into shipments with other items and shipped to the stores. In contrast, in a crossdocking operation, the incoming shipment would be unloaded, broken down and immediately reassembled into outbound shipments to the stores. In the words of Peter Drucker, 'in transportation parlance, the warehouse has become a switching yard rather than a holding yard.' Crossdocking is not a new idea; in some industries it has been practised successfully for decades, even if only by necessity. In the case of highly perishable or time sensitive goods, for example, most distribution systems are designed to 'keep the inventory in motion'. In most cases, however, crossdocking on a large scale is quite difficult to arrange because of the high degree of coordination required. It is far easier, although not necessarily more efficient, to rely on storage (or the inventory function) to decouple the inbound receiving activity from the outbound shipping activity. However, the traditional storage-based approach will result in inventory holding costs, increased handling costs, higher loss and damage rates and longer total cycle times.

The Limited Stores is a classic example of a firm that competes with a cycle time compression strategy, and its logistics processes are an integral part of this total firm strategy. The Limited operates over 3,500 retail stores across the United States which carry moderately priced women's fashions. This is an intensely competitive marketplace, where fashion, quality and cost are all important marketing variables, and where spotting fashion trends and bringing new items to market quickly are vitally important. In this market, a new product's saleable lifetime is a matter of only a few months. The Limited has engineered its entire corporate strategy around speed in getting to market. About 50 per cent of its total volume is produced off-shore, at manufacturing facilities in Europe, South and Central America, Asia and the Pacific Rim.

All of the Limited's fashion goods are moved through a single cross-docking operation. Large orders of a given item or line, typically an entire season's worth, are assembled at a manufacturing point and shipped, usually via chartered air freight, to the Limited distribution centre in central Ohio. The single large shipment will usually involve dozens of different sizes, colours, fabrics and so forth. At the distribution centre the shipment is received and inspected, and is broken down into separate shipments for each of the thousands of stores, each of which is to receive a carefully predetermined assortment by size, colour and so forth. In addition, garments are normally unpacked, placed on hangers, and ticketed for sale, so that the receiving store need only hang the garments on the display rack. As shipments are built, individual truckloads are released on predetermined schedules and routes so that each store receives shipments of fresh merchandise at least weekly. No garments are stored in the facility; every item should move from the receiving dock to the outbound truck within 24 hours. The entire network is designed so that a production lot released for shipment from a production facility in, say, Malaysia, will be hanging on the rack in 3,500 Limited stores no more than ten days later.

The smooth operation of a system such as this requires a high degree of coordination and centralized control, as well as well developed data automation and telecommunications capabilities. A key element of the Limited system is that distribution requirements are centrally controlled by the merchandizing staff. The system does not operate in a standard replenishment environment. Rather, the standard procedure is to manufacture a single large batch of an item, distribute it to the stores and sell it to exhaustion. While the selling season proceeds, the production and distribution system moves on to the new items planned for the next season.

As a result of this finished goods deployment strategy, the Limited can:

- Keep virtually all of its inventory out on the floor where shoppers can see it and buy it.
- Get its product to market first, well ahead of its competition, so that style-conscious customers will buy from the Limited. By the time competitors get their products to the sales floor, the Limited can take

its first markdown on the item and continue to generate profitable sales.

- Rather than commit to large production runs early, when there is still considerable uncertainty about the market potential for an item, the Limited can order a small production sample and quickly test market it at selected stores throughout the United States. If the test item is successful, the Limited can quickly mass produce and distribute it in time to capture the market.

In this application, then, the crossdocking operation not only shortens the firm's production and distribution cycle time, it also makes a critically important contribution to the Limited's new product design and development cycle time.

The example of the Limited demonstrates the power of a crossdocking tactic where the product is low density, high value, and high margin. However, crossdocking is also applicable in other environments. For example, wholesale grocers are showing increased interest in crossdocking operations because of the potential to reduce operating costs and improve margins in this highly competitive business.

In the traditional wholesale grocery operation, whole pallet loads of single SKU products are received and put in storage, and individual store shipments are individually picked and assembled from the inventory. In the crossdocking operation, vendors assemble multiple SKU pallets by store. The pallets are shipped to the wholesaler and crossdocked with pallets assembled by other vendors. Pallets are assembled directly into store level shipments.

The crossdocking operation is potentially much more efficient to operate, since storage costs are virtually eliminated and handling costs are effectively halved. However, a crossdocking operation is also far more complicated to execute. Such a system will usually include:

- Common bar-coding and standard case marking standards.
- EDI linkages between the wholesaler and the stores as well as between the wholesaler and the vendors.
- Highly reliable carriers who can maintain the tight schedules mandated by such a system.
- Information system software which can support the high volume of data processing involved.

In an attempt to provide these capabilities, third party logistics providers are organizing in support of cycle time compression initiatives. For example, the Logistics Flow-Through Consortium has recently been formed to provide integrated support of these initiatives in the grocery and consumer packaged goods industries. The consortium includes Dry Storage Corporation, a logistics service corporation providing contract warehousing, transportation and EDI capabilities, and LogiCNet, an information services company which specializes in the design and installation of DRP software systems. The aim of the consortium is to be able to provide an integrated capability which will enable a set of trading partners to quickly establish an effective crossdocking operation.

Implementation Issues

Many American firms have embraced and employed supply chain management and cycle time compression strategies in their logistics operations with dramatically positive results. However, not all such attempts have been successful, nor has every implementation proven to be straightforward or simple. In this section we will offer a list of observations and conclusions we have drawn from our studies of scores of American firms which have implemented these logistics strategies.

- **Supply chain management and cycle time compression are complementary strategies** The logistics manager is not forced to choose between these two strategies on an either/or basis. In fact, the two strategies are often mutually supportive and self-reinforcing. The strategies are seen together so frequently that it can be difficult or arbitrary to distinguish between them. In the discussion of supply chain management at Target Stores presented above, for example, one might have focused on the fact that cycle time was dramatically reduced with the new procedures. In the discussion of cycle time compression at the Limited, one might have stressed the high degree of coordination and cooperation between the Limited and its vendor base which was needed to achieve the desired cycle time compression. In practice, the distinction between the two strategies is often blurred. A principal reason to develop supply chain management is often to capture and amplify the benefits of cycle time compression by applying the strategy at all levels in the chain.
- **Each strategy has common barriers to successful implementation** There are many possible pitfalls involved in employing these strategies, but the most significant problems are generally of two types:
  - *High complexity* The new systems are usually much more complicated than the systems and procedures which they replace. Supply chain management, as embodied for example in a quick response system, requires coordination of SKU level item flows across firm boundaries in near real time with great precision and reliability. Low inventory levels place the entire operation at risk to errors at any level in the system. New data systems and communications systems are needed to drive the logistics flow, and these systems must perform flawlessly. In a successful crossdocking operation, vehicle scheduling and dispatching is crucially important as well, and completely reliable carriers must be found.
  - *High trust* Supply chain management and cycle time compression must be based on high levels of trust within the various parts of a given firm, such as between production and distribution and between sales and distribution. In addition, very high levels of

trust must be established and maintained between buyers and sellers in the supply chain, as well as between shippers and carriers and warehousers. Supply chain members must share and safeguard highly sensitive sales data, and all parties must be given candid estimates of production schedules, shipping status and delivery dates. Inability or unwillingness to share these data will generally frustrate meaningful attempts to establish the close coordination implied by these strategies.

- **Information technology is the key enabling technology** Another common thread in the successful implementation history of these strategies in American firms is the reliance on fast and accurate information technology. Most such logistics systems use bar-code scanning or some other form of automatic identification to provide input of SKU level transaction data on sales, inventory and shipments. Data is normally telecommunicated between various operating operations, usually by EDI. In addition, some form of high level logistics system software is needed to guide the operation of the strategy.

  For example, Formica Inc, a leading manufacturer of plastic laminates used in counter tops, furniture and other products, faced a serious challenge from a new competitor in the field. Formica implemented MRP and DRP systems to compress its production and distribution cycle time within the firm. Next it developed a supply chain approach by directly tying its key vendors into its MRP system and by bringing its key distributors on line within its DRP system. In this way the MRP/DRP software becomes the formal mechanism by which a supply chain management strategy is implemented. This has become a fairly common approach. Pillsbury, for example, has simply modified its commercially provided DRP software package to accommodate and implement a quick response system it has developed for frozen and refrigerated grocery products.
- **Inventory reduction as a benefit** Most successful case histories of supply chain management or cycle time compression will include inventory reduction, but inventory reduction will not be the whole story. Generally, inventory reduction will be one item on the list of benefits and cost savings which were sought or obtained. In many cases the savings due to inventory reduction will be substantial, while in other cases inventory reduction may be a relatively minor consideration.
- **Successful logistics strategies must be integrated with production, marketing and total corporate strategy** Supply chain management and cycle time compression are strategies which are often highly compatible with the overall strategy being pursued by the firm. Compression of the logistics components of the firm's total cycle time is an integral component of the firm's overall strategy of time-based competition, as was demonstrated in the previous discussion of the Limited's distribution tactics. Logistics cycle time compression and supply chain coordination are also highly supportive of the general

strategy of flexible manufacturing which many firms are moving towards.

Many other American firms are moving towards a marketing strategy which looks beyond mere 'customer satisfaction' in an attempt to move past the competition by 'delighting the customer'. In this context, compression of logistics cycle time increases the responsiveness of the logistics system to the customer's desires. Incorporating the customer into the formal supply chain system should improve the level of support provided to the customer as well as increasing the customer's ability to convey its needs and wants to the firm and have them acted upon. In this way the supply chain approach will work to reinforce the marketing strategy. As we mentioned in the discussion on quick response at Target Stores, an important aspect of the supply chain relationship established between Target and its vendors was that the inventory replenishing system was designed to reinforce the marketing strategy of providing highly visible evidence of 'full' stockage in the stores, simply because customers like to see full shelves.

Supply chain management and cycle time compression are complementary logistics strategies which progressive American firms are employing in many different ways in many different settings. These strategies are not simply or easily developed, but the results achieved through their use are often dramatic. Any firm which is truly serious about competing in the American marketplace should very carefully consider the implications of these strategies for their operations.

References

Andrews, L R (1971) *The Concept of Corporate Strategy*, Dow Jones-Irwin.

Bowersox, D J (1989) *Leading Edge Logistics – Competitive Positioning for the 1990s*, The Council of Logistics Management.

Cooper, M C (1992) *Strategic Planning for Logistics*, The Council of Logistics Management.

Hammond, J H (1991) 'Coordination in textile and apparel channels: A case for "virtual" integration', in *Towards the Integration of the Logistics Pipeline*, Proceedings of the Twentieth Annual Transportation and Logistics Educators Conference.

La Londe, B J and Cooper, M C (1989) *Partnerships in Providing Customer Service: A Third Party Perspective*, The Council of Logistics Management.

La Londe, B J (1991) *The Evolution, Status and Future of the Corporate Function*, The American Society of Transportation and Logistics.

Lambert, D M and Stock, J R (1987) *Strategic Logistics Management*, Richard D Irwin.

Stalk, G (Jr) and Hout, T M (1990) *Competing Against Time*, The Free Press, New York.

Chapter 9

Logistics Strategies in Japan

Minoru Saito
Nittsu Research Centre

Logistics Problems in Japan

There have been serious logistical problems in Japan since the end of the 1980s. Most Japanese companies, including manufacturers, wholesalers, and retailers, have had a hard time maintaining logistics operations.

There are several important factors that have created these difficulties. First, the logistics service required by customers has become increasingly more complex and demanding. Second, the recent labour shortage and the sharp rise of land prices in Japan have caused a sudden increase in the cost of logistics.

The Increased Complexity of Logistics Services

The 'just-in-time' (JIT) concept was originally formulated to describe the production process in the automobile industry, being introduced by Toyota Motors for its assembly line operation. However, the concept has not remained confined to production processes and has gradually found application in other sectors of the Japanese economy. The position in Japan now is that it is taken for granted that customers of every industrial sector expect JIT delivery – even small retail store owners. When a retail store owner orders goods, he assumes that the delivery will be made by the next morning.

The demand for JIT delivery has transformed the quality of delivery service. As a result, deliveries have become more frequent, and the quantities delivered correspondingly smaller. Most companies are therefore performing frequent and small delivery services.

Figure 9.1 illustrates the increase in weekly delivery frequency over the three-year period. Figure 9.2 illustrates the corresponding decrease in the size of the cargo per delivery during the early and mid-1980s.

Companies are increasingly tending to avoid the accumulation of stock, which takes up space and increases cost. By means of efficient management, companies can eliminate stock-holding by implementing JIT delivery patterns, with more frequent deliveries of smaller cargoes.

Effects of Frequent Delivery of Small Quantities

As frequent delivery of small quantities increases, the efficiency of

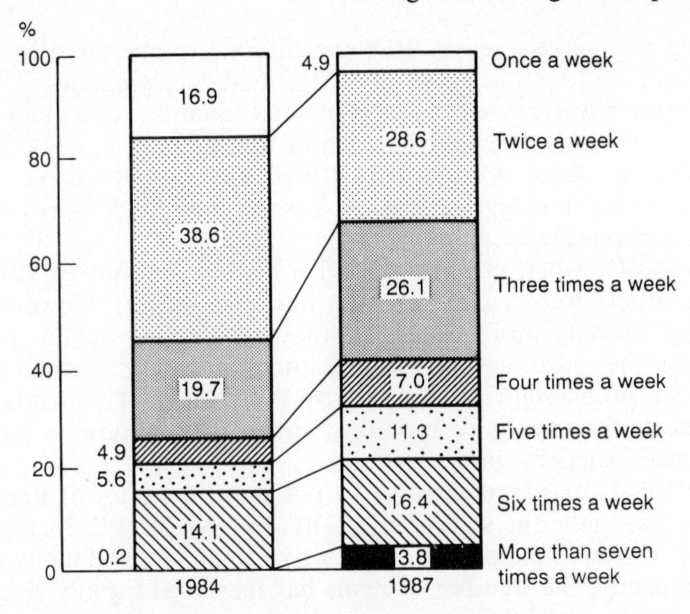

Figure 9.1 *Increase in Delivery Frequency*

Source: Research by questionnaire performed by the Ministry of Trade and Industry (September 1988)

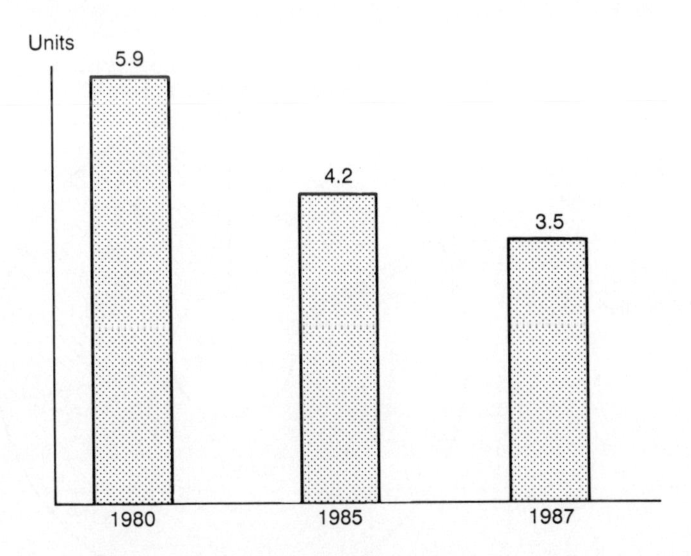

Figure 9.2 *Trend to Small Lot Shipment*

Source: Tokyo Route Truck Association

loading products decreases. It is very difficult to operate delivery trucks which are loaded to full capacity with small consignments.

The trend to frequent delivery of small quantities has had ramifications which extend beyond the area of transportation, to operations in warehouses, where products are stored and picked out according to customers' orders and sorted by destination. Such operations have become increasingly complex.

Previously, when customers held a certain amount of stock themselves, orders were typically in the unit of a carton. However, as JIT delivery prevails more generally, they now order by the piece. For example, instead of several cartons, two bottles of shampoo and three bottle of rinse might be ordered by the retailer. This leads to more complicated operations, requiring more labour power for picking individual orders in the warehouse.

The trend for manufacturers to put more varieties of items on the market has made the warehousing situation worse still. In Japan, mass production has changed to production of small lots and many products. Consequently, the number of items has increased rapidly (Figure 9.3). For example, a good processing company may produce more than 4,000 products. This is not abnormal, most manufacturers having increased the number of production items in order to expand their sales volume.

By increasing the number of products, not only the manufacturer but also the wholesaler and retailer have to expand space for storage, and warehousing operations become proportionately more complex.

In conclusion, customers' requirements of frequent delivery of small

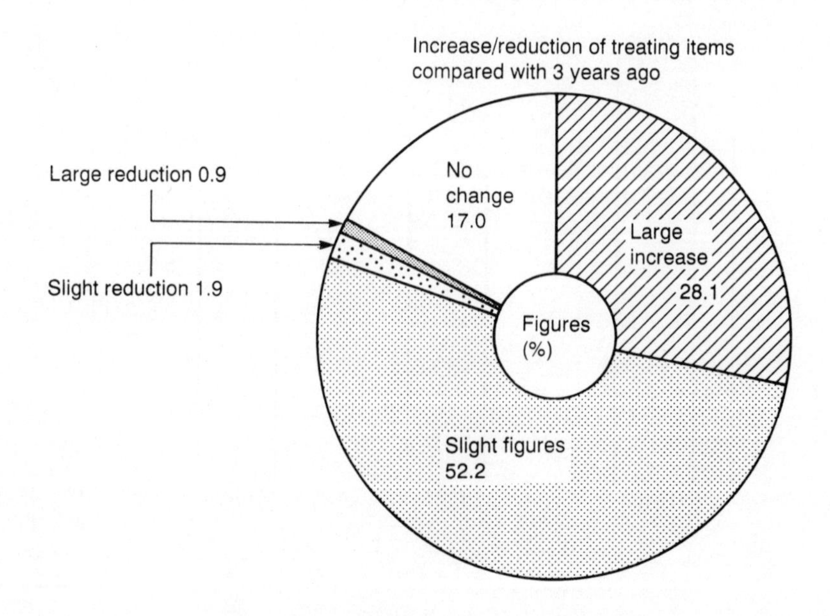

Figure 9.3 *Extension of variable items*

Source: Research by Road Economy Research Institute (1991)

quantities makes logistics operations complicated and troublesome. The increase in the number of products in the distribution system has aggravated this situation.

Labour Shortage and Increase in Land Prices

The economic boom of the late 1980s increased logistics costs, the increase in both wage and land prices having a bad influence on logistics operations. Compared with other Japanese industries, working conditions in the road freight industry are hard. Truck drivers always face the risk of traffic accidents, and in spite of long working hours, their wages are low by Japanese standards.

Consequently, many truck drivers have found jobs in other areas and the resulting shortage of truck drivers has become acute. In the peak season, trucking companies may be unable to carry all their cargo. In order to recruit truck drivers, wages increased rapidly. Not only haulage companies, but also companies transporting their own goods, were distressed by the serious labour shortage and wage rises.

Land prices, as well as wages, influence the operations of logistics. The boom in the Japanese economy brought about an increase in land prices. In and around Tokyo especially, where business activity is concentrated, the sudden rise of land prices has imposed further hindrances on the efficiency of logistics operations.

Companies tend to desire to improve their logistics facilities because they do not have enough space at present to handle the increase in products. In and around Tokyo, it is very difficult to find affordable land on which to carry out logistics operations.

Companies face the same problem whether they are trying to rent or buy. Together with land prices, rents have gone too high to be affordable. Companies accordingly have to locate new distribution centres far from the central Tokyo area.

Figure 9.4 sets out the responses to a questionnaire submitted to companies based in Tokyo. The data show that the most serious problem companies face is the insufficiency of labour to work in their logistics facilities. The labour shortage applies not only to the pool of truck drivers, but also to warehouse staff. Another major problem concerns the increase in the number of products, for which there is not enough warehouse space.

Logistics Strategy and Distribution Channels

The emergence of these logistics problems has impressed upon Japanese companies the importance of logistics strategy in management. Although new ideas have emerged in logistics strategy, companies have been unable to quickly improve their logistics systems.

Several companies, however, having recognized the importance of a successful logistics strategy before logistics problems began to be experienced, have been able to innovate advanced logistics systems.

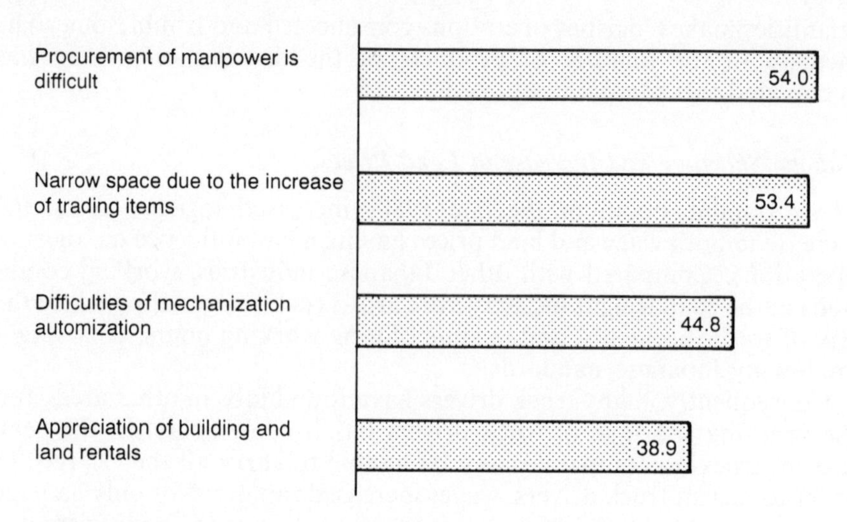

Figure 9.4 *Problems encountered by logistics facilities (percentages)*

Source: Research performed by the Road Economy Research Institute (1991)

Analysis of these systems makes clear the characteristics of successful Japanese logistics strategy.

Japanese companies have introduced information systems to improve their logistics. It is in fact true that companies have made rapid progress in adopting these information systems. Nevertheless, it has been impossible to improve the logistics systems unless the company also improve their distribution channels.

The logistics system is closely intertwined with the distribution channel. Japanese companies have found that they have been unable to improve their logistics systems in isolation from their existing distribution channels.

Logistics has not been able to advance much recently because of the great complexities of the distribution channels. A product's typical distribution channel starts with the manufacturer, passes through the wholesaler, and ends with the retailer. The distribution process is thought to have become overly complex because of the dual intervention of wholesalers in the distribution level. Put more explicitly, a wholesaler may sell goods not only to retailers, but also to other wholesalers – there are primary and secondary wholesalers. The Japanese distribution channel is long and complicated.

Japanese companies have no alternative but to rationalize the present distribution channel if they are to achieve an advanced logistics system. Companies which have been outstanding in regard to their logistics have accordingly been trying to change the distribution channels.

Advanced Logistics in Retailing

One of the first advanced logistics systems to meet the eye in Japan is to be found in retailing. One new type of retailer has developed especially quickly – the 'convenience store'. Such shops have spread throughout Japan and are influencing the way that the rest of Japanese retail business is being structured. This new type of retailing business has necessitated the use of new logistics techniques in order to ensure a smooth supply of various goods to the stores.

Synopsis of Seven-Eleven Japan

Seven-Eleven Japan is the organizer of the convenience store chain which has the most advanced logistics system in Japan. Originally Seven-Eleven was a well-known convenience store in the USA; it was introduced into Japan by Itoyokado, a major Japanese retailer. Seven-Eleven Japan was founded as a subsidiary company in 1973.

Seven-Eleven Japan organizes independent stores into the Seven-Eleven format. An independent owner of a small retail store, such as a grocery or a liquor store, typically initiates contact with Seven-Eleven Japan, and has the company rebuild his store into a Seven-Eleven outlet according to Seven-Eleven Japan guidelines. Seven-Eleven Japan subsequently provides uniform standard sales techniques to the individual outlets and decides for the retailer what items will be sold in his outlet.

The Seven-Eleven chain store has become especially popular as a new retailer for the younger generation and has expanded rapidly, becoming the leading convenience store company in Japan. At present there are more than 4,000 Seven-Eleven stores in Japan.

The Necessity of Frequent, Small Delivery Systems

Convenience stores depend on frequent delivery of smaller quantities; only with the use of advanced logistics systems has it been possible to develop convenience store chains, because it is the logistics system which makes possible the frequent delivery of small quantities.

The typical Seven-Eleven convenience store outlet is very small, average floor-space amounting to only about 100 square metres. Nevertheless, such stores will offer more than 3,000 product items, displaying practically every item that is needed for daily life.

Although the convenience store provides so many items, it typically does not have a storage room. Stockrooms are considered to be dead space, playing no immediate role in sales activity. The sales floor must in principle be as large as possible in order to promote the maximum number of goods for sale.

In consequence, all of the various goods must be capable of being replenished very rapidly by delivery from the distribution centre. If a customer visiting the store cannot find some item which should be available, the store loses an opportunity to make a sale and suffers an injury to its image as a convenience store. All retail businesses think that this is the sort of event which must be avoided above all else.

The just-in-time system is not merely a matter of the delivery time itself; it also involves techniques for the most rapid means possible of receiving orders from the individual outlets through an information network, and the most efficient technique for gathering the various items according to each specific order. This depends on a very advanced logistics system.

Improvement of Distribution Channels

The main responsibility of Seven-Eleven Japan is to provide for the efficient supply of all sales items to each outlet. Its first function is to obtain the various items, either from wholesalers or directly from manufacturers. Its second function is to distribute the items to each store according to need. The distribution centre operates as the coordination centre for these two functions.

Seven-Eleven Japan had to streamline its existing distribution channels in order to secure an efficient supply of the items. Many Japanese wholesalers used to characterize themselves as the exclusive agents of particular manufacturers, being allowed to deal only in the products of a single manufacturer.

Under this system a retailer usually had to deal with many different wholesalers in order to carry a range of products. Delivery of goods to the retailer was extremely inefficient, each wholesaler delivering goods by a separate truck. Furthermore there was no certainty that the deliveries of each wholesaler would arrive in time. People tended to overlook the inefficiency of the delivery system.

The Seven-Eleven Japan innovation consisted in integrating and reorganizing the distribution channels. Figure 9.5 illuminates how a given wholesaler in the new distribution system is allocated a certain area of sales activity and is given the freedom to deal in goods from different manufacturers without any restrictions. Furthermore, Seven-Eleven has been able to develop efficient distribution channels for their outlets by arranging the terms of sale with both wholesalers and manufacturers.

The wholesalers operate the distribution centres to provide delivery to the convenience store outlets. Seven-Eleven Japan itself has not invested in the distribution centres, even though they make up the core of the distribution channel. It is the wholesaler, not Seven-Eleven Japan, who has the distribution centre constructed at his own expense and then operates it under the supervision of Seven-Eleven Japan.

Through this arrangement, Seven-Eleven Japan has been able to create an efficient distribution system for its outlets without having to bear any heavy investment burden. Many wholesalers are willing to make the necessary investment in distribution centres in order to incorporate with Seven-Eleven Japan. In return, wholesalers gain access to a big market.

Seven-Eleven Japan has reorganized the wholesalers as well as the retailers, transforming the pre-existing distribution channels. In so doing, Seven-Eleven Japan has put in place an advanced logistics system, implementing an effective technique for storing a wide variety of goods and efficiently distributing them to all of the convenience store locations.

One reliable indicator of how advanced its logistics system is can be

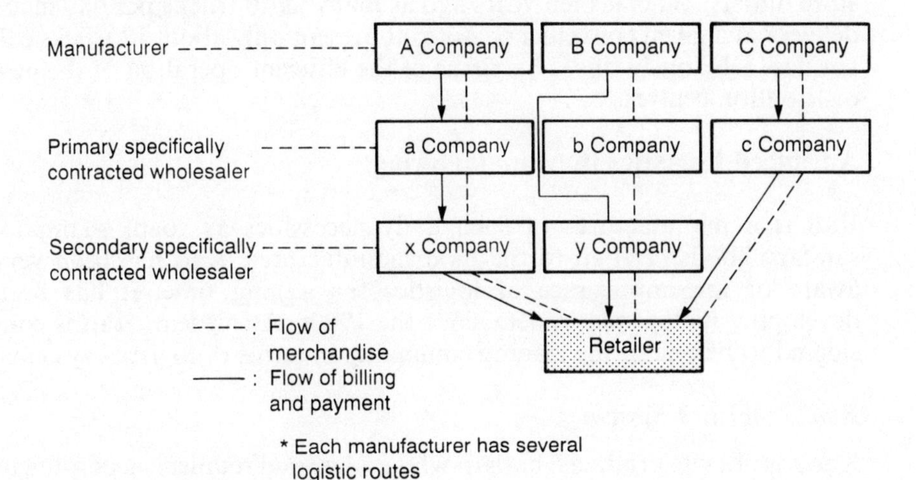

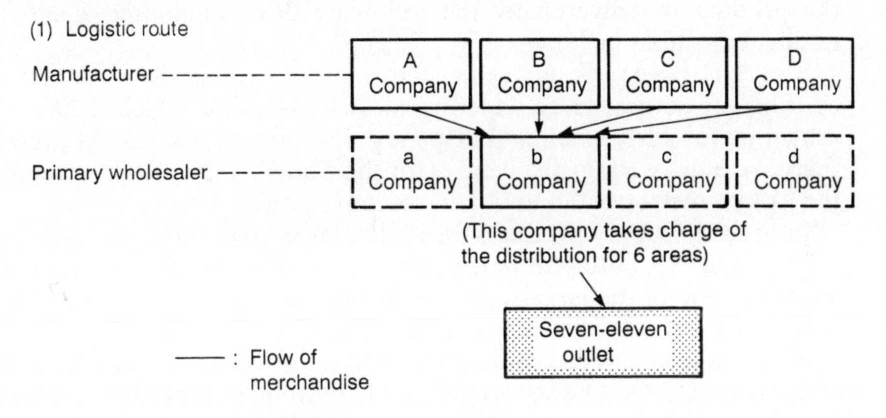

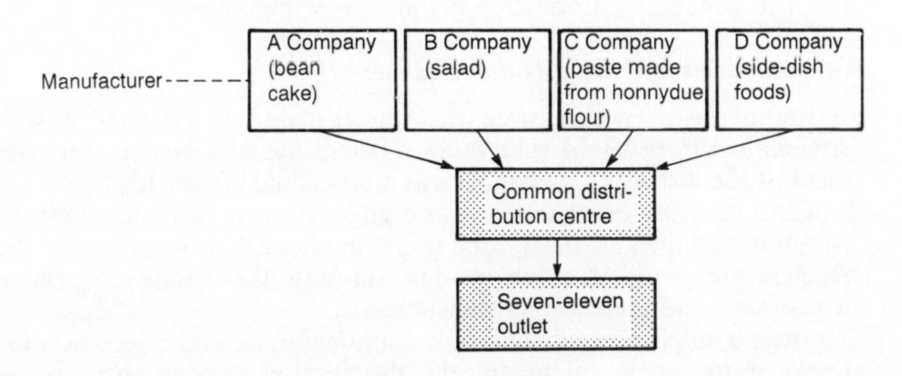

Figure 9.5 *The New Distribution Channel of Seven Eleven Japan*

seen in the decrease in the number of truck deliveries to the convenience store outlets. Whereas ten years ago as many as 70 trucks per day made delivery at a given convenience store, at present only about 12 trucks call per day. Obviously this is by virtue of the efficient operation of the new distribution centres.

Advanced Logistics in Manufacturing

Kao is a manufacturer of such daily necessities as soap, shampoo, sanitary goods, and so forth. As a manufacturer, Kao has been very aware of the importance of logistics for a long time; it has been developing its logistics system since the 1960s. At present, Kao is considered to be one of the leading companies in terms of logistics systems.

Kao's Logistics System

Kao supplies its products, both to wholesalers and retailers, according to a policy of next-day delivery. If, for example, a retailer should order a quantity of even less than a carton of Kao products, Kao sees to it that the product is delivered by the following day, no matter where the retailer is located in Japan.

Kao has been able to achieve this impressive level of service by establishing several large-scale logistics centres, into which it has integrated its formerly small and dispersed distribution centres. At present, there are only two logistics centres for the whole Kanto region, including the Tokyo metropolitan area and six more prefectures.

In order to supply products for such a large area, the logistics centres are so large that automation is necessary to secure efficient functioning. Thus, in spite of the large-scale supply operation it has been possible to reduce the amount of manpower required.

Needless to say, state-of-the-art information systems are applied to the supply operations. Orders originating from retailer terminals are transferred immediately to the logistics centre. All of the information about orders according to product is transmitted directly to the factories, in order to streamline production planning (see Figure 9.6).

Streamlining of the Distribution Channel

It cannot be overemphasized that the distribution channel must be streamlined in order to achieve an efficient logistics system. Improvement of the distribution channel was a crucial factor for Kao.

Kao's distribution channel was no different from most Japanese distribution channels in being long and complicated. Kao products only reached the retailers after passing through the hands of primary wholesalers and then secondary wholesalers.

Given a situation such as this, a manufacturer cannot keep accurate track of its stock volume in the distribution process, because the wholesalers handle their stocks independently from each other. Thus the long and complicated distribution channel in effect prevents the manu-

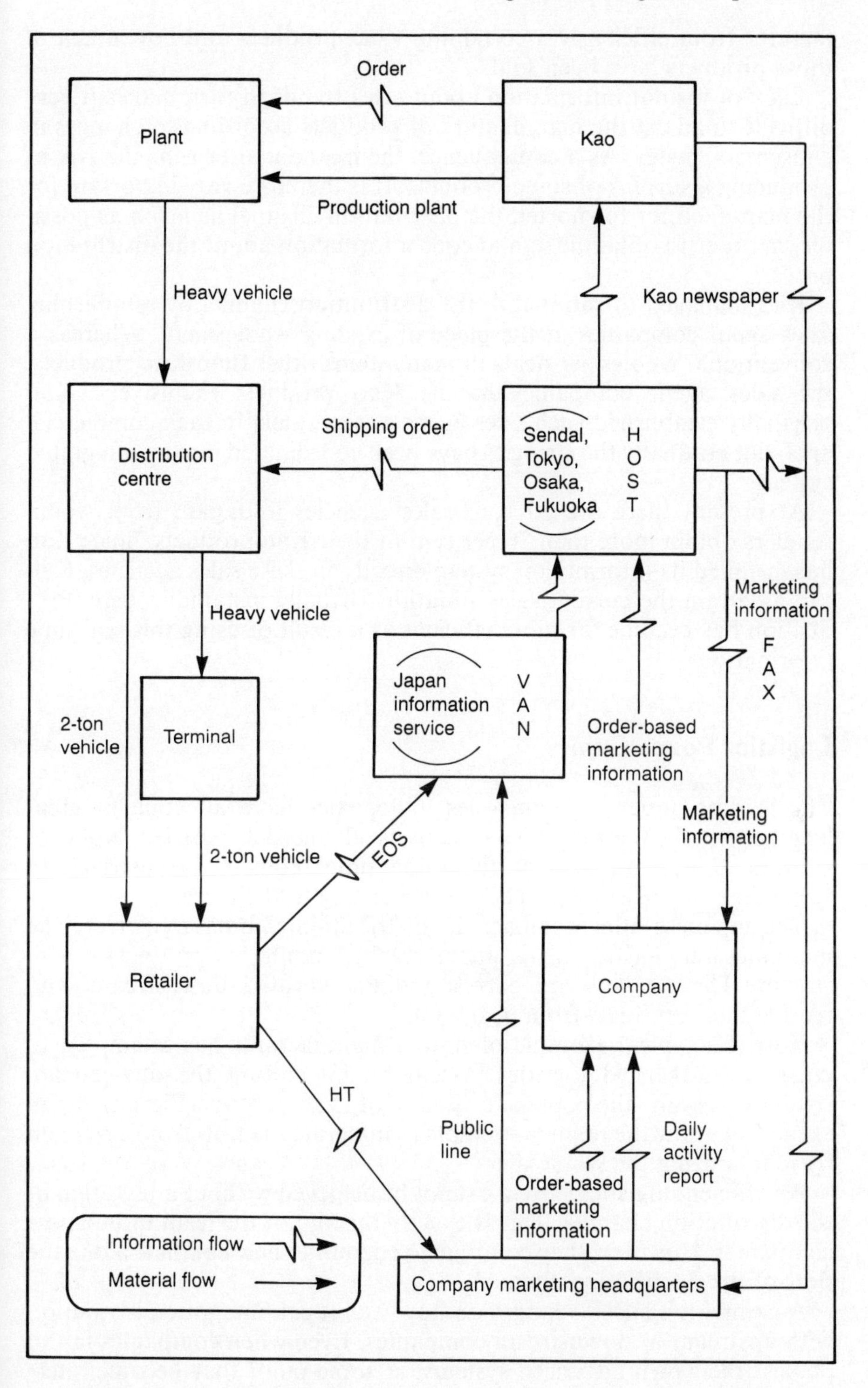

Figure 9.6 *Information and physical distribution network of Kao Corporation*

facturer from efficiently ascertaining what products and how much of those products have been sold.

Lack of instant information about sales trends in turn makes it very difficult to adjust the manufacture of products according to changes in consumers' tastes. As a consequence, the manufacturer runs the risk of producing a surplus of some products. It is therefore very important for the manufacturer to shorten the distribution channel as much as possible, in order to obtain instantaneous information about the distribution process.

Kao managed to rationalize the distribution channel by establishing sales agent companies in the place of existing wholesalers. Whereas a conventional wholesaler deals in many items other than Kao products, the sales agent companies handle Kao products exclusively. Kao originally established such sales agencies separately in each commercial area, but gradually the agencies have been coordinated into an integrated system.

At present there are 20 Kao sales agencies in Japan, from whom retailers obtain more than 70 per cent of their Kao products. Since Kao has installed its information system directly in these sales agencies, Kao can ascertain the current sales situation virtually instantaneously. Production has become far more efficient as a result of using this real-time information.

Logistics Power Games

The leading Japanese companies in logistics have all gone to great lengths to make their logistics systems as advanced as possible. Not only manufacturers, but also at the same time retailers have striven to streamline the distribution channel according to their needs.

The Japanese often compare the distribution channel to a river. The manufacturer, located in its upper reaches, pours his products downstream. The retailers are correspondingly located downstream, and receive their products from upstream.

Kao is a typical example of how a manufacturer has attempted to create an advanced logistics system by integrating the downstream retailers. From the opposite point of view, Seven-Eleven Japan exemplifies how the retailer attempts to integrate the flow from upstream by reorganizing the wholesalers.

An efficient logistics system cannot be achieved without integration of the distribution channel. This is exactly the aim of the leading Japanese companies. However, they continue to encounter new conflicts along the flow of the distribution channel.

A company's success hinges on how well it can integrate distribution with upstream or downstream companies. Even when companies fail to possess their own advanced systems, at some point they become interrelated with companies which do have advanced logistics systems, and there is a tendency for conflicts to arise with companies that have the more advanced logistics systems. This has become a sort of logistics power game in Japan.

Summary

- In recent years, logistics operations in Japan have become increasingly difficult, due to customers' requirements becoming more demanding, and to labour shortages and rising land prices
- The demand for JIT necessitates increasingly frequent delivery of smaller cargoes, making efficient transport operation harder to achieve
- At the same time, the number of products stocked by shops has increased. Warehousing operations have become correspondingly more complex.
- The increase in land values has forced logistics companies to operate from bases located far from Tokyo
- Effective logistics strategies have become vital. Some of the companies examined in this chapter have successfully utilized new technology to rationalize their distribution channels.

Chapter 10

Environmental Concern: Implications for Supply Chain Management

Ivy Penman
Head of International Planning, Exel Logistics

Introduction

Concern for the environment is increasing at what appears to be an exponential rate. Some companies have taken a leadership role in voluntarily adopting environmental policies. Others – too many others – have preferred to wait before acting. Many in this group believe environmental initiatives will cost money – often wrongly, since a great deal of environmental action is extremely cost effective and can often improve bottom-line profits.

These environmental 'laggards' have a difficult task on their hands. The environment is an extremely wide and complex subject. The topics of global warming, depletion of the ozone layer, acid rain, landfill site exhaustion – to name but a few – are complex. Scientific viewpoints can conflict and change. For example, there is no universal agreement that global warming is taking place. What *is* beyond doubt, however, is that many of the factors which lead to global warning, such as increasing carbon dioxide emissions, are taking place. In addition, any action a company takes can set in motion a complex environmental chain of events. A seemingly 'good' action can create a negative environmental effect somewhere else. Nowhere is this more true than in logistics, where the benefits of recycling – using fewer natural resources – must be balanced against the additional transport requirements involved in collection of packaging for further processing.

The Key Issues

Since logistics embraces management of the whole supply chain, a wide range of environmental considerations apply. Physical distribution, manufacturing, retailing must all be considered. In short, the supply chain as a whole must be viewed as a series of interlinking parts.

To date, considerable environmental developments have taken place within discrete elements of the supply chain. Transport has been addressed in detail, resulting in the introduction of aerodynamic kits, the fitting of speed limiters, the use of fuel additives – all designed to reduce fuel consumption and in turn to reduce emissions of carbon dioxide and other pollutants. Ever-improving vehicle utilization is being practised, for example by collecting from suppliers on return trips to retailers' regional distribution centres. Vehicle route-scheduling systems are constantly being improved and in-cab communication can help contain congestion – estimated to cost British industry £15bn per annum.[1] The introduction of 44-tonne heavy goods vehicles to the UK in 1999 will reduce total vehicle numbers by 9,000.[2] Manufacturers are working hard to improve fuel consumption – to very good effect – and are recycling a growing proportion of their vehicles, while others are extending vehicle life. Fuel suppliers are also reducing the noxious emissions created by burning fuel. Operators are using ever more flexible delivery scheduling, with night drops and early morning starts helping to reduce congestion. The impact of transport on the environment is addressed in more detail below.

Energy conservation is now being practised on a wider scale. Not only are the cost implications of wasting energy recognized, but the adverse environmental implications are also now being appreciated. Excess lighting, heat loss through poor insulation and the deliberate use of more energy in order to reach a lower cost tariff are now recognized as depleting the earth's natural resources.

It is now accepted that CFCs damage the earth's ozone layer when released to the atmosphere. Although a universal alternative has not yet been developed, work is in hand and precautions are now widespread to minimize CFC release and stimulate recapture wherever possible.

Together with transport, an issue which has received widespread attention is recycling. With the realization that landfill sites are in some areas nearing saturation, and the increasing difficulty of achieving new start-ups, recycling is now receiving considerable attention. In addition to the merit of using fewer virgin resources, recycling is being viewed as increasingly attractive and is being pursued with vigour in Germany, for example.

The real danger, however, lies in viewing any of these aspects in isolation. Although the benefits of recycling are recognized, more transport activity will follow as matcrial for rccycling is collcctcd and taken to processing sites. The energy used in the recycling process can sometimes be greater than that used in the original manufacturing of new materials.

If one looks strategically beyond the immediate environmentally-driven aspects of existing supply-chain management, a number of key factors can be identified which have far-reaching and mostly negative implications. These are:

- Stock reduction programmes
  - JIT/quick response
  - centralization of inventory
- Manufacturing economies of scale

- Wider sourcing
- Legislation – for example, tighter and wider application of temperature control.

All of these factors are leading to increased transport activity. Stock levels can only be minimized by incurring the expense of more frequent deliveries. Although the financial cost of increased transport activity is often fully evaluated, the environmental cost implications are not. Similarly, a company rarely looks further than its own costs or the environmental implications of its actions, but the impact on those throughout the supply chain must be considered. Thus, the centralization of inventories so admirably introduced by the major UK retailers has had a strong impact throughout the grocery and non-food supply chains. Previously, suppliers delivered direct to thousands of outlets, many of which were in high street locations. Congestion resulted, with excessive use of energy and the creation of noise. Now manufacturers deliver to regional distribution centres. Although frequent deliveries are often required – to enable retailers to minimize their stocks – the larger drops compensate. Where smaller drops prevail there are opportunities for manufacturers to consolidate loads, using third parties. Thus all sides involved in the grocery supply chain in the UK benefit – retailers, manufacturers and third party primary trunking transporters.

In the industrial manufacturing sector the picture is possibly less attractive. Again, the pressure to reduce inventories is making manufacturers such as vehicle producers insist on just-in-time deliveries from suppliers. Although financially beneficial to the vehicle manufacturer, such demands can be unwelcome to the suppliers, who sometimes choose to hold additional stocks adjacent to the factory. The alternative is ecologically unsound – lots of small drops, leading to increased transport activity.

'Quick Response', originating in the USA, is also leading to more and more frequent small drops to grocery and other retailers, driven by consumer purchases. In both JIT and Quick Response, an environmentally friendly option is to consolidate different suppliers' products, using a third party warehousing and transport consolidation service. This is a solution which is attracting considerable attention at present, but of course very advanced information systems are required to achieve optimum results.

Manufacturing economies of scale are driving manufacturers to use ever bigger factories. Pan-European facilities are now being established all over Europe, many specializing in the production of single-source products. Again this trend is significantly increasing transport activity, both inbound and outbound.

Similarly, with ever-wider sourcing, transport activity is again increasing. As economies concentrate on those products which they can produce with a competitive advantage this trend will continue on a global scale. The chief executive of a leading British grocery multiple recently conceded that approximately 40 per cent of British consumed products were imported, although substitutes for many were available in the UK.

Transport's Impact on the Environment

Transport activity increased dramatically throughout the 1980s. As nations in the developed world grew richer, consumer demand increased and was satisfied by an ever-increasing range of goods. Although the consumer is delighted to have an ever-increasing choice, the down-side of increased transport activity is not so welcome. In the UK in particular, the problem is exacerbated by the uneven population spread, giving rise to acute congestion in the overcrowded South East. It is further accentuated by the very high proportion of road transport in the UK, as opposed to the more environmentally friendly rail or inland waterway traffic, used to a greater extent in continental Europe.

Road transport means cars, buses and lorries, bringing obvious problems such as visual intrusion and noise. Lorries are often dirty, and are certainly perceived to be so, and they contribute to environmental damage. But cars are also involved, and by virtue of their sheer number contribute to the following environmental problems:

- Global warming
- Pollution
- Depletion of the ozone layer
- Depletion of resources
- Congestion
- Waste

Global Warming

Possibly the biggest single threat to the environment is that of global warming. During the course of this century, average world temperatures have risen. Carbon dioxide (CO_2) emissions, together with methane, nitrous oxide and ozone have been classified as 'greenhouse gases' – they remain in the lower atmosphere, retaining heat produced by the sun. Carbon dioxide is the most significant greenhouse gas, and road transport is currently responsible for 21 per cent of the UK emissions of this gas. It has been estimated that even if all further CO_2 emissions were miraculously stopped, we are already committed to temperature rises of between 0.5°C and 1.5°C. The resultant long-term effects of sea level rises and the shifting of existing climatic zones could be devastating.

Pollution

The noise caused by lorries has already received considerable attention, and improvements in technology have recently been made by most vehicle manufacturers. More are under way.

Road transport is a significant contributor to air pollution, being responsible for the following proportions in 1988:

- Carbon monoxide (CO): 85 per cent
- Oxides of nitrogen (NO_x): 45 per cent
- Smoke: 34 per cent
- Volatile organics: 30 per cent
- Sulphur dioxide (SO_2): 1 per cent.

Carbon monoxide (CO)
Toxic carbon monoxide is produced when fuel is burned inefficiently. UK output of CO has risen by 10 per cent in the last ten years, due in the main to a 20 per cent increase in road transport.

Cars, predominantly, are responsible for CO production, not lorries, and future trends should show a decrease, as catalytic converters have been mandatory on new cars in the UK – as in the rest of the EC – since 1992.

Oxides of nitrogen (NO_x)
Road transport is now the largest producer of NO_x, which is a major cause of acid rain, petrol engines contributing 23 per cent and diesel 22 per cent of all 1988 UK output. The United Nations has imposed a target to contain 1994 levels to those of 1978, with further reductions thereafter.

Smoke
Road transport produces 34 per cent of smoke or suspended particulate matter in the UK. This causes respiratory ailments and is possibly carcinogenic. Road transport has increased its proportion of total smoke production as the Clean Air Act has brought about a decline in emissions from traditional 'smoke stick' industries.

Volatile organics
Road transport again is a major contributor, producing 30 per cent of volatile organic compounds, such as benzene. More than two-thirds of these are produced by petrol engines, but 1993 legislation should reduce these emissions, leaving diesel engines as the main culprits.

Sulphur dioxide (SO_2)
Sulphur dioxide is released during the burning of sulphur-containing fuels such as coal and oil. Prolonged exposure can cause breathing problems. Road transport is a low contributor to SO_2 pollution in the UK, and projected improvements in the sulphur content of diesel fuel will further improve the position.

It is apparent that although road transport is a major cause of air pollution, much of this is produced by cars. Emissions legislation already in place for the first half of the 1990s will considerably reduce this problem.

Vehicle manufacturers, petrochemical producers and others who are developing products such as fuel additives and particular traps are working hard to further reduce pollution produced by diesel engines.

Depletion of the Ozone Layer

The ozone layer, 15–50 km above the earth's surface, forms a protective shield against the sun's harmful ultra-violet rays. Only recently have the ozone-depleting properties of CFCs become known, and as common vehicle refrigerants, the distribution industry is a potentially harmful contributor.

In addition to their use as vehicle refrigerants, CFCs are used widely within the supply chain – in cold stores, chilled warehousing and in blown foam insulation.

With considerably increased demand for chilled foods, and new legislation relating to their temperature control during transit, refrigerated vehicles will continue to play a vital role in food distribution.

However, the role of the distribution industry in contributing to ozone depletion must be put into perspective. CFCs are only harmful when they are released into the atmosphere. Therefore safe disposal on 'reefer' decommissioning and leak-proof systems should minimize the adverse impact of CFCs from this source.

It is also important to emphasize that the distribution industry is only one user of CFCs. Other applications are:

- Propellants in aerosols
- Coolants in air conditioning
- Refrigerants, especially in domestic refrigerators
- Blown foam production
- Manufacture of silicon chips
- Solvent production.

HCFCs – a recent invention which claimed to have considerably lower ozone-depleting potential – are now being decried by Friends of the Earth.

'Drop-in' replacements or substitutes are eagerly awaited by users who are reluctant to write off their existing assets. To date, the only true alternative to CFCs is ammonia, used extensively as a cold store refrigerant. Vehicle refrigerants still use CFCs.

Recycling and Waste Reduction

A number of important initiatives are taking place across Europe with regard to recycling and waste reduction – particularly with regard to packaging. Unfortunately, they have developed in a piecemeal fashion, with each country acting autonomously. In some cases government legislation has been applied, in other countries manufacturers have formed alliances to preclude the threat of legislation. The EC is struggling to agree a new directive on packaging waste, while some countries have made remarkable advances. The most ambitious countries, for example, are devising regulations that will compel manufacturers to take back and recycle cars, tyres, batteries and electronic parts in washing machines and computers.[3]

The most advanced initiatives are taking place in Germany, the richest EC country, where a strong green lobby has existed for some time. A key trigger factor was unification, when the former West Germany realized it had inherited one of the most polluted landscapes in Europe – the former East Germany.

A three-phase packaging ordinance is being implemented, designed to reduce household rubbish by 25–30 per cent within four years of the December 1991 start-up. This obliges retailers to take back packaging from consumers, manufacturers to retrieve it from retailers, and packaging companies to take it back from manufacturers. Thus by 1993 the actual containers holding products – even including items such as toothpaste tubes – will be subject to a deposit to encourage recycling. German FMCG manufacturing industry has joined forces to form Duales System Deutschland (DSD) which is funding a joint household collection scheme by means of a levy on the goods, indicated by a green dot.

There are important supply-chain implications to the DSD concept and the German recycling legislation. The cost of retrieving packaging initially, then containers, is prohibitive to small foreign competitors. Recycling economies of scale, together with kerb-side collections, will result in a dramatic increase in transport.

Other countries take a different attitude to reducing waste. Some countries, such as France and Italy, take account of the energy produced during incineration to help achieve target waste reduction levels.

Possibly the most dramatic effects on supply chain management will be felt when automobile recycling takes place. Already 70 per cent of a car is metal and thus theoretically recyclable. In practice, full recycling is only now being introduced, including recycling of all other car components. Special vehicle stripping lines are being developed, with Volkswagen claiming that a worker can strip down a car in 20 minutes. The company also now takes back its cars for recycling, free – initially this applies only to its most recent models, but this will be extended to earlier models.[4]

The Volkswagen disassembly plants which the company aims to license will therefore form another, separate link in the supply chain. BMW plans to set up its first British dismantling operation in the UK from 1993.

Motor cars, by nature of the landfill space they use, are good targets for recycling, but this is now extending to other non-FMCG products. B&Q, the DIY retailer, is experimenting at one British store, taking back half-used cans of paint.

Conclusions

Certain elements of logistics have been addressed in detail, with innovative companies leading the way, such as Exel Logistics where a comprehensive environmental policy is reducing fuel consumption, saving energy, reducing waste and containing and minimizing CFC usage. TNT and Transport Development Group have subsequently launched green policies which concentrate on fuel minimization. However, the impact of such policies will be only modest if manufacturers continue to increase their transport activity by building ever-larger factories. Similarly, the additional transport activity associated with recycling could cancel out the benefits.

With the different European countries pursuing different policies with regards to recycling and waste reductions, it will become increasingly complicated for suppliers to evaluate and enter new markets. Similarly, different technical standards will be required in various countries, for example such as those for parts which can be recycled. This will jeopardize the viability of future pan-European single product factories. Perhaps the only solution will be that adopted by many car manufacturers when California enforced new emission standards – produce to the highest required specification.

The environmental benefits of rail are barely being realized. With the UK arguably being too small to make rail handling economically viable, rail and combined transport accounts for an extremely low and declining proportion of freight. Even on the Continent, where long lengths of haul make rail economically feasible, the differing technical standards of the various nations' railways, lower speeds, poor reliability and inflexibility, make rail an unpopular and declining option. Yet combined transport, offering the flexibility of road with the environmental benefits of rail, could be an attractive option provided these disadvantages are overcome. With the threat of a carbon tax and the introduction of road pricing there is an ever-increasing incentive to take freight off the roads.

Similarly the economics of recycling will change as volume throughput increases. There is a view that recycling is only an intermediate solution to packaging within the supply chain. A better solution is to reduce the amount used. Modular, reusable systems can be reused for up to ten years. The only drawback again is the additional transport which will be incurred in returning the modules to the manufacturer.

A true economic and environmental cost benefit analysis is required to evaluate such developments. By looking at the impact across the whole supply chain, true environmental evaluation can take place. As companies increasingly take an integrated approach to logistics, there is an increasing likelihood that this will happen.

The threat of increasing legislation, imposed by governments or by the EC Commission, which focuses on only one aspect of logistics, thus preventing all those involved across the whole supply chain from acting together to minimize environmental harm, is a real worry.

Summary

- Concern about damage to the environment is growing, and is focused

on a number of areas, including global warming, atmospheric pollution and depletion of the ozone layer
- Companies which voluntarily adopt environmental policies can find these cost effective. Environmental effects are complex, however, and many issues are clouded by controversy
- In the field of transport, technological advances in mechanical efficiency and in utilization have made possible worthwhile financial savings through greater efficiency, helping to conserve energy
- Recycling of obsolescent vehicles and packaging material is another response to demands for environmental sensitivity
- Certain logistics strategies, such as stock reduction programmes, JIT and centralization of inventory have negative environmental implications through their greater demands for transport.

References

[1] CBI estimate
[2] Freight Transport Association (FTA)
[3] Cairncross, F., 'Four corners', *Harvard Business Review*, March–April, 1992.
[4] Cairncross, op. cit.

Chapter 11

Planning the Location of Depots

C D T Watson-Gandy
Director, Burman Associates

Introduction

There are many reasons for making changes to a distribution system, and particularly to the location of depots. Some of the more obvious reasons are:

- The end of a lease
- Changes in the law
- Substantial changes in costs, eg fuel
- The creation of development areas or enterprise zones
- Changes in the transport network, eg new motorways
- The introduction of a new transport system or mode, eg containers, the Channel Tunnel, or intermodal possibilities
- New technology, eg in vehicles or warehousing or information
- More use of third party logistics providers
- Global sourcing and marketing.

But most often the distribution system will simply slip imperceptibly away from the optimum arrangement, as the market and the products change. For instance, an article in *Management Today* has suggested that if a company has not looked at its distribution system for more than four years, it could well be paying 200 per cent more than is necessary.[1] The article was written in 1976 and reflected the fourfold rise in oil prices at that time, so is perhaps a little dramatic. Nevertheless it is always worthwhile making a periodic check on the distribution system, not only to keep a finger on the pulse of that part of the business but also to ensure that the system is serving the needs of the company efficiently.

Considerable work has been done in the area of facility location since the pioneering work of Alfred Weber in 1909. The whole area of distribution was effectively stimulated by Drucker in 1962, when management was made aware of the immense potential for both cost savings and the creation of new business opportunities.[2] Sadly, many companies still have a long way to go in properly grasping these opportunities – perhaps being unaware of the adverse impact that wrongly located facilities, both of production and of warehousing, can have on the marketing opportunities and profits of the company.

This chapter is designed to encourage distribution management to look again, critically, at their distribution systems by describing the more modern approaches to the task. The chapter starts by discussing the total cost concept, which provides an overview of the objective of the task. It then describes some of the factors which affect the choice of depot locations, and finishes with a discussion of the distribution modelling techniques which are used to determine the correct number and location of factories and warehouses – the linchpins of an efficient distribution system.

The Total Cost Concept

It is a truism that we should examine carefully how changes in one part of a system impact on other parts, to the benefit or detriment of the whole. This is particularly true of logistics systems, the economics of which consist of complex and interrelated parts. Too much improvement in one part of the system can often adversely affect other parts. Examples of this happening abound in the literature and in logistics folklore, a classic one being the balance of transport costs from depot to customer. Local distribution costs are inversely related to the number of depots, but the depot costs themselves obviously increase with the increased number of depots. An important step forward in the management of logistics systems was made when it was first appreciated that a balance can be found between these two types of cost, to give an overall cost-effective system.[3] A less obvious example is that improving the speed of delivery of customers can increase sales, but at the expense of increased delivery costs.[4] Savings achieved by being more economical with packaging can lead to serious losses through increased breakages and the consequent loss of customer goodwill. Savings on inventory can lead to unsatisfied customers, but 100 per cent order satisfaction means unacceptably high inventory costs. Furthermore trade-offs of this kind occur not only within the logistics system but also across functional boundaries within the company, and may even transcend company boundaries. Several examples of the different kinds of trade-off are given in Watson-Gandy.[5]

Clearly, then, in examining a logistics system care must be taken not to increase the total costs by optimizing one part of the system in isolation. One must ensure that all the parts of a distribution system (a list of these elements is given in Watson-Gandy[6]) work together to form a cohesive and cost effective whole in conjunction with one's counterparts in other functional areas of the organization. But perhaps even more importantly it is necessary to look backwards and forwards along the supply chain to ensure that any changes made do not adversely affect either the sourcing system or the service provided to customers.

Location Factors

There are many factors which will affect the choice of location for a warehouse. Some of these factors are broad in their effect; that is to say, their consideration will indicate only a general area in which a site should be found. Other factors are more detailed and will point to specific sites. In addition, many of the factors are closely related to the purpose for which the warehouse will be used. This is an area which often deserves close scrutiny in the light of possible alternatives. There are several important factors.

Market Orientation

It is sensible to locate warehouses close to customers, in order to provide a good service to those customers. There are often sound economic reasons to do so, as well. Customer orders are frequently smaller than a lorry-load and are delivered in smaller vehicles which are often more expensive per tonne-kilometre to operate than trunk vehicles. It pays, then, to minimize the workload of those small vehicles by bringing the warehouse closer to the customers.

Production Orientation

A warehouse with this type of orientation usually ships in bulk, ie in lorry or container loads, to retailers, wholesalers, or break-bulk depots as well as to its own distribution depots. This type of warehouse should be located as close to the end of the production line as possible, to minimize the cost of movement between the two points.

The Nature of the Product

The type of products being handled will have a profound effect on the number of warehouses required. If the product is, for example, perishable, then it is important to deliver to the customers as quickly as possible, perhaps within a day. Warehouses facing this sort of delivery constraint will need to be small and numerous. Warehouses serving as common stock rooms for several high street shops are also of this kind. By contrast, warehouses handling consumer durables, where a fast delivery service is unnecessary, can be larger and fewer.

Communications

Present and planned road and rail networks can have a strong locational influence on the warehouse. In particular, the speed with which goods can be delivered in bulk will have a direct bearing on stock-holding. This factor may be critical in just-in-time operations.

Financial Considerations

Development incentive or rate 'holidays' can also influence where a warehouse is sited. However, this type of incentive may only influence the choice of site in a quite localized way.

The Type of Warehouse

In many cases it may be possible to operate the distribution system using either conventional warehouses or highly automated warehouses. The latter are very expensive, which means there must be fewer of them.

Local Considerations

The above six points will influence companies in their choice of area when looking for a suitable site. There are, of course, many more detailed factors which will determine the choice of the actual site to be used:

- Availability of buildings
- Local site values and the attitude of local government towards building development and use
- Availability of labour with the right skills
- Ease of access, and traffic congestion
- Expense of building, including drainage, access to power supplies, etc
- Ancillary services, including the availability of facilities for vehicle repair or the repair of specialized equipment
- Local communications, eg travel facilities for employees.

Modelling the Distribution System

The principal reason for modelling the distribution system is that a company will wish to obtain the best possible guidelines before starting to make expensive changes to the system. It is possible, by building a model of the distribution system, to forecast the effect of alternative changes and scenarios in a series of 'what if?' questions. Hence more thoughtful decisions can be made on the future form of the system and how it can be made to best serve the needs of the company.

The variety of elements that make up a logistics system and the factors which influence the choice of warehouse location combine to present a system which is difficult to model in its entirety. The approach most frequently used, therefore, is to concentrate on the more important strategic decisions, assuming the more tactical variables to be fixed. This is a reasonable approach because, for example, there is little point in collecting information on available plants, depots or sites before it is known where one should be looking. Once some possible locations have been indicated by the model, a check should be carried out to see whether the assumptions made earlier are still valid. Hence an iterative process can, perhaps, be started. The most critical of all strategic decisions is the choice of the number and location of the facilities in the system, and it is here that the most work has been applied.

Facility location models can be characterized by four non-exclusive attributes.

The Objective Function

Depot location models can be divided according to the objective required, particularly with reference to the local distribution costs. The two approaches are called colloquially 'Minisum' and 'Minimax'.

Minisum problems assume that the local distribution costs can be represented by a function of the sum of all the costs of delivering to each customer in turn, and it is this function that is minimized – hence the name. Most distribution systems fall into this category.

Minimax problems appear to be concerned less with the cost of supplying all the customers than ensuring that no customer receives too bad a service. The function that is minimized in this case is the maximum distance to a customer. This type of model is more usually seen in the public domain, with the location of police stations, fire stations, ambulance centres or schools. However, the model can also be of importance in the private sector for the location of maintenance or service centres. For example, expensive, heavy equipment is often sold because the purchaser is assured that, in the event of a breakdown, an engineer can be quickly on the scene to effect repairs.

A further categorization can be made according to whether the distribution system is regarded as a profit or a cost centre; in other words, whether the objective of the model is to maximize profits or to minimize costs. The very great majority of depot-location models are designed to minimize costs. There is one exception, however, and that is where sales depend on the location of the depot. Profit maximization is a more suitable objective here; one such model is described by Watson-Gandy and Dohrn.[7]

The vast majority of the models available examine and optimize on one single objective, be it cost minimization or profit maximization. However, a number of researchers have recognized that the problem of locating facilities has a number of different facets – for example, cost, customer service, risk and environmental impact. These facets are not necessarily measurable in comparable ways, eg money, and the optimum result for each factor is unlikely to be achievable simultaneously in the same site. An analysis of several papers examining multiple objectives is given by Current, Min and Schilling.[8]

The Distribution Plan

Clearly any changes made to the distribution system must be planned to cope with the demands expected when the new system is fully operational. Analysts approach this problem in two different ways, with models which are either 'static' or 'dynamic'.

Static models examine essentially one period of time, like a snapshot, although the period of time is often a whole year. To develop a distribution plan over a longer planning horizon it is necessary to take a series of snapshots and then derive a plan from these afterwards.

Dynamic models examine the whole planning horizon in one go and produce a plan for the complete period. Such a plan might be of the form: close depots in Edinburgh and Rotterdam now; next year open a depot in Bruges; open depots in Milan and Berlin in three years; and close the depot in Rouen in year 5; and so on.

Dynamic models are less commonly used at present, principally because of the increased scale of the problem to be solved. However, with increasing computer power and new methodology, dynamic models will become more common. Of course, regardless of the method used, the plan will still depend on forecasts and must be updated on a regular basis as the information improves. Dynamic models are described by Van Roy and Erlenkotter[9] using mathematical programming, and Frantzeskakis and Watson-Gandy[10] using dynamic programming.

Depot Locations

Depot location models can also be distinguished according to the attitude taken towards the choice of location. The approach may be either 'continuous' or 'discrete'. The continuous models basically assume that a depot may be located anywhere, whereas in discrete models, a list of preselected sites is required from which to choose the best subset to use.

The discrete models were developed in order to incorporate precise costs associated with a specific geographical area, particularly rent, which are otherwise catered for rather imprecisely in continuous models. For discrete models the list of possible sites may be obtained from an estate agent, and will consist only of sites which are known to be suitable for the products to be handled and for which all the costs are also known. This is an attractive argument in favour of discrete models but one which loses strength when it is appreciated that the sites will not necessarily stay vacant while the study is carried out. Both methods, then, are best used with rather broader cost estimates to indicate only where a site should be sought.

Discrete models can handle all transport costs as point-to-point costs because the location of the depot and the customer are known, and this is particularly useful if a haulage contractor is used to move goods. Continuous models, on the other hand, require the transport costs to be calculated as a function of distance. This restriction, however, provides additional flexibility because it is very simple then to cost alternative solutions in a series of 'what if?' questions. Point-to-point costs can become very cumbersome when looking at alternatives.

In some situations, the choice of which approach to use is determined by the requirements of the model. All dynamic models, for example, fall into the discrete category. Otherwise, the best choice may well be the type the analyst feels most at home with.

Discrete algorithms using mathematical programming methods are described by Khumawala using the primal form,[11] and Erlenkotter[12] or Bilde and Krarup[13] who make use of the dual form. The simplest of all continuous models, namely the centre of gravity model, is still advocated by some authors (see Coyle, Bardi and Langley[14]), although the model has serious modelling restrictions – for example, the method locates only one facility and ignores any interaction with other facilities. More complex continuous models are described in detail in Chapters 3 and 4 of Eilon, Watson-Gandy and Christofides.[15]

The Optimizing Process

For all problems – and distribution is no exception – there are two approaches to optimization: 'exact' procedures and 'heuristic' procedures.

Exact solution procedures are defined as those procedures which can be demonstrated as always giving the optimal solution to the problem. Heuristics are essentially rules of thumb, which will usually give a good if not optimal solution. However, counter examples to heuristic procedures can often be found; that is, a problem (perhaps contrived) for which the method will give a clearly bad solution.

Obviously most people would prefer an optimal solution to the depot location problem and this leads to the adoption of an exact procedure. Unfortunately, the choice is not always so straightforward. In terms of discrete location models, the principal technique for obtaining an exact solution is a form of mathematical programming called mixed integer programming. This method requires that the costs be linear, that is, they increase directly with the level of activity. However, in warehousing, for example, there are economies of scale. This can, of course, be usually accommodated by using a piece-wise linear cost curve. But there are often non-linearities in local distribution which are not easily catered for (eg the model may be required to reflect sales declining with distance from the depot). In such cases, mixed integer programming is virtually impossible at present.

The basic question then concerns the degree of accuracy with which one needs to model the distribution system. The answer to that question will lead directly to the choice of an exact or heuristic procedure. A simplified cost model may be used to provide an exact solution, but to optimize accurate representations of most real distribution systems means using an heuristic procedure.

Exact discrete models are given by Khumawala, Erlenkotter, and Bilde and Krarup, as mentioned earlier. For discrete heuristic methods, the 'add' heuristic of Kuehn and Hamburger,[16] and the 'drop' heuristic of Feldman, Lehrer and Ray[17] are still good procedures. It is worthwhile trying both approaches in any problem, as the methods are likely to provide different answers, which could lead to a deeper understanding of the problem. A more consistent discrete heuristic (using consistent in the sense of obtaining optimal or near-optimal solutions more reliably) is described by Captivo.[18] Heuristics for the continuous models are described in Eilon, Watson-Gandy and Christofides.[19] Only very small continuous problems may be solved exactly, unless the problem is subject to a constraint on the maximum distance between customer and depot (see Watson-Gandy[20]).

Modelling Distribution Costs

The different approaches that may be used in depot location studies have been briefly mentioned above. It is useful also to examine the principal costs of a distribution system and to see how they can be represented in the model. The cost elements can be grouped into four main parts which go together to model the whole system. These four costs are the local delivery costs, trunking costs, warehousing and inventory costs. A location study would be incomplete without collecting such cost data. It is, perhaps, important to note here that the data should be collected for at least two time periods. The first period should be the current period. These data are used to validate the model, for it is only with current figures that the accuracy of the predictions from the model can be tested. When the model is considered sufficiently (rather than totally) accurate, the model can be used with the second (and other) set(s) of data to examine the future operations. The second set of data must, therefore, be forecasted data, predicting, as well as is possible, the requirements for the system when it will be in operation. The four types of cost are now examined in turn.

Local Delivery Costing

Technically, this is perhaps the most interesting problem. Eilon, Watson-Gandy and Heilbronn have demonstrated clear causality of transport costs with mileage.[21] Hence the objective is to transform the forecasted market data, available in the form of customer locations and demands, into an estimate of the route mileage required to service those demands. There are currently three different approaches.

The most popular approach is to assume that vehicles visit customers on a there-and-back basis. This is perfectly valid if the number of customers on a trip is small, eg two or three. Alternatively, the customers may be grouped together and the costs estimated from the distance to the group, plus a constant term for travelling within the group. Note, however, that the approach is still valid even if the customers are not grouped, but then the mileage (and the cost) is likely to be an overestimate. The distances involved may be measured as crowflight distances appropriately modified, or taken from a computerized road map, or alternatively great circle distances can be used to give a more accurate measurement in international problems.

A more accurate but cumbersome approach is to use a vehicle scheduling package in a simulation mode. That is to say, it is desired to compare two (or more) possible sites by deriving, using historical customer order data, the routes which would have been run if the alternative sites were actually being used. The routes may then be costed very precisely. The approach does require the collection of a considerable amount of data and is expensive in computer time. Furthermore the method does not predict future costs.

The final approach is to use a function which relates distances between customers and depots to route distances. Such a function is proposed by Christofides (Chapter 8 in Eilon, Watson-Gandy and Christofides[22]). This function is, however, difficult to optimize but has been used successfully to cost alternatives,[23] and some empirical evidence of the accuracy of the function in reality is provided by Stokx and Tilanus.[24] Other functions have been used with some success, but this is an area where further research is needed.

Trunking Costs

Trunking costs are usually conveniently modelled in the same fashion as local distribution costs, and usually in the form of the there-and-back approach mentioned above, as a trunk vehicle seldom visits many depots on one trip. Alternatively, when different modes of transport can be and are used – for example, if owned transport and third party operators are used as and when convenient – then a sample of typical route costs can be subjected to regression analysis to determine a suitable function.

Warehousing Costs

These can also be represented by a function derived from regression analysis using existing costs and throughput. This approach, however, must be used with caution if the existing depots are few in number or the new depots are likely to be operated in a different fashion – for example, if a significant degree of automation is to be incorporated in any new warehouse.

Inventory Costs

The cost of inventory held, although not usually appearing in the distribution manager's budget, is a significant cost borne by the company and must not be forgotten. It is well known that there are economies of scale in inventory – that less inventory needs to be kept in a few large warehouses than in many small warehouses, in order to service the same demand. Usually the inventory cost is catered for by the inclusion of a square root term, in keeping with inventory control theory.

Finally, other relevant data relating to the operation of the system must be considered and collected. These items will include the service policy requirements, the estimated rate of future growth, the product mix and likely changes to that mix, the number of special and emergency deliveries (if only to consider how to reduce them), the cost of overnight stops, whether a haulage contractor is used and when, and many other items which affect or constrain the way the system is operated.

Conclusions

The modelling of a distribution system is taken most seriously when changes are being considered to the system. Several models and approaches have been described to attack the most critical of the planning problems, namely that of determining the number and location of factories and warehouses to meet the future needs of the company's distribution system both economically and efficiently. The models described can be used in a wide variety of situations.

Models are often used to effect one-off changes to the distribution system, and in that they are very effective. The savings achievable by a study of the distribution system are difficult to predict, depending as they do on how uneconomical the current system is – and this cannot be foretold without optimizing the system. Nevertheless, savings of 20 per cent are not uncommon, and indeed savings of the level of the 200 per cent mentioned in the introduction to this chapter are not impossible. These same models can also be usefully employed in an ongoing situation to maintain close control over the system. So once the model has been built, the good distribution manager will continue to use it to keep not only the model up to date, but also his distribution system.

Summary

- Regular modifications to distribution systems are necessary if they are to operate efficiently
- The complexity of logistics systems makes it difficult to achieve improvement in one respect without some undesirable implications in another, through the various trade-offs that occur
- Factors affecting warehouse location include the extent of market or production orientation, the nature of the product, quality of communications, financial considerations, the extent of warehouse automation, as well as local considerations
- There are various modelling techniques available to aid choice of location.

References

[1] Caulkin, P., 'Delivering the goods', *Management Today*, January, 1976, pp. 89–94.

[2] Drucker, P., 'The economy's dark continent', *Fortune*, 72, 1962.

[3] Watson-Gandy, C.D.T., 'The planning and development of warehousing policies', *Freight Management*, June, 1969, pp. 37–41.

[4] Watson-Gandy, C.D.T. and Christofides, N., 'The choice of service level', *Retail and Distribution Management*, 2 (5), 1974, pp. 51–5.

[5] Watson-Gandy, C.D.T., 'Logistics and the supply chain', in *Operational Research Tutorial Papers 1992*, ed. M.E. Mortimer, Operational Research Society, 1992.

[6] Watson-Gandy (1992), op. cit.

[7] Watson- Gandy, C.D.T. and Dohrn, P.J., 'Depot location with van salesmen – a practical approach', *Omega*, 1 (3), 1973, pp. 321–9.

[8] Current, J., Min, H. and Schilling, D., 'Multiobjective analysis of facility location decisions', *European Journal of Operational Research*, 49, 1990, pp. 295–307.

[9] Van Roy, T.J. and Erlenkotter, D., 'A dual-based procedure for dynamic facility location', *Management Science*, 28 (10), 1982, pp. 1091–1105.

[10] Frantzeskakis, M. and Watson-Gandy, C.D.T., 'State space relaxation for the dynamic depot location problem', *Annals of Operational Research*, 18, 1989, pp. 189–211.

[11] Khumawala, B.M., 'An efficient branch and bound algorithm for the warehouse location problem', *Management Science*, 18 (12), 1972, pp. B718–31.

[12] Erlenkotter, D., 'A dual-based procedure for incapacitated facility location', *Operations Research*, 26 (6), 1978, pp. 992–1000.

[13] Bilde, O. and Krarup, J., 'Sharp lower bounds and efficient algorithms for the simple plant location problem', *Annals of Discrete Mathematics*, 1, 1977, pp. 79–97.

[14] Coyle, J.J., Bardi, E.J. and Langley, C.J., *The Management of Business Logistics*, 5th edition, West Publishing Company, 1992.

[15] Eilon, S., Watson-Gandy, C.D.T. and Christofides, N., *Distribution Management – mathematical modelling and practical analysis*, Charles Griffin & Co., London, 1971.

[16] Kuehn, A.A. and Hamburger, M.J., 'A heuristic program for locating warehouses', *Management Science*, 9(4), 1963, pp. 643–66.

[17] Feldman, E., Lehrer, F.A. and Ray, T.L., 'Warehouse location under continuous economies of scale', *Management Science*, 12 (9), 1966, pp. 670–84.

[18] Captivo, M.E., 'Fast primal and dual heuristics for the p-medium location problem', *European Journal of Operational Research*, 52, 1991, pp. 65–74.

[19] Eilon, Watson-Gandy and Christofides, op. cit.

[20] Watson-Gandy, C.D.T., 'The solution of distance constrained mini-sum location problems', *Operations Research*, 33 (4), 1985, pp. 784–802

[21] Eilon, S., Watson-Gandy, C.D.T. and Heilbronn, A., 'A vehicle fleet cost model', *International Journal of Physical Distribution*, 1 (3), 1971, pp. 126–32.

[22] Eilon, Watson-Gandy and Christofides, op. cit.

[23] Watson-Gandy and Dohrn, op. cit.

[24] Stokx, C.F.M. and Tilanus, C.B., 'Deriving route lengths from radial distances', *European Journal of Operational Research*, 50, 1991, pp.22–6.

Chapter 12

Making Warehouses Work More Efficiently

John Oxley
Cranfield Centre for Logistics and Transportation
Cranfield School of Management

Introduction

Effective logistics in business enterprises are vital to success. The cost of logistics operations, and their direct impact on the ability or otherwise to achieve customer service, have made industry internationally aware that the planning and management of logistics must be carried out with the same expertise and professionalism as the other major areas of commercial and industrial management such as production, marketing and finance. Logistics must also integrate into the overall strategy of industrial enterprises. Failure to do so can result in business failure.

More recent issues which are increasingly bearing on the logistics function are quality management, environmental issues including packaging and waste management, and health and safety. These issues also illustrate the need for logistics managers to keep abreast of standards, legislation and codes of practice, not only in their own countries, but also, with the increasing internationalization of trade, in the other countries and markets where they operate. This growth of multinational activities can bring its own problems, an example being the different standard sizes of unit load, especially pallets, used in different European countries which can complicate decisions on warehouse storage and handling equipment sizing for companies trading internationally.[1]

Warehousing is an integral part of the logistics supply chain, and it is important that it be seen as such, and that the planning of warehouse design and operations should be within the overall context and objectives of the total supply chain. Unless this happens, there is the risk of sub-optimizing warehouse operations, at the expense of overall supply chain objectives.

Warehouse Objectives

The objectives of most warehouses will generally include:

- Customer service
  - speed of delivery

  - consistency of delivery
  - completeness and quality of order fulfilment
  - customer/supplier communication, including accurate and timely information about goods and services provided, and flexibility
- Costs controlled and to a budget
- Effective and safe use of resources – people, equipment, building space
- Minimum inventory levels consistent with service
- Control of stocks and movements, with up to the minute information about orders status, stock status and stock location.

An overriding consideration must be that warehouse performance to meet the objectives should be monitored on a routine and regular basis to identify inefficiencies and to maintain required levels of performance.

In addition, there is the requirement to work within the laws, standards, and codes of practice laid down by the relevant bodies on such matters as quality, safety, environment and waste, and good working practice.

Technology in the Warehouse

It is probably not too much to claim that for many years the warehouse function, together with its associated handling systems, were perceived as the bit on the end of production into which finished goods were routed before eventually finding their way to the customer. Significant management resource was not allocated to it, financial and other performance controls were rudimentary or not in place, and the significance of warehousing for customer relations and service was hardly recognized. Only a minimum level of capital was considered to be necessary, and technical development and innovation were slow in coming.

The first industrial powered truck with lift capability, the counterbalanced fork-lift truck, appeared only in the mid-1930s. This enabled more effective use of building height by stacking and ultimately by using racking structures, and it encouraged the concept of load unitization, with standardization of handling and storage equipment, and minimization of movement in warehousing and handling. Subsequent developments of reach trucks, double-reach trucks, high-rack stacker trucks and stacker cranes have refined our ability to use expensive building space more effectively while still retaining easy and rapid movement and access to stock, as have the introduction of mechanized and computer-controlled storage systems such as carousels. The use of automated guided vehicle systems (AGVs), conveyor systems and barcoding techniques has enabled easier movement and movement control to be achieved.

Engineering developments continue to enhance equipment performance, but many current applications are using established types of equipment in increasingly sophisticated ways by building on the opportunities presented by the quick and up-to-the-minute availability of information provided by using computers. An example of this is the sorting of pre-allocated incoming goods as they arrive at a warehouse, using conveyors, followed by direct despatch – in some cases utilizing techniques such as bar coding to identify quickly and accurately the product items as they come into the system. This bypasses the need to stock and subsequently order-pick the pre-allocated goods, greatly increases the speed of throughput from supplier to final end user, reduces the total labour requirement for the operation, and increases the stock-turn.

Information Technology in the Warehouse

Applications such as that just mentioned continue the process of improvement in operating efficiencies by enabling faster movement of goods with less handling, better use of space and other resources, and continuing improvement in cost effectiveness and in customer service.

However, the effectiveness of a warehouse system, of whatever level of technical sophistication, depends totally on the quality of the supporting information and communication systems, and the most technically engineered and advanced system will not be able to work effectively unless driven by a good information system, and that effectively means a computer-based system.

In some industries it is not uncommon for suppliers to guarantee that orders received by, say, 5.00 pm on a particular day will be delivered the following day. This sort of performance is unlikely to be achievable, whatever the level of technical engineering sophistication in the warehousing and handling operations, unless they are supported by the appropriate information system.

It is worth noting that there are two basic types of computer application in warehousing:

- Where the computer handles the warehouse operational information on such things as order processing, stock location, stock rotation, order picking, and load marshalling, as a basis for planning the warehouse operations and optimizing the use of people and equipment, tracking the movement of goods, and ensuring that stock replenishment is carried out to time. The processed information is then communicated by means of radio data communication, visual display units, or computer print-outs to the warehouse staff to implement the planned work.
- Where the computer controls the physical movement of unmanned equipment such as stacker cranes working in high-rise installations. This application usually incorporates the functions described above.

The consequences of inadequate information systems in warehousing can include:

- Delay
- Stock-outs and shortages
- Inaccuracies in order fulfilment, and incomplete orders
- Slow response to customers and inflexibility

Since the warehouse is often the last stage in the supply chain before transport and the customer, these inadequacies can result in poor service, lost sales, and often, lost customers.

Today's business environment encompasses continuing customer demands for better service, including concepts such as just-in-time, for quality, for flexible response to customers' requirements, whilst at the same time reducing total inventory and minimizing logistics costs. There is also increasing scope and opportunity for suppliers to operate more and more widely across international boundaries, but also the need to meet not just national but international competition. To meet these conditions demands, above all else, information systems which are:

- Fast, flexible and with rapid response times
- Accurate
- Up to the minute and therefore probably 'on line'
- Capable of sorting and presenting information where and when it is required.

Speed and Flexibility

Computers are fast and can accept and process large amounts of information, which they make instantly retrievable. Computing speed enables rapid collation and sorting of information into required sequences (eg for stock replenishment, kit marshalling, order picking), and rapid updating and checking of information (eg credit ratings, stock balances, reorder triggers)

Manual systems often require information to be transferred from one document to another, eg from order document to goods received note to stock records to supplier account clearance. This takes clerical effort and time, and introduces potential for error. Because of their capacity and speed, computer-based warehouse management and information systems reduce clerical effort and are much more accurate.

The other side of this is that because computers can handle so much information so quickly, there is a temptation to load more and more work onto the system, to call for more and more routine reports, producing more and more print-outs, which become so bulky and numerous that managers become overloaded and cease to use the resulting information.

Accuracy

Computer systems which reduce clerical effort, cutting out duplication of data logging and the need to transfer information from one document to another, are inherently more accurate than manual systems. The increased accuracy and reliability of such systems (eg for stock and location records) gives more confidence in managing operations, reduces the incidence of mislocated stock, and leads to more accurate and complete order fulfilment.

Research data derived some time ago suggested error rates:

- Written entry: 25,000 per 3,000,000
- Keyboard entry: 10,000 per 3,000,000
- Bar code: 1 per 3,000,000
- Transponders: 0.1 per 3,000,000.

Immediacy of Information

Early IT systems ran on a batch basis and the information, for instance, concerning stock levels, was only updated perhaps once every 24 hours. Consequently the stored information was always, to an extent, out of date. Modern systems tend to be on-line, giving the opportunity of keeping records much more up to the minute, and this is vital when working with minimum stock levels and very fast service and order to delivery times. One company introduced a computer-based paperless system for stock location for incoming pallets, with the objectives of reducing the clerical effort involved in making out two-part pallet tickets and then updating stock records, improving the accuracy of stock location, and increasing the productivity of their fork-lift trucks by enabling more double cycling (return loads). These objectives were achieved, and the virtually instant updating of stock location records (whether any particular pallet location was full or empty) enabled empty locations to be reoccupied much more quickly than with the old system and the company claimed an effective increase of warehouse storage capacity of 5 per cent.

This aspect of getting information into and out of the system as rapidly as possible, and of transmitting information or instructions to operators or other users, is greatly enhanced by the use of techniques such as radio data communication, in which the warehouse computer can 'talk' directly to individual work stations, fork-lift trucks, etc, via a transmitting/receiving base station and remote terminals at the work stations. Similarly, techniques such as bar coding greatly speed up data entry and product and location identification, give much improved accuracy in information handling, and can be used for routeing and tracking the movement of goods through a warehouse. A further benefit of these methods of transmitting information can be the virtual elimination of paper in the warehouse, with operators taking instructions from visual displays, and 'talking' to the warehouse computer by means of a keyboard.

Improved Management Control

Effective management control requires that up-to-date and accurate information is available when needed, so in addition to routine processing of orders, stock levels, picking instructions etc, management and information systems should have the facility to be interrogated to pull out specific required information.

To conclude this section, it is emphasized that, because communication and the use and manipulation of data are so vital, the design of information, management, and control systems must be carried out very thoroughly. Account should be taken of the objectives of the warehouse system (within the overall logistics objectives) and also of the people who will have to run the systems, who should also be trained, or have the appropriate skills to exploit the potential of the installed system.

Warehouse Information and Management Systems

When considering operating efficiency, it is worth noting that, of the total annual cost of running a warehouse, building and building services can account for up to 40 per cent and direct labour up to about 50 per cent, half of this latter being taken up by order-picking staff.[2] Hence working methods which facilitate the effective use of people's time and of building space are likely to have a direct impact on operating efficiency and costs.

The first applications of computer information handling in the warehouse were for stock control and location, leading to greater accuracy, less paperwork and clerical effort, more up-to-date records and faster response times. These have led on to packages for order-processing, tracking the location and movement of goods through a warehouse, for identifying when particular stock items need to be replenished, for maintaining stock rotation or 'sell-by' dates, for routeing and planning of order-picking activities – all designed to minimize work-loads, and to provide up-to-date information on the status of stocks and of orders.

There are now many off-the-shelf computer packages for warehouse management and control, and a number of software houses have their own versions having a variety of features.

Stock Control

- Recording of receipts and confirmation against purchase orders
- Allocation of stocks
- Recording of issues/despatches, proof of delivery
- Maintaining and reporting on stock balances, reorder levels, back orders
- Stock location and location verification
- Batch traceability
- Stock and throughput analysis – Pareto classification
- Interface to mainframe computer, to order processing and sales ledger
- Multi-site and in transit stock.

Warehouse Management

- Selection of optimal locations for stock to comply with pre-determined location rules, eg locate reserve stock as close as possible to the order-picking fixed location; to maintain location by zone
- Location verification (to ensure that a fork truck driver has correctly located a pallet, he records a random check code which is printed on to the location, and the code is correlated by the computer to the actual location code in the data files – if the two match, the correct location has been found)
- Stock rotation, first in first out, maintain sell-by dates
- Replenishment of order-picking stock, based on next day's orders, or by continuous subtraction of goods issued from residual picking stock balances
- Order-picking work-load allocation and routeing to satisfy whatever picking regime is in use. (The author likes the system of a computer picking list printed onto sticky labels. As the picker selects each item from stock, the appropriate label is stuck to it and the picker moves to the next item. When all labels are used up, the pick sequence is complete and any unused labels give automatic indication of shortages, ie items not picked)
- Allocation of tasks to each item of handling equipment
- Reports on productivity and resource utilization measures such as picking rates, daily pallet movements, orders despatched, fork truck utilizations, space utilization, man hours by function/operator
- Wage payment schemes linked to productivity measures

Some of the above features are self-evident and basic requirements of a well-managed warehouse, whether a computer based or a manual system is used. However, there are warehouses which, for example, do not have a location system and rely on operator memory for knowing where stock is located. The risks are obvious, and misplaced stock, which cannot be found when required, can so easily result in an incomplete order, and if this persists, in loss of customers. The author can vividly remember spending one afternoon accompanying an order-picker as he travelled the picking face. On every single order there was at least one item whose nominated location was empty, or which contained the wrong product, and the picker had to return to the office to be redirected to an alternative location – and not all these were correct or had sufficient stock either. This represented wasted time, unnecessary travel, delay in order completion, and some incomplete orders being despatched – and operator frustration. Also, in this case, no attempt had been made to use the available, throughput and order data to design a lay-out for the picking stock which would minimize the order-picker's travel time. In another case seen by the author, the use of throughput data to identify the popular items in a range of paint products enabled a revised lay-out of the product in the picking face which resulted in a reduction in the order picker's travel distances of the order of 40 per cent. In another instance, a food company which implemented a computer system to record stock balances and locations to achieve faster and more accurate information handling, also found that stock write-offs from out-of-date products were significantly reduced.

The potential benefits of effective management and information systems include:

- Accurate stock balance and location records
- Fewer stock-outs
- Stock rotation, meeting sell-by dates
- Accurate knowledge and tighter control of operations
- Better utilization of warehouse space and of storage and handling equipment
- Performance monitoring for operators and for equipment
- Tracking of goods through the system
- Lot and batch traceability
- Less clerical effort.

A final cautionary tale concerns the implementation of systems. A company using on-board terminals to transmit picking instructions – location, product, quantity – to driver/operators on narrow aisle picking cranes, considered, correctly, that it would be technically possible to get the computer to control the crane movement, leaving the operators free to pack, label, and stack the picked goods while the crane moved to the next location. However, it was found that this so de-skilled the job, downgrading the operator's role, that problems of motivation and lack of interest quickly developed, performance fell away, and in the end the task of driving the cranes had to be returned to the operators. One moral of this experience is that it is not good management, nor good human relations, to de-skill jobs to the extent that the operator is being used in a very low-grade role, and further that it is always sound practice to consult with, and get the ideas of the operators and others concerned with an operation before introducing change.

Advanced and Automated Warehouse Systems

The technology of automated warehousing has been with us for about thirty years. Japan has more installations than any other country, followed by the USA, and in Europe the major user is Germany. Such technology can enable very effective use of ground area – automated warehouses tend to be high – they generally require fewer operators than their conventional equivalents, and they lend themselves to 24-hour operation. They also have lower operating costs in terms of heating, lighting and ventilation requirements. They can operate fast, accurately, and are secure.

The other side of the argument is that they tend to have high capital costs, can be inflexible for future change, can be very unforgiving to badly stacked, wrapped or damaged unit loads such as pallets, and require more highly qualified operators. Generally, if things go wrong it is with the computer control systems, and these also can require a long commissioning time.

The main components of automated warehousing systems are:

- Input device
  - — conveyors
  - — automated guided vehicles (AGVs)
- Storage/retrieval machine
  - — stacker cranes
  - — driverless fork lift trucks
  - — in-rack trolleys
- Storage medium
  - — high bay racking
  - — carousels
  - — minitrieve storage
  - — small parts storage racking/shelving
- Output device
  - — conveyors
  - — automated guided vehicles (AGVs)
- Controlling computer.

These components work as an integrated system, controlled by the computer, which monitors the status of the components and issues commands based on decision rules in the control system, on the demands coming into the system, and on feedback signals from the components. The computer also acts as a management information system. Types of automated warehousing include the following:

Automated Storage and Retrieval Systems (ASRS)

- For palletized loads with random access, eg high-bay racked warehouse accessed by stacker cranes
- Block storage for full pallets with internal trolley movement or input and retrieval by controlled overhead crane
- Long load storage using pigeon-hole racking with stacker crane access or longitudinal racking accessed by overhead crane
- Small parts storage systems using carousels or miniload.

Order-Picking Systems, generally for case and small part picking

- Horizontal and vertical carousels. These can be used on manual or on computer control
- Miniload, ie a mini-stacker crane working inside small parts storage shelving
- Automated dispensers with computer-controlled discharge, feeding out to sequentially controlled powered conveyors which ensure order separation on the conveyors, then feed individual orders into empty boxes or cases on a cross conveyor

- Pick-by lights for manual picking, with operators guided by lights which display the required pick quantity at the required picking locations.

Sortation Systems

- Conveyors with diverters and bar code technology for applications such as parcel sortation, for routeing of material to required locations, and for sorting/picking of goods prior to order assembly.

Robotics

- Robotic picking, eg a rail-guided trolley-mounted robot which can pick from either side of an aisle using a vacuum gripper head, with video camera vision guidance
- Auto stacking/destacking of pallet loads to pre-set patterns

When a company decides that it requires in-house warehousing capacity and will have to acquire or build it rather than use third-party distributors, some of the key decisions include location, size/storage capacity, and throughput capacity. The other major issue is the type of technology to use, between the extremes of low-level traditional and flexible systems, probably requiring comparatively little capital but with high operating cost, and high-level technology, probably requiring greater capital, but with low labour and operating costs. This is necessarily a sweeping general view, and every individual case must be evaluated on its own merits, taking account of the particular circumstances that apply.[3]

Warehouse Simulation

Increasing use is being made of the techniques of computer simulation to help determine the suitability of the design and technology to be used in a given warehouse application. The operation of different designs can be simulated to assess the probable operating characteristics, to identify potential constraints and hold-ups, to get a measure of probable working storage and throughput capacities, and of equipment utilizations. 'What if?' questions can be explored and various different operating scenarios tested to define the most suitable design configuration and equipment before finalizing the design and committing capital resources.

The use of visual interactive simulation, using computer graphics to produce a continuous moving representation of the system, provides a useful visual impact and can assist in diagnosing where and why problems or hold-ups occur. It also provides a useful training medium.

Summary

- Planning and design of warehouse systems must be integrated with the overall objectives of the supply chain

- Account must be taken of requirements and constraints of customer service, cost, resource utilization, quality, safety and environment
- The appropriate level of technology to adopt is a key decision and must be backed up by an appropriate information and communication system
- Information technology allows monitoring of performance as well as optimization of customer service and resource utilization
- Logistics managements are required to keep abreast of increasing legislation, standards and codes of practice, from both national and international bodies.

References

[1] Institute of Materials Management Monograph No 3, *The European Pallet Dilemma: Costing the Alternatives*, 1992
[2] Institute of Materials Management Monograph No 1, *Towards More Efficient Order Picking*, 1988
[3] Institute of Materials Management Monograph No 4, to *The Principles of Warehouse Design*, published April 1993

Chapter 13

Distribution Round the Clock*

James Cooper
Director, Cranfield Centre for Logistics and Transportation

and

Geoff Tweddle
Institute for Transport Studies,
University of Leeds

Introduction

In the manufacturing industry, many companies run expensive plants both by day and night. By spreading fixed costs, notably the capital costs of machinery, companies reduce their unit production costs and this helps keep them competitive. The distribution industry is also a user of expensive capital equipment, particularly vehicles. But it is the norm within the industry to use vehicles only during the daytime.

The reason for restricting vehicle use to the daytime is often an obvious one: customers such as high street retailers will only accept deliveries when they are open for business. Yet there are circumstances when vehicles can be scheduled for two, or even three, shifts during a 24-hour period, resulting in reduced costs for the operator.

Multiple shifting is a particularly promising prospect when the operator controls both the origin and destination of goods (eg in an own-account national depot system), or when a substantial number of customers can offer round-the-clock facilities for goods reception (eg continuous process manufacturers). However, in this chapter, the intention is not so much to identify potential opportunities for multiple shifting, but rather to consider the costs and benefits of switching to this type of vehicle operation when the opportunity arises.

The discussion is separated into three parts. Firstly, there is an assessment of the operational benefits that can result from scheduling vehicles at night: multiple shifting will invariably mean operating vehicles through at least part of the night. Secondly, there is an appraisal of the consequences of multiple shifting for the composition and financing of the transport fleet. Thirdly, there is the potential savings in inventory

* This chapter is based upon the results of a research programme which examined the impact of night operations by goods vehicles on distribution operations. The research programme was funded by the Science and Engineering Research Council.

costs. For some companies, this will be the most important consequence of operating vehicles around the clock.

Benefits in Vehicle Operation

If vehicles are double-shifted from, say, 0800–1600 hours and 2200–0600 hours, then drivers on the second shift will enjoy virtually congestion-free conditions on the road.[1] Even end-on double-shifting (eg 0600–1400 hours and 1400–2200 hours) will mean vehicles avoiding some of the high levels of daytime traffic congestion. The absence of congestion can be of potential benefit to companies since reductions in fuel consumption and journey times might be expected.

As part of a Science and Engineering Research Council project on night operations by goods vehicles, the authors carried out a survey of benefits to operators. The general consensus amongst operators taking part in the survey was that greater fuel economy was unlikely to be achieved where motorway running prevailed. But if other inter-urban and urban roads were to be used extensively, then worthwhile savings could be counted upon.

One dairy company, for example, quoted the average figure 7.7 mpg for night deliveries in Central London. Daytime work to the same locations and using the same vehicle would return an average of 6.7 mpg. This would result in an annual saving per vehicle of about £1940, given an annual mileage of 50,000 miles and a bulk diesel price of £2.00 per gallon.

Another company had carried out tests on a double-shifted vehicle to evaluate the benefit of aerodynamic aids fitted to the vehicle. The results of the tests are summarized in Table 13.1.

Table 13.1 shows that the impact of running at night gives benefits in fuel consumption which parallel those resulting from the attachment of aerodynamic aids to the vehicle.

The same company also examined the average speeds recorded by day/night and with/without aerodynamic aids. Table 13.2 summarizes the results.

Again, night-time operation gives a similar range of benefits to the fitting of aerodynamic aids.

Another company had carried out a very detailed monitoring of journey times on two of its regular routes, London to Wiltshire and Northampton to Wiltshire.

The first route, much of which involved use of the M4 motorway,

Table 13.1 *Results of fuel consumption test (miles/gallon)*

	Aerodynamic Aids	
	With	*Without*
Daytime operation	6.70	6.27
Night-time operation	6.97	6.66

Table 13.2 *Results of speed tests (miles/hour)*

	Aerodynamic Aids	
	With	*Without*
Daytime operation	40.05	38.92
Night-time operation	40.56	39.90

showed little difference between day and night average journey times.* Moreover, on the Northampton–Wiltshire cross-country route, night running offered only a small reduction in average journey time. More significantly, perhaps, it was the variance in journey time which was reduced through night running. Table 13.3 summarizes the results of the company tests for the Northampton– Wiltshire route.

For many operators, reduced variance in journey times will be a more compelling reason to adopt night operations than a small reduction in average journey times. This will particularly be true when depots are sited distantly from one another. Here, it may be difficult to keep within drivers' hours limits when daytime variance for journey time is high. Night-time operation, with reduced journey time variance, is a better guarantee for keeping within the regulations.

Fleet Composition and Financing

Fleet size reduction is frequently the major consideration for an operator switching from a single day shift to two or three shifts spread over 24

Table 13.3 *Journey times between Northampton and Wiltshire depots*

a) Northampton to Wiltshire

Shift	*Day*	*Night*	*Saturday*	*Sunday*
Sample size	37.00	93.00	30.00	31.00
Mean (hours)	3.04	3.06	2.79	3.07
Sample Standard Deviation	0.26	0.19	0.23	0.20
Variance	0.07	0.04	0.05	0.04
95% Confidence Interval	2.98–3.08	3.04–3.08	2.75–2.83	3.03–3.11

b) Wiltshire to Northampton

Shift	*Day*	*Night*		*Saturday*	*Sunday*
		Empty	*Loaded*		
Sample size	37.00	93.00	58.00	30.00	31.00
Mean (hours)	3.08	2.99	3.03	2.88	3.05
Sample Standard	0.32	0.18	0.18	0.25	0.29
Deviation Variance	0.10	0.03	0.03	0.06	0.08
95% Confidence Interval	3.03–3.13	2.97–3.01	3.00–3.05	2.83–2.93	3.00–3.10

* Note: the company took care to schedule vehicles so that they did not have to operate in London during peak traffic conditions.

hours. The scale of the fleet size reduction can be considerable. An operator going over to double-shifting, with the work-load evenly split between the shifts, could expect a reduction in the order of 40 per cent. (Because of the intensive use of double-shifted vehicles and the need to provide back-up for fewer vehicles in the event of breakdown or maintenance, it is rare for an operator to halve his fleet.)

The important financial implication of multiple shifting is that less capital will be tied up in the purchase and ownership of vehicles. Intensive working of the vehicles may result in more frequent replacement but, at any one time, there will be a smaller capital commitment to vehicles by the company, giving it the opportunity to invest the capital saved elsewhere within the company. Since a single 38-tonne articulated vehicle can cost about £65,000, the reduction in capital tied up with the vehicle fleet can be considerable.

A smaller fleet will also mean that the operator will need to pay less in Vehicle Excise Duty (VED) and vehicle insurance premiums. At present, the maximum annual VED payable on a 38-tonne articulated vehicle with five axles is £3,100. For the same vehicle, *Commercial Motor* cost table put the annual insurance at £5,500. The operator therefore stands to save about £8,600 for each articulated vehicle that multiple shifting makes redundant.

But not all is gain to the operator. He will need the same number of drivers as before, and those working unsocial hours will have to be paid a premium. If double-shifting means a night shift, for example, drivers on the night shift can command 25 per cent extra on their wages compared with their daytime colleagues. According to the *Commercial Motor* tables, this can mean £4,600 annually for every night driver employed by the operator.

Also, it will often be the case that additional supervision and security will be required as a consequence of night operations. This adds again to the wages bill. Some investment in equipment may also be required (eg further semi-trailers to allow pre-loading for vehicles scheduled at night). Yet, overall, potential savings in operating cost are available from multiple shifting. The following example illustrates the likely scale of savings.

Consider a hypothetical national distribution operation where about 90 trunk movements are required every 24 hours. Two possible options are open to the company:

- Purchase 100 vehicles and operate them on the basis of a single day shift. (The surplus of vehicles over movements reflects the need to have back-up in case of accidents/maintenance.) Renewal of the fleet would take place, say, every five years
- Purchase of 60 vehicles and operate each of them for two shifts per 24 hours. Renewal of the fleet would be every three years, reflecting the higher wear and tear on vehicles working on two shifts.

Let us take first the fixed cost items where there is a readily quantifiable difference in levels of expenditure between single and double-shifting (ie fleet purchase cost, VED, insurance, drivers' wages). (Note: for illustration purposes, drivers' wages are assumed to be paid at the beginning of each year, in line with the other expenditures.) Table 13.4 shows the streams of expenditure that result over a 15-year period.

This stream of expenditures, with different amounts being spent in different years, can best be compared by making two gross present value (GPV) calculations, one for the single-shift and one for the double-shift.[2] GPV is calculated according to the formula:

$$GPV = \sum_{t=o}^{t=n} \frac{A_t}{(1+r)^t}$$

Using a time span from year 0 to year 14, a discount rate of 10 per cent (r = 0.1), and designating the expenditure in any year t as A., this formula gives us:

	GPVss = £20,236,900	(single-shift)
and	GPVds = £17,977,200	(double-shift)
making	GPVss – GPVds = £2,259,700	

Table 13.4 *Differences in expenditure between single and double-shifted vehicle fleets*

	Single shift	*Double shift*	
Year 0	£6,500,000	£3,900,000	vehicles
	£860,000	£516,000	VED/insurance
	0	£207,000	night wage supplement
Year 1	0	0	vehicles
	£860,000	£516,000	VED/insurance
	0	£207,000	night wage supplement
Year 2	0	0	vehicles
	£860,000	£516,000	VED/insurance
	0	£207,000	night wage supplement
Year 3	0	£3,900,000	vehicles
	£860,000	£516,000	VED/insurance
	0	£207,000	night wage supplement
Year 4	0	0	vehicles
	£860,000	£516,000	VED/insurance
	0	£207,000	night wage supplement
Year 5	£6,500,000	0	vehicles
	£860,000	£516,000	VED/insurance
	0	£207,000	night wage supplement
Year 6	0	£3,900,000	vehicles
	£860,000	£516,000	VED/insurance
	0	£207,000	night wage supplement

Table 13.4 *Continued*

	Single shift	*Double shift*	
Year 7	0	0	vehicles
	£860,000	£516,000	VED/insurance
	0	£207,000	night wage supplement
Year 8	0	0	vehicles
	£860,000	£516,000	VED/insurance
	0	£207,000	night wage supplement
Year 9	0	£3,900,000	vehicles
	£860,000	£516,000	VED/insurance
	0	£207,000	night wage supplement
Year 10	£6,500,000	0	vehicles
	£860,000	£516,000	VED/insurance
	0	£207,000	night wage supplement
Year 11	0	0	vehicles
	£860,000	£516,000	VED/insurance
	0	£207,000	night wage supplement
Year 12	0	£3,900,000	vehicles
	£860,000	£516,000	VED/insurance
	0	£207,000	night wage supplement
Year 13	0	0	vehicles
	£860,000	£516,000	VED/insurance
	0	£207,000	night wage supplement
Year 14	0	0	vehicles
	£860,000	£516,000	VED/insurance
	0	£207,000	night wage supplement

This shows that there is a clear financial benefit from double-shifting, according to the assumptions used in the illustration.

However, the importance of the assumptions in determining the scale of the benefit must be acknowledged. Three particular assumptions (which will be interdependent to some extent) are likely to have the greatest impact. These are:

- Frequency of vehicle replacement
- Residual values of vehicles
- Uncertainty over levels of future costs incurred by the company.

For example, it is assumed that *vehicle replacement* is every three years for double-shifted vehicles while single-shifted vehicles are replaced every five years. This replacement cycle is based upon industry observations and it shows that mileage is not the sole criterion used in making replacement decisions: the age of vehicles is a further, important criterion. Yet, even if it is assumed that single-shifted vehicles can be kept for six years, then there are still financial benefits from double-shifting. A recalculation of the above example shows the difference in GPVs between single and double-shifting to be £1.46 million against the earlier £2.26 million.

In the worked example, it is assumed, for simplicity, that *residual values* are the same for double- shifted and single-shifted vehicles at the time of their replacement. Yet, in practice, a three-year-old vehicle will usually be worth more than a five-year-old one when the mileages are similar. The differential may be in the order of £3,000. Reworking the example to take account of differing residual values gives:

	GPVss = £20,236,900	(single-shift)
and	GPVds = £17,606,700	(double-shift)
making	GPVss – GPVds = £2,630,200	

Therefore, if residual values are included in the calculation at different levels for single-shift and double-shift vehicles, the attractiveness of double-shifting is improved, albeit marginally.

The last factor, which might affect the attractiveness of double-shifting, either for better or worse, is *uncertainty*. There may, for example, be some future reason to alter the discount rate. The rate of VED may also change, but in which direction?

Uncertainty on these issues can make companies unwilling to adopt double-shifting solely for the financial benefits which are expected within transport operations: the scale of benefit may not be sufficiently high. Even a saving of £2.26m is only about 11 per cent of total operating costs (expressed as a GPV) spread over a 15-year period. The equivalent percentage for savings of £1.46m is 7 per cent, and this may be too low for companies to consider a major change in operating practice.

However, even at this lower level, double-shifting may still prove to be worthwhile for a company, but only if it looks outside transport for the savings that can result. A particularly promising area for achieving those savings is in inventory management.

Potential Savings in Depot and Inventory Costs

Double-shifting not only reduces transport operating costs, but also gives companies scope for bringing down delivery lead-times. In many cases, overnight delivery effectively reduces lead-time by a full working day compared with single, day shift delivery.

Faster delivery lead-time has important implications for inventory holdings, particularly for carriers of high value products. An example is probably the best way of simply illustrating the point.

Consider, as a starting point, our 100 vehicle company where transport operations are confined to a single, daytime shift. Suppose that the company trades in high value products and the turnover is £1 billion per annum. The company (which we may call PCL Products) turns over its stock ten times a year.

Two other assumptions we need to make are that PCL Products trades on 250 days of the year and an interest rate of 10 per cent applies to its inventory holdings. (Stock interest paid on non-working days is treated here as an unchanging element of company overheads and so is not included in the exercise.)

Two fundamental outcomes of PCL Products' distribution strategy are:

- Average stock in hand is £100,000,000
- Average time in stock for each stock item is 25 days.

If double-shifting allows for a reduction in delivery lead-time of one day, then it follows that the company can benefit through a reduction in its stock in hand. If the average time in stock for each stock item is reduced to 24 days, then the stock in hand becomes:

$$\text{New stock in hand} = 24/25 \times £100{,}000{,}000 = £96{,}000{,}000$$

Clearly PCL Products benefits from being able to reduce its average stock in hand by £4m since the keeping of it no longer has to be financed. On the assumption of a 10 per cent interest rate, the company saves £400,000 per year.

Over 15 years, annual savings on this scale give a GPV of £3.4m, which is rather more than the expected savings in transport operating cost brought by the double-shifting of vehicles (£2.26m or £1.46m, depending on the length of time vehicles are kept, *see* above).

However, the less valuable the stock, the lower the potential for inventory savings. Figure 13.1 illustrates the relationship that would exist between turnover and savings in inventory using the parameters of the above example.

Furthermore, it is interesting to note that the savings in inventory appear to be independent of the number of stock turns. This can be demonstrated using some basic algebra:

Let Annual turnover = T
Annual stock turns per year (working days only) = n
Annual number of working days = W
Rate of interest on stockholding (over working year) = R

then Average time in stock = W/n

and Savings on inventory by reducing delivery time by a full day (S)

$$= \left[T/n - \frac{T/n(W/n - 1)}{W/n}\right] \times R$$

$$= \frac{T \times R}{W} \qquad \text{which is independent of n}$$

There is, however, an important qualification that must be made to savings in inventory resulting from the double-shifting of vehicles. This qualification relates to cash flow.

A company will only achieve the potential savings in inventory cost if

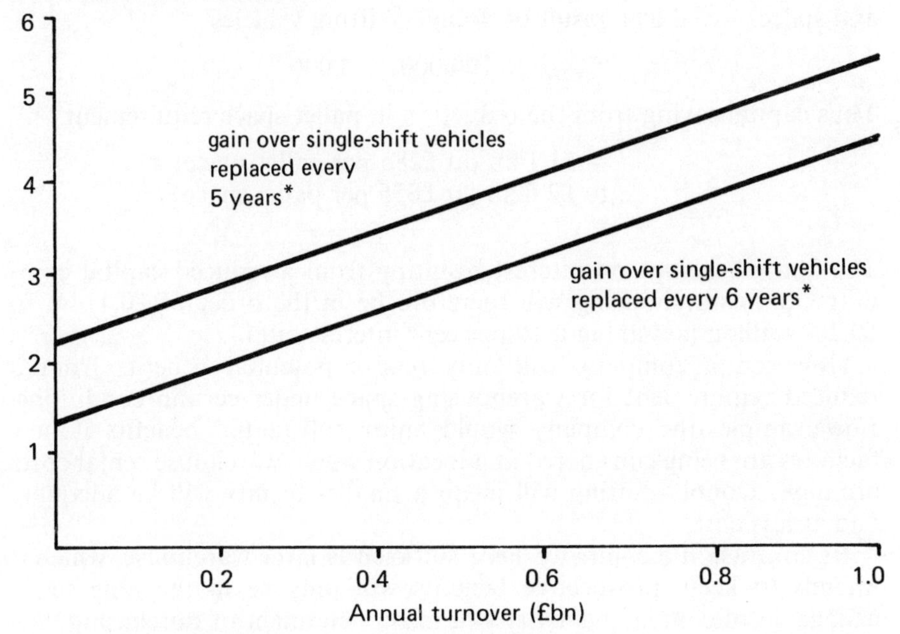

* See text for other assumptions

Figure 13.1 *Savings resulting from the double-shifting of vehicles*

the timing of payments and receipts is kept in line with the reduced time of stockholding. So if the average time of stockholding is reduced by one day, the period of time between paying suppliers and receiving payment from customers for the goods must also be reduced by one day. Any failure to keep cash flow in line with changes in stockholding time will reduce the potential inventory benefits of double-shifting vehicles.

Cash flow control is, therefore, the key to achieving substantial savings and companies should carefully examine their control practices to ensure that the potential benefits of double-shifting are translated into real gains. This examination should, of course, apply no less to internal company transactions than to external relationships with suppliers and customers.

In addition to direct savings in inventory holding resulting from double-shifting, there is also the possibility of achieving savings in storage space. Reduced stock in hand will reduce the average storage space required for stock. In the worked example, the double-shifting allows a $^{1}/_{25}$ reduction in stock.

According to a survey carried out by the Institute of Physical Distribution Management, the capital cost of providing space for storing one pallet is in the range £285–£655.[3] If it is assumed in our example that the average value of stock held on a pallet is £1,000 then

Average number of pallet spaces required for stock in hand

$$= £100m/£1,000 = 100,000$$

and spaces saved as a result of double-shifting vehicles

$$= {}^{1}/_{25} \times 100,000 = 4,000$$

Thus capital saving from the reduction in pallet space requirement

= £1.14m (at £285 per pallet space)
to £2.62m (at £655 per pallet space)

The annual savings on interest resulting from a reduced capital commitment to warehousing will therefore be in the order of £0.114m to £0.262 million (assuming a 10 per cent interest rate).

However, a company will only realize potential benefits from a reduced requirement for warehousing space under certain conditions. For example, the company would enjoy substantial benefits if new facilities are being considered at a location where warehouse rental costs are high. Double-shifting will mean a smaller facility will be adequate and at less cost.

By contrast, if a company has a sufficiently large warehouse, which it intends to keep, prospective benefits will only be in the long term: expansion of company activity can mean deferment of purchasing new warehouse capacity for perhaps a number of years. In the short term, when the double-shifting of vehicles can create even more excess capacity, it could even be argued that costs are increased as the warehouse will be operated even more sub-optimally than before. Clearly any assessment of potential savings in warehouse costs resulting from the double-shifting of vehicles must be undertaken with considerable caution.

On the other hand, in cases where the operations undertaken at small depots can be transferred to larger neighbours with spare capacity, then satellite distribution methods can be introduced. The satellite depot can then be supplied during the night with pre-assembled loads ready for delivery locally.

Drawbar vehicles using demountable bodies are generally accepted as being most suitable for this type of operation. The trunk vehicle can either specialize in feeding the satellite depot both day and night, or be used on delivery rounds during the day. Whether the trunking vehicle is based at the main depot or at the satellite will be determined by the workload which can be achieved in each individual case.

This system not only extends the use of vehicles beyond the day shift, but can eliminate expensive regional depots and reduce inventories. Obviously increased costs at the remaining depots may be incurred, but supplying satellite depots will spread the window for picking and load assembly operations, with possible productivity improvements.[4]

The distance from the main depots to satellites can be relatively short in circumstances where productivity of delivery vehicles is low. An example is that of brewery drays, which spend a considerable amount of time standing outside public houses undertaking delivery and collection work. They also carry a crew of two or possibly three draymen. If a system of feeder services is instigated, one man can carry out the stem of delivery rounds using a vehicle carrying two or three preloaded demountable bodies. Such operations are not new in the brewing industry,[5] but more recently both Whitbread and Joshua Tetley have been undertaking trials of variations on this theme.

Although drawbar operation tends to be favoured for satellite operation, it is perfectly feasible to trunk by articulated vehicle, transhipping the load to a number of delivery vans. However, this usually requires a covered facility, which can be dispensed with when using preassembled loads on demountable bodies. Which method is chosen depends on the merits of each individual case.

Lastly, any analysis of the consequences of introducing multiple shifts for vehicles may need to consider potential benefits outside of distribution. Shorter lead-times, for example, may make the company more competitive in the market-place. It is therefore important to emphasize that *all* the potential benefits should be assessed because trade-offs between different components of business activity are vital considerations. So there could even be an increase in transport operating cost, but this may be more than compensated for by savings in, say, warehousing and inventory or growth in sales. By taking a broader view, more companies could find operating vehicles around the clock an attractive proposition.

Summary

- Benefits in fleet operation can arise when vehicles are run at night as part of a multiple shift system. Worthwhile reductions in fuel consumption can be achieved, together with reduced journey time and journey time variance
- The multiple shifting of vehicles can also bring financial benefits to companies by reducing fleet size, but the magnitude of savings crucially depends on assumptions made with respect to key variables, especially vehicle replacement
- The multiple shifting of vehicles, by reducing delivery lead-time, can bring down stockholding time and cut the size and cost of inventory. In the long run, warehouse capacity can be reduced
- Savings in inventory cost are wholly dependent upon cash flow timing being kept in line with the reduction in delivery lead-time
- The largest inventory savings will be achieved with high value products. Increasing the number of annual stock turns does not improve the inventory savings that can result from the introduction of double-shifted vehicles.
- The number of depots can be minimized by using night trunking to satellite depots, reducing the fixed and operating costs of the distribution system, possibly at the expense of higher transport costs
- The attractiveness of using vehicles around the clock should only be

determined by a comprehensive assessment of a wide range of distribution and non-distribution factors.

References

[1] Tweddle, G. and Cooper, J.C., 'Recent trends in lorry traffic by night', *Traffic Engineering and Control*, **26** (1), January, 1985.
[2] Hawkins, C.J. and Pearce, D.W., *Capital Investment Appraisal*, Macmillan, 1971.
[3] Institute of Physical Distribution Management, *Survey of Distribution Costs*, 1983.
[4] Cooper, J.C., 'Vehicle pre-loading: theory and practice', *International Journal of Physical Distribution and Materials Management*, **13** (3), 1983.
[5] Howell, T., 'Coping with the demands of improving service standards at reducing cost', *Focus*, 5 (4), 1986, pp. 27–36.

Chapter 14

Quick Response: The Road to Lean Logistics

Matthew Walker
Logistics Consulting Services
P-E International

Introduction

The term 'Quick Response' (QR) describes a number of recent developments in the business of logistics. It has specific and general logistics applications and furthermore has implications at both operations level and for company strategy.

Specifically, QR was first used in the fashion apparel sector. Here information technology has been used to improve stock control and service, reduce operational costs and thereby increase profits. For companies like Wal-Mart and Target in the United States QR is fulfilling the logistics ideal of improved service and increased sales with a reduced stock-holding. As Liam Strong, the Chief Executive of Sears plc in the UK, puts it: 'We have already proved we can sell more by stocking less.'[1]

A QR strategy not only enables companies to become logistically more efficient, but also changes the way in which they do business. For example, the faster and more accurate information made possible by QR systems is enabling companies to become much more responsive to fluctuating demand. Previously, such companies bought products speculatively and then tried everything to sell them. As Strong continues, 'It is essential to buy what we sell, not sell what we buy.'

More generally, however, QR can be applied to logistics improvements in a wide range of sectors. These improvements are initiated by investments in inter-company, intra-company and indeed international company information flows. The first key feature of QR is the faster and more accurate transfer of information both within and between all the players in the logistics chain. In all cases, from fashion houses through to food retailers, QR's impact on business has been immense. Recent studies in the US have suggested that not only will the majority of retailers be QR retailers within a few years, but that together they will achieve annual operational savings of US$9.6 billion by implementing these strategies.[2] In the UK, one company, has reduced its stock holding by the equivalent of US$34 million through adopting a QR strategy.

This chapter sets out to describe and explain the current interest in QR strategies and also provides a framework for future logistics developments. The first part of the chapter provides background material into logistical cost analysis and argues that the time has now come for the full implementation of QR. Recent developments in logistics, the costs of operations and the building of the logistics information chain are dealt with, and the speed with which change is taking place is demonstrated. The suggestion is made that traditional logistical systems have concentrated too much upon operational efficiencies in the traditional physical parts of operations such as transport. The QR revolution concentrates on the cost of holding stock and logistics administration.

The second part of this chapter provides a strategic framework for analysis and uses examples to demonstrate the benefits currently being achieved through QR.

Distribution Cost Structures

Logistics operations have always been about cost trade-offs. These trade-offs may be internal, that is within a company, or external, that is between various partners in logistics. But to understand the trade-offs we have to appreciate the costs and cost alternatives. True logistics costs are often difficult to measure, because of imprecise definitions of the logistics chain and the fact that they are incurred by all the players in the chain. The internalized physical distribution costs of individual companies, however, are easier to appreciate and provide a useful starting point for an analysis of the benefits of QR. A variety of recent surveys have shown that these internal distribution costs have been falling for the last decade.[3] The typical range of distribution costs for most companies is between 6 and 9 per cent of sales revenue.

Whilst there are obvious differences caused by product and service characteristics, and some companies may have a cost in excess of 20 per cent of sales, typically a company spends about 7 per cent of its sales revenue on distribution.[4] This cost includes the true full costs of distribution, not just the freight and warehousing (or 'wheels and sheds', as they are referred to by some QR gurus). In addition to these costs there are the costs of inventory control, order processing, the computer and communication costs, distribution administration and customer service. Taken together, these costs are likely to be 7 per cent of sales.

Most companies understand the costs of the physical side of moving goods, namely transport and warehousing, and have concentrated great effort in reducing these costs over the last few years. In future it will most likely be harder to continue to make further reductions; yet few companies fully understand or have explored these other costs.

The cost of holding stock is not usually incurred by the distribution department, but it is an essential cost. A standard pan-European Data base of distribution costs charges inventory at 18 per cent of the value of the average stock-holding. This is typical of the charges many organizations register internally and also reflects the opportunity cost of the capital tied up in stock. The financial cost of inventory in the chain and

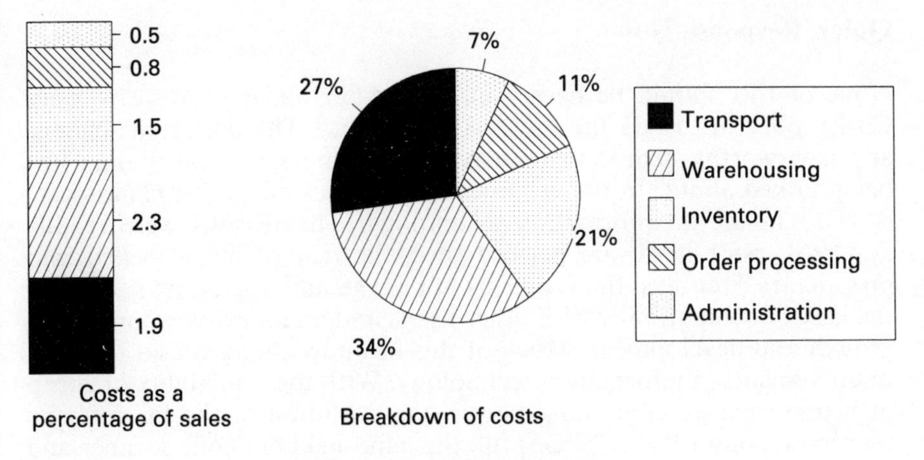

Figure 14.1 *Distribution Costs*

Source: ELC Database

order processing may account for 2 per cent of a manufacturing company's sales revenue. It is therefore clear that inventory and the cost of order processing and support can account for between a quarter and a third of total distribution costs. A typical cost structure is shown in Figure 14.1.

Time-Based Competition

Understanding and addressing these key costs is one factor of concern to management, but so is the need to consider time. There is increased corporate pressure to respond to customer demands faster. Yet many companies underestimate the time taken to process an order internally. A recent study for a leading European manufacturer revealed that the time involved with order capture and processing was five times longer than the finished goods transit time. So reducing both communications and processing time would help meet increased customer requirements.

Traditional distribution cost studies have tended to concentrate on incremental improvements to operational aspects such as transport and warehousing. Over the course of time it becomes increasingly difficult to achieve further significant savings. With mature distribution networks and a free market in transport, companies are looking to other areas of cost for savings. Consequently the impetus will be concentrated in two areas: an examination, firstly, of inventory and order processing policies and costs, and secondly efficiencies in the whole logistics chain, rather than just internal distribution chains. This strategic shift in analysis makes QR, with its emphasis on speed, inventory reduction, information chains and partnerships, the focus of attention and the route to future success.

Quick Response Now

None of this should be news; yet it is. After all, it is 20 years since Christopher described the information chain.[5] The important change and newsworthy item is that today QR is happening, rather than just being talked about. In the seventies and eighties many companies were slow to invest in information technology. The reasons were readily apparent: poor hardware performance, the fear of being locked into proprietary products, the problems of change and upgrading resources, the lack of compatibility with other users, and an inflexible approach to growth and development. Much of this has now changed as a result of improvements in information technology. With the availability of cheap high-performance computing power, the evolution of the PC into the electronic point of sale (EPOS) till, the hand-held bar code scanner and the integrating revolution brought about through 'open systems' and electronic data interchange, the QR revolution has begun.

Quick Response relies upon the creation of an information chain between the manufacturer's 'mill', through distributors and suppliers, to the retailer's 'till'. Elements of this information chain will include universal product coding (UPC), electronic point of sale (EPOS) shop tills, hand-held scanners or bar code readers, electronic data interchange (EDI) networks, forecasting software, agreements on data exchange protocols, the use of value added networks (VANS) and increased information sharing. But QR is not principally about technology *per se*; it is about enhancing logistical performance through the use of this technology. It requires vision and a willingness to change, based upon the creation of a seamless and transparent information chain.

Electronic Point of Sale

This information chain begins at store level, because QR is about creating a demand-driven logistics chain. Here retailers are investing heavily in second- and third-generation electronic point of sale equipment. The rate of EPOS installation in recent years has speeded up immensely. Many companies are now engaged in a four- or five-year rolling programme to invest in EPOS equipment.

In the mid-1980s the Article Numbering Association reported that Boots the Chemist had two stores fitted out with EPOS equipment. These were essentially test-bed operations. By the middle of 1992, all of Boots' stores were fitted with EPOS and they had invested in over 12,000 tills.[6] In the process they have invested over £70 million, with an annual operating cost of £8 million. Yet their director for information services stated that in 1993 these systems would account for £90 million worth of profits.

Electronic Data Interchange

The increase in EPOS tills is matched by growth in the number of companies wishing to use electronic data interchange (EDI). Here, data is moved between one company's computer application and another in an agreed format and usually via a third party. Companies like British Telecom, IBM, Istel and INS are all supplying inter-company links or value added networks. Currently growth in the EDI user base is between 25 and 33 per cent per annum. By 1995, it is estimated that the UK EDI user base will exceed 15,000 companies.[7] For example, ASDA, one of the leading grocery retailers, is committed to a three-year rolling programme to place its top 750 suppliers on EDI, and Tesco, another supermarket chain, recently announced that it already has 1,000 suppliers on EDI.

For some, EDI has become the normal way of life. B&Q, a leading UK home improvement retailer, has imposed EDI as a condition of trading on its suppliers. Toys 'R' Us, the US retailer, with a rapid expansion programme in Europe, has a policy of charging suppliers US$25 every time it has to process a piece of paperwork.

The Long Road to Quick Response

Although the technology for QR is now available, many companies still have a long way to go. Whilst the use of EDI is well known in certain sectors such as the automotive industry and food retailing, some manufacturers appear to be slow to implement EDI. Recent research has shown that over half of manufacturing orders are still received by telephone.[8] Surprisingly, the second most important method remains the postal service, with all its inherent variability in lead time. This is followed by EDI, which today accounts for only 13 per cent of all received orders.

Even those companies that are using EDI are failing to use it to its full potential. A recent survey of the benefits of EDI ranked faster transactions, reduced administration and improved service as the three most important features. Reduced stock levels and partnership development came later.

Clearly EDI is being used to improve existing processes by speeding them up. 'Time', it has been suggested, 'is the next source of competitive advantage'.[9] Food retailers can now place orders and receive deliveries within 16 hours. High street pharmaceutical dispensaries can process orders and receive them in a few hours. This is only possible with EDI.

Saving time is not the only benefit. Cost savings, too, can be substantial. Sears in the US demonstrated that it costs them US$52 to process a paper order and US$5 to process an EDI order.[10] One British company was able to reduce its telephone charges by nearly US$2 million as a result of installing an EDI system.

Given its vast potential, the use of EDI is at present fairly limited. Baker describes the process from simple EDI to Quick Response as a long road, and cites General Motors in the US, who have been using EDI for over 20 years.[11] Currently most companies using EDI have fewer than ten trading partners, and these are usually confined to the companies' immediate suppliers. Only 15 per cent of companies use EDI on an international basis, and at the moment EDI is largely justified only by its reduction in clerical errors and to support administration. Yet EDI visionaries know that it can be used to request information, update prices, book transport services, request a delivery slot at a depot, invoice, transfer funds, offer advice, and answer queries – in fact almost anything that we currently assume has to be done by phone or fax. Yet surprisingly the road down which EDI and EPOS can be used to create lean logistics operations and Quick Response remains largely untrodden.

The full logistical system benefits of reduced stock levels are not yet widely enjoyed, yet they are available. A comparative study of two blue chip UK-based manufacturers, both of which sell similar products to the same customers, demonstrated the clear benefits. One of the companies is an extensive user of EDI and renowned for its use of information technology. The other relies heavily on the telephone and the postal service. The non-EDI user was found to spend twice as much on order processing as the EDI user. The EDI user could control stock levels more efficiently, and the rival was holding twice as much stock as the EDI user. In all, these differences accounted for a cost difference of nearly US$8 million per annum on distribution cost. Figure 14.2 illustrates the typical savings that can be achieved through QR.

The growing use of EPOS sales data to provide more accurate forecasts and the linking of retailers and suppliers will help shorten the road to QR. Quick Response will soon come about, and within the next few years it will change the way many logistics operations are undertaken. However, a key requisite to exploiting the full logistical benefits of EDI will be a new approach to the commercial relationships between many of the players in the logistics chain. As the amount and extent of information flowing electronically between companies grows, so does the trust and desire to undertake other tasks electronically. This often leads to a strategic alliance between the players.

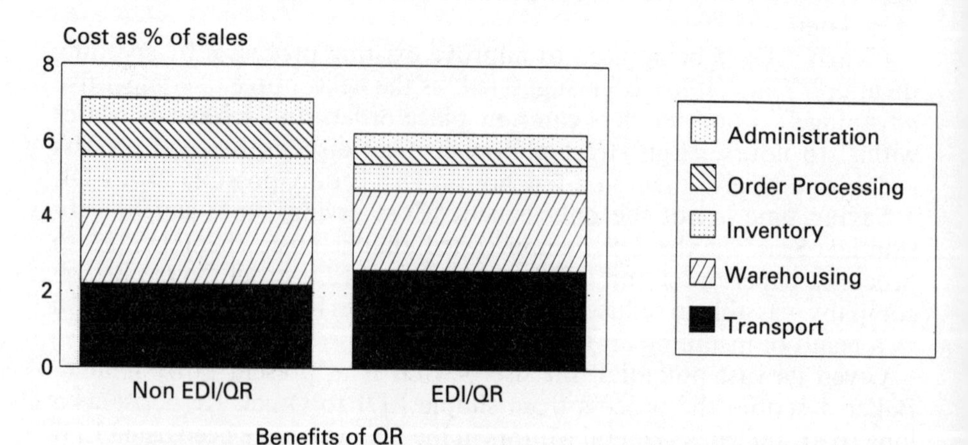

Figure 14.2 *Cost reduction through QR*

Source: P-E International Distribution Cost Database

The Role of The Strategic Alliance in QR

Strategic alliances are typified in the UK by the agreement between the manufacturer Pedigree Pet foods and the retailer Tesco. They can achieve significant benefits. As the jointly produced forecasts get better, so safety stock cover and ultimately cost levels can be reduced. The Pedigree and Tesco partnership led to total stock being reduced by 50,000 cases and produced a cost saving of nearly US$600,000.[12] Between them, the two companies have reduced the average stock holding on certain lines from 1.79 weeks to 1.04, creating a truly lean logistical operation between two players. This stock is therefore turning over 50 times a year. Tesco already have the best stock turnover of any grocery retailer, with an average of 30 turns per year as Figure 14.3 shows. Tesco are one of the few UK companies to have an acknowledged QR programme, and have won a number of awards for their use of information technology.

In the apparel sector the integration of the information chain has provided buyers with more timely and accurate sales details about colour, style and line. This too has led to more accurate forecasting, improved allocation and a better level of sales. The extent of markdowns, the garments that have to be discounted after their selling season, has been reduced by up to a half in some cases. And for these same companies, stock availability has also improved, from 75 per cent to 95 per cent and beyond. So they are selling more while stocking less.

Quick Response builds upon the technology and information supplied by the rapidly expanding EPOS and EDI systems. But QR is more than just operational issues. Quick Response starts at the adoption of automation in the retail supply process and continues through to manufacturing companies. For companies like the jeans manufacturer Levi-Strauss, and General Electric, QR has become a corporate philosophy.

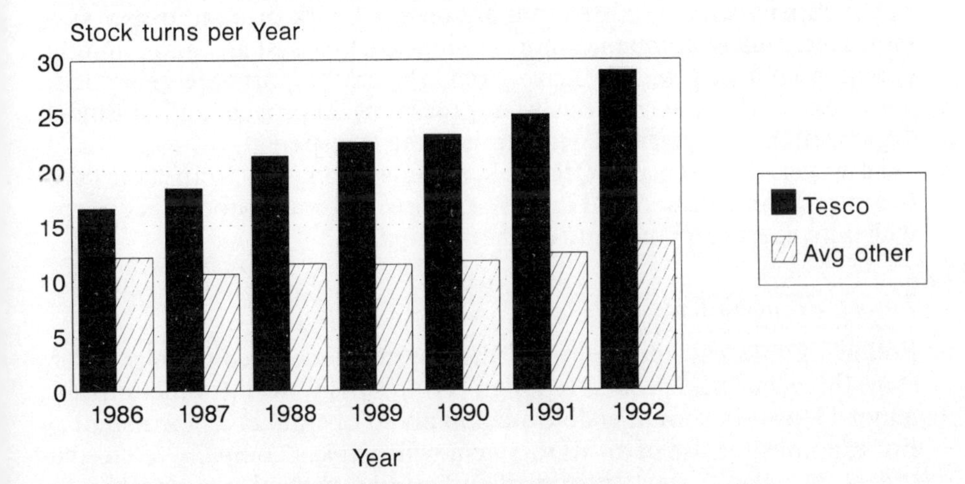

Figure 14.3 *Stock turnover, Tesco plc*

Source: IGD Research Services

Quick Response as a Strategic Weapon

Quick Response is a strategic business opportunity to alter existing business practice. It is best explained by a process highlighted by the Massachusetts Institute of Technology (MIT), which examined corporate response to developments in Information Technology.[13] This study provides a convenient framework with which to examine QR.

MIT put forward a five-stage process by which companies assimilate the consequences and benefits of IT. These stages are:

- The localized exploitation of IT
- The internal integration of IT
- Business process redesign
- Business network redesign
- Business scope redefinition.

These are dealt with in turn.

Localized Exploitation of IT

The first stage of development is described as the localized exploitation of information technology. This involves using information technology to help solve a single logistics business problem. This might be the installation of a warehouse control computer, or perhaps a vehicle routeing program. These stand-alone systems are typical of stage one development being localized and highly focused applications.

Internal Integration of IT

Second stage development is described as the internal integration of information technology. This is perhaps best described as the installation of a company-wide database running on a network or a multi-user system. Here, many companies are moving to open systems and running common company-wide systems from which all reports are generated. As a result the internal business process is improved and business organization and functions start to become transparent.

However, the essence of QR lies in moving a company from stage two, the internal integration of IT, to stage three, business process redesign, which involves reaching out to other companies.

Business Process Redesign

Following internal integration of their systems many companies enter stage three 'business process redesign'. At this point the introduction of a major IT project should enable a company to operate in a new manner. For example, the use of an EDI system will enable a company to receive orders 24 hours a day, instead of just during normal working hours. Many retailers are able to poll or download their orders several times a day. In such cases the order lead time may be reduced to minutes. Such a system has many benefits. It will speed up the order capture because peaking and batch processing can be reduced or eliminated, but it can also help with other matters. Credit-checking procedures can also be simplified and improved as the data does not need to be rekeyed. It remains the case that typically 70 per cent of a company's information is rekeyed by an operator, yet this ordering process is automated, so staff can be redeployed to assist with merchandising and forecasting. Suddenly they are adding value, not cost, and the existing processes have been changed or redesigned. This happened to Wal-Mart in the US, who were able to redeploy 500 staff from administration to sales monitoring and forecasting.[14]

In the US the transparent information link has led to the development of the 'rebuy' function. This process gives the manufacturer the right to trigger store orders of their product without the retailer's direct involvement. Whilst retaining the right of veto, the retailer has given the manufacturer full responsibility for sales of the manufacturer's product. The manufacturer is paid only on recorded sales through the EPOS tills in the store, not on delivery to depot. The roles and responsibilities in the logistics chain have been altered and the business process has been redesigned.

Business Network Redesign

Stage four of the MIT study is described as 'business network redesign'. This refers to the impact on physical distribution or logistical networks. Quick Response programmes in the US have forced manufacturers to restructure their physical distribution operations. Because manufacturers are now required to ship products with shorter notice and in smaller volumes, many of them have found that their existing logistics network and handling procedures could not cope with the change in operational requirements. Companies like Ever Ready have been compelled to redesign their network.[15]

Manufacturers have traditionally shipped stock orders in full truck loads of palletized products to retailers' central warehouses. At these warehouses the retailer might hold four weeks' stock. A Quick Response strategy might require the manufacturer to deliver shop-assembled orders for transhipment at the depot, or increasingly in the US, direct store delivery. Changes in handling techniques are also required and the use of layered pallets of product and slip sheets is increasing. In the UK, consideration is being given to manufacturers supplying retailers with shop-picked goods in the retailer's roll cages. The consequences for both parties are considerable, and there is a trade-off between a reduction in stock-holding and an increase in transport costs.

Within the UK we are starting to see some examples of changes in the role of warehousing. This is indicative of the adoption of Quick Response strategies. There is a clear trend towards the adoption of stockless warehouses, where product is simply transhipped or cross-docked. Many retailers have realized that they have depots designed to hold several weeks' stock, yet with QR their stock levels will drop, and they will have the wrong depot layout.

There is also a revival of interest in automatic sortation systems, particularly by food retailers. Systems like that being used by Stewarts Supermarkets in Northern Ireland will become more popular as a result of QR. Littlewoods, a British retailer, has established wide-ranging EDI links even with their Italian hosiery supplier. As a result of their adoption of QR they had to invest heavily in automatic sortation facilities in their warehouses. Already 80 per cent of their orders are transmitted via EDI, but the demands of QR have meant that they have had to address the problems caused by peaking in the physical distribution system.[16] A traditional warehouse operation would simply have been unable to cope with the peak work loads. Over two-thirds of their product arrives direct from suppliers and is redespatched within a few hours. The solution they have sought is based around technology used in the express parcels sector. They have invested in the automatic sortation equipment that handles 4,000 items per hour. As well as helping them move to QR, the sortation technology has also saved them US$1.5 million per annum.

Primark, another clothes manufacturer, has gone one step further and completely eliminated warehousing from their operation. Orders are collected and consolidated by a third-party transport contractor and delivered directly to the high street; so it is clear that there is also a changing role for third party carriers in meeting the challenges of QR. Certainly there appears to be scope for the increased use of third-party consolidation centres, as stock levels decline and service levels increase.

Business Scope Redefinition

The final development stage is defined as 'business scope redefinition'. SeikoMart are a Japanese convenience food retailer who appreciate the critical role of IT in their company. In fact IT is really their business. They have franchised their outlets so they do not own any shops and they have also contracted out much of their transport to another company, so they neither own nor operate any physical distribution operations. What they do own and operate is the information network. They have transformed themselves from a physical retailing operation to a systems house or network provider, redefining their role in the logistics chain.

The Implications of QR for Logistics

The full benefits of QR are brought about through stages three and four referred to in the MIT study. A QR strategy includes many factors, some of which are internal and some of which are external. For example, a reorientation of company organization and staffing will be required. Information systems and organization must become transparent, and IT skills must be widened, decentralized and spread throughout the business functions. Increasingly the business functions of IT and logistics need to become closer and are often given sole responsibility at board level. And some companies such as Black and Decker have established QR responsibility at board level.

A further impact will be on the staffing of companies. The logistics staff engaged in QR will need new skills and will require to be proactive analysts of information, rather than reactive processors. Increasingly it will be the case that data will be abstracted from the public networks and manipulated into forecasting modules.

Companies must also share sales information with suppliers in order to get more accurate forecasting. They should set up joint working parties to explore this and further opportunities. The MIT study shows that the impact of information technology on companies can be considerable. Information technology enables QR to take place, but to reap the considerable potential benefits of QR, changes in business operations, organization, distribution structures and relationships with other members of the logistics network are essential.

Conclusion

Quick Response can be applied in most sectors and to most products. However, technology aside, the issues are ones of suitability of product and the ability to form partnerships with the other players. QR is about forming an integrated information chain, from 'mill to till'. It involves integrating retailer information chains with distributors and suppliers. Integration of information ensures clearer ordering and stock control, and speeds and smooths the logistical flows. The rewards of QR will be less stock holding, faster ordering and delivery, a reduction in costs, and increased profits.

With this timely and more accurate information, some considerable benefits are available in terms of more accurate stock control and forecasting. Indeed we will rapidly see the introduction of advance shipping notices as warehouses are advised of inbound movements combined with product tracking systems and automatic replenishment systems.

Other improvements to current practice will also come about. These might include EDI invoicing, self-billing procedures, joint forecasting, or even allowing the manufacturer to undertake the rebuy function. Put simply, QR involves changing the way a company undertakes its business. It requires a shift from traditional adversarial roles to a more open partnership arrangement. And the bond in this partnership is the information link.

It is this partnership of supplier, retailer and distribution that will help gain the full benefits of QR by redesigning the way in which business takes place. As a result of implementing QR new operating methods or networks may be necessary. This will enable further benefits to be gained.

As a simple overstatement, the 1980s can be viewed as a decade when companies were encouraged to think about logistics principles. Yet in reality, there was very little work undertaken which we might describe as true or integrated logistics management. This was the case for a number of reasons, such as management structure, economies of scale in production, service considerations, geographical, cross-function and internal political problems, which often prevented full logistical trade-offs being implemented. Yet by far and away the biggest problem was simply the lack of information, without which it was impossible to plan and cost alternative courses of action.

With the completion of the information chain between the players in the logistics chain, true logistics operations will be introduced. The 1990s will be about implementing the new logistics techniques that much of the 1980s was spent discussing. And those logistics techniques and attitudes are called Quick Response.

Summary

- Quick Response has specific and general logistics applications, enabling companies to become logistically more efficient and changing the way in which they do business
- Key features of QR include the faster and more accurate transfer of information within and between partners in the logistics chain
- Areas of potential savings through increased efficiency include inventory control, order processing, distribution administration and customer service. Reduced communications and order-processing time are key areas of competitive advantage
- In recent years there has been heavy retailer investment in electronic point of sale equipment. These companies are increasingly requiring their suppliers to adopt electronic data interchange technology, leading to faster transactions, reduced administration and improved service. Cost savings can be substantial
- EPOS/EDI users have the potential to enjoy substantial logistical system benefits through reduced stock levels. This implies a closer strategic alliance between retailers and manufacturers
- Because QR requires manufacturers to deliver products at shorter notice and in smaller volumes, they are compelled to redesign their logistical networks
- It has been suggested that companies assimilate the benefits of information technology in five stages: localized exploitation, internal integration of IT, business process redesign, business network redesign, and business scope redefinition.

References

[1] Article in *Electronic Trader*, November/December, 1992.
[2] Dolen, P., Grottke, R., Lucker, *Quick Response: A Cost Benefit Analysis*, Arthur Andersen, London, 1990.
[3] Institute of Logistics *Annual Distribution Cost Survey*, 1992.
[4] European Logistics Consultants Distribution Cost Data Base, 1992.
[5] Christopher, M.G., *Total Distribution*, Gower Press, Aldershot, 1971.

[6] Hopwood, D. and Carter, V., 'EPOS and its impact on the retail environment' in *Handbook of Retailing* by A. West (ed.), Gower Press, Aldershot, 1988.
[7] PFA Research Ltd, 'UK state of the nation', *Electronic Trader*, 10, 1992.
[8] Walker, M., 'The distribution implications of quick response', Quick Response Conference, London, 1992.
[9] Stalk, G., Jr. 'The new manufacturing, time the next source of competitive advantage', *Harvard Business Review*, 1991.
[10] 'Quick response, the path to better customer service', *Chain Store Age Executive*, 3, 1991.
[11] Baker, R., *The Long Path to Quick Response*, McGraw-Hill, Maidenhead, 1991.
[12] 'Supply chain partnerships', Institute of Grocery Distribution Annual Conference, 1991.
[13] Morton, S., *The Corporation of the 1990*, Oxford University Press, 1991.
[14] Kramer, S., *Quick Response, An Implementation Guide*, Retail Systems Alert Special Report, Newton, MA, 1990.
[15] Davis, H., 'Quick response now', *Davis Database*, 3, 1992.
[16] Metzgen, F., *Killing the Paper Dragon*, Heinemann, London, 1990.

Chapter 15

Developments and Perspectives of Medium Sized Logistic Service Providers in the Netherlands*

Jos J M Vermunt
Manager of Strategic Innovation, PTT Post

Cees J Ruijgrok
Professor, Tilburg Institute of Advanced Studies, Tilburg University

Introduction

Making choices is an essential aspect of the strategic management of every company. Logistic service providers are no exception to this rule, especially as their environment quickly changes and without adaption to changing circumstances their existence might very well be endangered. Logistic developments are quickly emerging, together with the demand for improved logistic services.[2]

The emergence of logistics in industry and the increasing role it plays inside every firm demonstrate clearly the importance of control of flows as a strategic issue. After a period of steady development, the economic climate in many countries has changed into one of harsh conditions of increased international competition and shrinking opportunities to make profits by developing sales. The need for cost reduction is greater. Shippers, be they industrial firms, wholesalers or retailers, are trying to reduce the cost of the physical circulation of goods. At the same time, they are looking to increase the service levels they are able to give to their customers. They are also trying to offer products and services that are better adapted to the fluctuations and movements of markets, which are themselves diversifying and becoming more fully international. What were once seller's markets are tending to become buyer's markets, with the logical consequence of this being more obvious customer service requirements.

Shippers are reconsidering the entire production and distribution logistic system. Shippers are no longer concerned with providing a transport-only service, but with offering complete logistic solutions. These new concepts include services that were previously considered to be subsidiaries to transport. This trend now affects the whole field of

* This chapter is based heavily on the PhD thesis that Jos Vermunt recently finished,[1] supervised by Cees Ruijgrok.

logistic services; increasingly, long-term logistic partnerships between service providers and their contractors are being formed.[3]

Logistic service providers have to position themselves in the market. They have to develop from being simple operational transportation firms, to fully equipped on-line control companies that deliver extensive logistic services. This requires extensive investment in people, equipment and systems. In some cases the nature of the return on investment is unclear, and the actors have to select the timing and optimal design of these investments quite carefully. The market for logistic services certainly is not a homogeneous one and what is a good strategy for one firm could well prove disastrous for another. For some firms, an ideal strategy would be to focus on a dedicated device to specific clients; for others, more generic services are appropriate.

In this chapter an attempt is made to clarify some of the typologies in logistic service demand that can be distinguished, the associated typologies of logistic services, and the most appropriate strategies that can be distinguished, given the different starting points and associated restrictions on the strategical decision-making of companies. The focus is specific to medium-sized (between 50 and 500 employees) Dutch logistic service providers that deal with general cargo using road transport as their main mode of distribution. Smaller companies are left out of the analysis, because in many cases they are not able to formulate strategic decisions; the few companies that are larger than 500 employees are left out because in general they are conglomerates of smaller companies with the same characteristics as the target group.

Up until now, very little serious research has been undertaken to investigate the strategic developments in this sector, which is considered to be very important to the Dutch economy. Most of the research has been of a general or empirical nature and misses a theoretical background. Consequently, after a brief description of the structure of the Dutch market for logistical services, emphasis is given to a description of logistical concepts considered relevant to likely and strategic decisions in the foreseeable future. Empirical evidence presented in this chapter is heavily based on a survey of 61 logistic service providers which took place in 1990.

The Structure of the Dutch Logistic Service Industry

As in many other countries, the road transport market is largely dominated by small and medium-sized companies. On average, Dutch road transport companies have nine employees. In total, there are about 7,000 road transport companies, of which about 2,500 also operate internationally. The target group on which we have focused (those with between 50 and 500 employees) is much smaller in size (about 250 companies), but we estimate that this group accounts for a 5 billion guilder turnover, thus representing about 45 per cent of the total contribution of Dutch road transport companies to Dutch GNP.

Seventy-five per cent of the turnover from the target group stems from transport-related activities. The rest comes from warehousing and distribution control activities. The share of non-transport activities, however, is quickly growing (70 per cent of the companies experienced an increasing share of non-transport activities in the period 1985–90 and 68 per cent expected a further growth in the period 1990–5). The majority of these companies (77 per cent) expect a considerable growth of their activities in the period 1990–5, notwithstanding low profitability. The mean profitability was around 2.5 per cent in the period 1983–9 and has been decreasing since then.

The profitability of international transport activities was slightly better than this, until recently, and the market share of Dutch transport firms in intracommunity freight transport has been relatively high (the Netherlands is responsible for 36 per cent of international transport within the EC, whereas its GNP is only 5 per cent of the GNP of the EC as a whole). The large majority of companies surveyed expected that the share of international transport in their total revenue would grow in the period 1990–5 to exceed the 60 per cent share for which it accounted in 1985. The Single European Market is seen as both a threat and an opportunity to the strong position of Dutch trucking firms. Only a minority (12 per cent) of the companies expected to maintain their independence in the coming years. The rest saw cooperation or take-over as the only way to survive in the enlarged market with growing competition. Recent years have seen a considerable number of joint ventures and take-overs involving both Dutch and foreign companies.

Concepts Relevant for the Logistic Service Industry

In order to describe strategic developments of logistic service providers, it is useful to explore the typology of the demand and supply side of logistic services. The **elementary functions** of logistic operations (transportation, handling and warehousing) consist of the following activities:

- Stabilization (inventory control)
- Translation (geographical rearranging)
- Transformation (changing the appearance).

An important concept is the **handling unit**. Distinctions can be made between:

- Product units (articles)
- Packing units (box, crate, tray)
- Loading units (pallet, container)
- Transport Units (container, demountable, trailer, wagon)
- Modality units (train, ship, truck-combination).

In Figure 15.1 the functionality of **logistical nodes** (terminals) is set out.

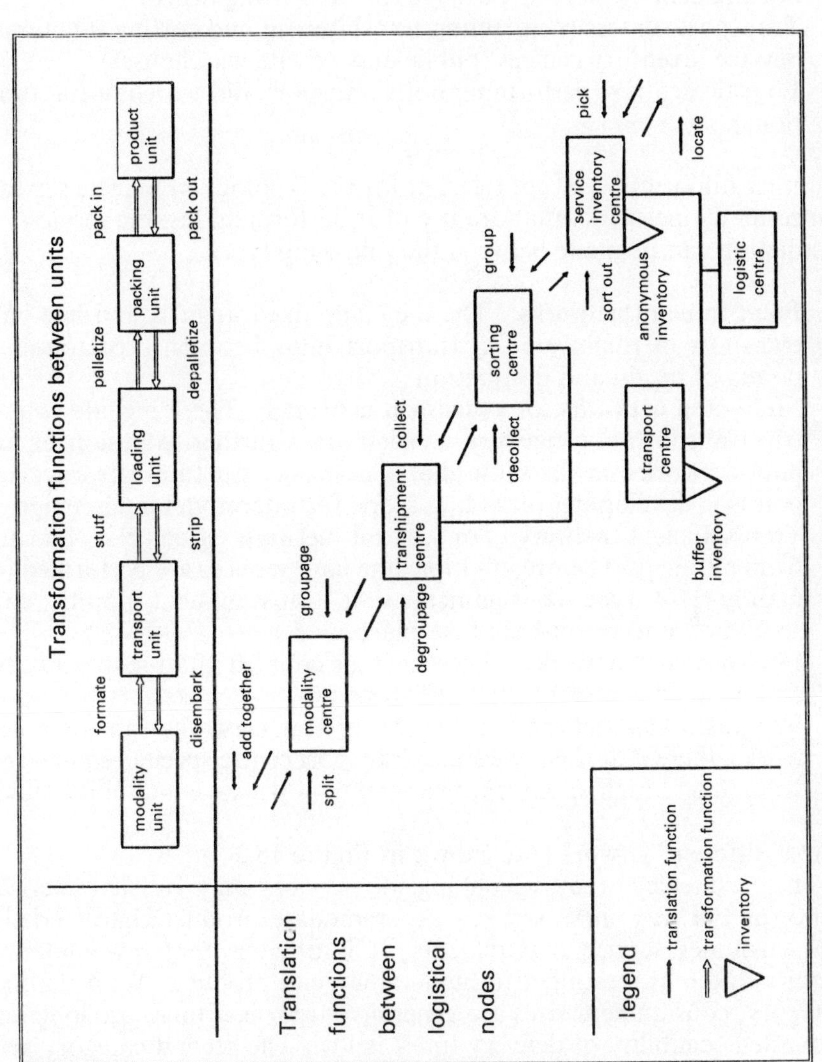

Figure 15.1 *Typology of logistical nodes in relation to their elementary functions*

In these terminals changes of type of handling unit take place. The type of elementary function that is performed there determines the character of this terminal. A distinction is made between:

- Modality centres (such as railway yards and harbours)
- Transhipment centres (stuffing and stripping of containers)
- Sorting centres (sorting packages at the sorting office)
- Transport centres (performing transhipment and sorting functions)
- Service inventory centres (public and private warehouses)
- Logistic centres (performing both transport and warehousing functions).

Another important concept relevant for the typology of logistic services concerns the networks that are used for performing logistic services. A distinction can be made between the following types:

- **Point to point networks** These include fixed, regular and line haul transport of (mainly FTL) transport units between predetermined points of origin and destination
- **Multi-stop networks**, or **round-trip networks** These include round-trip transportation networks, which are a further extension of line haul networks, in the sense that a network structure between fixed points is developing, providing scope for intermodal interchange.
- **Transshipment networks**, or **central network structures** Starting from a transport centre, multiple line haul services are performed for mainly LTL-type consignments. At transshipment points, consolidation and break-bulk take place.
- **Inter-terminal networks** These include coupled multi-stop networks and coupled transshipment networks.
- **Integrated hub and spoke networks**, or **star networks** In these networks, there is at least one super transport centre specialized in large-volume and high-speed transshipments of package and unit loads.

These different networks are shown in Figure 15.2

The next element by which logistic services may be characterized concerns the way these services accommodate product characteristics and customer service requirements. It is obvious that raw materials require different treatment to high-valued end products. With the first category, consignment sizes are generally large, lead times are long and requested reliability of delivery times is low. The second category generally has small consignment sizes, short lead times and high reliability requirements. These characteristics have a strong influence on the type of distribution channel chosen, and this of course is reflected in the type of network used. Raw materials are often transported with low frequencies, directly from producer to customer. End products usually pass one or several nodes in a logistical network before they reach the final customer. It depends upon the 'push' or 'pull' character of the logistical flow whether or not the character of these nodes takes the form of a depot

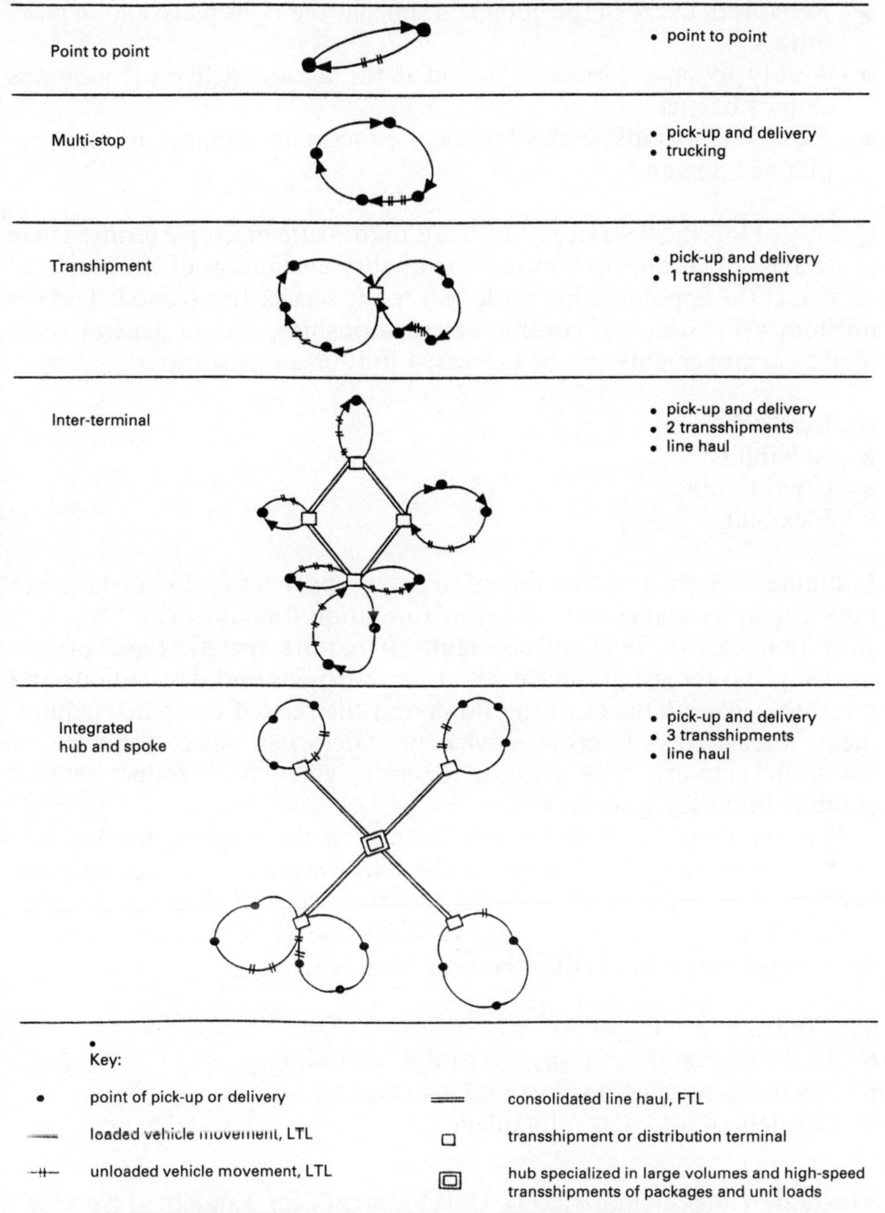

Figure 15.2 *Different types of transport networks*

Source: OECD, *Advanced Logistics and Road Freight Transport*, Paris, 1992

with unlabelled inventories, or transshipment points where inventories only fulfil a buffer function.

It is also clear that improved reliability can in general only be achieved using advanced logistical information systems, especially if there is a large level of variation in logistical requirements.[4] Important elements in logistical control include:

- Reliable delivery of the goods (in time, at the right place and in good order)
- Ability to take corrective action if the agreed delivery conditions cannot be met
- Flexibility to adjust the logistical process to changes of the pre-planned demand.

Quality of logistical services is difficult to measure in simple terms. There is always a relationship between the quality evaluation of the logistical service at the appointments made before the service has started. There is an immense variety of contractual relationships, but in general these quality arrangements can be expressed in four dimensions:[5]

- Lead time
- Reliability
- Conditioning
- Flexibility.

In Figure 15.3, the functionality of road transport networks in relation to the elementary translation and transformation functions is shown. It is clear that specific types of consignment require specific types of networks, given the geographical structure of origins and destinations and given the characteristics of the flows and the related customer requirements themselves. Logistic service providers can select the type of transport network they want to operate, given the product market combination they want to serve.

This typology bears some resemblance to the product market segmentation developed by Cooper in the Eurofret study.[6] He distinguishes between the responsibility of the logistical control function (haulier versus client) and the specificity of facilities reserved for special clients or for general purpose. He differentiates between:

- Contract hire transport
- Dedicated contract transport and distribution
- Shared contract transport and distribution
- Specialized and general haulage.

Strategic Choices and Likely Developments for Logistical Service Providers

According to classical theory of firm behaviour, in general three types of choices are defined for companies that wish to adapt their product market combinations in reaction to external developments.[7]

- **Vertical integration** This means the combination of adjacent activities in the production process from raw material to end products

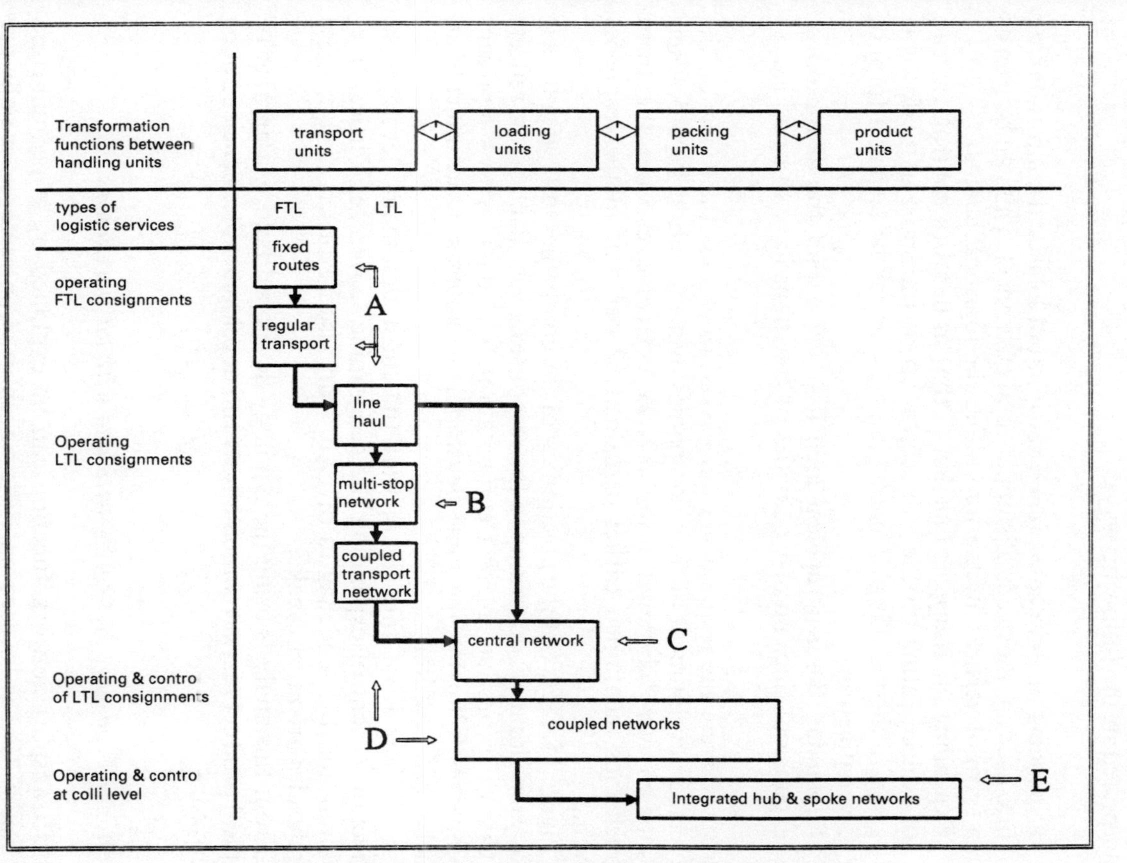

Figure 15.3 *Typology of road-related logistic services*

- **Diversification** The incorporation of new activities that have no direct relation with the present core business
- **Expansion** The expansion of the activities of the company in terms of market share or turnover, within the present activity pattern.

For the logistical service providers, these main strategy directions can be interpreted in the following ways:

- **Expanding the warehouse function** to that of logistical control, taking into account the needs of shippers and customers. This can be seen as a form of vertical integration (along the logistical chains)
- **Expanding the transport function** to that of network control. Instead of concentrating on the transportation of transport units, focus is given to the handling of loading units. This can be seen as a form of diversification
- **Expanding the geographical area** fits well within the definition of expansion, since no new activities or functions have to be added.

In our survey, the respondents were asked to express their view on the expected development of their companies over the period 1990–5. Their responses were clustered using ANOVA techniques, and the three dimensions mentioned earlier explained 52 per cent of the responses given.

Figure 15.4 sets out the positioning of the companies in 1990 and their likely development according to the responses given. Each arrow reflects a change in product–market combination. The thick arrows represent companies following the same development patterns. Dots indicate an unchanged position.

It is clear from this figure that the most dominant development direction is that of expanding the geographic[4] coverage. Vertical integration and the tendency to diversify can also be observed, but these tendencies are much weaker.

From this analysis using the typology developed before, a number of typical product market combinations and development tendencies can be derived.

National Transport Networks, with and without warehouses

This transport network function can be exploited by a medium-sized company that is focused on FTL transport. Contractors normally are producers or large wholesalers based in the Netherlands. There is a tendency for the shippers to want to outsource their warehousing, and thus to shed some of their overheads. In general, the logistical control function is still in the hands of the shipper. The marketing effort of these companies relies strongly on achieving a favourable price-performance ratio.

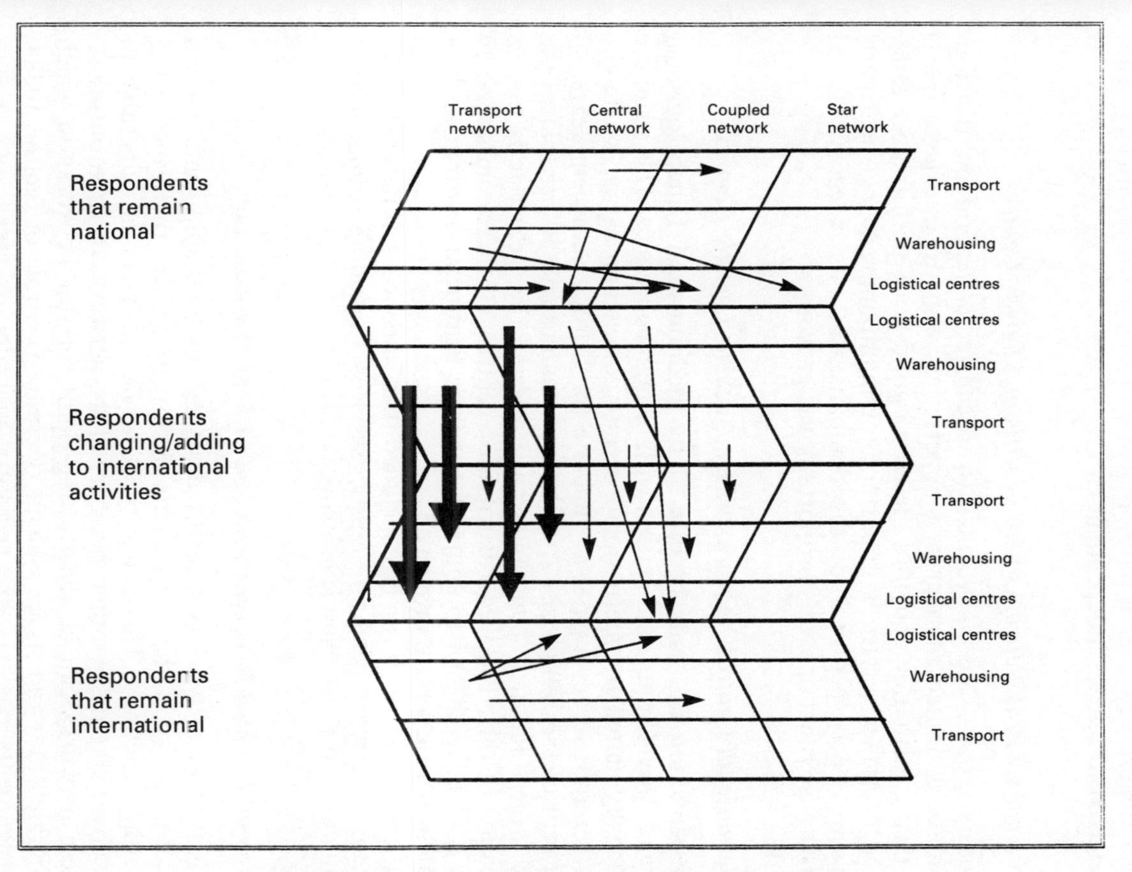

Figure 15.4 *Positioning and prospects of respondents*

International transport networks with or without warehousing

This category is a logical extension of the first category. The main difference is the inclusion of the concept of multimodality. A possible development from this position would be to develop an international coupled network. Only a minority (20 per cent) of the respondents within this category saw such a development as realistic for themselves. They preferred to remain independent.

National Central Networks with or without Logistic Centres

This category is especially suited to specialized collection and distribution for a limited number of shippers that want to outsource (part) of their distribution activities. Besides a good price–performance ratio, good customer service is important for maintaining a logistical partnership. Forty per cent of the companies in this category offered warehouse functions; this proportion was growing.

International Central Networks with or without Logistic Centres

This function can only be offered by medium-sized Dutch logistical service providers in combination with foreign colleagues. This structure is ideally suited to international or intercontinental flows, where the Netherlands serves a gateway function for Europe. In recent years, 40 per cent of the 500 largest American companies and 30 per cent of the 300 largest Japanese companies have selected the Netherlands for the location of their European distribution centres. Of these companies, 39 per cent have chosen to contract out their European distribution to a Dutch logistic service provider.[8]

From the survey it can be concluded that 50 per cent of the companies in this category perform logistic services (including administrative control), and their share is growing.

National Coupled Networks with and without Warehousing

This type of network is specially designed for LTL shipments. Only a small minority of the respondents in this group also performed warehousing functions. This category of service provider is vulnerable to take-over activity by other members of the network, or from outsiders. These networks can be the starting point for star networks in which integrated hub and spoke systems operate. As a rule of thumb, 10,000 consignments per day are necessary in order to make such a step profitable.

International Coupled Networks

This is an extension of the above category. The combination with warehouse function hardly exists.

National Star Networks with or without Warehousing

The medium-sized Dutch service provider will be too small to perform this function independently. In reality, only three or four Dutch companies are able to maintain such networks (PTT, VGL, NPD). This market segment is characterized by heavy investments in terminals and information systems. In order to maintain partnership relations with large clients, innovation in advanced logistical information systems is a prerequisite to remaining competitive.

International Star Networks with and without Warehousing

This category is the big brother of the above category; only internationally active integrators can offer such a service. The role of medium-sized Dutch service providers is limited to that of subcontracting.

Conclusions

With regard to the formation of logistical and transport networks, the Dutch market of road freight operators and logistic service providers is rather well developed. Their position in the international market is strong only in transport networks.

It is anticipated that competition, both within the Netherlands and with foreign companies, will intensify. A growing percentage of companies is expecting a take-over or a joint venture in the near future. The alternative for survival is cooperation. One third of our respondents saw this as a realistic alternative, partnership with a shipper being the most popular cooperation envisaged. Cooperation with colleagues was seen as a less favourable option, because of the lack of trust in each other and the fear that it might lead to a take-over.

The majority of respondents expect that the large companies and networks will expand their activities, and that the role of most of the medium-sized companies will be downgraded to that of subcontractor.

The importance of external logistic relations will continue to grow; it is also likely that independent departments of large shippers (producers and also wholesalers) will enter this market and try to develop their own profit centres.

Summary

- Shippers are under pressure to reconsider their entire logistics systems and to offer their customers complete logistic solutions. Their share of non-transport activities is growing
- Increasingly, long-term partnerships between service providers and their contractors are being formed
- The Single European Market is seen as both a threat and an opportunity by Dutch transport firms. Most anticipate joint venture or take-over as being the only way to survive in the enlarged market

- Different types of transport networks can be identified, depending on factors such as product characteristics and customer requirements
- A variety of strategic choices confronts providers of logistics services: expanding the warehouse function, expanding the transport function or expanding the geographical area of operation.

References

[1] A.J.M. Vermunt 'Wegen naar logistieke dienstverlening' ('Ways to logistical services'), PhD thesis, Tilburg University.
[2] OECD, *Advanced Logistics and Road Freight Transport*, Paris, 1992.
[3] La Londe, B., and Cooper, M.C., 'Partnerships in providing customer service: a third-party perspective', Report prepared for the Council of Logistics Management, Oak Brook, Il., 1989.
[4] OECD, op. cit.
[5] De Leijer, H., Janssen, B. and Ruijgrok, C., 'Loper: an instrument to measure logistical performance', paper presented at the WCTR, Lyon, 1992.
[6] Cooper, J., Browne, M. and Peters, M., *European Logistics, Markets, Management and Strategy*, Blackwell Business, Oxford, 1991.
[7] Breukink, H., *Verkenning van ondernemingsgrenzen*, ('Exploration of boundaries for corporations'), Tilburg University Press, 1992.
[8] NDL, *The Netherlands: Europe's Distribution Centre*, NDL, The Hague, 1990.

Chapter 16

Effective Inventory Management

C D J Waters
Faculty of Management,
University of Calgary

Introduction

Inventory control is one of the most common problems faced by managers. It tends to be viewed as a modern problem, but in reality it has been around for a long time.

Over time, views of stock-holdings have changed considerably. The main objective of inventory managers now is to minimize stock levels, while maintaining an acceptable level of service. A huge effort has gone into solving this problem. Much early work was theoretical, but technological advances have now made it possible to implement many of the findings. We might expect to find, therefore, that aggregate stock levels have been declining. This chapter looks for evidence to see if this has happened.

There is evidence to suggest that inventory control is generally improving. Aggregate stock levels in most industrialized countries have followed a similar pattern. In this chapter we select one country, the United Kingdom, to illustrate specific trends, and then do some international comparisons which show that these are common to a range of countries.

Changing Views of Inventory

It seems reasonable to suggest that the effectiveness of inventory control can be judged by how well it achieves its objectives. We should start by discussing what these objectives are, and by noting how they have changed over time.

Problems of inventory control have been around for a very long time. The need to collect food when it is readily available and then store it for times of shortage is, perhaps, the oldest inventory problem, one which confronts almost every living creature. The implicit objective of this problem is to have as big a store of food as possible, as those with the largest stocks have the highest chance of surviving during periods of food shortage. This view, that high stock are beneficial, has been applied to all types of goods. For most of history, accumulating possessions at times when they are not needed has been a measure of personal and collective wealth.

High stock levels are sensible when supply or distribution of goods is uncertain. During the nineteenth century, however, supply and distribution became more organized and, provided a stable monetary system was in place, third parties could be entrusted to hold enough stock to moderate the tensions between variable demand and uncertain supply. These intermediate stock-holders removed the need to buy goods when they were available, rather than when they were actually wanted. The resulting stability allowed a change of view, so that inventories became expensive and needed formal planning.

The importance of this change was recognized with the growth of manufacturing at the end of the last century. Much of this industry used large-scale batch production, so that stocks of various kinds became inevitable. Scientific inventory control was developed to regulate these stocks by determining 'optimal' stock levels which minimized associated costs. One recurring difficulty, however, is to get agreement about what is meant by 'optimal'. Harris is often credited with the derivation of the economic order quantity formula in 1915,[1] and this gives one view of an optimal stock policy. Equivalent results were developed independently by many others, and by 1931 Raymond was able to write the first reasonable book on inventory control.[2]

Sometimes the distinction between minimizing costs and minimizing stocks was not appreciated, and during the 1920s many companies reduced stocks to levels which made it impossible to operate effectively. For some time it was felt that a fixed accelerator might be used to define an optimal stock level as some fixed proportion of sales.[3] This approach proved unworkable, however, and a flexible accelerator was suggested to allow for time delays, random effects, differences between aims and actualities, and so on.[4] This also proved to be of limited practical value.

More recently, industry has moved to the view that stocks are inherently wasteful. A number of control methods, including dependent demand inventory systems, have been developed with the aim of reducing stocks. Material requirement planning, for example, links stocks directly to planned production, while just-in-time systems can work with almost no stocks at all. The objective of these approaches is normally to minimize stocks, while maintaining an acceptable service.

This brief review has shown how opinions on stocks have changed over time. For most of history, stocks were seen as beneficial, and they were kept as high as possible. From the end of the nineteenth century they came to be considered expensive, so controls were developed to ensure 'optimal levels' which minimized costs. More recently, stocks have come to be considered inherently wasteful, and controls have been developed to minimize them. We should now check to see if the available controls are actually working and achieving this goal.

Achieving Low Stock Levels

Organizations may have a clear objective of minimizing stock levels, but this can be difficult to achieve in practice. Until the 1960s, most inventories were controlled manually, and it was difficult to store and process all the information needed for effective control. When computers appeared they revolutionized the area, and within a few years 90 per cent of stocks had some element of computerization. It now became possible to apply in practice the controls which in earlier years had only been theoretical proposals.

Computers also encouraged the development of new models and methods for inventory control. Less directly, they allowed changes in the operations for which stock is maintained. Automated production, for example, can ensure items of consistently high quality, thereby reducing the need for safety stock to cover for defects. Flexible manufacturing systems can significantly reduce lead times and, when linked with high quality and steady demand, can allow just-in-time systems which virtually eliminate working stocks.

The following list contains developments which have allowed stock levels to be controlled more effectively:

- Widespread use of computerized inventory control systems
- Availability of better models to represent real problems
- Development of models for an increasing range of problems
- Reliable and timely data from improved management information systems
- Improved forecasting methods
- More educated workforce, aware of stock-holding costs and the need to control them
- Integration and automation of many operations (in flexible manufacturing systems, computer integrated manufacturing, and so on)
- Growth of materials requirement planning and extensions (such as MRP II)
- Emphasis on quality, which is lowering the need for stocks to cover for defects
- Reduced lead times
- Growth of just-in-time systems.

Whenever there is uncertainty in operations or lack of control, organizations tend to be cautious and hold more stock than is necessary. Only when an effective control mechanism is in place can they reduce stocks and remove the extra cushion of safety. The ability to control stocks has clearly been rising. This, together with an objective of reducing stocks, should give a general reduction of stock levels. We could hypothesize, then, that from the 1920s onwards, and particularly since the widespread use of computers in the 1960s, inventory control procedures would steadily improve and there would be consistent reduction in stock.

Many companies have significantly reduced their inventories, but a broad picture of the effectiveness of stock control can only be found by looking at a national scale. Then a useful measure would compare the aggregate national stock to the overall economic activity of the country.

To be specific, we could measure the ratio of aggregate stock to gross domestic product.

Because it is easy to move goods and information between countries, we would expect to see similar patterns in any industrialized country. Initially it is easier to look at figures for one country, and then to compare these with other countries. In the first instance, then, we will describe figures for the United Kingdom, which has a history of publishing reliable statistics. Later in the chapter we will confirm that similar results could be found for other countries.

Aggregate Stock Levels in the United Kingdom

Figure 16.1 shows the book value of aggregate stocks held in the United Kingdom as a percentage of GDP from 1949 to 1991.[5]

Considerable care is taken by the British authorities in compiling these statistics. They are, however, open to misinterpretation and should be used with care, particularly noting all the conventions used. Notwithstanding this warning, there is a clear underlying pattern to the figures. At the end of the 1940s and into the early 1950s there was a rapid decline in stocks, which can be attributed to the economy returning to normal after the Second World War. From the early 1950s to the early 1970s there was a further steady decline, which is evidence of improving inventory control. In the early 1970s, however, there was a sudden change of pattern. This was caused by the rapid increase of oil prices and the economic disruption which followed. At this time, costs of raw

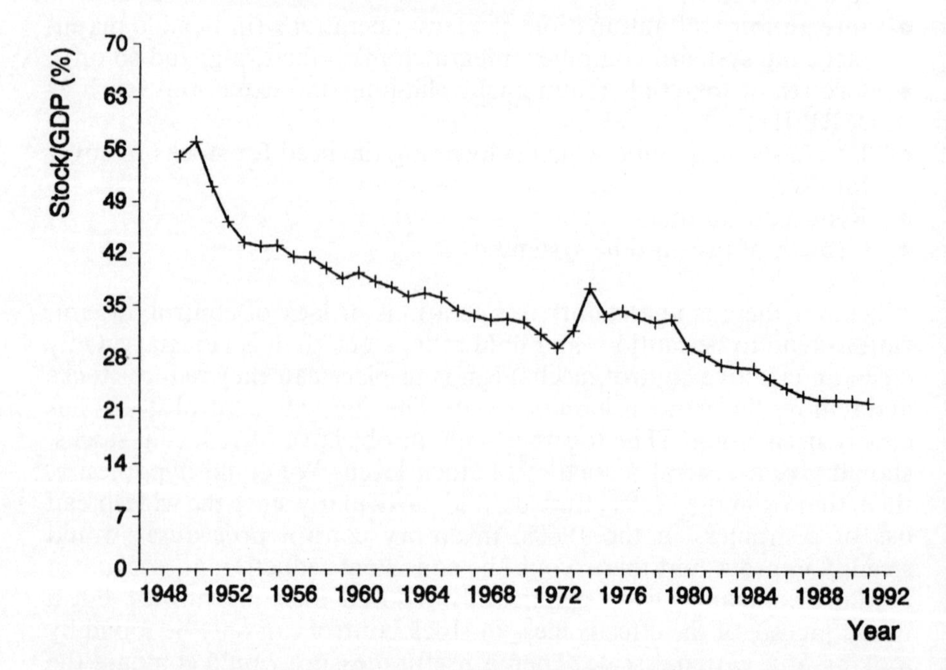

Figure 16.1 *Aggressive stock as a percentage of GDP in the UK from 1949 to 1991*

materials rose sharply and there were frequent shortages, while declining sales left finished goods unsold. This meant that rational policies were often rejected; in particular, raw materials were hoarded, to allow uninterrupted operations. This sudden discontinuity must, however, be considered a short-term fluctuation on an underlying downward trend, which resumed throughout the 1980s. In the past few years there seems to have been a slight levelling of the graph, and this is presumably a reflection of the substantial economic depression affecting the UK in the early 1990s.

In general, then, the ratio of aggregate stock to GDP follows the downward trend expected, but there are a number of short-term fluctuations superimposed on the trend. These result from wider economic influences, over which individual organizations have no control. It is often suggested that these fluctuations are related to the general business cycle. A precise relationship between stocks and business cycles has not been found, and there is a widespread belief that each business cycle is in some way unique. Nonetheless, business cycles and stock levels do seem closely related, and in particular inventory levels, as one of the easiest factors to change, tend to fluctuate more than the business cycle itself.

The underlying downward trend seems to give strong evidence that stocks are declining as a result of improved inventory control. There are, however, a number of other reasons which could be suggested. It might be, for example, that the structure of industry has been changing, and as a higher proportion of the GDP now comes from services, so the amount of stock needed has been declining. A range of other economic factors might also have an effect on UK stock levels, including:

- Consolidated membership of the European Community, including controls imposed by the Exchange Rate Mechanism
- Following a period of rapid expansion in the 1960s, GDP rose very slowly or even declined during the 1970s and again at the end of the 1980s
- The contribution of manufacturing to GDP continues a steady decline
- The contributions of the service sector and oil-related industries have grown in relation to GDP
- Governmental policies have had widespread effects (on, for example, inflation, unemployment rates, government spending and interest rates).

If true, arguments which suggest that changes in stock levels simply reflect changing circumstances are cause for some concern. The implication is that changes are essentially reactive and *ad hoc*, and are not necessarily the result of improved control procedures or more rigorous planning. In that event, British industry might not be improving its competitiveness, but rather continuing with existing practices.

Such possibilities certainly contain some element of truth, and a full explanation for reducing stock levels would probably include a combination of many factors. However, our initial view that inventory control policies are steadily improving still seems valid and gives a reasonable explanation for observed patterns. We can examine this view in more detail by looking at one sector of the economy.

Stock-Holdings of Manufacturing Industry

The proportion of stocks held by different industries has changed considerably over time. In 1965, for example, agriculture and forestry accounted for 15 per cent of aggregate stocks, but by 1990 this had declined to 3 per cent. Conversely, over the same period, stocks in the construction industry have risen from almost nothing to 11 per cent of the total. The 1990 aggregate stocks in the UK are classified in Table 16.1, while Figure 16.2 shows how some of these have changed since 1965.[6,7] Values are in current prices, so the rising value of stocks is caused partly by increased quantities and partly by higher prices.

Manufacturing is a key sector of industrialized economies. Although it accounts for only 20 per cent of GDP in the UK, it holds over 40 per cent of aggregate stocks. This pattern is found in most industrialized countries as their economies progress beyond manufacturing and towards service industries. Because of their large stock-holdings, much work in inventory control has been aimed at manufacturers. This would seem an important sector of industry to look at in more detail.

Although manufacturers are the dominant stock holders, Table 16.2 shows that the proportion of stock held has declined steadily. This is partly explained by the following contribution of manufacturing to GDP, but it is probably true to say that inventory control has improved more in manufacturing than in other sectors of the economy

If we now break down the classification of manufacturing stocks into raw materials, work in progress and finished goods, the changes in the proportions of each might be useful in indicating whether stock changes have been planned (resulting from long-term strategic plans and improved inventory control) or have just happened (short-term

Table 16.1 *Classification of stocks in the UK*

Industry	*Stock-holdings (£ million)*	*Percentage of aggregate stock*
Agriculture and forestry	3,692	3.0
Extraction (minerals, oil, gas)	204	0.2
All other energy and water	4,969	4.0
Manufacturing	52,650	42.4
Construction	13,730	11.1
Wholesale and distribution	21,854	17.6
Retail and repairs	21,255	17.1
Other industry	5,372	4.3
Central government	490	0.4
Total	124,216	100.0

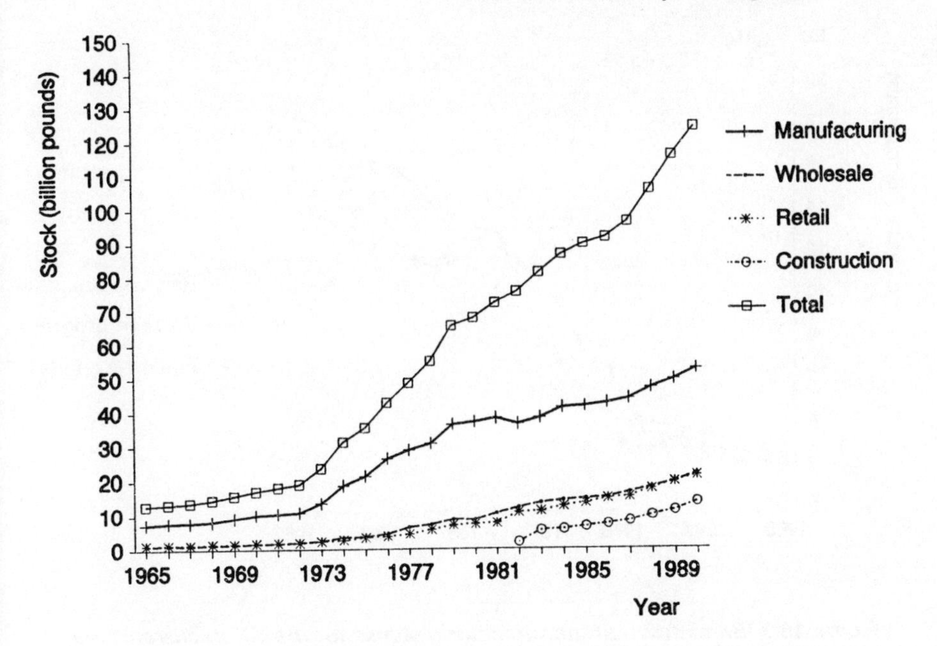

Figure 16.2 *Breakdown of aggregate stock by industry*

responses to economic factors and market forces). One view suggests that stocks of raw materials, for example, should decline with planned changes, but increase if responding to deteriorating market conditions. Similarly, work in progress should decline if production is carefully planned, or increase if a consequence of significantly slowed production rates. Figure 16.3 shows how these stock levels have changed in recent years.[8,9]

The three components of stock follow similar patterns. Stocks of raw materials show a slight decline relative to the others and this is consistent with manufacturers exerting better control over those stocks which are most easily handled. Then in the early 1970s there are sudden jumps in all stocks, particularly raw materials. This was caused by the economic disruption which encouraged manufacturers to hoard available materials and thus ensure continued production. High stocks were also encouraged to some extent by inflation rates at that time of well over 20 per cent a year.

The next obvious feature starts in the late 1970s and lasts for a decade, during which stocks, again led by raw materials, showed a decline. There

Table 16.2 *Proportion of aggregate UK stock held by manufacturing industry*

Year	*1979*	*1980*	*1981*	*1982*	*1983*	*1984*	*1985*	*1986*	*1987*	*1988*	*1989*	*1990*
% of aggregate stock	55.5	54.6	52.9	48.4	47.2	46.9	46.5	46.5	45.6	44.5	42.7	42.4

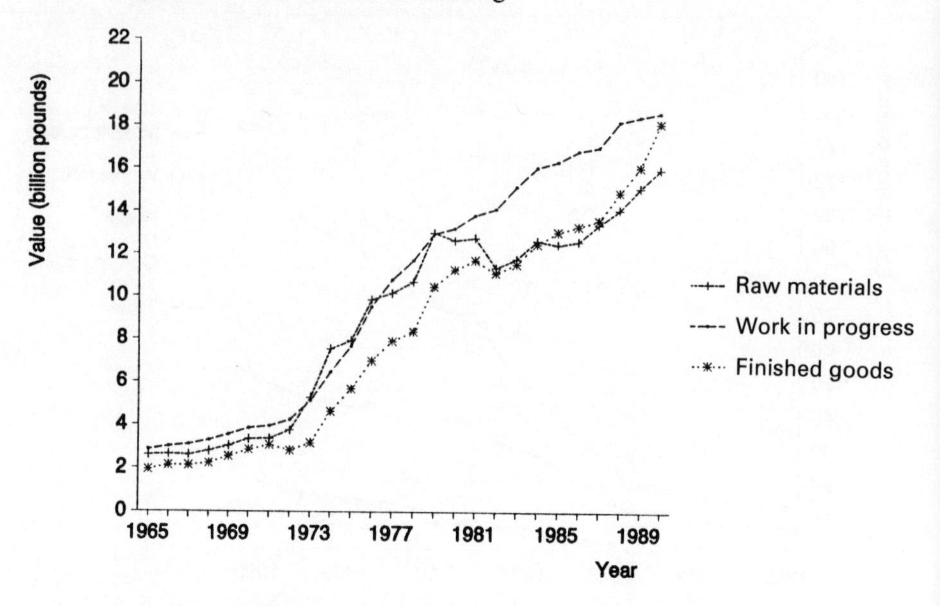

Figure 16.3 *Breakdown of manufacturing stocks for the UK in current prices*

are no obvious economic changes to explain this, and the results are strong evidence of improved inventory management. More recently the stocks of raw materials have stayed relatively low, stocks of work in progress seem to have been levelling out, and stocks of finished goods are rising. The first two of these can be seen as signs of improving control, while it seems likely that competition has increased the need to provide customer service and hence hold larger stocks of finished goods. Unfortunately, it might also be argued that higher stocks of finished goods indicate an economy which is slowing down and leaving its finished goods unsold.

Some of these patterns become clearer if inflation is discounted, so Figure 16.4 shows the same results in constant 1965 pounds.

Overall, there is strong evidence to suggest that inventory control has improved. There is a clear reduction in aggregate stocks, and moves towards comparatively lower stocks of raw materials and higher stocks of finished goods. This may not be conclusive, but the argument certainly seems convincing.

International Comparisons of Stock-Holdings

So far we have illustrated the pattern of stock-holdings in industrialized countries by reference to the UK. The patterns seen in other countries will, with minor variations, be similar, so we could probably have used any industrialized country. This can be demonstrated by making some direct international comparisons.

It must be emphasized that international comparisons of this kind are extremely difficult. Required information is often not available, or is in

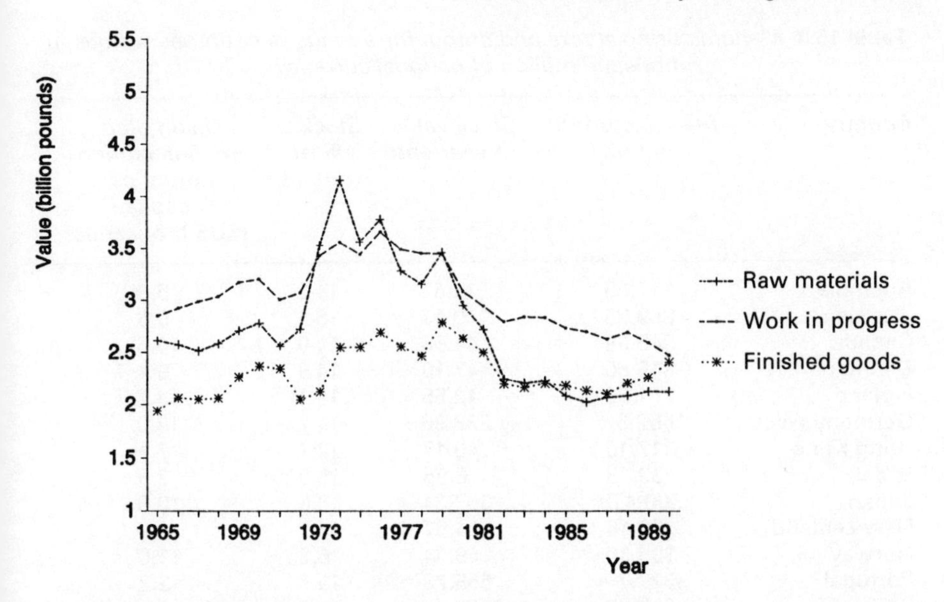

Figure 16.4 *Breakdown of manufacturing stocks for the UK in 1965 pounds*

the wrong form. More frequently, apparently useful information is available, but when examined in detail it is found to be strictly non-comparable. When, for example, we look at the stocks held by manufacturing industry we find that countries define 'manufacturing industry' differently; some exclude small companies, others include mining but exclude electricity generation, and so on. Even basic figures like GDP may not be comparable as they may be based on different accounting conventions to value outputs (which might be at factor value, present value, discounted real value), or may include only manufacturing industry, exclude primary industries, include investment income from overseas, be seasonally adjusted, be income- or expenditure-based, and so on.

Figures from different national publications would not give reliable comparisons, but international bodies collect more useful data. The United Nations, Organization for Economic Cooperation and Development and the International Monetary Fund present information which should be reasonably consistent. They use standard conventions which should be applied to each country's figures, but even so the results must be viewed with caution. Another obvious drawback in using these sources is the time taken to collate and analyse returns; the results may be several years out of date before they are published.

We can start by confirming that UK aggregate stocks of manufacturing industry, at about 17 per cent of output, are typical of industrialized countries. The United Nations and World Bank give the figures in Table 16.3 for a range of countries.[10,11]

Considering the diversity of the countries listed, there is a surprising similarity in the amount of stock held. The mean is 15.2 per cent of GDP,

Table 16.3 *Manufacturing stocks and output for a range of countries (values in thousand million of national currency)*

Country	*Manufacturing output*	*Stock value at year-end*	*Stock as % of output*	*Estimated manufacturing output per capita ($US thousands)*
Australia	117.39	16.67	14.2	5.3
Austria	869.35	140.17	16.1	9.6
Canada	345.99	41.58	12.0	10.5
Denmark	315.80	47.16	14.9	9.4
Finland	281.50	42.55	15.1	13.7
Germany (West)	1652.6	233.96	14.2	18.0
Hong Kong	317.10	40.17	12.7	7.1
Israel	33.13	6.05	18.3	3.8
Japan	300,418	25,831	8.6	18.6
New Zealand	36.16	4.87	13.5	6.9
Norway	305.10	49.34	16.2	11.0
Portugal	3327.7	655.28	19.7	2.2
Spain	22,500	3153.7	14.0	5.4
Sweden	560.87	102.74	18.3	11.0
Turkey	70,164	11,005	15.7	0.6
UK	285.12	49.37	17.3	8.3
USA	2781.0	379.76	13.7	11.2
Venezuela	757.66	144.24	19.0	0.9

with a range from 8.6 per cent to 19.7 per cent. These differences seem small enough to be explained by random fluctuations and differences in conventions used to compile the statistics. A closer look, however, shows that Japan, which has a history of innovative and efficient inventory control, has low stocks, while Portugal, which does not have such a history, has relatively high stocks. Moreover, those countries with strong economies (such as West Germany, USA and Hong Kong) generally seem to perform better than those with weaker economies (such as Venezuela and Turkey). This view is confirmed when a regression is drawn between the value of stock as a percentage of output and the estimated manufacturing output per capita. The coefficient of correlation is 0.58, showing that 33 per cent of the variation is explained by the regression. In other words, those countries with higher manufacturing output per capita seem to control their stocks more efficiently. This does not, of course, mean that one effect causes the other, but the relationship between two measures of economic performance is interesting.

Now we can take a sample of countries and confirm that their aggregate stocks have fallen over time. The United Nations collects these figures, so if we concentrate on the G7 countries, only France and Italy do not supply enough information. Figure 16.5 shows the ratio of manufacturing stock to output for the remaining five countries. All five countries follow a generally declining pattern, but this is most obvious in the UK and least obvious in the USA.

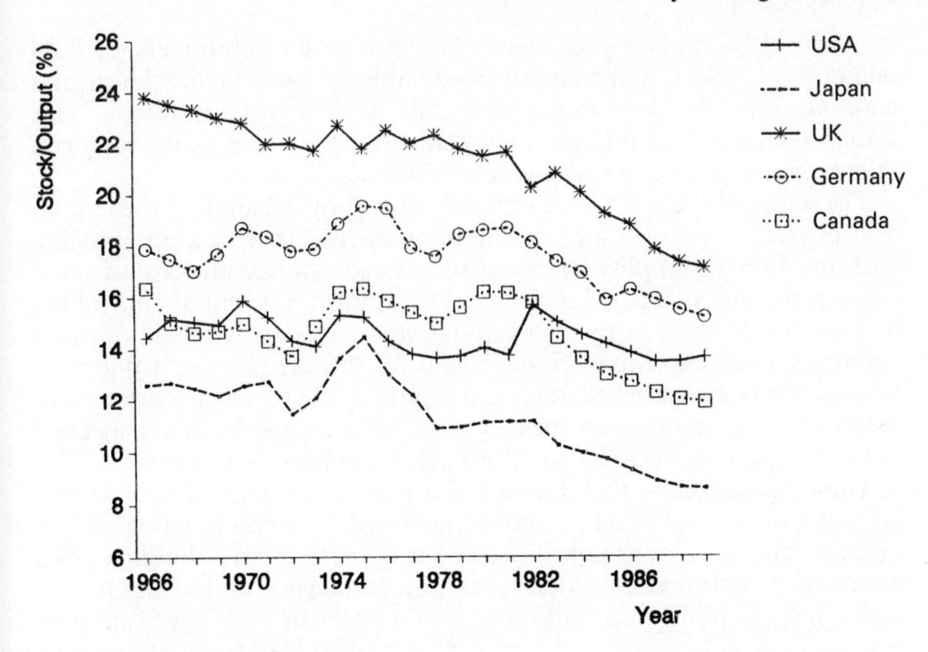

Figure 16.5 *Ratio of manufacturing stocks to output (%)*

There are several possible reactions by countries with relatively high stocks. The first is to suggest that the figures are not sufficiently reliable to allow valid comparison. There is some basis for this view, but international agencies like the UN do attempt to validate data and the figures represent the best evidence available. Another reaction is that variations are simply a consequence of the current stage of industrialization and outside influences: over time, most countries are improving their inventory control, and those countries which are currently lagging will catch up in the future. This complacent view may be over-optimistic and, of course, it ignores the likely continued improvements in countries which are already performing well.

Another reaction would be to suggest that aggregate stock levels are not important. This view is considered in the following section.

Stock Levels and International Competitiveness

Excess stocks are wasteful. They tie up capital, increase costs unnecessarily, reduce profitability, and, in a wider context, have a marked effect on national economies.[12,13] We have already seen this to some extent, where there was a positive correlation between manufacturing stocks and output per capita. Now we can see if there are other relationships.

Surveys[14,15] suggest that annual stock-holding costs, excluding finance, are typically about 17 per cent of value held. Assuming borrowing by manufacturing companies costs somewhat more than bank base rate, then average stock-holdings will cost between 25 per cent and

35 per cent of value a year. This may be a major component of final selling price, and if some countries are able to reduce stock levels and maintain services, they would obviously have a cost advantage. This should increase their international competitiveness and in the long run take business from countries with higher stock levels.

The scope of these effects can be illustrated by calculating the overall cost of stock-holdings in a sample of countries. If we assume holding costs are 17 per cent plus finance costs, we can estimate the cost of stock holding per unit of sales. Japan seems to be most efficient at controlling its inventories, so we can then estimate the cost disadvantage of other countries relative to Japan. Some results for this are given in Table 16.4. In practice, actual interest rates paid by manufacturers are difficult to determine, and change very quickly. For this comparison an average real bank interest rate over the past four years has been estimated.

These figures show that Japan has a price advantage of several percentage points over other countries, achieved by a combination of low interest rates and low stock levels. To suggest that stock-holding costs alone affect national competitiveness, or are even a major factor, is a gross over-simplification. Differences of 1 per cent and 2 per cent here are probably not enough to be important when added to all other costs, and would hardly be enough to affect national economic performance. Nonetheless, such variations could indicate more widespread effects which together measure the efficiency of industry. In this case there may be a correlation between the aggregate stock and other economic meas-

Table 16.4 *Estimates of stock-holding costs as a percentage of sales*

Country	*% of output held as stock*	*Average bank interest rate*	*Cost of stock (% of value)*	*Cost of stock (% of sales)*	*% Japan advantage over other countries*
Australia	14.2	16.5	33.5	4.75	2.86
Austria	16.1	6.5	23.5	3.78	1.89
Canada	12.0	12.0	29.0	3.48	1.59
Denmark	14.9	9.5	26.5	3.95	2.06
Finland	15.1	14.0	31.0	4.68	2.79
Germany (West)	14.2	6.5	23.5	3.34	1.45
Hong Kong	12.7	6.0	23.0	2.92	1.03
Israel	18.3	17.0	34.0	6.22	4.33
Japan	8.6	5.0	22.0	1.89	–
New Zealand	13.5	15.0	32.0	4.32	2.43
Norway	16.2	11.5	28.5	4.62	2.73
Portugal	19.7	13.0	30.0	5.91	4.02
Spain	14.0	14.5	31.5	4.41	2.52
Sweden	18.3	11.5	28.5	5.22	3.33
Turkey	15.7	48.0	65.0	10.21	8.32
UK	17.3	14.0	31.0	5.36	3.47
USA	13.7	9.0	26.0	3.56	1.67
Venezuela	19.0	18.0	35.0	6.65	4.76

Table 16.5 *Economic performance related to stock-holdings*

Country	*Stock value/ output*	*Average annual economic growth (%)*	*Index of exports*		*Index of imports*		*Index of exchange rates*	*Average annual rate of inflation*
			quantity	*value*	*quantity*	*value*		
Australia	14.2	3.3	140	160	187	161	100.5	7.6
Austria	16.1	2.8	174	109	152	107	100.0	2.6
Canada	12.0	3.8	124	108	137	111	103.1	5.0
Denmark	14.9	0.8	142	149	123	136	108.0	4.8
Finland	15.1	4.3	121	156	143	126	102.8	6.6
Germany (West)	14.2	2.9	152	120	140	106	109.6	2.8
Hong Kong	12.7	9.3	348	167	299	168		9.7
Israel	18.3	3.3	160	111	159	104		20.2
Japan	8.6	4.5	153	84	165	55	104.9	2.3
New Zealand	13.5	0.7	138	178	124	159	114.7	5.7
Norway	16.2	3.8	187	118	117	149	104.4	4.6
Portugal	19.7	4.7					109.1	12.6
Spain	14.0	4.9	147	205	148	166	110.5	6.8
Sweden	18.3	2.4	147	172	143	155	108.2	6.4
Turkey	15.7	5.2						69.6
UK	17.3	4.0	141	146	177	149	107.1	7.8
USA	13.7	3.6	112	127	171	118	69.6	4.8
Venezuela	19.0	2.3					51.1	84.5
Average	15.2	3.7	159.1	140.7	159.0	131.3	100.2	14.7
Coefficient of correlation	–	−0.22	−0.1	0.22	−0.21	0.38	−0.22	0.39

ures. Table 16.5[16–19] shows a series of economic indicators for different countries. Average values have been taken over the past five years of data, while trade indices are based on 1980 as 100 and exchange rates are based on 1985 as 100.

There are no obvious patterns in these figures. We cannot say, for example, that one country has a low aggregate stock, so we would expect a high growth of exports. If there are such patterns, they are difficult to identify. When lines of best fit are drawn through the data the coefficients of correlation are small. This suggests that the amount of stock held has little direct effect on wider economic performance. This should not be surprising, even though some correlations are perhaps high enough to raise questions. Economic conditions in countries are so complex, and are affected by so many factors, that to expect stock-holdings in manufacturing industry to have a dominant effect would be extremely naive. The best that can be said is that overall stock-holdings may have some effect on a country's economic performance, but details of the relationships and interactions are not yet clear.

Summary

- Problems of inventory control have been worked upon for many years. Most problems are well understood and the results are widely used
- Current views are that stocks are inherently wasteful and should be kept as low as possible. Recent developments, particularly in computer systems, have allowed much more effective control of stocks
- Stock levels in industrialized countries have been falling for many years. In the UK, for example, levels have fallen from 40 per cent of GDP to 20 per cent over the past 30 years. Valid international comparisons are difficult, but available evidence suggests that stock levels in other industrialized countries also follow this pattern
- The manufacturing industries of industrialized countries contribute a declining proportion of GDP. Nonetheless they still hold a large part of aggregate stocks. These have generally declined in relation to output, and there has been a shift from holding raw materials to finished goods
- Some countries, particularly Japan, seem to be controlling their stocks better than other countries. This gives a price advantage which could affect their long-term competitiveness. However, the precise effect of aggregate stocks on national economies is difficult to assess.

References

1 Harris, F., *Operations and Cost*, A Shaw & Co., Chicago, 1915.
2 Raymond, F.E., *Quantity and Economy in Manufacture*, McGraw-Hill Book Co., Chicago, 1931.

[3] Abramovitz, M., *Inventories and Business Cycles*, The National Bureau of Economic research, New York, 1950.
[4] Lovell, M.C., 'Manufacturers' inventories, sales, expectations and the accelerator principle', *Econometrica*, 29, 1964, pp. 293–314.
[5] Central Statistics Office, *Economic Trends*, HMSO, London, 1971–92.
[6] Central Statistics Office, *National Income and Expenditure*, HMSO, London, 1966–83.
[7] Central Statistics Office, *United Kingdom National Accounts*, HMSO, London, 1984–92.
[8] CSO 1966–83, op. cit.
[9] CSO 1984–92, op. cit.
[10] United Nations, *Industrial Statistics Yearbook*, UN, New York, 1991.
[11] World Bank, *World Tables*, Washington D.C., 1991.
[12] Ray, D.L., 'Assessing UK manufacturing industry's inventory management performance', *Focus on Physical Distribution*, 27, 1981, pp. 5–11.
[13] Waters, C.D.J., *Inventory Control and Management*, John Wiley, Chichester, 1992.
[14] McKibbin, B.N., 'Distribution cost survey', *Proceedings of Institute of Physical Distribution Management Annual Conference*, Brighton, 1984.
[15] O'Brien, J., '1985 survey of distribution costs', *Focus on Physical Distribution*, 5, 1986, pp. 16–19.
[16] International Monetary Fund, *International Financial Statistics*, IMF, Washington, 1992.
[17] United Nations, *International Trade Statistics Yearbook*, UN, New York, 1991.
[18] United Nations, *Industrial Statistics Yearbook*, UN, New York, 1991.
[19] United Nations, *National Accounts Statistics*, UN, New York, 1991.

Chapter 17

The Purchase of Logistical Services

Dr Alan C McKinnon
Heriot-Watt Business School, Edinburgh

Over the past decade, a broad consensus has developed in business circles that firms should concentrate their resources on core activities and contract out ancillary functions. As logistics is often regarded as a supporting rather than mainstream function, it has been an obvious candidate for externalization. For many firms, logistics has ceased to be an activity that they directly manage and has become something that they purchase from outside specialists. Even firms that have retained an in-house logistical operation often make extensive use of contractors. The manner in which transport, warehousing and related services are purchased can, therefore, have a major influence on the overall quality and efficiency of logistical systems. This chapter will review recent trends in the purchase of logistical services and outline various ways in which firms buying and selling logistical services can develop more stable and co-operative relationships.

Increasing Externalization of Logistical Functions

There is a long tradition of firms contracting out freight transport operations. In many countries, however, external purchases of freight transport services have been constrained by government controls on the capacity of the road haulage industry. These controls have generally excluded lorries operated on an 'own-account' basis and thus encouraged firms to internalize their road freight operations. The deregulation of road haulage in countries such as the UK, the USA, Canada, Australia and the Netherlands has made it much easier and more attractive for firms to contract out the transport function. The recent growth in contracting out cannot simply be attributed to deregulation, though. In the UK, for example, road freight traffic remained fairly evenly divided between 'own account' and 'hire and reward' operations for a decade after the liberalization of the road freight market in 1970. Only since 1980 has there been a significant and sustained increase in the proportion of road freight tonnage handled by outside contractors, from 50 per cent in 1980 to 60 per cent in 1990.[1] The swing away from in-house transport had to await the general change in managerial attitudes to contracting out that occurred in the late 1970s and early 1980s.

Freight transport statistics present only part of the picture because, in addition to giving contractors greater responsibility for transport, firms have been externalizing related activities such as warehousing, stock control, materials handling and order processing. This is in keeping with one of the fundamental principles of logistics, which stipulates that the management of transport, stockholding and other related activities should be closely coordinated. A recent survey of 300 British firms undertaken by PE-International[2] found that 19 per cent of firms contracted out all their transport and warehousing, while a further 12 per cent outsourced their entire distribution operation.

The externalization of logistics has become a two-dimensional process, with firms increasing both the range of services that they source externally, and the volume of traffic handled by outside agencies. These two dimensions can be used to differentiate firms' externalization strategies. The vectors labelled A to G in Figure 17.1 represent typical strategies, ranging from a gradual increase in reliance on contractors for a single activity (A), to an abrupt switch to an integrated contract distribution operation (G). There is no ideal strategy; the externalization 'route' that a firm follows will reflect its particular circumstances.

It is difficult to assess the proportion of physical distribution services purchased from outside agencies, partly because of a lack of data, but

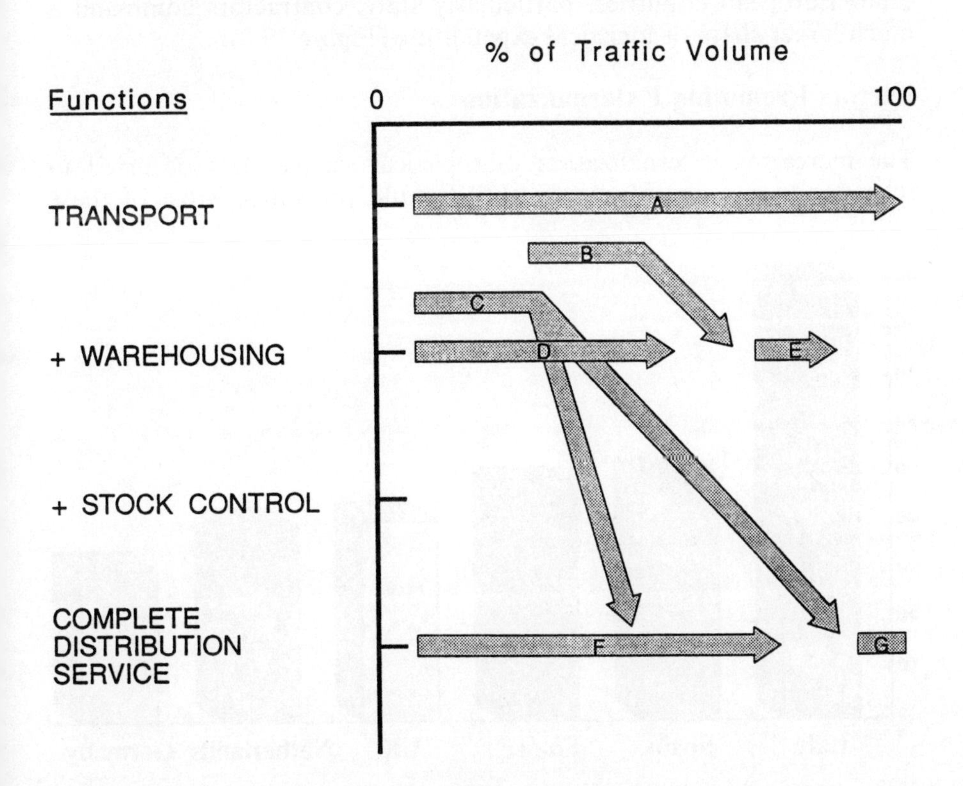

Figure 17.1 *Increasing externalization of logistical services by function and traffic volume*

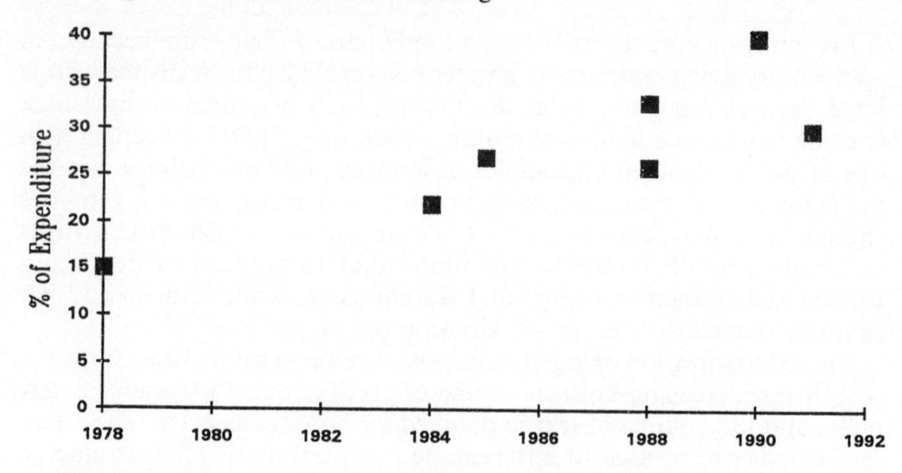

Figure 17.2 *Estimates of contractors' share of transport and warehousing expenditure in the UK*[4]

also because the extent of the total market is ill-defined.[3] Nevertheless, on the basis of data drawn from several sample surveys, it appears that contractors' share of total UK expenditure on transport and warehousing has increased significantly over the past decade (Figure 17.2). In other European countries, particularly Italy, contractors command a much larger share of logistical expenditure (Figure 17.3).

Factors Promoting Externalization

The increasing externalization of logistical services has occurred in response to a range of supply and demand pressures. Most of these

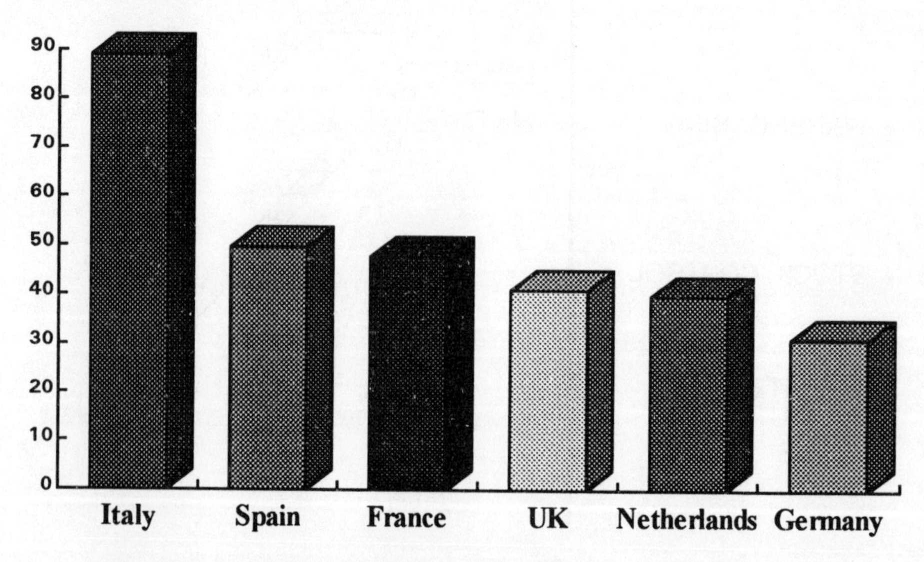

Figure 17.3 *Contractors' share of total expenditure on transport and warehousing, 1991*[5]

pressures are fundamental and widespread, though some are associated with particular developments in individual countries.

On the supply side, there have been major improvements in the nature of the third-party logistical services on offer. Standards have undoubtedly risen and operations become more efficient. New types of service have been developed which are more closely tailored to clients' requirements. Logistical services are being marketed much more skilfully and aggressively today than in the past.

Many transport firms have diversified into related activities such as storage, stock control, goods handling and order-picking in an effort to escape the rigours of the general haulage market. In most countries, the general road haulage industry is characterized by low entry costs, high rates of entry and exit, intense competition, heavy reliance on spot-hiring, low returns on capital and slim profit margins. By trading up into integrated distribution, the larger carriers have been able to add value to their services, create niche markets with much higher entry costs and secure longer-term contracts with clients. This has enabled them to improve both their profitability and their growth prospects.

On the demand side, financial conditions during the 1980s encouraged firms to concentrate capital investment in their core businesses and to pay for ancillary activities like distribution on a current cost basis. For some firms, the use of outside contractors not only averted the need for new investment in logistical facilities, but also released some of the capital already tied up in warehousing and vehicle fleets. In the UK, changes in corporate taxation introduced in the 1984 Budget reinforced this trend away from own-account operations. The phasing out of capital allowances, coupled with the reduction in corporation tax, had the effect of redirecting tax incentives away from simply owning assets towards maximizing their contribution to profit.[6] This discouraged firms from making further investment in in-house distribution facilities and strengthened the relative economic advantage of contract services.

The management of in-house distribution operations has also been made more difficult by rising customer expectations, the proliferation of regulations on vehicle operation and product handling, the rapid rate of technological change in this area and uncertainties about future trends in fuel and other costs. These developments have increased the relative attractiveness of contracting out logistics to specialist agencies, which are better equipped to cope with these mounting challenges and to assume the associated risks. Contracting out can also help firms overcome internal industrial relations problems by increasing their leverage in trade union negotiations and making external back-up systems available for use in the event of a strike.

New ways have been found of overcoming the natural resistance to contracting out in firms with extensive and/or long-established own-account operations. Much of this inertia has stemmed from a reluctance to relinquish control over the logistics function.[7] This has become less of a concern in recent years, partly as a result of growing confidence in the way that contract distribution operations are managed, but also because of advances in information technology. These have made it possible for firms to monitor and control contract distribution operations almost as closely as in-house systems.[8]

In some countries, particularly the UK, structural change in the retail supply system has also promoted the use of contractors. As the proportion of retail supplies being channelled through retailers' centralized distribution systems has risen, manufacturers have found it increasingly difficult to operate their own in-house delivery systems efficiently and have been forced to rely more heavily on 'groupage' services provided by outside contractors.[9] Meanwhile, the large retailers that now control physical distribution upstream of their shops have shown a high propensity to contract out its day-to-day management.[10]

There is also an important international dimension to the externalization of logistical services. Manufacturers tend to rely heavily on contractors both for international transport and for the distribution of their products within foreign markets. In the EC, for example, contractors handle around 96 per cent of the international movement of freight by road, as opposed to 58 per cent of road freight movement within countries.[11] Roughly a third of the European distribution centres used by American and Japanese manufacturers are managed by specialist contractors.[12] The steep upward trend in global sourcing and distribution is therefore inflating the demand for contract services at both the international and national levels.

The Process of Externalization

Own-account operators have often been deterred from contracting out by an unwillingness to dispose of existing logistical assets, shed staff and risk disruption of their operations during the transitional period. It is possible, however, for firms to minimize these adverse effects by adopting one of the following strategies:

- **System take-over** Some of the larger contractors now have sufficient resources to buy out a firm's complete in-house distribution system, comprising vehicles, depots, equipment and much of the existing workforce. Following a take-over of this type, the system may continue to be operated on an exclusive basis for the 'divesting' firm, or the contractor may share the use of the acquired facilities with other clients, thereby improving utilization and spreading overhead costs.
- **Joint ventures** Some clients prefer to retain part-ownership of distribution facilities and to maintain close involvement in the logistical operation. For them, joint ventures with contractors offer a more attractive means of injecting outside capital and expertise.[13]
- **System 'spin-off'** Tucker and Zivan[14] advocate the 'spinning-off' of firms' in-house logistical systems as separate subsidiaries. They consider this to be the 'most likely scenario' for the externalization of the logistical function, both in the US and elsewhere. In some

countries, however, most notably the UK, the greater development of contract distribution firms and their willingness to enter into buy-out deals has reduced the need for corporate 'spin-offs'.

- **Management-only contract** Firms wishing to retain ownership of logistical assets can still contract out their management. This has become a popular strategy among large retailers in Britain and other EC countries,[15] many of whom see contracting out more as a way of upgrading the management of their distribution operation than of releasing capital for other uses.

Recent Trends in the Purchase of Logistical Services

The recent increase in the level and diversity of firms' external expenditure on logistical services has been accompanied by important changes in the way they purchase them and in the nature of their relationship with outside contractors. Five changes have been of particular significance.

Increase in the Proportion of Logistical Services Bought on a Contractual Basis

Road hauliers providing a basic 'truck-load' service have typically been employed on a spot-hire basis to handle individual deliveries. Such services are fairly standardized and generally purchased at minimum price. The high degree of fragmentation in the road haulage industry ensures that there are numerous small hauliers available to provide an economical service at short notice.

Buying haulage services in this way, however, has serious shortcomings. The need to deal with large numbers of separate carriers on a daily basis both inflates transaction costs and makes it difficult to ensure high delivery standards. In practice, even within the spot market, firms have been able to alleviate these problems by making regular use of the same set of hauliers. Even in the absence of formal contracts, manufacturers have tended to exhibit a high degree of 'source loyalty' to particular carriers.[16]

Where firms demand more specialist services tailored to their particular requirements and often involving capital investment on the part of the carrier, they must be prepared to enter into longer-term contracts. In the case of transport operations dedicated to a particular consignor, a contractor would like ideally to secure a contract at least as long as the working life of the vehicles, though, given the competitive conditions in the haulage industry, the typical duration of contracts is usually much shorter.[17] Even where contractors invest in warehousing facilities for the exclusive use of a particular client, contracts seldom extend beyond five years, though generally they require the client to assume responsibility for the lease in the event of non-renewal. In situations where the third-party operator merely provides a management service, contracts are usually much shorter, two to three years being the norm. A substantial proportion of distribution contracts, nevertheless, have no fixed time limit and are simply considered to be 'ongoing'. According to the study by PE-International,[18] approximately 37 per cent of contracts in the UK fall into this category.

Reduction in the Number of Contractors Used

In both the 'spot' and 'contract' markets, the average number of carriers used has been declining. One large food manufacturer in the UK reduced the number of road hauliers in regular use from around 120 in 1978 to only five in 1991, and is now proposing to single-source its entire road freight requirement. On the basis of a large survey of American manufacturers, La Londe and Cooper[19] predicted that the average number of carriers used would decline by around 36 per cent by 1995. Concentrating purchases of logistical services in this way enables firms both to reduce transaction costs and improve the standard of service.

Transaction costs
In Germany, Sweden and several other European countries a substantial proportion of domestic road haulage services are purchased from freight forwarders, who act as middle men in the freight market. This greatly reduces the number of direct transactions between consignors and hauliers. There has also been a sharp increase in the number of freight brokers in the United States since the deregulation of its trucking industry in 1980.[20] In Britain, on the other hand, the brokerage services of freight forwarders tend only to be used for international distribution. There has been a tradition in the UK, as far as domestic transport operations are concerned, of dealing directly with numerous hauliers. This has enabled firms to secure lower freight rates, but at the expense of higher transaction costs. In their pursuit of low haulage prices, many firms under-estimate the total cost of buying-in road haulage in this way.

It is, nevertheless, possible for firms to streamline the purchase of haulage services, while continuing to exploit the very competitive rates available in the general haulage market. Under a 'freight management' arrangement, some of the larger contractors, such as Exel Logistics, will, on a particular client's behalf, subcontract trunk haulage operations to smaller carriers. Similar 'one-stop shipping' services are provided by the new generation of third-party logistics firms that have emerged in the US over the past decade.[21]

Standard of service
The more hauliers a firm employs, the more time it must spend vetting them and monitoring their performance. Concentrating traffic on a smaller number of more reliable hauliers simplifies these tasks. It can also win a greater commitment from these hauliers to maintain or improve the quality of service.

Firms purchasing logistical services on a contractual basis employ relatively few outside agencies. In the UK, around 38 per cent of them single-source these services, while a further 41 per cent employ between two and five contractors.[22] Many of the firms using more than one distribution contractor, however, are not multiple-sourcing in the conventional sense. When applied to the supply of material goods, the term 'multiple-sourcing' generally means obtaining identical products from different suppliers. Where a firm employs several distribution contractors, however, they seldom provide parallel services. Various studies have established that the dominant motive for using several contractors is to subdivide distribution operations geographically.[23] Where more than one contractor is used, it is common for each to be given exclusive responsibility for distribution within a single region. The nature of local storage and delivery operations makes it possible to split a distribution contract geographically among several agencies at little or no extra cost. Purchasing contract distribution on a regional basis can yield important benefits by reducing the risk of the entire system being disrupted by, for example, industrial disputes or company failure, and permitting interfirm comparisons of rates and service standards.

More Rigorous Selection of Contractors

Numerous studies conducted over the past 30 years have shown that many firms opt for particular transport modes or carriers without fully appraising the available alternatives.[24] The observed deficiencies in the selection procedure may be partly explained by the fact that many firms' total expenditure on freight transport represented a small proportion of total costs, and because differences in rates and quality of service, particularly among road hauliers, were perceived to be small. Now that firms are contracting out a broader range of distribution-related services, total external expenditure on logistics has begun to figure more prominently in their budgets. This, combined with the greater emphasis being placed on quality of service, the reduction in carrier numbers and the shift to contractual relationships, has made the choice of carrier a much higher-order decision, requiring a more thorough review of the market and more formal selection procedures. Research by Whyte[25] also suggests that the calibre and status of staff purchasing distribution services has been improving.

Closer Involvement of Contractors in the Design of Distribution Systems

In purchasing component parts, many manufacturers are replacing the traditional 'design specification', which describes the required item in detail, with the more open 'performance specification', which outlines the function the part has to perform.[26] This gives suppliers greater freedom to innovate and develop parts that meet the customer's requirements more economically and effectively.

A similar development has occurred in the purchase of physical distribution services. It is now quite common for firms externalizing their distribution operations to involve contractors in system design. The decision to externalize is often made at the same time as the decision to restructure the distribution system.[27] Moreover, as one of the major reasons for using contractors is to exploit their specialist expertise, it is hardly surprising that firms should seek their advice when revising their distribution strategies. Outside contractors can also take a more objective view of firms' distribution needs than in-house managers.

Participation in system design can be a mixed blessing for contractors. On the positive side, it gives them the opportunity to set up a system in which they have confidence and which they believe they can operate efficiently. The broad terms of reference also enable them to compete at a strategic as well as an operational level for what is then a higher value-adding service. The main disadvantage is the higher cost of preparing a tender containing proposals for the strategic redesign of a firm's distribution system. Such costs can be in the region of £50,000–100,000 and easily deter smaller contractors from tendering for the business. Even some of the larger operators, wary of providing an expensive consultancy service without any guarantee of securing the final contract, now impose a separate charge for the development of a distribution plan. This charge is usually waived, however, where the contractor is awarded the business.

Greater Emphasis on the Development of Longer-term Partnerships

It can be just as important for a firm to develop close, mutually beneficial relationships with suppliers of logistical services as with suppliers of products. Many such relationships have already been established and go beyond the formal terms of the logistics contract. Expressions such as 'partnershipping' and 'co-shippership'(!) have been coined to describe the new consignor–carrier links that have been formed.

These relationships are most likely to develop where logistical services are provided on a dedicated basis for the exclusive use of individual clients. As Cooper and Johnstone point out, 'compartmentalisation of the contractor's capacity between clients means that the service needs of any one client will not be compromised by the conflicting needs of other clients, such as may occur when capacity is shared.'[28]

While this usually ensures a high standard of service, it also usurps one of the contractor's traditional functions, that of consolidating many clients' traffic and thus running distribution facilities at a lower unit cost than in-house operators. Increasing numbers of manufacturers and retailers are, nevertheless, prepared to incur the higher costs of dedicated services in order to maintain high levels of control and service quality.

In 1991/2, British firms' expenditure on third-party transport and warehousing was divided evenly between dedicated and shared operations.[29] In other European countries, such as France and Germany, much smaller proportions of distribution services are provided on a dedicated basis (Figure 17.4).

Several recent developments have been conducive to the formation of closer partnerships between distribution contractors and their clients.

Adoption of the just-in-time principle

One of the prerequisites for a successful JIT system is the fast and reliable delivery of supplies. In the absence of buffer stocks, production and distribution operations become much more vulnerable to deviations

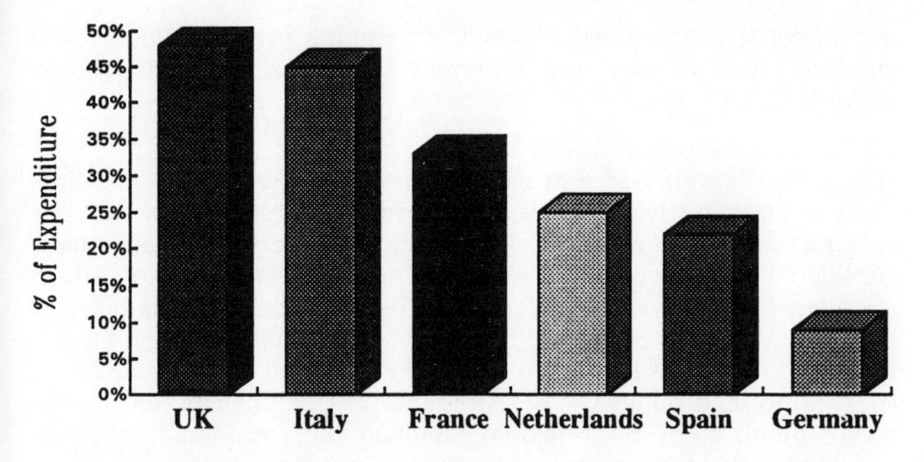

Figure 17.4 *Proportion of contract distribution expenditure on dedicated services, 1991*[5]

from the delivery schedule. Ansari and Modarress found that 53 per cent of a sample of large American corporations implementing JIT purchasing experienced difficulty in getting carriers to provide services of the required standard.[30] This has forced them to change the way in which they purchase transport services. In addition to greatly reducing the number of carriers employed and increasing the proportion of work done on a contractual basis, they have tried to forge 'closer, long-term and more interdependent' relationships with transport firms.[31]

Development of electronic data interchange

Many contractor–client relationships have been reinforced by the establishment of EDI links, particularly where the contractor provides an integrated distribution service. By making the flow of materials through the contractor's system more 'visible' on a day-to-day, or even hour-to-hour, basis, EDI increases the client's confidence in the contract operation. The integration of the contractor's and client's computer systems also strengthens the operational bond between them and makes it difficult for either party to break-off the relationship at short notice. As Ellram and Cooper point out, 'The integration of information and operating systems creates a relatively unified system that is difficult and costly to replicate should the partnership dissolve.'[32] There has, nevertheless, been some disagreement between contractors and their clients over the allocation of EDI costs, particularly in the case of shared-use services, and a feeling on the part of some contractors that their clients are under-estimating the true benefits of EDI.[33]

Increasing specialization of logistical equipment

Technological developments in the fields of transport and materials handling are making it possible to tailor equipment more closely to individual firms' logistical needs. Such 'client-specific' equipment is an example of what Williamson calls an 'idiosyncratic asset'.[34] He argues that the inclusion of such assets in a transaction greatly increases the likelihood of a 'relational contract' developing between supplier and customer. This is borne out by recent experience in the distribution sector.[35]

Change in the degree of interdependence

It is generally supposed that close, cooperative relationships are more likely to develop where there is a high level of interdependence between customer and supplier. As Rinehart notes, consignors have traditionally considered themselves to be less dependent on carriers than carriers considered themselves to be dependent on consignors.[36] This reflected consignors' perceptions of the road haulage market as being a buyer's market in which business could easily be transferred between carriers at short notice and minimal cost. Although, as Cunningham and Kettlewood found, many firms seldom exercised this freedom, they nevertheless regarded themselves as being in the stronger position.[37]

The externalization of a broader range of physical distribution services to a much smaller number of contractors has increased clients' dependence and made it much more difficult for them to sever their links with a contractor, at least in the short term. Within the contract distribution market, contractor–client relationships tend to be unbalanced in the opposite direction from those in the general road haulage market. Companies outsourcing their distribution operations either on a national or regional basis to a single contractor become completely reliant on that firm within the area in question. As a result of the high degree of concentration in the contract distribution sector, major contractors can have an extensive client portfolio (Table 17.1). Even quite a large manufacturing or retail client might therefore account for only a small proportion of the contractor's total business. This differs from the situation outlined by Ellram and Cooper,[38] where the shipper is the dominant party and has a tendency to behave opportunistically. Many distribution contractors are now large enough to exert countervailing power and win favourable terms from major corporations.

The fact that the pattern of interdependence between client and contractor remains asymmetrical does not appear to be hindering the development of close relationships. Nor is there any evidence to suggest that, in choosing contractors, firms have a preference for smaller operators over which they can exert greater bargaining power. It should be noted too that, despite the strengthening of contractual and operational ties between clients and third-party operators, only a small minority of firms externalizing distribution services perceive themselves to be 'locked-into' a particular contractor's system.[40]

The Promotion of Longer-term, Cooperative Relationships between Suppliers and Users of Logistical Services

Despite the major changes in the logistical services market described above, doubts remain about the long-term stability of many contractor–client relationships. The PE-International survey revealed that, in the

Table 17.1 *Client portfolios of major distribution contractors in the UK, 1991*[39]

Exel Logistics
Argos, BBC Books, Beefeater, Bird's Eye Walls, BMW, Boots, Brooke Bond Foods, Cadbury, Chrysler, Comet, Fiat, Lancia, Findus, Hershey Chocolate, Ind Coope, Johnson Wax, Kelloggs, Kimberly Clark, Lever Bros., Marks and Spencer, Mirror Group Newspapers, Nabisco, Nissan, Panasonic, Pizza Hut, Procter and Gamble, Safeway, Sainsbury, Scottish and Newcastle, Sharp Electronics, Suzuki, Tesco, Thorn Lighting, Toyota, Unisys, Van den Berghs & Jurgens, Vauxhall Parts, Whitbread, Woolworth.

Federal Express Systemline
Land Rover Parts, Sanyo, Ferguson, Saab, Volvo, Massey Ferguson, Lucas Automotive, Kenner Parker Tonka, Rowenta, Boots, Applied Chemicals, Yamaha Kemble, TKN Automotive, Aiwa, Matchbox, Champion Spark Plugs

Hays Distribution Services
Waitrose, Tesco, Seagram UK, Ford Motor Co., Lyons Tetley, New Zealand Lamb, Eurobands, Moët et Chanson, Anchor Foods

Tibbett and Britten
Marks and Spencer, Tesco, Asda, Sainsbury, Waitrose, Littlewoods, Sears, Swaddlers, HP Foods, Whitbread, Woolworths, C&A, B&Q, IBM, Black and Decker, Elida Gibbs, Colgate-Palmolive, Elizabeth Arden

TNT Contract Distribution
Ford, Volkswagen-Audi, Cow and Gate, Rover Group, Thermalite, MFI Group, Lever Industrial, Grand Metropolitan, Hobart Manufacturing, Wickes, Boddingtons Brewery, Victoria Wine, John Cotton.

UK, approximately 70 per cent of the users of these services were seriously considering changing contractors when the existing contract expired.[41] This was surprising, as almost two-thirds of the firms consulted were 'generally satisfied' with the service they were receiving. It seems, therefore, that many firms believed that, while their existing contract distribution package was adequate, other contractors might be able to improve upon it. There are several ways in which the quality and stability of contractor–client relationships can be enhanced.

Improved Contractor–Client Communications at All Levels

Inadequate communication is frequently cited as the main barrier to the development of close relationships between suppliers and users of logistical services. Contractors often claim that they are not given sufficient information about short- to medium-term changes in the client's pattern of business and longer-term strategic developments. Their clients, on the other hand, often complain that they are not informed quickly enough about system failures.

Healthy, long-term relationships between shippers and carriers tend to be 'very information-intensive'.[42] Information flows freely between the two organizations at different levels in the management hierarchy. This should be combined with vertical communication within each company to ensure that internal perceptions of the relationship are consistent. It is not uncommon, for example, for senior management to rate a relationship much more highly than employees with first-hand experience of its operational shortcomings.

More open discussions at a strategic level and the sharing of forecasts can help contractors become more proactive. Given their intimate knowledge both of general developments within the distribution industry and of a particular client's distribution operation, contractors are ideally placed to provide expert advice on an ongoing basis. Several contractors have gone so far as to set up 'think tanks' which meet regularly to explore ways of improving the service to individual clients.

They could also exploit more fully their role as intermediaries within the supply chain. This role could extend beyond simply managing freight flows on a routine basis. Beier, for instance, contends that they should 'include problem solving and experience savings among their services'.[43] He concludes that as 'carriers see the logistics flow from a different perspective from either consignor or consignee ... their function should be to act as consultant-middlemen in synchronizing all phases of goods movement between consignor and consignee'.

More Precise Contract Specification

Many of the early distribution contracts were inadequately specified at the outset. This has led to a good deal of misunderstanding and dissatisfaction. The British distribution contractor Christian Salvesen, for instance, has claimed that the misspecification of contracts is one of its most serious problems.[44] Both contractors and clients have learned from this experience and are now less likely to repeat earlier mistakes. Attempts have also been made to compile fairly comprehensive checklists of points that firms should bear in mind when drawing up distribution contracts.[45]

As distribution relates closely to other functions, particularly production, marketing and sales, it is important that the decision-making unit with responsibility for the purchase of distribution services contains representatives of these activities. It is also important to consult customers at the receiving end of the new delivery operation. As 'customers' throughout the supply chain are imposing tighter constraints on incoming deliveries, it is essential that their views are canvassed.

Refinement of Appraisal Schemes

Short-term auditing of contract distribution operations, using standard performance indices such as average transit times, adherence to delivery schedules and stock-out levels, does not provide an adequate basis for assessing the quality of longer-term relationships. As Kleinsorge, Schary and Tanner explain, in appraising this type of relationship, firms must take both a short-term/operational and a long-term/strategic perspective and supplement 'the "hard" and more tangible parameters of statistically measured operating dimensions' with 'less tangible measures of satisfaction'.[46] They present a new framework for evaluating 'shipper–carrier partnerships' which incorporates qualitative as well as quantitative measures.

Adoption of Open-book Accounting

Although survey evidence[47] suggests that the level of charges is not a major source of contention among users of third-party logistical services, the choice of pricing system can strongly influence the quality and stability of contractor–client relationships, particularly in the case of dedicated services. One of the disadvantages of single-sourcing logistical services is that firms then have difficulty comparing contractors' rates. They therefore need frequent reassurance that they are getting value for money. Increasing numbers of contractors are offering this assurance by giving their clients detailed cost break-downs and negotiating their management fee as a separate item.This system of open-book accounting is only appropriate, however, in the case of dedicated operations, where the costs of serving individual clients can easily be isolated. Even under these circumstances, it does not necessarily eliminate conflict between contractor and client. As Newson explains, conflict can still arise 'if improvements in operating efficiency which lead to substantial savings are claimed by one side as entirely due to its initiative, yet the open book contract states that such benefits shall be shared in preordained proportions'.[48] To operate effectively, therefore, open book accounting must be accompanied by an arrangement whereby benefits are fairly divided in relation to the costs and risks that each party bears.[49]

Conclusion

Since the early 1980s, the management of logistics has been radically reorganized. An important feature of this reorganization has been the externalization of many activities previously performed in-house. The resulting growth in the level and variety of external expenditure on logistics has induced important changes in the way that these services are purchased. Fewer carriers are being used; more of the work is being performed on a contractual basis; contractors are being given greater say in the design of distribution systems and greater emphasis is being placed on the development of longer-term, cooperative relationships. The relationships between distribution contractors and their clients are thus evolving in a similar way to the links between suppliers and customers of material goods. More needs to be done, however, to ensure the longer-term stability of these relationships and to exploit more fully the potential contribution of third-party logistics firms to improved supply chain management.

Summary

- Logistics services are now commonly contracted out by firms; the manner in which transport, warehousing and related services are purchased can have a major influence on the quality of logistical systems
- Changes in managerial philosophy have also led to contracting out of stock control, materials handling and order processing
- The externalisation of logistical services is being promoted by both supply-side and demand-side pressure
- Structural change in the retail supply system has also promoted the use of contractors
- Recent trends in the purchase of logistical services include an increase in the proportion of logistical services bought on a contractual basis, a reduction in the number of contractors used, more rigorous selection of contractors, closer involvement of contractors in the design of distribution systems and greater emphasis on the development of longer-term partnerships.

References

1. Department of Transport, *Transport Statistics Great Britain: 1980–1990*, HMSO, London, 1991.
2. PE-International, *Contract Distribution in the United Kingdom: What the Customers Really Think*, Egham, 1991.
3. Fernie, J., 'Third party or own account – trends in retail distribution', in Fernie, J. (ed), *Retail Distribution Management*, Kogan Page, London, 1990.
4. Buck, D., 'Changing to contract distribution' in Cooper, J.C. (ed), *Logistics and Distribution Planning*, Kogan Page, London, 1990; Kitcat and Aitken, *Distribution: A Revolution in Motion*, London, 1987; Corporate Development Consultants, *The United Kingdom Market for Contract Distribution*, 1988; Institute of Logistics and Distribution Management, *Survey of Distribution Costs*, Corby, 1991 and 1992.
5. Institute of Logistics and Distribution Management/Touche Ross, *European Logistics: Comparative Costs and Practice*, Corby, 1992.
6. Jones, A.B., *Financing the Acquisition of Commercial Vehicles*, Ernst and Whinney, London, 1986.
7. McBeath, J., 'Maximising own account operations', *Logistics Today*, 4 (4), 1985, pp. 811-10; Murtagh, J., 'Coca-Cola & Schweppes Beverages: Own Account Distribution', *Logistics Today*, 10 (2), 1991, pp. 21–3.
8. Quarmby, D.A., 'Distribution, the next ten years – the market place', *Focus on Physical Distribution and Logistics Management*, 4 (6), 1989.
9. McKinnon, A.C., *Physical Distribution Systems*, Routledge, London, 1986.
10. Fernie, J., 'Contract distribution in multiple retailing', *International Journal of Physical Distribution and Materials Management*, 19 (7), 1989.
11. *Motor Transport*, 6 September, 1990.
12. Holland International Distribution Council, *Holland: Europe's Distribution Centre*, The Hague, 1991.
13. Buck, 1990, op. cit.
14. Tucker, F.G. and Zivan, S.M., 'Create integrated logistics third parties: spin

them off', in J. Williams (ed), *Proceedings of the 7th International Logistics Congress*, IFS, Bedford, 1987.

[15] Rendell, J., 'Battle for Europe's middle ground', *Transport Week*, 16 February, 1991.

[16] Cunningham, M.T. and Kettlewood, K., 'Source loyalty in the freight transport market', *European Journal of Marketing*, 10 (1), 1976; La Londe, B.J. and Cooper, M.C., *Partnerships in Providing Customer Service: A Third-Party Perspective*, Council of Logistics Management, Oak Brook, Il., 1989.

[17] Cooper, J.C. and Johnstone, M., 'Dedicated contract distribution: an assessment of the UK market place', *International Journal of Physical Distribution and Logistics Management*, 20 (1), 1990.

[18] PE-International, 1991, op. cit.

[19] La Londe and Cooper, 1989, op. cit.

[20] Ibid.

[21] Sheffi, Y., 'Third party logistics: present and future prospects', *Journal of Business Logistics*, 11 (2), 1990.

[22] PE-International, 1991, op. cit.

[23] Corporate Development Consultants, 1988, op. cit.; Cooper and Johnstone, 1990, op. cit.; PE-International, 1991, op. cit.

[24] Bayliss, B.T. and Edwards, S.L., *Industrial Demand for Transport*, HMSO, London, 1970; Sharp, C., *The Allocation of Freight Traffic*, Ministry of Transport, London, 1970; Pike, J., *Major Factors Influencing Modal Choice in the UK Freight Market*, Research Report 52, Transport Operations Research Group, University of Newcastle upon Tyne, 1982.

[25] Whyte, J.L., 'Characteristics of transport managers which influence haulier selection', *International Journal of Physical Distribution and Logistics Management*, 22 (5), 1992.

[26] Ramsay, J., 'Purchase specifications and profit performance', *International Journal of Physical Distribution and Logistics Management*, 21 (1), 1991.

[27] Benham, P., 'The benefits of logistics partnerships in European distribution', *Focus on Physical Distribution and Logistics Management*, 9 (7), 1990.

[28] Cooper and Johnstone, 1990, op. cit.

[29] ILDM, 1992, op. cit.

[30] Ansari, A. and Modarress, B., *Just in Time Purchasing*, Free Press, New York, 1990.

[31] Crum, M.R. and Allen, B.J., 'The changing nature of the motor carrier–shipper relationship: implications for the trucking industry', *Transportation Journal*, 30 (2), 1991.

[32] Ellram, L. and Cooper, M.C., 'Supply chain management, partnerships and the shipper–third party relationship', *International Journal of Logistics Management*, 1 (2), 1990.

[33] McKinnon, A.C., 'Electronic data interchange in the retail supply chain: the distribution Contractor's Role', *International Journal of Retail and Distribution Management*, 18 (2), 1990.

[34] Williamson, O.E., 'Transaction-cost economics: the governance of contractual relations', *Journal of Law and Economics*, 22, 1979.

[35] Aertsen, F., 'Contracting out the physical distribution function: a trade-off between asset specificity and performance measurement', *International Journal of Physical Distribution and Logistics Management*, 23 (1), 1993.

[36] Rinehart, L.M., 'Organisational and personal factors influencing the negotiation of motor carrier contracts: a survey of shippers and motor carriers', *Transportation Journal*, 29 (2), 1989.

[37] Cunningham and Kettlewood, 1976, op. cit.
[38] Ellram and Cooper, 1990, op. cit.
[39] *Freight Management*, May 1991.
[40] PE-International, 1991, op. cit.
[41] Ibid.
[42] Ellram and Cooper, 1990, op. cit.
[43] Beier, F.J., 'Transportation contracts and the experience effect: A framework for future research', *Journal of Business Logistics*, 10 (2), 1989.
[44] *Motor Transport*, 28 May, 1992.
[45] Farmer, D. and Ploos van Amstel, P., *Effective Pipeline Management: How to Manage Integrated Logistics*, Gower, Aldershot, 1991.
[46] Kleinsorge, I.K., Schary, P.B. and Tanner, R.D., 'The shipper–carrier partnership: a new Tool for performance evaluation', *Journal of Business Logistics*, 12 (2), 1991.
[47] PE-International, 1991, op. cit.
[48] Newson, P., 'What happened to goodwill?', *Distribution*, 4 (4), 1991.
[49] La Londe and Cooper, 1989, op. cit.

Chapter 18

Retail Logistics

John Fernie
Dundee Business School
Dundee Institute of Technology

During the last 10–15 years the retail sector in many countries of the world has been at the forefront of logistical innovation. Like their counterparts in the manufacturing sector, innovative retailers have recognized the benefits of supply chain management in being able to meet changing customer needs as quickly and efficiently as possible. While the buzzword of the manufacturing sector in the 1980s and 1990s has been JIT, retailers have coined the phrase 'Quick Response'. Boardrooms around the world have included a new position – the logistics or supply chain director, whose position is not solely to manage the secondary distribution function from warehouse to store, but to oversee the whole chain from procurement to delivery to the final customer.

In the tough economic climate of the late 1980s and early 1990s, many of the success stories in retailing have been companies which were willing to provide customers with high-value products, reliably available at reasonable prices. The speciality 'category killers' such as Wal-Mart (discount department store), Nevada Bob (golf equipment), Costco and Price Club (warehouse clubs) have performed exceptionally well in the USA through aggressive pricing. Their success, achieved through the 'productivity loop',[1,2] is geared to generating volume business at low gross margins in large-scale retail formats. Thus 'category killers' can maintain or even improve net margins by gaining efficiencies throughout the supply chain and by achieving higher asset turns. For example, Wileman shows how a warehouse club in the USA competes with a traditional supermarket (Table 18.1.)[3] In terms of sales volume, the warehouse club is nine times higher on a gross margin of 9 per cent compared to the 22.5 per cent of the supermarket. Operating margins, however, are the same at 4 per cent and the warehouse club's sales density and stock-turn are around twice that of the supermarket.

'Category killers' are gaining an international presence. The two best-known are Toys 'R' Us and Ikea. The success of either company could not have been achieved without efficient control of the supply chain. In each sector – toys and home furnishings – the companies sell a wide range of quality products at prices (normally) below that of the competition. The customer feels confident that not only will the desired product be cheaper, but it will be available. Consequently both companies satisfy the basic tenets of a sound supply chain management

Table 18.1 *Warehouse club and supermarket comparison*

	Warehouse club	*Full-price supermarket*
$m Sales	90	10
% Gross Margin	9%	22.5%
% Operating Profit Before Property Costs	4%	4%
Stock Turn	14x	8x
$ Sales Density	700	350
% Operating Return on Net Assets (incl Property Assets)	35%	10%

strategy, namely to provide products at the right place at the right time at the right price. To support their trading philosophies, they can aggressively manage the supply chain because manufacturers can respond quickly to customer demands, and can be guaranteed volume sales, albeit at discounted terms, to these retailers.

This kind of trading format is not the only example of excellence in retail logistics. The performance of British food retailers throughout the 1980s, when net margins rose from around 2–3 per cent at the beginning of the decade to 6–7 per cent by 1990, can be partly attributed to a major transformation of a complex supplier-driven distribution system to one which is streamlined, efficient and retail-controlled. It is perhaps no coincidence that the food retailers which have performed more poorly in recent years have had problems with their distribution (Asda and Budgen). In non-food retailing, new concepts such as catalogue shops have thrived because of the importance of distribution in the marketing strategy of the leading players (Argos and Index). Some traditional retailers with falling market capitalization values in the late 1980s and early 1990s have turned their attention to improving their distribution to stores. In some cases, such as with Storehouse and Laura Ashley, this has meant the contracting out of this part of the business to third party distributors. While Benetton is often cited as the model of efficiency in controlling product flow from its factories to its shops, Laura Ashley clearly experienced graver difficulties in managing a vertically integrated system, and Federal Express hope to be able to trim 10 per cent off its annual £15 million distribution bill through streamlining the current supply chain network.

The remainder of this chapter will discuss retail logistics at two levels. In the first instance it is necessary to provide a macro-view of the retail environment in order to be able to understand the type of logistical support required by different types of business. Factors which shape the very nature of the distribution function include industry structures in different countries, the extent of own-label penetration, the degree of control of the supply chain by retailers, sophistication of the logistics industry, and levels of regulation by country. The issues discussed at this level should explain the differences which do occur in retail logistics throughout the world. The second part of the chapter builds upon this overview to detail the types of distribution operation, drawing extensively from the author's own research, particularly in grocery distribution in the UK.

Retail Structure

The degree of concentration in retail markets is a major influence on the development of marketing channels and the associated logistical support function. The more fragmented the industry structure, the more likely it is that a complex physical distribution system will exist; conversely, markets with a high degree of concentration tend to have a more efficient channel network. The difficulty in trying to make international comparisons on this subject is the incomparability of data between countries. This is highlighted by various recent papers and reports on grocery retailing,[4,5,6,7] which have all produced different figures to justify the point that countries in Northern Europe have a few major operators accounting for a high proportion of national sales. But in some cases these companies are either a grouping of affiliated independents or a combination of sales for the cooperative movement. The overall effect of defining markets in this way is to come up with similar concentration ratios in most Northern European countries. If concentration is defined by the degree of multiple groups' penetration in retail markets, a different picture emerges, with the UK standing out as the market with the greatest concentration of trade in the hands of large multiple chains.[8] To further complicate matters in the UK, the Institute of Grocery Distribution has proposed a new definition on how to measure market share in food retailing. As the market categories include chemists and off-licences, the net effect is to reduce the market share of the largest multiples by 6–7 percentage points.

Ohbora, Parsons and Riesenbeck have compared consumer markets in Germany with those of the US and Japan.[9] They claim that concentration levels in food markets in Germany is twice that of the US, and eight times that of Japan. Thus Japanese distribution and retail channels are fragmented and inefficient; for example, the US has 145,000 food stores to serve a population of 250 million, compared with Japan's 620,000 for a population of one half of the size. Concentration, however, is not perceived to benefit the consumer. The authors argue that German retailers have used their power to stifle new product development by manufacturers, which in turn limits consumer choice. By contrast, Japanese consumers' desire for new products has led to product proliferation and high birth and death rates in product life cycles. Although Japanese supermarkets are only one-third the size of their US counterparts, they hold 30,000 SKUs, 50 per cent more than in the US. This places great strain on the logistical system, especially as marketing channels are highly fragmented, with a multilayered network of manufacturers, wholesalers and retailers. Ohbora, Parsons and Riesenbeck claim that these long-term relationships, or *Eigyou*, place too much emphasis on high-cost supplier-driven channels, at the expense of relationships with customers.

The Retail Offer

In order to give customers value in the market-place, the retail offer has to be sufficiently distinctive to attract consumers and encourage them to be loyal to the retailer's store. For instance, the 'category killers' unique selling proposition is built around giving customers quality products at competitive prices. Trading formats, product policy and positioning of the retail offer in marketing terms will contribute to explaining the role of the distribution function. In town or out of town, narrow or wide product range, fast-moving or slow-moving lines, discount or value-added pricing, private label or manufactured brands; all these factors impact upon logistical support to stores. For example, the hard grocery discounters represented by Aldi, Netto and Norma in Europe offer low prices and limited ranges of fast-moving tertiary brands in fairly austere premises. This contrasts with major UK grocers, with their emphasis on quality own-brands, wide product ranges and large edge-of-town superstore environments. The logistics back-up to the latter has been the investment into massive regional distribution centres (RDCs), with a streamlined supply chain of large RDCs supplying large stores in large vehicles. By contrast, the discounter has a large number of warehouses serving a complex network of small stores with a large number of vehicle movements.

Manufacturer–Retailer Relations

The evolution of distribution networks is also a function of the changing balance of power in the marketing channel between retailer and manufacturer. In the last 20–30 years, retailers in many markets have grown from small, regional, family-run businesses to become national or international corporations. Commensurate with this growth has been an increase in retailers' buying power and a jousting with suppliers for responsibility for aspects of the value-added chain, namely product development, branding, packaging and marketing.[10]

These changes in supplier–retailer relationships vary in time and space according to the extent of retail concentration and the degree of fragmentation of suppliers' markets. Ohbora, Parsons and Riesenbeck maintain that this power struggle is finely poised in the US, where a combination of brand pull and innovative product development by manufacturers continues to ensure that suppliers' products reach retailers' shelves.[11] They contrast this situation with that in Japan and Europe, where the balance of power is uneven. In Europe, for example, supermarket chains have steadily eroded manufacturers' brands in many areas. Figure 18.1 shows a strong relationship between own-label share of grocery markets and retail concentration. Indeed, Wileman maintains that concentration is a necessary prerequisite before developments such as own-labelling.[12]

The concept of the retail brand rather than the manufacturers' brand has attracted much academic interest in recent years;[13,14,15] however, comparability of own-branding levels between countries suffers from similar definitional problems to that of measuring retail concentration. What is a retail brand? Davies lists four attributes:[16]

- The brand can be differentiated
- It is capable of a separate existence
- It can command a premium price
- It offers the customer some psychic value.

This form of retail branding creates a process brand where the retail name generates customer flow, customer loyalty and higher expenditure. While many authors attribute a high level of retail private labels in countries of Northern Europe (see Figure 18.1), many companies would not pass Davies' test of retail branding. For example, brands in both France and Germany, whether private label or manufacturers', are often used as promotional tools to gain market share over competing retailers. Bedeman has argued that German consumers have no sustainable loyalty to any particular store, as they seek the cheapest promotional offers.[17] This contrasts with the UK, where retailers' brands comply with the Davies' definition of retail branding with the offer of value-added brands, which are not a cheap alternative to the leading manufacturers' brands. In grocery retailing, Wileman has shown that in France it is not uncommon for a leading brand to command a price premium of 20–50

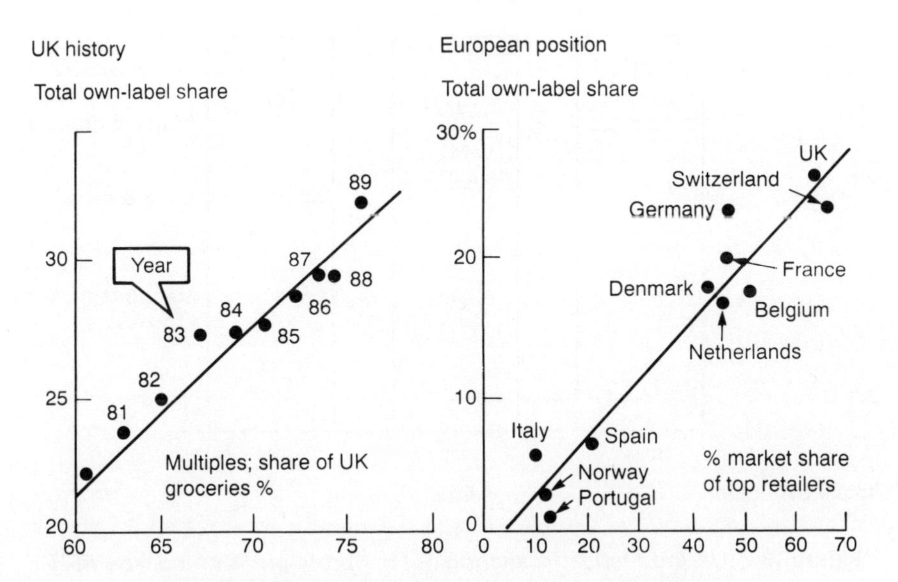

Figure 18.1 *Own-label and retail concentration*

per cent over its own-label counterpart, whereas in the UK there is often no price differential at all between high-quality brands and own-label brands.[18] The French situation may be changing, however, with both Carrefour and Casino investigating ways of developing their private brands.

The UK can be considered unique in the positioning of its brands, especially in grocery markets. Figure 18.2 indicates how this power balance has changed during the last ten years in terms of the profits generated in the UK food industry. Although the total market has grown, benefiting all channel members, it is clear that multiple grocers have been increasing their share (from 21–40 per cent), at the expense of their suppliers (from 76 down to 58 per cent). This shift in the balance of power is also reflected in the increased importance of brand advertising by retailers. Table 18.2 shows that retailers dominate the list of top advertisers in the UK, with much of this advertising spend focusing upon 'branding' rather than specific promotions.

It is clear from this discussion that the balance of power has swung towards the retailer in recent times. Wileman believes that this trend is likely to continue, but for long-term success in consumer goods markets, partnerships and collaborative arrangements between members of the supply chain will be essential to contain costs and improve customer service levels.[19] Speaking at an international conference in October 1992, Drayer of Procter and Gamble states that:

> experience has taught us that recognition of interdependence, good communication and the elimination of mistrust and arrogance between manufacturer, wholesaler and retailer is absolutely crucial to mutual success.[20]

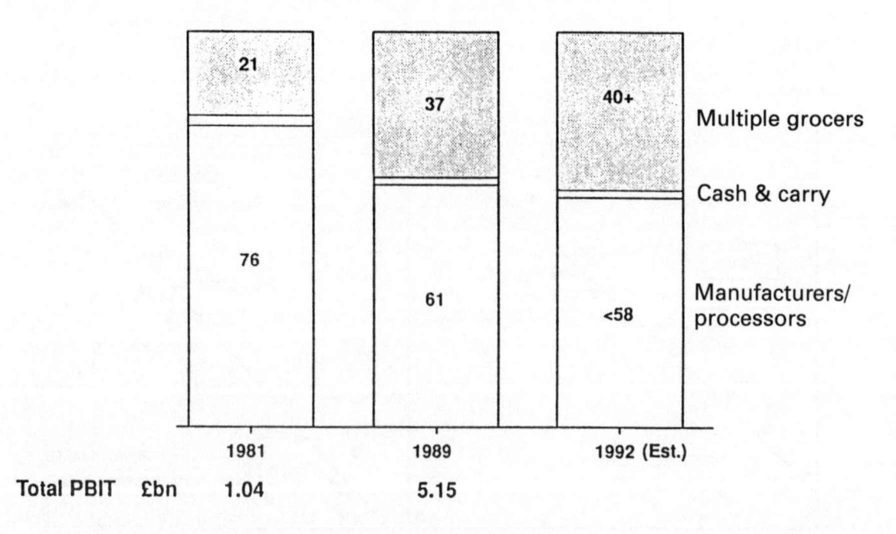

Figure 18.2 *UK food industry: sharing out the profit pie % of industry PBIT*

Source: Wileman, 1992

Table 18.2 *Top 300 brands, ranked by 1991 advertising spend*

Rank 1991	*Rank 1990*	*Brand*	*Spend 1991 (£000s)*	*Spend 1990 (£000s)*	*% change 1990/91*
1	1	Tesco	23,781	26,313	–10%
2	7	B&Q	19,765	14,012	41%
3	11	Texas Homecare	16,876	12,528	35%
4	3	McDonalds	16,833	16,930	–1%
5	4	Woolworths	15,466	16,322	–5%
6	–	Nat West Corporate	15,366	N/A	N/A
7	13	Comet Store	14,805	11,625	27%
8	15	Sainsbury's	14,581	10,435	40%
9	–	Conc. Persil Auto. Powder	14,543	N/A	N/A
10	12	Currys	14,147	11,893	19%
11	22	Boots Retail	13,997	9,623	45%
12	10	MFI/Hygena	13,905	12,745	9%
13	5	Asda	13,644	14,568	–6%
14	38	Safeway	12,640	7,342	72%
15	18	Dixons	10,790	9,859	9%
16	23	Debenham Group Store	10,712	9,603	12%
17	6	Benson & Hedges Special	10,678	14,317	–25%
18	–	BT Share Offer	10,652	N/A	N/A
19	17	Franklin Mint Mail Order	10,494	10,245	2%
20	–	American Airlines	10,419	N/A	N/A

Source: Retail Week, 5 June, 1992

This approach is gaining acknowledgement by major retailers in their quest to achieve even greater efficiencies in primary distribution to their warehouses.[21] The key to achieving this goal lies in the sharing of retail generated data to enable suppliers to plan production accurately enough to shorten lead times and reduce inventory through the supply chain.

Information technology will be a major facilitator in achieving such efficiencies, especially EPOS to capture product sales data, and EDI to speed up communication between retailers and their suppliers.

Who Controls The Supply Chain?

It follows from previous sections that firms in countries with greater retail concentration and a high level of retail branding will assume greater responsibility for distribution support to their stores. In the UK the transition from a supplier-driven distribution system to one that is retail-controlled is almost complete in nearly every sector of retailing. This process has been well documented.[22,23,24] The author is currently completing a study of the distribution strategies of UK retailers, and the majority of companies have over 90 per cent of their products channelled through distribution networks either run by retailers or operated on their behalf by third-party contractors. In the grocery sector, the largest chains operating superstores have invested heavily in the construction of large composite warehouses. These RDCs incorporate all product ranges, from ambient to frozen foods, under one roof, and these products are then distributed to stores in specially designed trailers which can accommodate a mix of products of different temperature ranges.[25]

The extent of retail control of the supply chain is much less in other parts of Europe and the US. Recent reports and papers suggest that in Europe, retail control is more evident in the Benelux countries, followed by France, Germany, and the Scandinavian countries, with the southern European countries of Italy and Spain continuing to be dominated by a supplier-led distribution system.[26,27,28] Wilman,[29] for example, claims that it is still possible to find sales and merchandising forces of 3,000 people providing direct coverage of 80–100,000 retail outlets in Italy and Spain. The growth area in retail distribution in both of these countries is the common user 'groupage' service, which was prominent in the UK in the 1960s and early 1970s. The concept of common user or shared distribution has been largely superseded by dedicated distribution in the UK. This means that contractors working on behalf of the client provide a dedicated service to only one company, rather than a consolidation service for a variety of customers.

It can be hypothesized that as retail and distribution markets become more sophisticated, a greater integration of the supply chain occurs as retailers seek to improve service levels and drive down costs. In practice, however, several obstacles exist to achieving integration rather than fragmentation of the supply chain. Penman[30] has shown how the British approach to logistics is markedly different from that of the US and Continental Europe. Jourdan and Irving[31] have arrived at similar conclusions, stating that in the US, for example, the long distances involved and the strength of manufacturers' brands have led to reducing the costs of individual components of the supply chain, rather than trying to reduce overall costs throughout the whole supply chain.

The situation is complex and is dependent on a range of factors pertaining to individual countries and the associated costs attributed to elements in the supply chain. It is not surprising that the UK, Japan and the Benelux countries have the so-called just-in-time (JIT) method of delivery to stores, working to fast replenishment of stock at stores from distribution centres. These countries are small and densely populated, land costs are high in prime retail locations, and road transport dominates in the distribution of consumer goods to retail outlets. In these countries there is an incentive to maximize sales space and carry minimum stock in store. By contrast, in the US and the larger European countries, the equation pertaining to land costs and freight costs will be different. Logistics costs vary according to these and other factors such as the level of interest rates, freight costs and the degree of regulation in specific countries.[32]

The UK's unique position can also be attributed to some of these macroeconomic factors, in addition to retail concentration, branding, etc. For example, UK interest rates have been much higher than those in most other countries during the last two decades, thereby encouraging retailers to reduce stockholding levels. Also, the deregulation of transport markets which occurred 25 years ago has produced a highly efficient, innovative and professional industry which has developed partnerships with retailers to improve supply chain efficiencies. Bedeman[33] calls the UK model the 'Rolls-Royce' of distribution and contrasts this approach with the low-cost model adopted by most other European countries. He argues that the Continental approach, with its emphasis on promotional items, puts much more stress on the supply chain than is the case in the UK. French retailers, for example, he claims hold 12 to 16 weeks' worth of bulk stock to support promotional campaigns; Bedeman questions whether the increased sales and savings in discounts can be compensated for by costs of financing, handling and storing this stock. By comparison, most major grocery retailers in the UK hold around two weeks' worth of stock, on average, in their warehouses.

The Role of The Third-Party Operator

The difference in approach to retail logistics in the UK compared with other countries is also evident in the role of the logistics contractor, as Cooper *et al.*[34] point out:

> A switch to third-party logistics services can enable a manufacturer and retailer to concentrate on their core business, and while contracting out the entire logistics operation is largely a UK phenomenon this can be expected to spread as deregulation develops. As a consequence, opportunities for mega-carriers will grow.

Cooper *et al.* and also Penman,[35] have shown that the UK is fairly unique, in that professional contractors provide a dedicated distribution service to retailers, that is the management of RDCs and transport to stores, compared with a more fragmented support function found in the rest of Europe and North America. In the US and mainland Europe, most warehousing is own-account, while the transport is contracted out. Trucking in the US is predominantly carried out by owner-drivers, and the deregulation of transport markets has led to competitive pricing for freight services. Similarly, the progressive deregulation of EC transport markets should provide opportunities for the efficient UK operators, which have enjoyed deregulation of their own market for a long period of time. The pre-1992 situation fostered nationally protected markets, which tended to hamper innovation, with the net effect that Europe continues to be dominated by general haulage services.

Other reasons why contracting out is more important in the UK are the need for more sophisticated distribution support to run composite RDCs, rather than low specification 'sheds', and the differential in profitability between the UK retail industry and the distribution sector. For example, retailers can achieve a higher return on investment by opening a new superstore, rather than a new warehouse. This differential in profitability between industrial sectors is less marked in mainland Europe than in the UK. The differences in accountancy practice between nations can also influence the decision-making of companies. For example, in the UK, changes in accountancy practice in the 1980s tended to favour 'off balance sheet' financing, that is companies did not own a particular asset, but utilized it fully (an expense). This improved the return on capital figures. German companies, on the other hand, have tended to prefer large balance sheets.

The differences between countries in their approach to contracting out are largely related to the sophistication of their markets. It has been shown that there is a strong relationship between retail concentration of markets, level of own-branding and the degree of control of the supply chain. NFC[36] studied five grocery markets in Europe; Figure 18.3 shows that there is a strong relationship between concentration of grocery markets by multiples and the degree of third-party penetration.

Retail Logistics at The Company Level

Although the previous sections have highlighted the differences in distribution 'culture' between countries, individual firms face the challenge of improving efficiency in the logistical support to stores. The nature of this support is largely a function of the following factors:

- Product categories: fast movers or slow movers, number of SKUs, products requiring 'specialist' distribution provision
- The geographical spread of stores, and increasingly, location of suppliers to facilitate backloading
- The relative costs of the component variables which contribute to total logistics costs, for example the cost of labour, land, capital and transport
- The trading formats of stores and constraints, if any, on delivery.

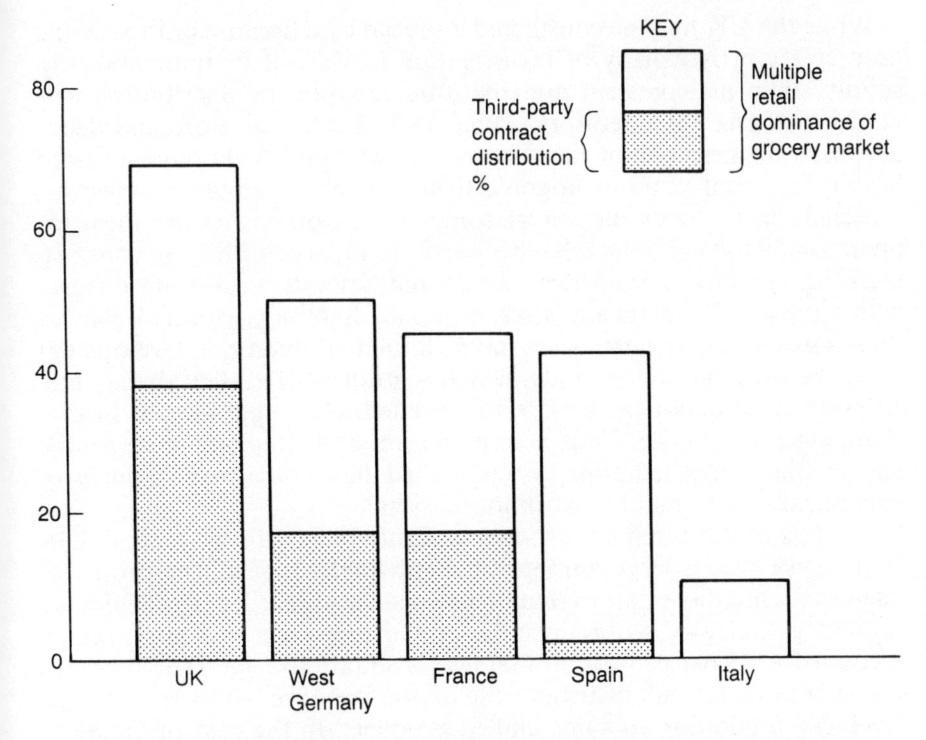

Figure 18.3 *Major retailer market share, including proportion of third-party distribution*

Source: NFC Contract Distribution Report, 1989

Although managers use the terms 'quick response', 'time compression' and 'logistics', most directors are only responsible for the distribution costs associated with secondary distribution. Initially their efforts focused upon issues such as number and location of depots, direct versus centralized distribution and the degree of contracting out. More recently, greater coordination of the supply chain has been taking place, with the backloading of goods from suppliers, and coordination through retail alliances to reduce inventory levels and shipment costs in global sourcing.

Clearly the approach adopted is largely dependent upon the retail sector under consideration. At one extreme the mail order operator's distribution costs will be the highest, as a tier of sortation/returns warehouses feed a network of depots for onward distribution to people's homes; at the other extreme, the specialist non-food retailer will be able to supply its stores from one or a few depots, according to the geographical spread of stores. In the UK, Simkin *et al.*[37] and McKinnon[38] show that the majority of British retailers operate from one site, with only the food retailers and the mixed retail business chains operating from multi-sites. More recent work by Fernie and McKinnon[39] suggests that the trend to larger RDCs and the use of transshipment depots will continue, as retailers seek to maximize the use of their transport assets.

While the UK may be considered a special case because of its size, the grocery sector is worthy of investigation in view of its innovations in supply chain management and the differences in the distribution networks of the major operators. Table 18.3 profiles the store and depot networks of these companies. Tesco, Safeway and Asda have invested heavily in recent years to upgrade their existing distribution networks, especially in the construction of composites. Composites are ideal for operators like Asda, which have a portfolio of large stores. By contrast, the other 'majors' – Sainsbury, Tesco and Safeway – have more stores with a range of formats and sizes, especially Safeway, with its legacy of Presto stores. These companies have all focused upon the development of superstores, but unlike Asda, which centralized late, they already had an established depot network which needed to be upgraded to meet a changing store profile. Thus a combination of a changing store profile and an inherited distribution system has led these operators to a policy of maximization of existing distribution assets.

The rest of the companies shown in Table 18.3 (with the exception of Wm. Low) have a large number of small stores. Indeed, the profile of Gateway is not dissimilar to that of Tesco a decade earlier. The 27 depots supplying Gateway stores include 11 Gateway-operated sites, which account for 85 per cent of all Gateway's square footage. The other 16 sites consolidate and distribute all of the produce, meat and frozen products in addition to some chilled products. In the case of Gateway and the other small-store format retailers the building of composites has not been possible, although mini-composites, grouping frozen and dry grocery products, has been implemented by Iceland. The profiles of CRS, Iceland and Kwik Save are more representative of the distribution networks of companies on mainland Europe, with their large number of

Table 18.3 *Profile of store and depot characteristics (1991)*

Operator	*No of stores*	*Av Selling space of store (000 sq ft)*	*No of depots*	*Size range (000 sq ft)*	*No of composites*
J. Sainsbury	303	22.9	21	64–440	7
Tesco	389	25.2	18	110–350	8
Safeway*	500	14.4	14	20–510	4
Asda**	206	43.5	8†	180–370	6
Gateway	727	9.2	27	5–245	0
Kwik Save	710	6.5	11	90–250††	0
Iceland	519	4.1	6	45–195††	0
Wm. Low	63	12.2	3	120–220	0
CRS	472	5.4	20	15–180††	0

* The Safeway figures include Safeway and Presto but not Lo-Cost. The 310 Safeway stores have an average size of 19,300 sq ft, compared with the 190 Presto stores average of 6,300 sq ft.

** Prior to the purchase of 61 Gateway superstores in 1989, Asda had 129 stores with selling space of 4,762,000 sq ft.,

† Does not include a transshipment depot

†† Does not include depots where chilled or frozen produce are consolidated by contractors

small supermarkets and discount stores. For example, Tengelmann has 15 general warehouses and 14 fresh food depots supplying its 3,501 stores which trade under a variety of formats and facias. The Netherlands, with its urbanized environment similar to parts of the UK, still has a fragmented distribution network in the grocery sector. Albert Heijn, the largest chain, has centralized 80 per cent of its distribution but its 443 stores range in size from 3,000 to over 30,000 square feet, making composite warehousing difficult to implement. Heijn's stores are supplied from four RDCs, five produce warehouses, a national distribution centre, and a centre which distributes cut flowers.

Even in France, the home of the hypermarket, the main operators serve their stores from product category warehouses similar to the small supermarket operators of the UK. This can partly be explained by the range of trading formats used by these companies – for example, Casino has 105 supermarkets and 225 neighbourhood stores, in addition to 41 hypermarkets. Cooper *et al.*[40] argue that the RDC concept has limited application in France and Spain because the hypermarket format has a stand-alone status within a region, negating another link in the distribution chain. This approach, however, is under review as French grocery retailers investigate the possibilities of building composites. In several cases (Casino, Auchan and Promodes), RDCs have been built to serve hypermarkets, and some of the non-food distribution has been carried out by British distribution companies.

Summary

- The extent of logistical support to stores has varied over time and space. Retailers' control of the supply chain increases with retail concentration, the level of retail branding and the quality of distribution service support
- The distribution 'culture' in the UK is different from that in the US and the rest of mainland Europe, where there is a more fragmented approach to distribution
- As retail markets mature and further concentration occurs, it is more likcly that rctail branding will bccome an important part of companies' retail strategies
- The pace at which retailers gain control over the supply chain will be influenced by the level of internationalization of retailing.

References

1. Mandel, S.F., Jnr 'A competitive challenge: how supermarkets can get into the productivity loop', *International Trends in Retailing* 18(1), Spring, 1991, Arthur Anderson & Co.
2. Rogers, D., 'An overview of American retail trends' *International Journal of Retail and Distribution Management* 19(6), 1991, pp. 3–12.

[3] Wileman, A., 'Destination retailing: high volume, low gross margin, large scale formats', *International Journal of Retail and Distribution Management* 20(1), 1993, pp 3–9.

[4] Martensen, R., *The Future Role of Brands on the European Grocery Market*, The University of Gothenburg, 1992.

[5] Europanel, *Manufacturers, Retailers and Consumers in Europe – Prospects for after 1993*, Europanel Database, London, 1992.

[6] Bedeman, M., 'Third party continues to strengthen European logistics', Press Release on Bedeman's conference paper at the Council of Logistics Management, San Antonio, Texas, 1993.

[7] MacLauchan, M., 'A city view of the European retail sector', paper presented at a Financial Times conference, Retailing in the 1990s, London, September, 1992.

[8] Fernie, J., 'Distribution strategies of European retailers', *European Journal of Marketing*, 26(8/9), 1991, pp. 35–47.

[9] Ohbora, T., Parsons, A. and Riesenbeck, H., 'Alternative routes to global marketing', *The McKinsey Quarterly*, 3, 1992, pp. 52–74.

[10] Stout, D., 'Where are we now', paper presented at a one-day debate 'Branded food and drink manufacturers and not retailers are better placed to take advantage of the emerging European market', London, May, 1990.

[11] Ohbora, Parsons and Riesenbeck, op. cit.

[12] Wileman (1993), op. cit.

[13] Davies, G., 'The two ways in which retailers can be brands', *International Journal of Retail and Distribution Management*, 18(2), 1992, pp. 24–34.

[14] Martensen, op. cit.

[15] Wileman, A., 'The shift in balance of power between retailers and manufacturers', paper delivered at Management Centre Europe, Brussels, June, 1992.

[16] Davies, op. cit.

[17] Bedeman, op. cit.

[18] Wileman (1992), op. cit.

[19] Ibid.

[20] Drayer, R., 'The emergence of supply chain management in North America', paper presented at a CIES conference, 'Integrating the Supply Chain', Rotterdam, October, 1992, pp. 3,4.

[21] Galloway, J., 'Asda's central distribution development over the last three years', Exel Logistics Distribution Forum, 26 July, 1991.

[22] Quarmby, D. A., 'Changes in the physical distribution of food to retail outlets', chapter 9b in Fernie, J.

[23] McKinnon, A.C., 'The advantages and disadvantages of centralised distribution', chapter 4 in Fernie, J. 1990 (ed.), op. cit. *Retail Distribution Management*, Kogan Page, London, 1990.

[24] Fernie, J. and McKinnon, A.C., 'The impact of changes in retail distribution on a peripheral region', *International Journal of Retail and Distribution Management*, 19(7), 1991, pp. 25–32.

[25] Williams, B., 'Composite warehousing and distribution in Britain', paper presented at a CIES conference, 1992, op. cit.

[26] Wileman (1992), op. cit.

[27] Jourdan, P. and Irving, R., 'Food distribution in the UK, Continental Europe and the US', paper presented at a CIES conference, 1992, op. cit.

[28] Cullis, R., *European Distribution Services*, IGD, Watford, 1992.

[29] Wileman (1992), op. cit.

[30] Penman, I., 'Logistics – fragmented or integrated', *Focus*, 10(9) 1991, pp. 21–4.
[31] Jourdan and Irving, op. cit.
[32] ILDM, *European Logistics Comparative Costs and Practice*, ILDM/Touche Ross, Corby, 1992.
[33] Bedeman, M., 'Logistics options in Europe' paper presented at a British Retailer's Association Conference, 'Logistics – the European Impact', London, May, 1990.
[34] Cooper, J., Browne, M. and Peters, M., *European Logistics: Markets, Management and Strategy*, Blackwell, Oxford, 1992, p. 202.
[35] Penman, op. cit.
[36] NFC, *Managing the European Supply Chain*, NFC Contract Distribution Report, Bedford, 1989.
[37] Simkin, L.P, Maier, J. and Lee, W.M., 'PDM and inventory management', *Retail and Distribution Management*, 15(1), 1987, pp. 57–9.
[38] McKinnon, A.C., 'The transformation of the retail supply chain: implications for regional development', in Moyes, A. (ed) *Companies, Regions and Transport Change*, IBG, Aberystwth, 1991.
[39] Fernie and McKinnon, op. cit.
[40] Cooper, Browne and Peters, op. cit.

Chapter 19

Monitoring Logistics and Distribution Operations

Alan Rushton
Cranfield School of Management

Introduction

Recent advances in information technology have focused attention on the importance of good information systems to support logistics and distribution activities. There has always been this requirement for information, but the computer has enabled the development of more sophisticated means of data storage, processing and presentation.

Information can be seen as being the lifeblood of a logistics and distribution system. Without the smooth flow and transfer of information it is impossible for a distribution system to function adequately and effectively. To this end, it is important that a company develops an appropriate corporate strategy for its information requirements. This plan will need to take account of a number of different objectives, from strategic planning through to operational control.

A typical framework is shown in the planning and control cycle of Figure 19.1.[1] This framework emphasizes the cyclical nature of the planning and control process, starting with the question 'where are we now?', where the aim is to provide a picture of the current status of an operation. This might be through an information feedback procedure and/or through the use of a distribution audit. The second stage is to identify the objectives of the distribution process. These should be related to such elements as customer service requirements, marketing decisions, etc. The third stage in the cycle is the process which includes the development of appropriate strategic and operational plans to achieve these objectives. Finally, there is a need for monitoring and control procedures to measure the effectiveness of the distribution operation compared to the plan. The process has then turned full circle and the cycle is ready to begin again. This emphasizes the dynamic nature of distribution, and the need for continual review and revision of plans, policies and their operations. This must be undertaken within a positive planning framework to ensure that continuity and progress are maintained.

This chapter begins by considering the need to monitor logistics operations, emphasizing the importance of identifying clear business objectives as the basis for setting up appropriate operational measures. A

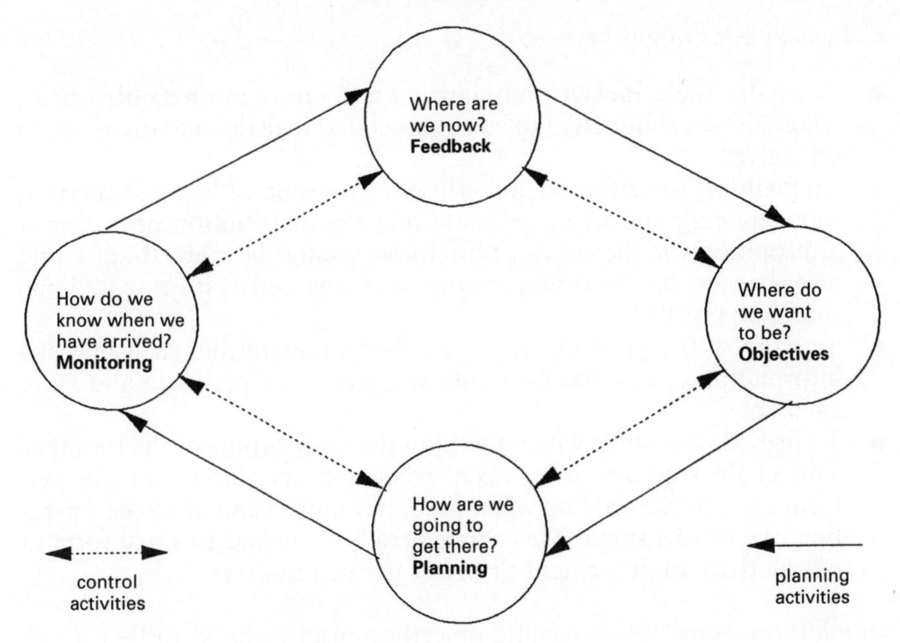

Figure 19.1 *Planning and control cycle*

formal approach for monitoring and control is outlined and the major comparative standards are discussed. The basis for a clear operational planning and control system is outlined.

Companies can be categorized according to the sophistication of their approach to the monitoring and control of their operations. These different categories are outlined. Some specific areas of good practice are considered. Although based on sound common sense, these factors are essential to the development of an effective monitoring system. In addition, a number of influencing factors are highlighted. These are used to help explain the differences that occur when systems are monitored for comparative purposes. Finally, a number of detailed and key monitoring and control measures are indicated.

Wherever possible, case examples are used, based on actual company operations and approaches.

Why Monitor?

To establish an effective system for cost and performance monitoring and control, there is a need to identify some overall guidelines or aims which the system is designed to fulfil. These are likely to reflect major business objectives as well as more detailed operational requirements. Thus it is important to be aware of the role of logistics and distribution within the context of the company's own corporate objectives. It is also essential that the control system reflects the integrated nature of logistics within an organization.

Typical aims might be:

- To enable the achievement of current and future business objectives, where these are directly linked to associated logistics and distribution objectives
- To facilitate the effective and efficient provision of logistics services, thus enabling checks to be made that the distribution operation is appropriate for the overall objectives ('doing the right thing'); and also that the distribution operation is run as well as it can be ('doing the thing right')
- To support the planning and control of an operation, such that any information can be fed back into the process of planning and management
- To provide measures which focus on the real outputs of the business. This enables action to be taken when the operations are not performing satisfactorily or when potential improvement to the operation can be identified. This will generally be linked to some form of productivity improvement or better use of resources.

In addition, some fairly specific objectives need to be identified which relate to the logistics operation itself. A major feature is likely to be measure actual progress against a plan. Typically, this will be to monitor the budget in a way that identifies if some change from plan has taken place, while also providing a useful indication of *why* actual performance or achievement does not reflect what was originally planned. Another feature may well be to highlight specific aspects or components of the system that need particular attention.

Care needs to be taken in identifying these broader objectives. They need to be meaningful. Examples which fail the test include:

- 'The aim for distribution is to minimize costs'. Is this to be at the expense of customer service? There needs to be a clearly identified relationship between cost and service requirements.
- 'The level of service is 'as soon as possible'. What does this really mean? Are all orders treated as urgent?
- 'Everything is to be delivered on our own vehicles.' Does this mean resourcing the fleet to cover peak demand all year round? This is almost certainly not a cost effective approach for determining transport requirements.

An example of carefully prepared objectives comes from a manufacturer and distributor of soft drinks, whose overall objectives were expressed in the following terms:

> To provide accurate, timely and useful information on Distribution Cost and Operational performance to enable:
>
> - the Business to monitor progress towards set objectives at the Total Distribution level

- the operational departments within Distribution to measure their performance against their objectives and targets, and to make operational adjustments as necessary
- the regular provision of information to other internal operations and functions to help assess wider trade-off opportunities
- [the creation of] a solid database of information for use in strategic and operational planning.

Overall the information must be quantitative and comparative wherever possible, relating to set objectives.

Monitoring and Control: A General Approach

The monitoring and control of logistics and distribution operations is often approached in a relatively unsophisticated and unplanned way. Control measures are adopted as problems arise, almost as a form of crisis management.

It is important to adopt a more formal approach, although this should not necessitate a complicated format. Such a simple and straighforward approach is shown in Figure 19.2.

The scope of distribution and logistics activities will, of course, vary from one company to another, as will the extent of integration. Because of this, it is impossible to identify a standard system that can be adopted generally. A company must first determine the scope of activities that need to be considered, taking into account the overall logistics requirements and objectives, as well as the traditional components of the functional sub-systems (trunking, depot operations, local delivery, etc).

More detailed departmental objectives should be defined. These will include considerations such as stock-holding policies by individual line or product group, customer service levels by product, by customer type or by geographical area, delivery transport costs, utilization and performance, etc.

Determine scope of logistics activities

↓

Identify organizational and departmental objectives

↓

Determine operating principles/methods

↓

Set productivity/performance goals
(using standards, etc)

↓

Measure and monitor performance
(develop MIS)

Figure 19.2 *Broad approach for a monitoring and control system*

Operating principles and methods need to be clarified with respect to the different logistics components, such as trunking and delivery transport, warehousing resources and usage, together with implications for seasonality, etc. These factors will provide the basis for establishing realistic and relevant measures.

Productivity and performance goals should then be set in relation to the detailed operational tasks which are performed and with respect to the overall output requirements for the integrated logistics system as a whole. These should cover all the essential aspects of the physical distribution system. It is often easier to categorize these under the major sub-systems of warehousing (order-picking performance, labour utilization, cost per case, etc); transport (vehicle utilization, cost per mile, fuel consumption, etc); and administration/stock-holding (customer orders received, stock-outs, percentage of orders fulfilled, etc).

Goals should be set based on some acceptable standards or comparative information. There are several different approaches used by organizations, and these are discussed below. They include:

- Measuring cost and performance against historic data
- Measuring against a budget plan
- Developing physical or engineered standards
- Using industry standards
- Benchmarking against 'best practice'.

Finally, key indices and ratios need to be developed to allow for appropriate monitoring and control to be undertaken (ie actual work against planned work, cost per case, cases per hour, tonnes per journey, etc). These need to be representative of the distribution operation, and they should be capable of clearly identifying *why* a deviation has occurred, as well as *if* a deviation has occurred.

What to Measure Against?

As already indicated, there are a number of different approaches that can be adopted to determine appropriate goals. These range in sophistication from very simplistic internal year-on-year comparisons, to quite detailed externally related engineered standards. Most well-developed systems are internally budget-oriented, but are also linked to external performance measures.

Historic data

Systems that merely compare overall activity costs on a period-by-period basis may not be providing any useful information with which to monitor operational performance. As an example, a measure may indicate that the cost of distribution for a company has been reduced as a percentage of total revenue for the current year compared to the previous year. Without any background to this measure, it is impossible to be sure whether or not this is an improvement in terms of distribution performance.

Budget

Almost all companies will have a budget plan, and this should include a breakdown of the logistics costs in appropriate detail – an activity budget. A traditional means of monitoring an operation is, therefore, to evaluate the cost of the logistics operation in relation to the expectations of the budget plan.

The budget approach has been developed in a variety of ways to enable more sophisticated and more meaningful measures to be created. The 'activity' concept means that the budget – and the respective measurement process – can identify and differentiate between functional activities (warehouse, transport, etc) but more importantly, across core business-oriented activities. This might, for example, be by product group or by major customer, thus allowing for very detailed measurements, reflecting the integrated nature of the logistics activities under scrutiny.

An additional development is the concept of flexible budgeting, which recognizes one of the key issues of monitoring – the need to be able to identify and take account of any changes in business volumes. This is particularly important in the logistics environment, where any reductions in volume throughput can lead to the under-performance of resources. The concept is based on the premise that budgets are put together with respect to a planned level of activity. The fixed, semi-variable and variable costs appropriate to that level of activity are identified, and form the basis of the budget. If activity levels fluctuate, then the planned budget is flexed to correspond with the new conditions. Thus, semi-variable and variable costs are adjusted for the change. In this way, the change in cost relationships which result from a change in the level of activity is taken into account automatically, and any other differences between planned and actual cost performance can be identified as either performance or price changes.

This approach is particularly applicable to logistics activities, as there is very often a high fixed cost element, and any reduction in levels of activity can increase unit costs quite significantly. With a fixed (eg non-flexible) budget system, it can be difficult to identify the essential reasons for a large variance. To what extent is there a controllable inefficiency in the system, and to what extent is there under-utilization of resources due to falling activity?

A typical example is the effect that a reduction in demand (throughput) can have on order-picking performance and thus unit cost. A flexible budget will take account of the volume change and adjust the original budget accordingly.

Finally, an effective budget measurement system will incorporate the idea of variance analysis. In the context of logistics activities, variance analysis allows for the easier identification of problem areas, as well as providing an indication of the extent of that variance, helping the decision process of whether or not management time should be assigned to solving that particular problem. As indicated earlier, an effective system will indicate if a variance has occurred, the extent of that variance, and also why it has occurred with respect to performance/efficiency change or price/cost change (or a mixture of both). Variance analysis is best used within the context of a flexible budget, because the flexible budget automatically takes account of changes in activity.

Engineered standards

A number of companies use internally derived measures for certain logistics activities through the development of engineered standards. This involves the identification of detailed measures for set tasks and operations. The means of determining these measures is a lengthy and often costly process involving the use of time and work study techniques.

When suitable and acceptable standards have been agreed for specific tasks, then a performance monitoring system can be adjusted to allow for direct measurement of actual performance against expected or planned performance. The advantage of using engineered standards is that each task is measured against an acceptable base. A monitoring system which measures against past experience alone may be able to identify improved (or reduced) performance, but it is always possible that the initial measure was not a particularly efficient performance on which to base subsequent comparisons.

Apart from cost, a potential drawback with engineered standards is that the initial time or work study data collection is difficult to verify. There is no certainty that an operative who is under scrutiny will perform naturally or realistically (whether consciously or otherwise).

Many logistics tasks do lend themselves to the application of engineered standards. Most warehousing activities fall into this category – goods receiving, pallet put-away, order-picking, etc, as well as driver-related activities – vehicle loading, miles travelled, fixed and variable unloading. For delivery transport, for example, standard costs can be related to measured or standard times, which should cover the three main operations:

- Running/driving time (speeds related to road types)
- Selection and delivery time (fixed and variable)
- Depot/loading time.

Standard time journeys can then be built up and can be incorporated with standard costs to give a standard cost per minute. Thus, the planned and actual performance are linked and variance analysis can be undertaken, providing for a stronger system of control.

External standards and benchmarking

Another approach to cost and performance measurement is to make comparisons against industry norms. The intention here is that a company's performance should be compared to similar external operations and standards, making comparison more realistic and therefore more valuable. For some industries, such as grocery retailing, these measures are fairly readily accessible through industry journals and associations. Examples of typical measures include order-picking performance (cases per hour), delivery cases per journey, etc.

A further development to this is the idea of 'benchmarking'. Here, the aim is to identify appropriate 'world class' or 'best in class' standards across a whole range of different organizations and operations. This enables a company's performance to be compared with the very best in any industry. It is a broader concept than merely identifying variations in performance, the intention being to identify the reasons why a certain operation is the best and to establish ways and means of emulating the operation. A number of 'benchmarking' clubs have been formed to this end.

Recent surveys have shown that there is still significant room for improvement for many companies in the context of the use of appropriate monitoring systems. Figure 19.3, which is based on the results of a survey of logistics productivity carried out by A T Kearney,[2] indicates that the majority of companies base their performance measures on past experience, or have no set standards at all.

An Operational Planning and Control System

The budget should be used as the basis for providing quantitative

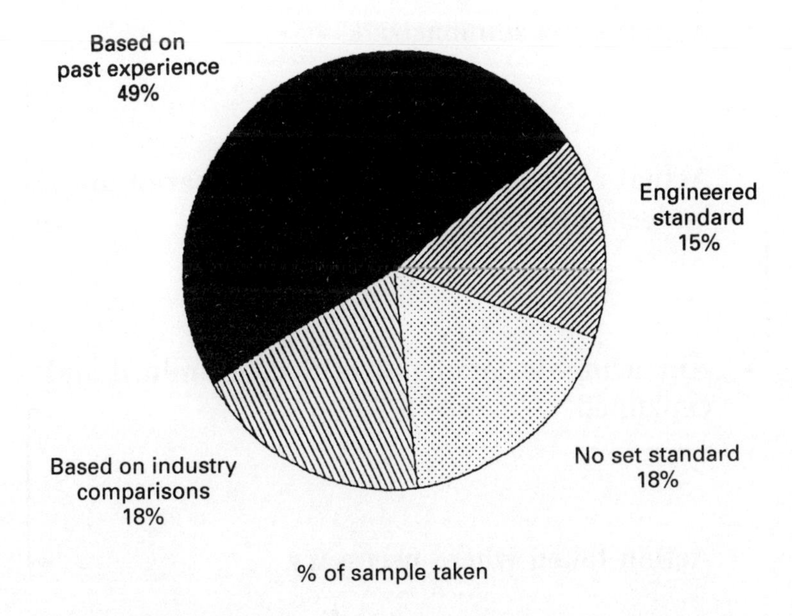

Figure 19.3 *Goal-setting basis used in sample UK companies*

objectives for the relevant elements within the logistics operation that are to be monitored. Linked to this should be any appropriate internal (engineered) or external standards that are deemed to be important measures of the business.

The operating plan should be drawn up, based on the above factors to indicate the operational parameters or cost centres. This will show how costs are to be split by period (week, month), by functional element (fuel, wages, etc). Also, the plan should show which key business performance indicators are to be used (tonne/miles delivered, etc) and demonstrate how those are linked to set standards.

The operating control system involves the process of identifying whether the operating plan has been adhered to – what deviations have occurred and why – such that they can be speedily remedied. Figure 19.4 outlines this process.

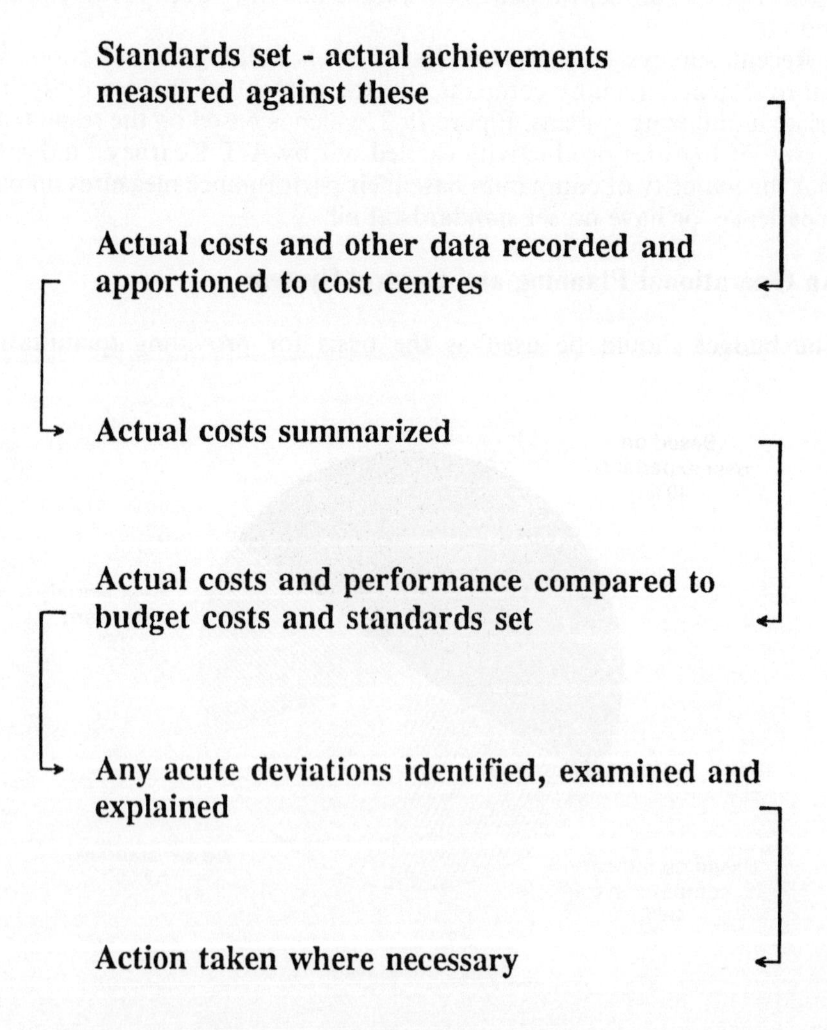

Figure 19.4 *Operating control system*

In measuring these deviations, it is important to be aware of three major causes of deviation:

- Changes in levels of activity (eg less work is available for a fixed capacity – labour, equipment
- Changes in efficiency or performance (eg the resource, labour or equipment, has not performed as expected)
- Changes in price (eg the price of an item, say fuel, has increased, so costs will increase).

Activity levels changes can, of course, be taken into account by the use of flexible budgets.

Key indices and ratios need to be developed to allow for appropriate monitoring and control to be undertaken (ie actual work against planned work, cost per case, cases per hour, tonnes per journey, etc). These need to be representative of the distribution operation, and they should be capable of clearly identifying why, as well as if, a deviation has occurred.

Leaders and Laggers

As with many aspects of business, companies vary in the extent to which they have developed the sophistication of their performance measurement. There are the leaders who have adopted a very forward-looking approach to the monitoring and control of their operations, and who have incorporated ideas such as flexible budgeting, variance analysis, productivity standards and integrated control measures. There are also the laggers, who do little more than compare broad costs on a period-by-period basis.

It is possible to identify discrete categories of companies indicating the different approach to, and different level of use of, cost and performance monitoring techniques. The emphasis is very much one of attitude to measurement and productivity performance. A T Kearney[3] have suggested four company categories:

- **Inactive companies** have few clear measures, and a tendency to react to crises as their sole means of monitoring. At the most, they will isolate very broad costs and link these to macro outputs such as sales revenue, subsequently comparing these over long time periods.
- **Reactive companies** have budget-based monitoring systems and tend to evaluate performance only against the budget. The approach is broadly one of historic cost accounting. Budgets are likely to be broken down into different functional activities, but will not reflect key core business activities. Companies in this category are positioned to pursue cost reduction programmes rather than productivity improvement programmes.
- **Proactive companies** will incorporate both measured/engineered standards as well as flexible budgets and variance analysis. The more

sophisticated will have moved towards industry-based standards and may have begun some benchmarking programmes
- **Integrative companies** will have adopted the same approach to measurement as the proactive companies, but rather than identifying and measuring the different functional activities in isolation, will have developed overall logistics-related measures. This will help provide the ability to monitor and plan in an integrated way, allowing trade-off opportunities to be identified and evaluated.

Good practice

There are a number of key areas of 'good practice' that need to be considered when developing the detail of an effective monitoring and control system. These are all fairly straightforward, but bear discussion. They can be broadly categorized as:

- Principles
- Content
- Output.

Principles

Most of the main principles associated with an effective system are based on sound common sense. They can be used to provide distinct guidelines for the development of an appropriate new control system, as well as to help identify reasons why an existing system is not functioning satisfactorily. They include:

- **Accuracy** The basic input data to the system must be correct. Inaccurate data will obviously produce incorrect measures, but will also undermine confidence in the system as a whole
- **Validity/completeness** The measures used must reflect a particular activity in an appropriate way, and must cover all of the aspects concerned. For example, a broad carton per hour measure for order-picking is clearly inappropriate if there is a substantial element of full pallet picking or broken case picking
- **Hierarchy of needs** Certain information is only required by certain individuals within an organization. To swamp individuals with unnecessary information is unnecessary, expensive and may diminish the usefulness of an information system. Typically, the higher the level of personnel within an organization, the more general or more aggregate is the information required. Figure 19.5 indicates this hierarchy, illustrating the relationship between what might be termed as command information and feedback/control information
- **Targeting the correct audience** Linked very much to the previous point is the need to ensure that the correct audience is identified and that all the key information is then directed to this audience.
- **User ownership** The fault of many an information system is to

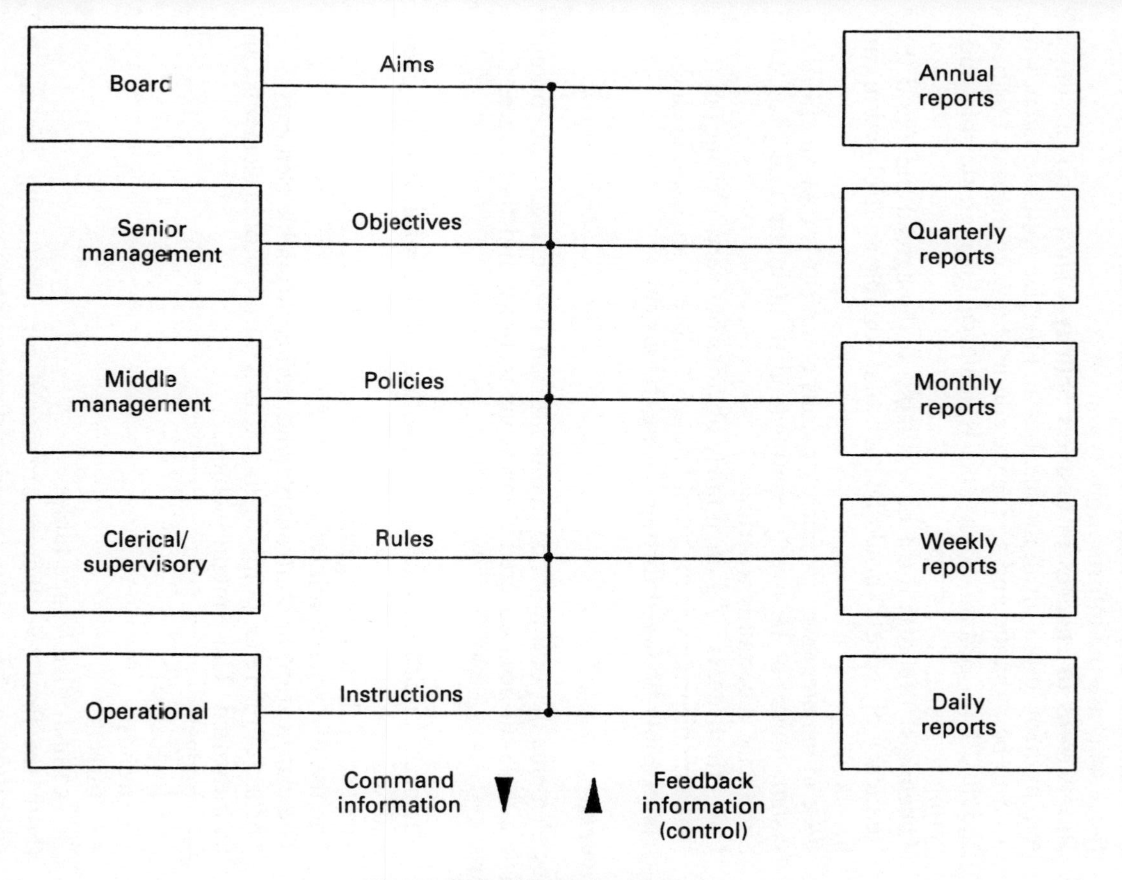

Figure 19.5 *Hierarchy of needs*

impose information onto individuals without first including them in the process of identifying and determining information requirements. This can be very demotivating. It is a very valid step to include potential users at the systems requirement stage, thus conferring user ownership of the information when the system is in place. The information should be useful and the detail should be understood by those who use the information

- **Reactiveness to changes in business activity** This is not a simple requirement to put into practice, but an effective control system will need to be dynamic and so take account of any changes in business activity. To a certain extent this is achieved through flexible budgeting
- **Timeliness** Reports must be available at the agreed time, and the frequency of reports should be such that suitable control action can be taken
- **Ease of maintenance** A fairly obvious comment is that an effective system must not be overly complicated to maintain and progress. Simplicity is certainly a virtue
- **Cost effectiveness** Again, a fairly obvious but very relevant point is that a monitoring system should not cost more to set up and run than can possibly be saved through using the system.

Content

The elements of good practice that come under the category of content have almost all been covered in previous sections, and they are as follows:

- The need for clear cost categories, with careful identification of fixed and variable costs
- The use of flexible budgeting
- The use of variance analysis
- The clarification of controllable and non-controllable elements
- The use of reference points against which the monitored elements can be measured. These might include:
  - budgets
  - forecasts
  - trends
  - targets
  - comparative league tables

  (both the final two factors are useful for monitoring contractor operations and for setting up inter-depot comparisons).

Output

The final aspect of good practice concerns the type of output that the system produces. This is the information on which any form of action is based. It has already been emphasized that this information must be relevant and useful:

- reports can vary, they may be:
  - summary: providing key statistics only
  - exception: identifying the major deviations from plan
  - detailed: including all information
- Reports should be made to a standard format – especially important where any inter-depot comparisons are to be made
- Data should be presented in whatever means is most appropriate to the eventual use of that data.

Some alternative forms of output are indicated below:

- **Trend data** Based upon moving annual totals to identify long-term changes
- **Comparative data** Data analysis over a short period (eg this month against last month), against a target (eg this month compared with budget), or against a measured standard (eg this month compared with standard). Comparative data analysis also identifies variances which indicate the degree of performance success
- **Indices** Data in statistical form compared with a base position over time
- **Ratio** A combination of two or more pieces of meaningful data to form a meaningful figure for comparison
- **Graphs** Comparative trends in pictorial form.

Characteristics of monitoring

What do companies see as being the most valuable characteristics of a good monitoring system? The example outlined below provides an indication.

An international manufacturer and supplier of computer equipment identified the need for a more adequate information system for monitoring and controlling performance in its three warehouses. The company set up a project team to investigate these requirements, and produced some interesting output.

Five key areas for measurement

- **Volume** What is moving through the warehouse?
- **Efficiency** How well is the operation being run?
- **Cost effectiveness** Is the cost reflecting the work being done?
- **Quality** How well are the service levels being met?
- **Stability** What does the staff turnover picture look like?

Outline requirements to help monitor the operation

- Overall business control
- Activity measures within business area
- Trend indicators and productivity measures.

Factors for consideration

- **Action** It should lead to a change in the current position. It should be used
- **Confusion** The system should filter out the irrelevant information which confuses and diverts attention
- **Comprehensibility** Everyone who receives information must understand it
- **Defensiveness** The defensive reaction to figures, especially adverse ones, needs to be overcome
- **Timelessness** The information has to be available in sufficient time for action to be taken
- **Validity** Actual changes in performance must be reflected by the system
- **Dynamism** The system must be sensitive to the changing internal and external conditions; tomorrow's problems cannot be solved with yesterday's measurement system.

Influencing Factors

Many monitoring systems are developed with a view to using them to enable comparisons to be made between different depots. Some companies will do this across their own operations. It is also common practice for some of the major users of dedicated contract operations to compare how well one contractor is performing against the others.

If this is the major use of a monitoring system then it is essential that there is a broad understanding of any different operational factors that might influence the apparent effectiveness or efficiency of one operation compared to another. Thus, a number of operational influencing variables can be identified, and may need to be measured, to enable suitable conclusions to be drawn and explanations given for any comparative assessments.

Any number of these may be relevant, but typical examples of these are:

- Throughput variability (by day)
- Product profile
- Order profile
- Store profile
- Store returns
- Special projects (promotions, alternative unitization)
- Equipment specification
- RDC design (building shape, mezzanines)
- Employee bonus schemes
- Methods (secondary sorts, etc)
- Local labour market (quality, need for training, etc)
- Regional cost variations (labour, rent, rates, etc)
- Staff agreements (guaranteed hours, etc)
- Unit definitions.

Detailed and Key Measures

For most logistics operations it is possible to identify certain key measures which provide an appropriate summary measurement of the operation as a whole and of the major elements of the operation. Detailed measurements are likely to differ from one company to another, dependent on the nature of the business.

Measures are generally aimed at providing an indication of the performance of individual elements within an operation, as well as their cost effectiveness. In addition, the overall performance or output is often measured, particularly with respect to the service provided, the total system cost and the return on capital investment.

Typical detailed and key measures that are used are summarized in three different case studies. These cover customer service requirements, a warehouse operation and a multi-depot delivery transport operation. Both the warehouse and the transport examples indicate adherence to the principle of the hierarchical nature of information requirements.

Case Study 1: Supplier of Consumables

Major customer service measurements:

- Percentage of orders satisfied in full
- Percentage of items supplied at first demand
- Percentage of overdue orders
- Numbers of stock-outs
- Orders delivered within set lead times
- Percentage of deliveries outside fixed delivery windows/times.

Case study 2: Grocery – Multiple Retailer

Measures taken are designed to assess the performance of the delivery transport system. They are aimed at measuring the cost effectiveness of the operation and also the quality of service. Note the hierarchical approach, and also the fact that there are no cost-related measures at the lowest level.

Director/head office (strategic planning and control)

- ROCE
- Cost/case (divisional)
- Cost/vehicle (divisional)
- Cost/value of goods delivered
- Cost as percentage of company sales.

Depot managers (management control)

- Cost/mile
- Cost/vehicle
- Cost/roll pallet

- Average earnings/driver
- Maximum earnings/driver
- Maintenance costs/vehicles.

Transport managers (operational control)

- Cost/mile
- Cost/case
- Cost/vehicle
- Cost/roll pallet
- Cost/journey
- Roll pallets/journey
- Journeys/vehicle
- Damage repairs/vehicle
- Miles/gallon per vehicle
- Damages in transit and cases delivered
- Percentage of cases out of temperature
- Percentage of journeys out of schedule.

Supervisors

- Overtime hours as percentage of hours worked
- Contract vehicles as percentage of vehicles
- Percentage of vehicles off road
- Percentage of drivers absent
- Percentage of vehicle fill
- Percentage of vehicles overweight
- Percentage of breakdowns
- Average hours worked/driver.

Case study 3: Manufacturer/supplier of FMCG

Information requirements related to the company's warehouse operations in terms of performance measurements and operating ratios.

CEO

- Profit
- Return on investment
- Growth
- Stock turnover
- Distribution cost
- Sales value.

Distribution director

- Service achievement
- Cost effectiveness
- Capital employed
- Stock turnover by depots
- Storage cost/unit

- Warehouse handling cost/unit
- Overall labour efficiency.

Warehouse manager

- Inventory level
- Stock availability
- Operating cost
- Operating productivity
- Actual hours and
- Standard hours for
  - — stock receiving and location
  - — order-picking
  - — packing
  - — despatch
- Warehouse cost/unit (order)
- Stock turnover.

Summary

- The approach to monitoring logistics and distribution operations has been pursued in this chapter, linked wherever possible to actual company practice. The need for monitoring and control procedures to measure the effectiveness of actual distribution performance against a prescribed distribution plan has been identified within the context of the framework of a planning and control cycle.
- The need to establish clear, business-related objectives has been emphasized. A formal approach for a monitoring and control system was outlined, but it was felt important that this should not be a complicated format.
- Several different means of identifying suitable goals were introduced:
  - — Measuring cost and performance against historic data
  - — Measuring against a budget plan
  - — Developing physical or engineered standards
  - — Using industry standards
  - — Benchmarking against 'best practice'.
- The major factors related to these alternatives were discussed, together with the relative advantages and disadvantages of the different approaches. An operational planning and control system was described, with the emphasis on the need to identify and measure what deviations had occurred, and why they had occurred. This should specifically consider changes in:
  - — Levels of activity
  - — Efficiency or performance
  - — Price or cost.
- It was noted that companies could be categorized according to whether they were leaders or laggers in the development of reliable cost and performance monitoring systems. One study was quoted which identified four main company categories:

  - Inactive
  - Reactive
  - Proactive
  - Integrative.
- A number of key areas of good practice were considered. These were deemed essential in developing the detail of an effective monitoring and control system. These were considered under the heading of principles, content and output. In addition, a number of influencing factors were highlighted as being important to help explain the differences that occur when systems are monitored for comparative purposes.
- Finally, a series of key and detailed cost and performance measures were considered. These were drawn from a number of specific case studies.

References

[1] Rushton, A. and Oxley, J., *Handbook of Logistics and Distribution Management* Kogan Page, London 1991.

[2] A T Kearney Inc., *Logistics Productivity: The Competitive Edge in Europe*, 1990.

[3] A T Kearney Inc., *Measuring Productivity in Physical Distribution* NCPDM, 1988.

Chapter 20

Planning for Urban Delivery

Kenneth W Ogden
Professorial Fellow
Monash Transport Group
Monash University
Melbourne, Australia

Introduction

Other chapters in this book have focused upon particular aspects of logistics and distribution planning from the viewpoint of the firm. The focus shifts somewhat in this chapter, in that we consider here the broader road and transport system context within which such distribution activities take place.

Such a perspective is important and will be relevant to the intended readership of this book. Nothing takes place in a vacuum, and distribution activities can only occur if there is a transport infrastructure, usually publicly provided, for freight deliveries to use. It is therefore relevant that those responsible for the (usually) private sector logistics management activities of the firm know something about the (usually) public sector responsibilities of transport infrastructure design and operation.

It is the writer's experience that there is all too little communication between logistics managers and transport system planners and designers. The latter (especially those in the roads field) concentrate almost exclusively upon catering for the private motorist; this is hardly surprising, since in Western countries private cars constitute the great bulk of the traffic stream. A consequence of this is that the problems of moving freight and the opportunities to contribute to economic, social and environmental objectives through a more efficient freight system are recognized all too rarely.

On the other hand, logistics people tend to accept the transport system for what it is. Poor road conditions, congestion, inadequate access, poorly designed terminals etc tend to be accepted as merely part of their operating environment, much like the climate. Since no single firm can gain a competitive advantage or disadvantage from, say, reductions in congestion levels, this is accepted by freight operators, and costs are passed on to their customers.

A prime purpose of this chapter therefore is to attempt to establish a link, albeit a tenuous one, between the two. If the readership of this book can gain some insight into the thinking of road system operators and planners, and of the opportunities available through better provision for freight activities, the beginnings of a more constructive dialogue may be possible.

In this context and with this objective, the chapter discusses the following issues:

- Truck routes
- Intersection design and operation
- Truck parking and loading
- Terminal design and location
- Emerging road system technology.

Truck Routes

Because trucks are bigger than cars, and are considered more environmentally intrusive, they are sometimes restricted to certain parts of the road network.

Designated Truck Routes

Truck routes may be of two forms, advisory or statutory. An advisory truck route system involves making particular routes attractive to trucks, with the aim of attracting trucks to it away from 'protected' routes. There are obvious enforcement advantages with this approach. In practice, this feature is very common, whether intended or not, in that certain routes are more attractive for trucks.

An advisory truck route network would usually include all motorways and major arterial roads in an area, and may encompass other road types where they extend into industrial areas or truck terminal locations. The network must be free of barriers to truck travel such as width or height restrictions.

A statutory truck route system is one which legally prohibits trucks from using routes other than those designated. In implementation, this approach tends to rely more on its corollary, ie particular areas (eg a local street network) are protected by an entry ban ('no entry except for access').

If a truck route network, whether advisory or statutory, is to be introduced, there are a number of factors to be taken into account in designating and promulgating it.[1] These include the need to serve major truck traffic generators, the need for adequate pavement design standards and road geometry, the desirability of avoiding sensitive abutting land uses, traffic control facilities, and the availability of truck and driver services. In implementation, the need for consultation between various local government authorities and with the industry is also important. The route must be adequately signed.

Hazardous Truck Routes

A particular category of truck route is the designation of specific routes for vehicles carrying hazardous goods (eg highly volatile, flammable or explosive goods, toxic wastes, etc), especially where the movement is frequent, eg between chemical plants, storage or disposal sites, etc.

The designation of truck routes and the development of management plans for the transport of hazardous materials should be based upon a risk assessment procedure, such as that developed by the US Federal Highway Administration.[2] In general, roads which are preferred for the transport of hazardous materials will be likely to include freeways and controlled access facilities, to avoid densely populated areas and sensitive land uses, to be of a high geometric standard, and to take into account relative levels of exposure to risk, as measured by distance, persons exposed to risk, time of day, etc.[3]

A hazardous truck network has both advantages and disadvantages. Among the former are the potential for increased public safety, reduced truck driver stress, attention to specific road and traffic measures to increase safety, and the focusing of emergency services onto a smaller part of the network.

On the other hand, there are some major disadvantages – principally a strong negative reaction from among those people who live and work along such routes. An attempt to develop and implement a hazardous truck route network must therefore devote much time and effort to community consultation.[4] In addition, transport costs are increased and operating freedom is reduced, and enforcement needs are increased. For these reasons, and particularly that relating to adverse community reaction, many cities do not designate an explicit network for vehicles carrying hazardous loads.

High Productivity Truck Routes

Another category of truck route is the designation of a network of roads which are available for use by high productivity vehicles. Perhaps the best example is the requirement for US states and cities to provide 'reasonable access' to Interstate and Federal-aid primary routes for the larger vehicles which are permitted on such routes by Federal law.[5]

Intersections

Intersections are a key consideration in road networks, since they are clearly the points at which traffic capacity is most constrained, and are also where crash exposure is highest. Design and operation of intersections should therefore take account of all road-user groups, including trucks.

Traffic Signals

Traffic signal design practices usually do not take explicit account of the needs of heavy trucks, in terms of such factors as braking and acceleration capability and the costs of stops. Current signal design practice concentrates on capacity maximization in the peak direction (usually radial), and this reduces the capacity in counter-peak and cross-town directions, the directions more likely to be used by trucks at peak hours.

Trucks are currently accommodated in traffic signal design mainly through the use of passenger car equivalents in capacity calculations (ie one truck is considered to be the equivalent of more than one car). Recent research[6,7,8] has shown that larger trucks have a higher through car equivalent value, and where a large number of heavy trucks use an intersection, existing design practices will overestimate the capacity of the intersection.

The potential exists to do more to cater for the needs of heavy vehicles at intersections, especially if signal equipment is modified to identify specific classes of vehicle (eg by number of axles). Potential changes might include the introduction of longer clearance or all-red times, to allow for lower speed and poorer braking for through trucks and slower acceleration of turning trucks; the use of dynamic truck detection and green phase extension so that signals do not turn yellow as a truck is approaching; adjustment of the gap and waste timers to allow for longer headways between vehicles (caused by slower truck acceleration); using turning phase warrants which take particular account of truck turning volumes; and adjustment of passenger car equivalent factors where there is a high proportion of trucks.

Increasingly, urban traffic signals are operated as part of a linked network. This provides progression along a route to improve the performance of the traffic system in terms of such parameters as reduced number of stops, reduced fuel consumption, reduced travel time and reduced accidents.

However, trucks can be disadvantaged by linked signal systems if the time offset between the commencement of the green at successive signals is set on the basis of car times which trucks, because of their slower acceleration, cannot match. Sometimes the settings are such that trucks in fact face a 'red wave' rather than a 'green wave', being stopped at perhaps every signal along a route.[9]

Trucks can be considered explicitly in linked networks in several ways: linking can be based on truck speeds; high-volume truck turning movements can be linked; linking can be based on counter-peak travel times when congestion in the peak direction precludes linking; and the density of signals (signals per kilometre or mile) can be minimized.

Intersection Geometry

Intersection geometry (ie layout and radius of right and left turns) also needs to take account of the requirements of large vehicles. All too often this is not the case, and trucks are expected to mount kerbs or raised traffic islands in order to negotiate an intersection. Guidelines and computer packages for the layout of intersections are available.[10]

Of course, there are sometimes situations where a deliberate decision is made to retain, or even install, an intersection which a truck has difficulty in negotiating, in order to discourage extraneous trucks from entering (say) a residential area. However, even in these cases, it is necessary to ensure that trucks with legitimate business in the area can gain access. In the case of roundabouts, for example, the central island should have a mountable curb so that a design vehicle (perhaps a large rigid truck) can get through the intersection; use of templates or computer packages, as described above, may be helpful here also.

Truck Loading and Unloading

Strategies for truck loading and unloading are critical, since the pick-up and delivery of goods requires trucks to stop at a convenient location, either at the kerb or off-street.

Kerbside Facilities

Kerbside arrangements include the provision of loading zones at selected locations, in which only commercial vehicles involved in pick-up and delivery operations are permitted, or the provision of loading zones for certain times of the day only, either to encourage delivery operations at those times or because other demands (eg clearway operations or exclusive bus lanes) take precedence at other times.

In determining kerbside loading arrangements, various factors need to be considered, particularly the variety of needs that have to be met (eg short-term pick-up and delivery operations such as courier or parcel delivery, longer-term requirements such as truckload deliveries, and service vehicle needs such as telephone, repair vans, etc); and the need for enforcement.[11]

Specific guidelines for the provision of kerbside loading zones have to be determined for each individual location. It always involves a trade-off between this use and other uses (especially car parking and, in peak periods, moving traffic).

Off-street Facilities

Major new commercial, industrial and retail developments should have adequate off-street loading and unloading facilities for trucks servicing the development. Since loading space is usually non-leasable, it is usually necessary for a public authority to prescribe its provision through the planning approval process.

The benefits of adequate off-street loading facilities include reduced costs of deliveries, and higher truck productivity; increased service quality to building occupiers; improved security for vehicles and goods; reduced on-street congestion (especially double-parking); and improved aesthetics of retail and commercial areas.

The need for off-street loading facilities varies widely, both between and within land uses, and planning for major new developments should be based upon experience or surveys of similar developments elsewhere. Guidelines showing the loading requirements for different land uses are also available.[12,13,14]

Terminal Design and Location

Although the design and operation of terminals and loading docks are usually the responsibility of the operator, there are planning and road design issues here as well. For example, many terminals are poorly sited, resulting in little if any opportunity for facility expansion or modification and also conflicts with other nearby land uses, or environmental impacts on adjacent premises from noise, hazardous materials storage, floodlighting, etc. Moreover, partly as a result of the locational aspect, access to many terminals, especially in the older areas of cities (typically near seaports or railway depots) can be quite congested. Terminal operations can also affect public infrastructure in a number of ways, such as damage to roads and bridges with overloaded trucks; damage to roadway signs, signals, poles, wires, etc; and problems at railway level crossings.[15]

Terminal Location

The location of freight terminals involves both operator concerns and land-use planning concerns. Ideally, a freight terminal should have the following characteristics:[16,17]

- Adequate site area of suitable shape and terrain
- Adequate local street and road capacity
- No restrictions on truck operations in the area
- Permitted access by largest vehicles likely to use the facility
- No adverse noise or zoning restrictions which might inhibit 24-hour terminal operations, such as restrictions based on noise or lighting.

These considerations usually imply a fairly large site in a suburban location, near freeways or arterial roads, and not abutting residential or other sensitive land uses.

Design

The design of loading bays and terminals is important to ensure efficient and safe operation. Some aspects of good design include the following:[18,19]

- Rear loading and unloading is more efficient and convenient than side loading
- Where trucks are required to reverse into a loading dock, the design should be such that the driver uses a right-hand lock on a right-hand drive vehicle (or a left-hand lock on a left-hand drive vehicle), so that the driver is on the inside of the turning manoeuvre (this ensures that the driver's view is not obscured by the vehicle or its load)

- Loading docks should be designed for the largest vehicle servicing a development
- The design should allow sufficient space for vehicles to easily manoeuvre into the loading docks
- Driveways and access roads should allow easy and convenient access to the dock area, and ideally should not be not used for car parking.

Road System Technology

Finally, it is relevant to note that there are a range of emerging developments in the technology of the road system itself. Primarily, these revolve around communication systems and electronic navigation and route guidance systems, but the technology is readily extendible to such applications as electronic logbooks, real-time road pricing and vehicle management. While the hardware and its proposed applications vary, several major research projects under way in the United States, Europe and Japan aim to have such systems operational within a few years.[20]

The generic term for these systems is 'Intelligent Vehicle/Highway Systems' (IVHS), or 'Telematics'. Five categories of IVHS may be defined:

- **Advanced Traffic Management Systems (ATMS)**, which activate traffic control and management strategies (such as traffic information, demand management, freeway ramp metering, arterial road traffic signals, and incident response procedures) in real time, based upon area-wide surveillance and detection systems
- **Advanced Traveller Information Systems (ATIS)**, which provide drivers with real-time information on congestion and alternative routes, navigation and location, roadway conditions, availability of parking, speed and occupancy traffic lanes, etc and a range of public transport information (eg bus location, estimated time of arrival of, the vehicle at a bus stop, etc)
- **Advanced Public Transportation Systems (APTS)**, which aim to improve the productivity, reliability and scheduling of road-based public transport operations
- **Advanced Vehicle Control Systems (AVCS)**, which aim to dramatically improve safety and highway capacity by ultimately providing complete control of the driving function, and even allowing for external (in-road) energy sources; in the mean time, the technology is applicable to collision avoidance systems
- **Commercial Vehicle Operations (CVO)**, which aim to improve the productivity, safety, and regulation of commercial vehicles.

Developments in the first three of these areas are proceeding rapidly, and there is a high degree of certainty about their introduction, in an incremental way. This has resulted, and/or will result in improvements of the following forms:

- Dynamic route guidance
- Speed guidance
- Traffic incident detection
- Signal priority to selected vehicles
- Real-time monitoring and control of traffic system performance
- Electronic citation for speeding and other offences
- Electronic detection of stolen vehicles
- Real-time information to travellers for improved trip-planning
- Electronic pricing of road use and parking
- Better information about traveller behaviour and travel demand.

These developments stand to benefit all road vehicles and road users. However, since commercial vehicle travel time and reliability of arrival time is probably greater for trucks than for most other road vehicle categories, these developments offer great promise to urban goods and service vehicles.[21]

Other chapters in this book have discussed the increasing importance of real-time information for control purposes in the overall logistics process. Applications in the fifth of the above areas, CVO, have the potential to complement and extend this information and control function to that part of the logistics chain which occurs on the road system. Freight-related aspects of IVHS are in three general categories: despatching and routeing; regulation and administration; and positioning and communications.

Despatching and Routeing

Real-time routeing and redirection of trucks in urban areas is fairly common using radio or (increasingly) cellular telephones, especially for those trucks on pick-up and delivery rounds. However, this is generally done without detailed knowledge of either current traffic conditions or the exact location of a truck at any point in time.

Real-time traffic information, perhaps supplemented by a route guidance system, would thus enable faster despatching, more efficient routeing, and more timely collections and deliveries.[22] This could involve either two-way communications between drivers and despatchers, using automatic vehicle location and tracking with in-vehicle text and map displays, or in-vehicle traffic information and route guidance displays (see below). A study of road freight transport operators in Australia indicated that real-time vehicle identification and location in urban areas was the industry's highest priority need from advanced technology.[23]

A particular application of truck routeing which is pertinent to IVHS is the potential for selective detection and priority for commercial vehicles. This is commonly done now for public transport operations, which are detected upon their approach to traffic signals, the operation of which is modified (eg green time is extended or cut short, depending upon where in the traffic signal cycle the vehicle is detected). Extension of this practice to other road vehicles is possible, and certain types of commercial vehicle operation are candidates for such treatment. Such type might include emergency vehicles, vehicles carrying hazardous goods (where a sudden stop might create a potential safety hazard), and high productivity vehicles such as medium or large combination vehicles, where there are economic advantages in avoiding stops and reducing delays.

Regulation and Administration

Among the earliest applications of IVHS technology were those directed at enhancing regulatory control of trucks and reducing the road freight industry's costs in complying with regulations. These essentially involve fitting the truck with a transponder which enables automatic vehicle identification (AVI) from roadside or in-pavement detectors. In those jurisdictions where trucks pass through various check points (eg US state boundaries, international borders), the documentation can be facilitated by electronic surveillance and monitoring. Such documentation might include driver licence validation, safety inspection certification, fuel tax and registration payments, load permit checks, customs and quarantine laws, etc. Full automation of the process could eventually lead to 'transparent borders'.[24] The well-known HELP/Crescent (heavy vehicle electronic licence plate) programme in the US, with its associated Crescent demonstration project, (involving all western US states between Texas and Washington, as well as British Columbia, Canada) is a prime example here.[25]

Similarly, the monitoring and control of hazardous material movements is enhanced with real-time detection. This not only facilitates the movement function *per se*, but also enables more rapid detection of incidents, and speedier response by emergency service personnel.

Weigh-in-motion (WIM) technology aims, as its name suggests, to weigh vehicles speedily, and to identify the truck type. It is also being used to provide valuable data on truck axle and gross loads, which is useful for road design and load enforcement purposes. Overloaded vehicles not only cause undue wear and tear on the road, but provide unfair competition to legally loaded vehicles. It is thus in the interests of both the public and private sectors to attempt to control or eliminate overloading.

Automated toll payments for toll facilities reduce or eliminate the need for trucks to stop to pay the toll, and obviate the difficulties of providing cash for toll payments to employed truck drivers (or of reimbursing them).

Positioning and Communication

Improved technology for truck positioning and communication is rapidly being adopted by the long-distance road freight industry, especially in the US. It incorporates three aspects: location (the current location of a vehicle is relayed to a central site); navigation (the location of the vehicle is known to the driver), and communications (data and voice transmissions to and from the vehicle).[26]

Systems in use are formatted to use satellites for vehicle position finding, and mobile cellular telephones for communication. Their main benefits are to long-distance trucking operators, and arise from reduced long-distance telephone charges and better truck productivity.

There can be improved customer levels of service, especially if these systems are linked via electronic data interchange (EDI) to customers' data base systems. There is also potential to link on-board electronic monitoring systems to base computers for such purposes as maintenance scheduling (engine monitoring systems), load control (eg refrigerated container temperature monitoring) and driver schedules.[27]

A related aspect is vehicle and load security. The ability of IVHS, suitably configured, to identify specific vehicles or containers (eg if tagged with a transponder) provides the opportunity to track or locate a specific vehicle. This would enable a despatcher to monitor the progress of a vehicle or a load, and could assist in the detection of stolen vehicles and loads.

Conclusions

Efficient and effective goods delivery involves both the private sector, through the logistics process, and the public sector, through the provision and operation of public infrastructure. There is much which the latter group can do to facilitate freight delivery, but this often requires explicit consideration of the needs of heavy vehicle in the traffic stream or at loading facilities.[28]

This chapter has attempted to outline possible ways in which freight activities can be improved through better planning and operation of the transport system, especially the road system. However, because there is a multitude of participants in the freight process, adequate resolution of planning issues is likely to involve input from all parties. To this end, a cooperative planning effort is more likely to be effective than for each party to attempt to act alone. There is increasing recognition from various agencies around the world that there are mutual benefits to be gained from a cooperative approach to urban freight problem identification and resolution. This may require the establishment of formal consultative mechanisms.

Summary

- Transport system designers and planners have frequently appeared to concentrate solely on the needs of private motorists, to the neglect of the needs of commercial freight operators
- Trucks can be disadvantaged by this bias, in particular by signalling systems and at road intersections
- Dedicated truck routes, intersection design and operation, truck parking and unloading, terminal design and location, and the

emerging road system technology, are all areas of interest to road system operators and planners
- Road system technology is extendable to such applications as real-time road pricing, vehicle management, traffic control and management, and general improvement of the productivity, safety and regulation of commercial vehicles.

References

1. Ogden, K.W., *Urban Goods Movement: A Guide to Policy and Planning*, Ashgate, Aldershot, 1992, p. 141.
2. Barber, E.J. and Hildebrand, L.K., *Guidelines for Applying Criteria to Designate Routes for Transporting Hazardous Materials*, Federal Highway Administration, Washington, DC, 1980.
3. Ogden (1992), op. cit., p. 145.
4. Kessler, D., 'Establishing hazardous materials truck routes for shipments through the Dallas-Fort Worth areas', *State of the Art Report 3: Recent Advances in Hazardous Materials Transportation Research*, Transportation Research Board, Washington, DC, 1986, p. 86.
5. Transportation Research Board, *Special Report 211: Twin Trailer Trucks*, TRB, Washington, DC, 1986, p. 50.
6. Kimber, R.M., McDonald, M. and Hounsell, N.B., 'The prediction of saturation flows for road junctions controlled by traffic signals', *Research Report 67*, Transport and Road Research Laboratory, Crowthorne, UK, 1986.
7. Molina, C.J., 'Development of passenger car equivalents for large trucks at signalized intersections', *ITE Journal*, 57(11), 1987, pp. 33–7.
8. Brown, G.E. and Ogden, K.W., 'The effects of vehicle category on traffic signal design: A re-examination of through car equivalents', *Proceedings of the 14th Australian Road Research Board Conference*, 14(2), 1988, pp. 27–34.
9. Ogden, K.W., 'Truck movement and access in urban areas', *ASCE Journal of Transportation Engineering*, 117(1), 1991, pp. 72–91.
10. Ogden (1991), op. cit., Ogden (1992), op. cit., p. 159.
11. Ogden (1992), op. cit., p. 165.
12. Ogden (1992), op. cit., p. 170.
13. Walters, C.H., 'Dallas urban goods movement changes: The decade after', in Chatterjee, A., Fisher, G.P. and Staley, R.A. (eds), *Goods Transportation in Urban Areas*, American Society of Civil Engineers, New York, 1989.
14. Rawling, F.G., 'Information needs for policy, planning and design', in Chatterjee A., Fisher, G.P. and Staley, R.A. (eds), *Goods Transportation in Urban Areas*, American Society of Civil Engineers, New York, 1989.
15. Staley, R.A., 'Urban intermodal freight management', in Chatterjee, A., Fisher, G.P. and Staley, R.A. (eds), *Goods Transportation in Urban Areas*, American Society of Civil Engineers, New York, 1989, p. 10.
16. Ogden (1992), op. cit., p. 231.
17. Muller, G.T., *Intermodal Freight Transportation*, Eno Foundation, Westport, Conn., 1989.
18. Stover, V.G., *Transportation and Land Development*, Institute of Transportation Engineers, Washington, DC, 1988, p. 204
19. Ogden (1992), op. cit., p. 171.

[20] French, R.L., 'Intelligent vehicle/highway systems in action', *ITE Journal*, 60(11), 1990, pp. 23–31.

[21] Walton, C.M., 'A concept of IVHS in commercial vehicle operation: The HELP/Crescent program', *Proc 2nd Vehicle Navigation and Information Systems Conference*, Vol 1, Society of Automotive Engineers, Warrendale, USA, 1991.

[22] US Department of Transportation, 1990, *National Transportation Strategy Planning Study*, p. 94.

[23] Pearson, R.A. and Associates, *Application of New Technology in Road Freight Operations*, Road Traffic Authority of Victoria, Melbourne, Australia, 1998.

[24] US Department of Transportation, op. cit., p. 96.

[25] Hill, C. and Davies, P., 'Help is on the way', *ASCE Civil Engineering Journal*, 60(2), 1990, pp. 64–5.

[26] Garrison, W.L. and Scapinakis, D., 'Adoption of advanced positioning and communications technology by the trucking industry', *Report Number UCB-ITS-RR-90-9*, Institute of Transportation Studies, University of California, Berkeley, 1990.

[27] US Department of Transportation, op. cit., p. 9.20.

[28] 'Issues and problems of moving goods in urban areas', *ASCE Journal of Transportation Engineering*, 115(1), 1989, pp. 4–19.

Index